Celebrating African-American Achievements

WHO'S WHO

in BLACK

Detroit.

THE INAUGURAL EDITION

JAN 2007 — CH

Celebrating African-American Achievements

WHO'S WHO
IN BLACK
Detroit®

THE INAUGURAL EDITION

Who's Who In Black Detroit®
is a registered trademark of
Briscoe Media Group, LLC

Purchase additional copies online @
www.whoswhopublishing.com

Who's Who Publishing Co., LLC
1650 Lake Shore Drive, Suite 250
Columbus, Ohio 43204

All Credit Cards Accepted
*Inquiries for bulk purchases for youth
groups, schools, churches, civic or
professional organizations, please call
our office for volume discounts.*

Corporate Headquarters
(614) 481-7300

**Copyright © 2006 by C. Sunny Martin,
Briscoe Media Group, LLC**

Library of Congress Control Number: 2006933778

Photo Credits
Monica Morgan, Vito Palmisano, Claudette de la Haye
Dave Hogan/Getty Images, Frederick M. Brown/Getty Images

ISBN # 1-933879-07-6 Hardback
$50.00 each-U.S. Hardback

ISBN # 1-933879-04-1 Paperback
$34.95 each-U.S. Paperback

Photography by Cladette de la Haye

Photography by Cladette de la Haye

Photo by Susan Stewart

CONTENTS

MEET THE TEAM

WHO'S *Who*
PUBLISHING CO., LLC

C. Sunny Martin
Founder & CEO

Carter Womack
Detroit Publisher

Detroit Sales Team

Ophelia Twine-Henry

Orena Perry

Marsha A. Brogdon

Ernie Sullivan
Senior Partner

Paula Gray
Columbus Publisher

Melanie Diggs
Executive Editor

Aaron Leslie
Production Manager

Christina Llewellyn
Graphic Designer

Tamara Allen
Senior Editor

Jeanne Goshe
Copy Editor

Elizabeth Harris
Graphic Designer

Sarah Waite
Webmaster

Ann Coffman
Executive Assistant

Nathan Wylder
Senior Editor

Erica Bowshier
Comptroller

CORPORATE OFFICE
1650 Lake Shore Drive, Suite 250 • Columbus, Ohio 43204 • (614) 481-7300
Visit Our Web Site - www.whoswhopublishing.com

THIS BOOK WAS MADE POSSIBLE BY THE GENEROUS SUPPORT OF OUR

SPONSORS

PLATINUM SPONSORS

Marriott.
DETROIT
AT THE RENAISSANCE CENTER

SHRG
Southern Hospitality Restaurant Group

DIAMOND SPONSORS

Fifth Third Bank
Working Hard To Be The Only Bank You'll Ever Need.

DAIMLERCHRYSLER

National City.

DaimlerChrysler Financial Services

LaSalle Bank
ABN AMRO

EMERALD SPONSORS

Blue Cross Blue Shield of Michigan

A nonprofit corporation and independent licensee of the Blue Cross and Blue Shield Association

Comerica Bank

UNVEILING RECEPTION SPONSORS

▼**nwa**
NORTHWEST AIRLINES®

DMC
DETROIT MEDICAL CENTER
WAYNE STATE UNIVERSITY

DTE Energy®

GREEKTOWN
CASINO
a Kewadin Casino™

CiNTAS®
THE SERVICE PROFESSIONALS

Turner
Building the Future

OnWheels
INCORPORATED

Huntington

The YES Foundation®
Youth Employment Services · Youth Education Services · Youth Enrichment Services

★macy's

DetroitMetro
CONVENTION & VISITORS BUREAU

VOICE OF THE COMMUNITY SINCE 1936
MICHIGAN CHRONICLE

STATE OF MICHIGAN
OFFICE OF THE GOVERNOR
LANSING

JOHN D. CHERRY, JR.
LT. GOVERNOR

October 2006

Greetings,

As governor of the state of Michigan, it is indeed an honor to congratulate you on the inaugural edition of *Who's Who in Black Detroit*.

For more than 300 years, Detroit . . . the Motor City . . . Motown . . . has been a center of inspiration and innovation and a leader in manufacturing, technology, the arts, education, business, the law, health care, and the music industry. It is with immense pride and heartfelt gratitude that we honor Detroit's African American leaders for their achievements and for their contributions to the city's rich and vibrant history.

The stories of their lives and their contributions to the city of Detroit and the great state of Michigan serve as stellar examples of what our youth – the future of our state and this country – can achieve through hard work and by putting their hearts into a lifetime of service.

Thank you for the opportunity to be a part of this wonderful project. Please accept my very best wishes as you continue to tell the inspiring stories of our country's great African American leaders.

Warm regards,

Jennifer M. Granholm
Governor

GEORGE W. ROMNEY BUILDING • 111 SOUTH CAPITOL AVENUE • LANSING, MICHIGAN 48909
www.michigan.gov

HOUSE OF REPRESENTATIVES
WASHINGTON, D. C. 20515

JOHN CONYERS, JR.

I am delighted to extend greetings and congratulations to both the publishers and the honorees of the Inaugural Edition of **Who's Who in Black Detroit**. For the past 17 years, Who's Who Publishing Co., L LC, has worked to illuminate the achievements of African Americans across the United States of America. I am thrilled to be part of the unveiling of a new publication that highlights the accomplishments of highly motivated Detroiters.

Who's Who in Black Detroit provides a unique opportunity to acknowledge the city's African-American men and women who have made significant contributions to our community. Each honoree stands as a living proof that one highly motivated person can indeed change the world.

The launch of **Who's Who in Black Detroit** affords us a rare opportunity to celebrate the achievements of Detroit's African-American citizens from a wide variety of career disciplines including; entrepreneurs, corporate executives, community leaders, media professionals, counselors at law, youth achievers, politicians and many other Detroiters who have made excellence a way of life.

Again, congratulations on your newest venture. I am thrilled that you have selected Detroit as the subject for your newest success story.

Very Truly

John Conyers Jr.

John Conyers, Jr.
Member of Congress

Congress of the United States
House of Representatives
Washington, DC 20515–2213

CAROLYN CHEEKS KILPATRICK
13TH DISTRICT, MICHIGAN

ASSISTANT WHIP

COMMITTEE:
APPROPRIATIONS

SUBCOMMITTEES:
FOREIGN OPERATIONS, EXPORT
FINANCING, AND RELATED PROGRAMS

TRANSPORTATION, TREASURY AND
INDEPENDENT AGENCIES

Greetings,

Congratulations on producing the inaugural edition of ***Who's Who in Black Detroit***! I am honored and pleased to support your efforts to celebrate the accomplishments and contributions of African Americans in Detroit.

This publication commemorates the lives and legacies of the many African Americans who have shaped our city. Many of our homegrown heroes and living legends have left an indelible mark on our country. Detroiters have used their drive and determination to improve the quality of life for those in our city and across the world.

Documenting the sacrifice, commitment, and vision of the pioneers and trailblazers in our community is a wonderful way to pay homage to their lives. This testament to Detroit's ability to produce leaders who have a positive influence in a variety of fields, including politics, business, fashion, and music, also challenges and inspires future generations of Detroiters to continue making history.

I commend Who's Who Publishing Company for expanding its efforts to document the achievements of African Americans to include Detroit. This publication will certainly be an important historical and networking resource for people in Detroit and others across the nation.

I also salute the many outstanding leaders who are recognized on these pages. Thank you for daring to dream and using your time and talents to strengthen our community. Together, we make Detroit great!

Sincerely,

Carolyn C. Kilpatrick

Carolyn C. Kilpatrick
Member of Congress

KWAME M. KILPATRICK, MAYOR
CITY OF DETROIT
EXECUTIVE OFFICE

September 6, 2006

Greetings:

As Mayor of Detroit, the city that moves the world, it gives me great pleasure to congratulate Who's Who in Black Detroit on the inaugural edition. Our city now has the opportunity through this dynamic publication to showcase our great business and community leaders, entrepreneurs, artisans, and individuals who have accomplished much as African Americans in our community.

The profiles and biographical information in Who's Who in Black Detroit reflect some of the best and brightest in the city of Detroit. It is my sincere hope that this publication is a success and that young and old will find inspiration in the achievements of the individuals portrayed in these many pages.

On behalf of my entire administration and the citizens of Detroit, please accept my best wishes for future success.

Sincerely,

Kwame M. Kilpatrick
Mayor

53 Investments in Diversity

At Fifth Third Bank, we subscribe to the definition of diversity
as the full utilization of all human resource potential.

It is understanding and valuing differences,
while mobilizing similarities effectively to achieve a common objective or goal.

CALL 1-800-246-5372 | **VISIT** www.53.com

Fifth Third Bank
Working Hard To Be The Only Bank You'll Ever Need.®

METROPOLITAN
DETROIT'S
101
BEST AND
BRIGHTEST
COMPANIES
TO WORK FOR
WINNER 2005

You're inspiring others to follow.

At DaimlerChrysler, we work hard to design, engineer, build and finance the best cars and trucks available. And it's all made possible through the dedicated work of each employee. That's why we're proud to support *Who's Who in Black Detroit*, and applaud our very own for their exceptional contributions to this community and beyond.

DaimlerChrysler Financial Services   DAIMLERCHRYSLER

Foreword

By The Honorable Judge Damon J. Keith

"Detroit is a city with both a rich history and a promising future."

It was a call heard around the country prompting thousands of southern blacks to migrate to Michigan: Ford Motor Company announces a "$5 a day" wage. In 1920 my father came to Detroit from Atlanta, Georgia to earn Ford's $5 a day. Upon settling in Detroit, my mother and siblings joined him. Thereafter, I was born, making me the only Detroit-born member of the family. I am proud I was born in Detroit at 3860 Hudson Street and went to public school from kindergarten at Columbian Elementary, to McMichael Intermediate School, to Northwestern High School. As a son of Detroit, I have seen this city give birth to many African-American successes in civil rights, business, music, law, drama, medicine, education, sports, journalism and politics.

Detroit has been blessed with a number of nationally-known black leaders in every sector of society, including a number of prominent black firsts. To name just a few, there was Charles W. Jones, Michigan's first black judge appointed to the Detroit Recorder's Court. Subsequently, Wade H. McCree Jr. became Michigan's first elected black judge when elected to the Wayne County Circuit Court, and he was also the first black appointed in Michigan to both the United States District Court for the Eastern District of Michigan and the United States Court of Appeals for the Sixth Circuit.

Other pioneers were Charles C. Diggs Jr., Michigan's first black congressman, whose father, Charles Diggs Sr., established one of the largest funeral homes in America. Cora M. Brown was the first black woman elected to the Michigan State Senate. William T. Patrick Jr. was the first black Detroit city councilman in the 20th century,

and Erma Henderson was the first black woman Detroit city councilperson and its first black president. Remus Robinson was the first black member of the Detroit Board of Education; later he became board president. Ozzie Virgil broke the Detroit Tigers' color barrier in 1958, opening the door for Detroit's own Willie Horton, a baseball superstar who helped the Tigers win the World Series in 1968. We had Nelson Jack Edwards, the first black international United Auto Workers vice president and Dr. D.T. Burton, the first black elected to the board of governors of Wayne State University. And finally, though this list is not exhaustive, there was Robert Hayden, the first black poet laureate in the United States; Dr. Haley Bell, founder of Detroit's first black radio station; and Tony award-winning director Lloyd Richards, the first black dean of the Yale University School of Drama.

Of course, when discussing the history of black Detroit, we cannot fail to mention great Detroit ministers like Reverend Albert Cleage Jr., who formed the Shrine of the Black Madonna, the centerpiece of the Black Christian Nationalist Church. We also had the great Reverend C.L. Franklin, the father of Aretha Franklin, the Queen of Soul. Reverend Franklin touched generations with his moving sermons and his activism, which included organizing Detroit's 1963 "Walk to Freedom," the largest civil rights march in any northern city. At this event, Dr. Martin Luther King Jr. delivered the precursor to his famous "I Have a Dream" speech.

Pioneer Rosa Louise Parks, the mother of the civil rights movement and a woman of quiet strength, made Detroit her home and taught us to stand up for what is just. Although we recently lost Mother Parks, her legacy of service to the civil rights movement and commitment to giving back perseveres.

In addition to giving this country some of its most important black leaders, black Detroit has also left an indelible imprint on the social and cultural fabric of this nation. Detroit introduced rhythm and blues and soul music to the world through Berry Gordy's Motown Records. We have the Charles H. Wright Museum of African-American History, the only museum of its kind in Detroit, dedicated entirely to the unique experiences and triumphs of African Americans. We had the black-owned Gotham City Hotel, a hotel as grand as any other in Michigan, which blacks patronized during a time when downtown hotels barred blacks. There is the legendary Emmanuel Steward's Kronk Gym, which produced world-class boxers like Thomas Hearns. And the *Michigan Chronicle*, led by its publisher Sam Logan, has spotlighted the trials and triumphs of black Detroit for more than seventy years.

As with any great success story, black Detroit has also endured adversity. I remember the hurt of never having a black teacher from kindergarten through high school and the Fisher YMCA across from Northwestern High School that blacks could not join. There was the segregated Detroit police department that had no black motorcycle or horseback patrolmen or integrated scout cars. We cannot forget the devastation of Black Bottom's and Paradise Valley's thriving, cultural and economic core when the Chrysler Freeway was built, destroying Hastings Street. Of course, black Detroit's greatest tests occurred during the 1943 and 1967 riots, after which, we witnessed the mass exodus of white residents and businesses from downtown.

Despite this, black Detroit would overcome. Today, we have the first black president of Wayne State University, Dr. Irvin D. Reid, and the first black female chief of police, Ella M. Bully-Cummings. There are black vice presidents at GM, Ford, and DaimlerChrysler. NBA hall of famer, Joe Dumars, is the first black president of basketball operations for the Detroit Pistons. We have a number of successful black-owned businesses. We have national leaders in United States Representatives

John Conyers and Carolyn Cheeks Kilpatrick. We have journalists like Rochelle Riley vigilantly reporting on the issues affecting black America. Twenty-two black female judges sit on the 36th District Court. Detroit-raised Dr. Benjamin S. Carson Sr. made his hometown proud when he was named the youngest chief of pediatric neurosurgery in the nation at Johns Hopkins Children's Center. And he continues to do so as the recipient of the 2006 NAACP Spingarn Award, its highest honor. We have the annual NAACP Freedom Fund dinner, the largest sit-down dinner in the country, which was co-founded under the leadership of former NAACP executive secretary, Dr. Arthur L. Johnson. And of course, since 1973, with the election of Coleman A. Young, we have had more than thirty years of continuous black mayoral leadership.

Mayor Young's legacy of helping black Detroit rise has continued under former Mayor Dennis W. Archer and current mayor, Kwame Kilpatrick. I had the pleasure of administering the oath of office to Mayors Young, Archer, and Kilpatrick at each of their inaugurations. All three exemplify strong black Detroit leadership! Today, under Mayor Kilpatrick's leadership, Detroit continues to shine, hosting Major League Baseball's 2005 All-Star Game and Super Bowl XL, proudly showing the world that Detroit is a city with both a rich history and a promising future.

It is a special honor for me to pen the foreword to the inaugural edition of **Who's Who in Black Detroit**®. As a lifelong resident of this great city, nothing makes me prouder than to introduce a volume celebrating black Detroit's numerous accomplishments. Since the days of slavery when Detroit was the final stop on the Underground Railroad to freedom, Detroit has served as a beacon of hope for blacks in this country. Those individuals honored in this volume are here because of this important legacy and as such, each of us must always "lift the generations we represent so that all whose lives come in contact with ours walk on higher ground."

Judge Damon J. Keith

A MESSAGE FROM THE

Founder & CEO

C. Sunny Martin

Detroit's Black Judges Worked It Out!

Welcome to the inaugural edition of **Who's Who In Black Detroit**®. Perhaps more than any other publication our company has undertaken, I have been most enthusiastic about seeing this Detroit publication come to fruition. Simply put, I jus' love me some Detroit black people!

A very special city, native Detroiters are a proud people. The Motor City has contributed so much to the soul of our nation and frequently throughout its more than 300-year history, has played a significant role on the world stage. In commerce, entertainment, fashion, sports and politics, Detroit has always found a way to contribute and represent the American spirit in a special way.

It was Chief Judge Sylvia A. James from Inkster, Michigan who first introduced me to Detroit. Having seen firsthand the quality of our publications, she had a sincere commitment and sense of pride when she contracted our firm to produce the nation's first directory to honor African-American judges with **Black Judges In America**®. Upon inviting me to Detroit and showing me around the city, she shared information about Detroit's rich heritage and made many key introductions that have proved to be extremely helpful in making this inaugural edition a reality.

Everyone knows him and everyone loves him— perhaps the greatest ambassador for the Motor City is none other than Judge Craig S. Strong. Judge Strong best epitomizes Detroit's sense of style and I am forever grateful to him for the many introductions he orchestrated on my behalf.

Additionally, we are extremely blessed to have Judge Damon Keith pen the foreword for this historic edition. Judge Damon Keith, at every turn and in every circle, folks in Detroit sincerely respect and appreciate your commitment to their community over the years.

I also want to thank our Detroit publisher, Carter Womack, for his tremendous effort in making this inaugural edition a reality.

It goes without saying that Detroit's judges and numerous other individuals have made Who's Who Publishing Company feel right at home. I welcome this edition into the Who's Who family of publications and look forward to working with your community for many years to come.

Live life to the fullest,

C. Sunny Martin

Criteria for Inclusion

Who's Who In Black Detroit® is an opportunity for us to afford a measure of recognition to the men and women who have made their mark in their specific occupations, professions, or in service to others in the Detroit community.

A sincere effort was made to include those whose positions or accomplishments in their chosen fields are significant and whose contributions to community affairs, whether citywide or on the neighborhood level, have improved the quality of life for all of us.

The names of those brief biographies included in this edition were compiled from customary sources of information. Lists of a wide variety were consulted and every effort was made to reach all whose stature or civic activities merited their inclusion.

In today's mobile society, no such publication could ever claim to be complete; some who should be included could not be reached or chose not to respond, and for that we offer our apologies. Constraints of time, space and awareness are thus responsible for other omissions, and not a lack of good intentions on the part of the publisher. Our goal was to document the accomplishments of many people from various occupational disciplines.

An invitation to participate in the publication was extended at the discretion of the publisher. Biographies were invited to contribute personal and professional data, with only the information freely submitted to be included. The editors have made a sincere effort to present an accurate distillation of the data, and to catch errors whenever possible. However, the publisher cannot assume any responsibility for the accuracy of the information submitted.

There was no charge for inclusion in this publication and inclusion was not guaranteed; an annual update is planned. Comments and other concerns should be addressed to:

C. Sunny Martin, CEO
Who's Who Publishing Co., LLC
1650 Lake Shore Drive, Suite 250
Columbus, Ohio 43204
Phone: (614) 481-7300

E-Mail: sunny@whoswhopublishing.com
www.whoswhopublishing.com

A MESSAGE FROM THE
Detroit Publisher

Carter D. Womack

The story continues. As we launch this inaugural edition of **Who's Who In Black Detroit**®, as historic as it is, it is certainly the continuation of a story. It is the story of a city and a race of people who were born here and moved here from all parts of America. Our ancestors arrived in Detroit with dreams to better themselves, their children and their children's children. They came to the Motor City, the soulful Motown city, to take jobs in an industry that replaced the horse and buggy and created within America, and ultimately the world, a love of automobiles.

With hopes for a better day, they came to take jobs in the factories and homes, not in the offices. Their story is one of migration, segregation, integration and endurance. As a result of their labors, we are here to celebrate African-American achievement in Detroit. Yes, we are still in the factories and the homes, but now we occupy the executive offices.

This story continues as we share with you, our readers, chronicles about past, present and future leaders who built and will continue to build Detroit into an even greater city. In the

celebration of our achievements, we have a greater opportunity to serve as strong role models for our young brothers and sisters. It is our responsibility to insure that the graduation rates for high school and colleges increase, the crime rates in our community decrease, we address the impact of AIDS, and we teach our young people the importance of being responsible and respectful.

I want to thank Judge Damon Keith for his support and agreeing to write the foreword for this issue. To my local team of Ophelia Twine-Henry, Orena Perry, Marsha Brogdon, Monica Morgan, and Coire Houston, the success of this book would not have been possible without your support – thank you!

Please enjoy this inaugural edition of **Who's Who In Black Detroit**® and share it with others, for truly, your story continues.

Carter D. Womack

Carter D. Womack

Here's to our VIPs (Very Important Partners).

Let The Party Begin!

Minority-owned businesses are making significant contributions to the development and construction of the new permanent Greektown Casino & Hotel. With the highest levels of skill, they are partnering with us to create a new centerpiece for the downtown area and are playing a key role in ushering in a new era for our city.

GREEKTOWN
CASINO & HOTEL
a Kewadin Casino ™

Located in the Heart of Historic Greektown, 555 E. Lafayette, Detroit, MI 48226
1-888-771-4FUN(4386)
www.greektowncasino.com

If you bet more than you can afford to lose, you've got a problem. Call 1-800-270-7117 for confidential help.

NOBODY CARES
(like we do)

St John HEALTH®

ST. JOHN DETROIT RIVERVIEW HOSPITAL

St. John Detroit Riverview Hospital is committed to serve the Detroit community with **reverence** in all that we do.

Whether you have an emergency, a new baby entering the world, or anything in between, you'll always receive the highest quality care from physicians, nurses, and associate staff – all dedicated to caring for YOU.

**Giving you the best care...from people who care.
That's what we call REAL MEDICINE.**

**1-888-440-REAL
www.realmedicine.org**

REAL MEDICINE™

"Be the change you wish to see in the world."

–Mahatma Gandhi

Congratulations to all the leaders who grace this book. Your contributions inspire us all.

Making more possible

LaSalle Bank
ABN AMRO

MIX 92.3
WWW.MIX923FM.COM

The Steve Harvey Morning Show
Mon-Fri 6am-10am
"The Mid-day MIX" with Frankie Darcell
Mon-Fri 10am-3pm
"Love, Lust & Lies" with Michael Baisden
Mon-Fri 3pm-7pm
"MIX Moods" with Keil Lamont
Mon-Thu 7pm-12am,
Sat/Sun 12pm-3pm
"All Night MIX"
with Tracey McCaskill
Tue-Fri 12am-6am, Sat 9am-12pm
"Back Jam" with Donafay
Fri 7pm-12am
"Saturday Night Live"
with Gerald McBride
Sat 7pm-12am
"Cruisin' with Foody"
Sun 7pm-12am
Chris Boyd
Sat 3pm-7pm
T. Williams
Mon/Sat/Sun 12am-6am
"Talk of the Town"
with Frankie Darcell
Sun 11am-12pm
Ramona Prater
Sun 3pm-7pm

Steve Harvey

Michael Baisden

Frankie Darcell

Keil Lamont   **Donafay**   **Gerald McBride**   **Foody**   **Marvin Winans**

Classic Soul & Today's R&B

A Historical Overview of

DETROIT

By John M. Green

*L*e détroit,

which means "the strait", was first explored by the French in 1701. They had learned to live with the Iroquois Indians, who were not really excited about foreign intruders invading their space.

Headed for Le Detroit, Antoine de La Mothe Cadillac, and his son, Antoine, left La Chine, a settlement on the northern shores of the St. Lawrence River, located below Montreal, Canada. His party consisted of 25 long canoes and 100 Frenchmen, who were probably voyageurs. Voyageurs were a hardy and rough group of men, ideally suited for exploring new areas. The journey to Le Detroit covered roughly 600 miles.

Detroit's early records indicate blacks were in the territory by 1750; however, there is no clear determination between free blacks and enslaved blacks or Indians. Ironically, early record keepers did not consider it important to maintain records on blacks or their activities.

Detroit, as we have come to know it, has a history that does not differ radically from that of Chicago, Cleveland or any other large northern industrial metropolitan city, except for the stellar role Detroit played in the history of the Underground Railroad. The following is a chronological order, by decade, of black history in Detroit:

1700–1749

1701 – Antoine de la Mothe Cadillac and his party of soldiers, fur traders and natives land at Le Detroit.

1736 – The first formal record of a person of African descent in Detroit.

1750–1799

1750 – First census by the French authorities: 450 free citizens; 33 enslaved people. The number of those of African descent or Indians is not known.

1757 – Jean Baptiste Pointe Du Sable, a free black fur trapper of Haitian origin, arrives in Detroit. In 1779 he established the trading post which grew into the city of Chicago.

1787 – The Northwest Ordinance prohibits the extension of slavery into the Northwest Territories, that is, no new slaves were allowed. The status of existing slaves did not change. This is the first antislavery legislation in North America.

1793 – Canada under British rule offered a safe haven to enslaved people who were able to free themselves. A terminal, Detroit was the end of the line on the Underground Railroad. It is estimated that more than 50,000 enslaved people escaped via the Underground Railroad to Canada prior to the Civil War.

1800–1849

1804 – The beginning of the Underground Railroad for slaves passing through Detroit.

1806 – Detroit becomes a city.

1807 – Peter and Hannah Denison, refugees from bondage, sue Catherine Tucker their former enslaver to gain their children's freedom. Judge Augustus B. Woodward's decision sets lasting precedent for the parameters of slavery.

1808 – Canadian merchant Richard Peterson attempts to recover refugees from enslavement who have come to the Michigan Territory from Upper Canada. Judge Augustus B. Woodward uses his *Tucker v. Denison* ruling to deny extradition.

1827 – The Michigan Territorial government implements an Act to regulate blacks and mulattoes and to punish the kidnapping of such persons.

1832 – First Baptist Church accepts William Butler as its first African-American member.

1837 – Michigan is admitted to the U.S. Three African-American members form the Colored American Baptist Church, later called Second Baptist Church, the first African-American church in Detroit.

1839 – The Colored Methodist Society forms and petitions the Common Council of Detroit, asking for use of the old military hall, which becomes the core of the Bethel African Methodist church.

1842 – Detroit establishes a system of free education, including one school for 86 African-American students.

Calvary Baptist Church

Chapel Hill Baptist Church
Rev. C.M. Newton Pastor, 1942

1850–1899

1859 – Abolitionist John Brown arrives in Detroit with 14 enslaved passengers. Abolitionist Frederick Douglass delivers lecture at the same time. They did not meet on this date in Detroit, contrary to the often told story.

1861 – The Civil War begins.

1862 – Congress allows blacks to enlist in the Union Army. Midnight, December 31, blacks gather at Second Baptist Church to hear the reading of the Emancipation Proclamation.

1870 – Michigan African-American males allowed to vote.

1882 – Dr. Samuel C. Watson elected first black member of the city council and served two terms.

1898 – Michigan Association of Women's club founded. Mary E. McCoy elected first vice president.

1900–1949

1903 – Educator Booker T. Washington speaks to city.

1910 – Blacks begin immigrating to Detroit. Detroit chapter of the NAACP established. Paradise Valley, a black entertainment hot spot, thrives.

1911 – St. Peter Claver Mission, a black Catholic group organizes.

1912 – Idlewild Resort area in Lake County, Michigan, which covers 2,700 acres, is developed for Detroit and Chicago's growing black middle class.

Grandmay Fair Victory Ball Exhibit

1915 – Carter G. Woodson establishes the Association for the Study of Negro Life and History.

Joe Louis

1916 – Vernor's begins bottling in Detroit. Detroit Chapter of the Urban League is founded. Frances Elliott Davis of Detroit is first black nurse accepted into the Red Cross.

1919 – Dunbar Hospital, the first hospital established by blacks, opens.

1925 – NAACP hires famous attorney, Clarence Darrow, to defend Sweet family, which was acquitted for killing a white man.

1929 – Ambassador Bridge is open to traffic. Cornelius Langston Henderson, a brilliant engineer, designed the Canadian approach to the Ambassador Bridge.

1931 – Charles Roxborough, a Republication attorney, becomes the first black elected to the Michigan Senate, serving one term.

1932 – Detroit track star, Eddie Tolan, sets two records in summer Olympics at Los Angeles.

1934 – Joe Louis, the Brown Bomber, wins first fight against Jack Kracken.

1937 – Charles C. Diggs, owner of House of Diggs Funeral Home, becomes the first black Democratic state senator.

1942 – Racial clash occurs at new federal housing Sojourner Truth Project, when blacks begin moving into new homes in all white neighborhoods.

1943 – Race riot and fights break out between white and black youth on Bell Isle; continues into the city for three days of bloody

Jenkins Family Reuinion

Detroit Quartet pose for photo at Adler & Adler Studio

fighting. Singer John Lee Hooker moves to Detroit and earns reputation as a great blues musician.

1945 – Detroit-born Dr. Ralph Johnson Bunche works with the United Nations in writing the charter.

1946 – Slade-Gragg Academy of Practical Arts opens as the first black vocational school in Detroit.

1947 – Beulah Cain Brewer becomes the first black principal in Detroit Public Schools.

1949 – Joe Louis retires from boxing.

1950–1999

1950 – Detroiter Charline Rainey White becomes the first black female elected to Michigan House of Representatives.

1955 – Charles C. Diggs Jr. becomes the first black member of Congress; serves until 1980.

1956 – Mother Waddles, a black minister, feeds needy Detroiters from Mother Waddle's Perpetual Mission, a privately-funded social service agency.

1957 – Attorney William Patrick, an African American, wins a seat on Detroit City Council. Rosa Parks, civil rights pioneer, moves from Montgomery, Alabama with her husband Raymond.

1958 – Dr. King preaches at St. John and St. Paul Episcopal Church.

1961 – Dr. King delivers address to the UAW on its anniversary. "Please Mr. Postman" puts the Marvelettes at the number one spot on the record charts.

1963 – Dr. King leads 125,000 in a march down Woodward Ave. prior to his famous "I Have a Dream" speech at COBO.

1964 – Motown's Supremes have three hit records on charts.

1965 – Dr. King attends funeral of slain civil rights worker Viola Luizzo, a white female from Detroit. Detroit physician Charles H. Wright establishes International Afro-American Museum on West Grand Blvd. and West Warren Ave.

1966 – Dr. King speaks at Cobo Hall.

1967 – Jerry Blocker becomes the first black television news anchor in the state of Michigan.

Ambrose Cartlege Furor Shop and his home

1968 – Dr. King delivers address to Grosse Pointe South High scholars, three weeks before he was slain. Michigan State Senator Coleman A. Young becomes the first black member of the Democratic National Committee.

1970 – Clara Staton Jones becomes the first black to head Detroit Public Library.

1972 – Erma Henderson is first black woman elected to Detroit City Council. Berry Gordy Jr. moves some of Motown to Hollywood.

1973 – State Senator Coleman A. Young (D) is elected first black mayor of Detroit.

1976 – Mayor Young appoints William L. Hart first black police chief of Detroit. Cassandra Smith-Grey appointed city's first black assessor; first female in nation to hold this job.

1977 – Coleman A. Young reelected to second term.

1978 – International Afro-American Museum leases land between John R and Brush Streets for new museum and cultural center.

1979 – Marilyn French Hubbard founds National Association of Black Women Entrepreneurs.

1981 – Coleman A. Young is reelected for third term as mayor of Detroit.

1982 – Coleman A. Young is sworn in for the third term. Betty Lackey elected first black female president of Detroit Chapter of the NAACP.

1985 – Coleman A. Young reelected for fourth term.

Ambrose Cartlege at a Fur Show with models

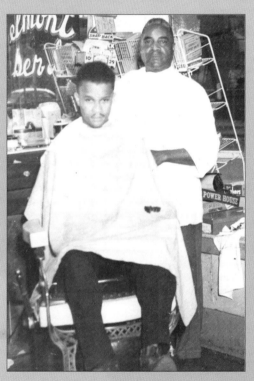

*Getting that Saturday hair cut
(local barber shop)*

1986 – Coleman A. Young is sworn in for a fourth term. The Joe Louis bronze arm is hung at the intersection of Woodward Ave. and Jefferson Ave.

1987 – Michigan is 150 years old! Museum of African American History opens new building in Cultural Center. Aretha Franklin, Detroit's famous "Queen of Soul" becomes the first woman inducted into the Rock & Roll Hall of Fame in Cleveland, Ohio.

1988 – Berry Gordy Jr. sells Motown to MCA records.

1989 – Coleman A. Young is elected for a fifth term. Detroit Pistons win NBA Championship.

1990 – Coleman A. Young is sworn in for a fifth term. Detroit Pistons repeat as the NBA Champs. The mayor welcomes Nelson Mandela to Tigers Stadium with overflowing well wishers. Nelson Mandela would later become the first black president of South Africa.

1993 – Former state Supreme Court Judge Dennis W. Archer is elected mayor of Detroit.

1997 – Museum of African American History is renamed Charles H. Wright Museum of African American History. Former five-term Mayor Coleman A. Young dies. Dennis Archer is reelected to second term.

1998 – Dennis W. Archer is sworn in for second term as mayor of Detroit. Detroit Shock becomes WNBA team.

1999 – Joe Dumars, longtime Piston player moves to the front office. Rosa Parks receives Congressional Gold Medal from Vice President Al Gore.

2000–Present

2001 – The Gateway to Freedom at Detroit's Hart Plaza and the Tower of Freedom at Windsor's Civic Esplendide is dedicated. Michigan House majority leader, Kwame Kilpatrick is elected mayor of Detroit. At 31 years old, he is the youngest mayor elected.

2005 – Mayor Kwame Kilpatrick reelected to a second term. The Mother of the Civil Rights Movement, Rosa Parks, dies. Jerry Blocker recognized by the Detroit Urban League as a Distinguished Warrior for his civil rights contributions.

Unique Perspectives.
Varied Cultures.
Innovative Ideas.

At Cintas, we capitalize on our greatest strength: **OUR PEOPLE**. As a leading provider of outsourced services, we embrace individuality in experience, age, appearance, physical ability, education, family status, and more. Our diversity has helped us become one of the most successful companies in the country. It allows us to serve our customers better and provide rewarding career opportunities for our employees.

For more information, please visit our website at www.cintas.com/wwp.

2005: INROADS honors Cintas CEO Scott Farmer with the prestigious "Frank C. Carr Award" for vision and commitment to diversity in corporate America.

2006: FORTUNE Magazine ranks Cintas among "America's Most Admired Companies" for the sixth consecutive year.

2006: Cintas records 37th consecutive year of growth in sales and earnings.

Where there is progress there is

growth

Joyce Hayes-Giles
Senior Vice President
Customer Service

Harold Gardner
Senior Vice President
Gas Operations

Larry E. Steward
Vice President
Human Resources

John S. Howell Jr.
Director
Regional Relations

Michael C. Porter
Vice President
Corporate
Communications

Teresa M. Sebastian
Assistant
General Counsel
Legal

Ronald L. Butler
Director
Gas Distribution
Operations

Reginald K. Pelzer
Controller
DTE Energy
Resources

Dennis L. Dabney
Director
Human Relations

Bridget J. Temple
Director
Customer Care

Kevin D. Ball
Director
Energy Distribution/
Energy Gas Supply Chain

George W. Jackson Jr.
President
Detroit Economic
Growth Corporation

Charles H. Hill Jr.
Director
Accounting
Operations

DTE Energy®

The Power of Your Community

dteenergy.com

Diversity makes us better.

At National City, we know that diversity makes us stronger and more competitive. It improves our communities and it opens our eyes to new possibilities.

Diversity contributes to a stronger workforce, creates thriving cities and builds a more vibrant region. So when a diverse company joins forces with a diverse city, great things happen.

National City Community Development Corporation (NCCDC), in conjunction with National City Mortgage, is pleased to be part of the Book-Cadillac renovation project in downtown Detroit. By providing equity, construction financing and discounts on mortgage loans for this project, we're making Detroit a stronger city. And that makes us all better.

National City®

Personal Banking • Business Banking
Investments • Mortgage Loans

An Extravagant Evening of Multicultural Diversity In the Auto Industry

The 11th Annual Urban Wheel Awards

Recognizing contributions made by companies and individuals committed to the growing multicultural automotive community

Tuesday, January 9, 2007 - 5 p.m.

Orchestra Hall at the Max M. Fisher Music Center
3711 Woodward Avenue • Detroit, Michigan

Held in conjunction with the
North American International Auto Show.

A great networking opportunity! Meet and greet national multicultural celebrities and auto industry leaders

Sponsorship Opportunities are still available. To learn more, contact:
Cindy Folson – (313) 963-2209   cfolson@onwheelsinc.com
Linda Witulski – (313) 963-2209 lwitulski@onwheelsinc.com
Tickets On Sale Starting October 20, 2006. Group rates available.

To purchase tickets
▶ Call On Wheels Incorporated at **(313) 963-2209**
▶ Visit: **www.onwheelsinc.com**

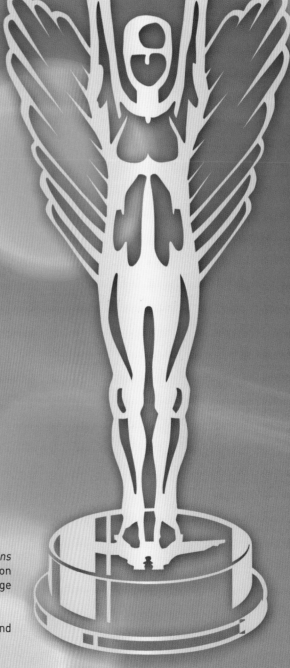

Presented by On Wheels, Incorporated, publisher of *African Americans On Wheels, Asians On Wheels* and *Latinos On Wheels*. On Wheels also manages the Edward Davis Education Foundation, which provides scholarships to students pursuing technical and college degrees in the automotive industry.

The Urban Wheel Awards honors multicultural diversity in the automotive industry and benefits the Edward Davis Education Foundation, a non-profit 501 (c) 3 organization.

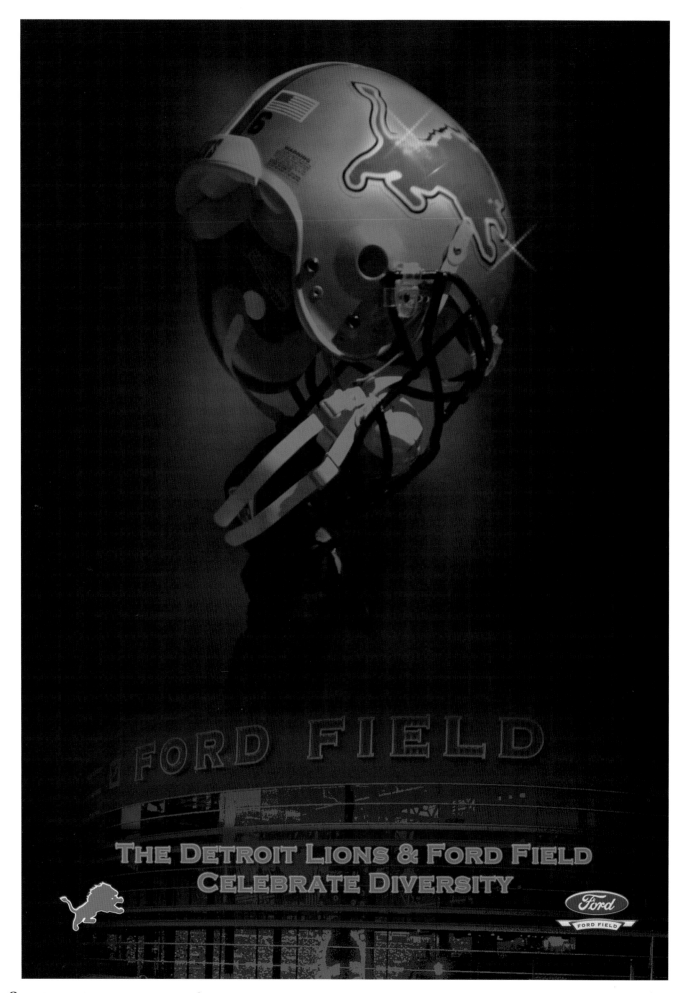

THE DETROIT LIONS & FORD FIELD
CELEBRATE DIVERSITY

Amazing Grace

Rosa Parks
MOTHER OF THE CIVIL RIGHTS MOVEMENT

By Karen Y. Perkins

"I was not the only person involved in starting the Montgomery Bus Boycott. I was just one of many who fought for freedom. Through our cause, many around me began to want to fight for their rights. Bitterness and fearfulness was turning into power. People started organizing and protesting, thousands were willing to make sacrifices. This was the modern mass movement we needed. I had no idea history was being made, we had just reached the point where we simply had to take action!" [1]

Rosa Parks was born Rosa Louise McCauley on February 4, 1913 in Tuskegee, Alabama to father James McCauley, a carpenter, and mother Leona Edwards McCauley, a teacher. At the age of two, her family moved to Pine Level, Alabama where she was educated in a one-room school house. At the age of 11, she was enrolled in The Montgomery Industrial School for Girls, which was a private school founded in 1886 by Alice White. The school was also known as Miss White's School for Girls. To attend school, she cleaned classrooms to pay her tuition. Years later she attended Alabama State Teachers College for Negroes in the 10th and 11th grade, but was forced to leave to care for her sick mother and grandmother, Rose Edwards. Her younger brother, Sylvester, worked to help support the family. Due to the time she missed in school while caring for her family, she was unable to graduate with her class. Years later, however, she finished her formal education and received her high school diploma.

On December 18, 1932 she married Raymond Parks, to whom she would remain married until his death in 1977. Raymond had very little formal education because of racial segregation, but his mother offered the encouragement and support he needed to educate himself. He was full of courage and inner strength and was extremely interested in changing racial conditions in the South. He became knowledgeable on current events and domestic affairs to the point where all who knew him believed he had attended college.

Raymond became an activist, involved in the effort to free nine young men referred to as "The Scottsboro Boys," which was a highly publicized case in the 1930s. These young men were convicted and sentenced to die for a crime they did not commit. Thanks in part to the efforts of Raymond and the NAACP, they were not put to death. Once their trial was over, Raymond and Rosa remained active with the NAACP and involved in civil rights issues.

Dubbed "The Mother of the Modern Day Civil Rights Movement," Rosa felt "If you don't stand for something, you'll fall for anything," or, more appropriately in this case, "If you don't remain seated for something..." This ideology took root on December 1, 1955 when Rosa had enough of Jim Crow laws, enough of paying her fare in the front of the bus and walking to the rear to board, enough of being left in the dust when the bus left before she could re-board in the back of the bus. With her quiet strength, dignity and resolve, she politely declined to relinquish her seat in the first row of the "Colored Section" to a white man on a crowded bus, and thus, gave birth to the Montgomery Bus Boycott. In her book *Quiet Strength*, Rosa makes it clear she was tired that day, but no more tired than any other day. What she was tired of, however,

was being treated like a second-class citizen. She was tired of mean-spirited acts of inhumanity, she was tired of this same bus driver, J.P. Blake, who decided to drive off after she paid her money, leaving her standing on the side of the road, and she was tired of giving in. It was time to take a stand, or "a seat," and this was the day that God gave her the strength and resolve to "just say no." This single act of courage brought civil rights issues to the forefront in the United States and provided a civil rights springboard to one of the most profound leaders of the 20th century, a young minister from Dexter Avenue Baptist Church in Montgomery, Alabama, the Reverend Dr. Martin Luther King Jr.

Rosa was arrested that day for violating segregation laws. She admitted that she did not get on the bus to get arrested; she just wanted to go home. Being arrested was not a happy experience for her, and during her ordeal she saw people that she knew on the bus who refused to help her or even let her husband know what happened to her. Her strong belief in God and the countless prayers she prayed as she sat alone in her cell are what got her through. That evening, under the direction of their newly appointed leader, Rev. Dr. Martin Luther King Jr., the Montgomery Improvement Association (MIA) was formed to start the Montgomery Bus Boycott.

The MIA printed flyers and spread the word throughout the Negro community, "Don't ride the bus on Monday." That Monday turned into 381 days and shined a spotlight on Jim Crow laws and segregation for the world to see. In November of 1956 a Supreme Court decision declared racial segregation on public transportation unconstitutional. The very next day, for the first time in her life, Rosa took her first ride on a non-segregated bus in Montgomery, Alabama. When asked how she felt about being a pioneer in the civil rights movement, Rosa said, "The thing that bothered me was that we waited so long to make this protest." But even though the battle was won, the war was not over. Laws changed, but hearts in the South did not. The harassment that had become a way of life continued even after the Supreme Court ruling, and in 1957 Rosa and Raymond moved to Detroit, Michigan.

In 1963 Rosa attended the civil rights march on Washington and worked closely with Dr. King. In 1965 she became a receptionist and office assistant to U.S. Representative John Conyers and remained in his employ until she retired in 1988.

In 1987 she co-founded the Rosa Parks Institute for Self-Development that sponsors a special program for young people between the ages of 11 and 18 called Pathways to Freedom. This program works with young people to study our history to understand the foundations of the civil rights movement. It traces the Underground Railroad into the civil rights movement and teaches youth about their history. The program provides young people a sense of pride in who they are and from where they have come. The need for this program was painfully evident when Rosa was attacked in her own home by a young man looking for quick cash.

At the age of 81, Rosa once again called on her will of steel and faith in God to stare down yet another act of hate. On August 31, 1994, while relaxing at home, Rosa heard a noise and went to investigate. She found a young black man standing in her living room. He claimed someone had broken down her door and he wanted to protect her. He asked for three dollars as payment. As she went to her room to get the three dollars, he began to attack. He started pushing her, and despite her 81 years, she pushed back. He smacked her; she screamed but no one heard her. He left after Rosa gave him all the money she had, which was $103. Instead of feeling anger and bitterness, she prayed for the young man and felt bad that conditions were such that he needed to rob her. Later she shared, "God protected me." Rosa felt that despite the violence and crime in our society, we should not let fear overwhelm us. We must remain strong, we must not give up hope, we can overcome.

In 1996 President Clinton presented Rosa with the Presidential Medal of Freedom, one of the two highest civilian awards in the United States. It is designed to recognize individuals who have especially made meritorious contributions to the security or national interests of the United States, world peace, or cultural or other significant public or private endeavors. She also received a Ccongressional Gold Medal in 1999.

Rosa Parks spent her remaining years in Detroit, Michigan. She passed away October 24, 2005 at the age of 92. Rosa was the first woman in American history to lie in state in the rotunda at the United States Capitol.

Photo courtesy of Monica Morgan

"There is work to do; that is why I cannot stop or sit still. As long as a child needs help, as long as people are not free, there will be work to do. As long as an elderly person is attacked or in need of support, there is work to do. As long as there is bigotry and crime, we have work to do.

I want to be remembered as a person who stood up to injustice, who wanted a better world for young people; and most of all, I want to be remembered as a person who wanted to be free and wanted others to be free. My fight will continue as long as people are being oppressed.[2]"

Rosa Parks

References
[1] Reed, Gregory J. and Parks, Rosa L. (1994). *Quiet Strength: The Faith, the Hope, and the Heart of a Woman Who Changed a Nation.* Grand Rapids, Michigan: Zondervan Publishing House, A Division of HarperCollins Publications
[2] Ibid.

Celebrating African-American Achievements

ACROSS THE NATION

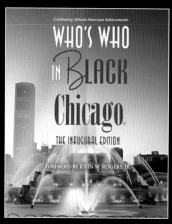

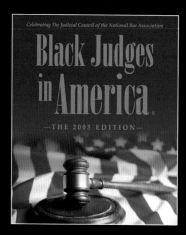

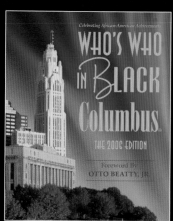

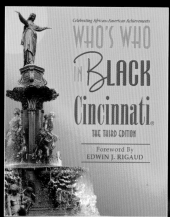

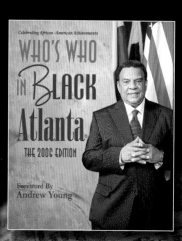

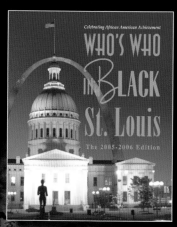

A Promise Delivered

At Turner we take great pride in the long-term relationships we have built in the City of Detroit. For over 30 years, Turner has worked on some of Detroit's finest landmarks and we look forward to our continued contribution to the Renaissance of the City. Our clients have placed their trust in us time and time again. They know that, at Turner, a promise made is a promise delivered. To learn more about Turner, visit www.turnerconstruction.com.

Building the Future of Detroit

Turner

SkyTeam®.
900 cities.
160 countries.
6 continents.

Northwest Airlines® is proud to be
a sponsor of Who's Who in Black Detroit.

Black Family Development, Inc.
Celebrating 28 Years of Service

To Strengthen and Preserve African American Families

Diana C. Jones
Board President

Gerald K. Smith
Board Vice President

Alice G. Thompson
Chief Executive Officer

Employment Opportunities
Seeking the "Brightest and the Best" sincerely invested in our community. Call: 313.758.0150

Administrative Offices
2995 East Grand Boulevard, Detroit, MI 48202
Email: info@blackfamilydevelopment.org

Visit our web site www.blackfamilydevelopment.org

SAVE THE DATE

Michigan Chronicle 70th Anniversary Gala

LEGACY in motion

November 10, 2006 • 7 pm to 12 am
The Roostertail

Sponsorship Opportunities Available

For more information, please contact
Karen Love or Rebecca Bare at 313.963.5522
or visit www.michronicle.com

a tribute to
COLEMAN A. YOUNG

Mayor Coleman Alexander Young
(1918-1997)

Introduction
By John M. Green

Coleman Alexander Young was elected the 55th mayor of Detroit, Michigan in 1973. As the first African American elected to this post, the door was opened for him to earn the distinction of being the longest serving top official – 20 years – in Detroit's 305-year history.

Mayor Young came into office only six years after the devastating civil riot of 1967, which only hastened the so-called "white flight" from the inner city. Perhaps the next bombshell for Detroit was the 1974 oil embargo, which shook the automobile industry, resulting in a tremendous impact on the economies of Detroit and Michigan.

Detroit was well into a decline when Young stepped in as mayor. Contrary to what many people believe, Detroit, for the most part, has been a deeply segregated enclave. The "white only" residential communities were stubborn in their resolve to allow blacks to reside in their communities.

Take, for example, the case of Dr. Ossian H. Sweet. The Water Works Improvement Association sought to prevent the black physician and his family from living in an all-white neighborhood on Garland near Charlevoix in 1925. White mobs surrounded Sweet's house, trying to force him out of the neighborhood.

Clarence Darrow, a well-known lawyer, successfully defended the Sweets, arguing for their right to defend themselves when their lives were threatened. Darrow's victory had far-reaching repercussions on the federal law, which negated Chief Justice Roger B. Taney's decision in the Dred Scott case. At that time, he declared that Negroes had no constitutional rights because the framers of the Constitution regarded them as inferior. This case captured headlines across the U.S. It helped establish a stepping-stone for Judge Frank Murphy, the presiding judge in Detroit's Recorders Court, who would hear Sweet's case. Murphy held a number of important political positions, including governor of Michigan, and eventually became a justice of the Supreme Court.

Despite this and other ongoing civil rights issues, America's political landscape was evolving with a new breed of politicians, particularly those of African-American descent. Faced with discrimination and segregation as a way of life, their politics were built on foundations that were designed to tear down the Jim Crow Laws and Black Codes and to rebuild others based on multicultural coalitions and grassroots organizing. It was in this environment that Coleman A. Young emerged.

His Life and Legacy
By Melanie L. Diggs

Detroit's first black and longest serving mayor was also one of its most controversial. Elected in 1973, Coleman A. Young served until 1993. His early encounters with racism stimulated a life of social activism and change in the labor movement, the military, and politics. Succinctly and summarily stated, the *Detroit Free Press* described him as "...revered and reviled, eloquent and profane, a leader and a loner. He dominated Detroit for 20 years, serving longer than any other mayor."[1]

Named in honor of his father and grandfather, Alex Young, Coleman Alexander Young was born May 24, 1918 in Tuscaloosa, Alabama to William Coleman and Ida Reese Young. Like thousands of blacks in the 1920s and 1930s, his father, frustrated with the Jim Crow laws of the South and looking for better economic opportunities, moved his family north. As destiny would have it, they moved to Black Bottom, an eastside Detroit neighborhood located a mere two miles from the mayor's office Young would eventually maintain for two decades.

The oldest of five children, his adversarial yet protective leadership abilities evolved from parental upbringing and experiencing discrimination first-hand in school. Young was denied scholarships to three area high schools despite his straight "A" average at St. Mary's Catholic School. In 1935 he graduated second in his class at Eastern High School, and once again was denied academic scholarships, this time to Wayne State University and the University of Michigan.

Young's activism began with organized labor, which he saw as a vehicle to fight discrimination and simultaneously earn good wages. As an automotive worker, his efforts as a union organizer for the Congress of Industrial Organizations (CIO) kept him unemployed and blacklisted. He was likewise fired from the U.S. Post Office for recruiting employees to form a union, and for his protests against racial segregation at Sojourner Truth, a public housing project in Detroit.[2]

His military career was equally controversial. At age 24, he enlisted in the U.S. Army during World War II. There, he received commission as a second lieutenant in the infantry, and subsequently transferred to the air corps. It was in the air corps that he became the nation's first black bombardier. He and his fellow black servicemen became known as the Tuskegee Airmen. Unfortunately, racism impeded them from their purpose. Instead of fighting Hitler and his forces, they fought the U.S. Army. With his organizational abilities, he and 100 black officers protested through a sit-in at an all-white Officers' Club in Freedom Field, Indiana.[3] Jailed, they avoided an attempt to be court-martialed and shot because of Young's ability to get their case in the headlines of black newspapers and his letters to the Adjutant General's office. As a result of failed efforts by the Army's investigative team and the negative publicity, they were released. Segregation at the Club ended, but according to Wilbur C. Rich in *Coleman Young and Detroit Politics*, the incident marked the beginning of "Young's first purely civil rights activity."[4]

Young picked up his union organization activities after the War, becoming director of the Wayne County AFL-CIO and a leader of the National Negro Labor Council. These roles landed him on the House Un-American Activities Committee's list of individuals thought to be communists. His defiance to their interrogation of him kept him blacklisted and invited the FBI to monitor him from the 1940s through the 1980s.

Young's subsequent political career was marked by a successful run for the Michigan Constitutional Convention in 1961; winning a Senate seat in 1964; becoming the Democratic floor leader in 1966; and in 1968 he became the first black member of the Democratic National Committee.

With racial tensions, rioting, and a steadily deteriorating relationship between the black community and Detroit's police department, Senator Young ran for mayor. Toughened by his past, the lack of finances did not hinder his bid. In 1974 at age 55 he became Detroit's first black mayor. His tenure was marked by the city's economic hardships and white flight to the suburbs. It was also highlighted by his creation of jobs for women and blacks in the police department, thus improving community relations. Under Young's leadership, the Detroit Police Department eventually became known worldwide for its crime prevention programs. Moreover, Young kept Detroit from bankruptcy, making alliances with leadership in the labor, business, political, spiritual and civic communities, and brought critical federal and state dollars to the city.[5] In the midst of several ongoing investigations by the media, the FBI, and other government agencies, he revived Detroit's riverfront, defused potential riots, and confronted his critics.

A constant warrior for racial and social justice, Young was elected mayor for five terms. Known for his colorful language and controversial nature he let any and everyone know he could not be intimidated. In his inaugural address he told all pushers, rip-off artists, and muggers, "It's time to leave Detroit; hit Eight Mile Road! And I don't give a damn if they are black or white, or if they wear Superfly suits or blue uniforms with silver badges. Hit the road."

For his efforts Young was awarded the NAACP Spingarn Medal in 1981, and received the "Mayor of the Year" award from the National Urban Coalition in 1984. Married and divorced twice, his marriages did not bear any children. After retirement from the mayoral office he wrote an autobiography, *Hard Stuff: The Autobiography of Coleman Young*, published in 1994. He was also a professor at Wayne State University. Wayne State, which previously denied him a scholarship, honored him with an endowed chair in urban affairs in his name.

Fighting to the end, Coleman A. Young lost his battle with emphysema and died November 29, 1997 of respiratory failure at age 79. A son, Coleman A. Young II, sisters Bernice Grier and Juanita Clark, sisters-in-law Elizabeth Young and Muriel Young, cousins Dr. Claud Young and Esther Walker, and his companion Barbara Parker survive him.

Notes

[1]*Detroit Free Press*, "A Life Remembered," 1997.

[2]Coleman A. Young Foundation, "Coleman A. Young Bio," www.cayf.org/bio_cay.htm (2001), accessed on February 3, 2005.

[3]Ibid.

[4]Wilbur C. Rich, *Coleman Young and Detroit Politics*, (Detroit: Wayne State University Press, 1989).

[5]Coleman A. Young Foundation, "Coleman A. Young Bio," www.cayf.org/bio_cay.htm (2001), accessed on February 3, 2005.

JAMES GROUP
International

We are a group of companies
offering a variety of services

4335 West Fort Street
Detroit, MI 48209 USA
(313) 841-0070
Fax: (313) 841-5074
www.jamesgroupintl.com

- Intermodal Services
- Logistics Management
- Transportation
- Warehousing/Distribution
- Consolidation & Exportation
- Deconsolidation
- Packaging
- Sequencing
- Sub-Assembly
- Light Manufacturing
- Building Materials Distribution

- Land Development
- Facilities Management
- Foreign Trade Zone

WHO'S NEXT?

The achievements and dedication of the 2006 Who's Who In Black Detroit honorees makes life better for all of us and leaves a lasting legacy for tomorrow. We salute you not only for being named Who's Who, but for inspiring Who's Next.

That's a mission worth investing in.

huntington.com

Huntington

A bank invested in people.®

Hotel Pontchartrain

Soon To Be A Sheraton Hotel!

Added conveniences after renovations will be:

- ✿ 70- 2 Room Suites newly designed, including microwave, refrigerators for extended stay
- ✿ New Indoor Heated Pool, Fitness Center and Dry Sauna
- ✿ LCD mounted Televisions in all guest rooms
- ✿ Executive level floor with club lounge and complimentary Breakfast & Cocktails
- ✿ A few steps from your door to our new casual dining "Bistro Restaurant"
- ✿ Evening turndown service available
- ✿ Valet Parking
- ✿ Directly across the street from Cobo Convention Center
- ✿ 5 minutes from live entertainment, Detroit Symphony, Theater District, etc.
- ✿ "People Mover" commuter to/from all major facilities in downtown area 1/2 block away
- ✿ Minutes away from Museum of African American History and Motown Museum
- ✿ 5 minutes to downtown casinos Greektown, Motor City, and MGM Grand
- ✿ Across the border from Canada, Windsor Tunnel just five minutes away
- ✿ 5-10 minutes to major sports arenas Ford Field, Joe Louis, and Comerica Park
- ✿ 20 minutes from Detroit Metropolitan Airport

In addition to lodging at its finest, the Sheraton Pontchartrain Hotel will offer elegant banquet and meeting space for groups from 5 to 400 people. Top of the Pontch features a spectacular view of the Detroit River and Windsor skyline and additional meeting rooms available plus our prestigious grand Ballroom.

Two Washington Boulevard ◆ *Detroit, Michigan 48226-4416*
313-965-0200 ◆ *fax 313-965-4557* ◆ *www.hotelpontch.com*

One Of Detroit's Finest Traditions

For Reservations

313-965-0200

With diversity,
we all stand taller.

SEE IT, KNOW IT, LIVE IT!

<u>Diversity Declaration</u>

We, the employees of Fifth Third Bank, Eastern Michigan, acknowledge the importance and vitality of diversity in our organization. Embracing diversity allows our company to integrate the unique variety of women and men in our workforce, marketplace and community to include individuals of all ethnic, cultural, and generational backgrounds. A culture of inclusion is built on a work environment where everyone feels valued and respected – not only because of their differences and their unique contributions, but also for their similarities and common experiences.

We subscribe to the definition of diversity as the full utilization of all human resource potential. It is understanding and valuing differences, while mobilizing similarities effectively to achieve a common objective or goal.

- As leaders, we will serve as role models. Not because we must, but because we believe in the principle of diversity.

- As managers, we will adhere to consistent practices that support and promote the values of diversity.

- As employees, we will seek to create an environment where there is an abundance of opportunities for diversity.

We, the employees of Fifth Third Bank, Eastern Michigan, are committed to permeating the principles of diversity throughout our company beyond our imagination.

PertussisProtection™
Around the Whole Family

Two steps to protect babies from whooping cough

A serious illness: Whooping cough (pertussis) is a serious illness in infants that can result in hospitalization and death. Children younger than 6 months old are at highest risk. In the United States (US), almost 80% of babies 6 months old or younger with whooping cough are admitted to the hospital.[1]

A continuing upsurge in whooping cough: In 2004, the number of reported cases of whooping cough reached a 45-year high.[2-4] Reported cases of whooping cough are highest among these groups: infants too young to be vaccinated, adolescents, and adults. A study has shown that babies often get whooping cough from their mothers or other family members.[5] The protection provided by childhood pertussis vaccines "wears off" in adolescents and adults, who may then spread the infection to infants. But there is a way to protect your baby.

Take 2 steps to protect your baby

Vaccination for children: Today, children in the US are routinely vaccinated with a combination vaccine for diphtheria, tetanus, and acellular pertussis (DTaP). The Centers for Disease Control and Prevention (CDC) recommends vaccination at 2, 4, 6, 15-18 months, and 4-6 years of age.[6]

Vaccination for adolescents and adults: Protection from pertussis "wears off" so predictably that, in 2005, the CDC Advisory Committee on Immunization Practices voted to recommend a single booster of tetanus, diphtheria, and acellular pertussis (Tdap) vaccine for adolescents and adults (11-64 years of age) who have close contact with infants less than 12 months of age.[6,7]

Please talk to your family doctor about immunizations to protect your baby from pertussis.

References: 1. Centers for Disease Control and Prevention (CDC). Rate of hospitalizations for pertussis among infants aged <6 months—United States, 1994-1998 and 1999-2003. *MMWR.* 2005;54:1027. **2.** CDC. Summary of notifiable diseases, United States 1994. *MMWR.* 1995;43:68-77. **3.** CDC. Summary of notifiable diseases—United States, 2003. *MMWR.* 2005;52:69-77. **4.** CDC. Final 2004 reports of notifiable diseases. *MMWR.* 2005;54:770-780. **5.** Bisgard KM, Pascual FB, Ehresmann KR, et al. Infant pertussis: who was the source? *Pediatr Infect Dis J.* 2004;23:985-989. **6.** CDC. Recommended childhood and adolescent immunization schedule—United States, 2006. *MMWR.* 2006;54:Q1-Q4. **7.** Advisory Committee on Immunization Practice recommends adult vaccination with new tetanus, diphtheria and pertussis vaccine (Tdap) [press release]. CDC; November 9, 2005.

Detroit's

INTERESTING PERSONALITIES

"Look Like You've Arrived."

JUDGE CRAIG STRONG

By Monica A. Morgan

It is not surprising that flashes go off wildly on the Shrine Auditorium's red carpet in Los Angeles as Detroit's own Judge Craig Strong struts by linked with Lynn Whitfield, Tyler Perry and Victoria Rowell. He stops to pose. The photographers love him – he is decked out in a black tuxedo with shimmering gold accents. "New York may be the fashion capital, but Detroit is the style capital in black America. Clothes may come out of New York, but people in Detroit know how to wear them. We are known for our hair and nails," shares Judge Craig Strong.

It also isn't surprising that Strong is in the limelight at the NAACP's 2006 Image Awards. No matter where he goes and amidst all the stars, he can't help but stand out.

The next day he attends a private soiree hosted by Judge Greg Mathis and takes a photo with Camille Winbush from *The Bernie Mac Show* – they were both dressed in orange.

"My generation, which benefited from their labor, dressed for success," says the Wayne County Circuit Court judge. "My mother used to say, the quickest way to get where you're going is to look like you've arrived."

At 31, Strong was elected judge of the Detroit Recorder's Court, at the time the youngest to serve in that capacity. He was reelected four times. At 30, he became the youngest president of the Wolverine Bar Association. He has since served as president of the Association of Black Judges of Michigan and chairman of the Judicial Council of the National Bar Association (NBA).

Strong served as an official observer in the 1994 first all-race elections for South Africa. His initial trip there was as an NBA delegate who met with lawyers from various countries to develop an International Bar Association. He even had a chance to sit on the Supreme Court of South Africa.

Strong is a retired commander in the U.S. Navy Reserve. During a five-year tour in the Navy Marine Corp Trial Judiciary, he was the only African-American judge to preside over special courts marshal. The dapper judge is also a 33-degree Prince Hall Mason, a lifetime member of the NAACP, and a member of Alpha Phi Alpha Fraternity, Inc. and the Navy Reserve Officer Association.

Although he is busy, he always finds time to give back as he considers Detroit a great place to be entertained, live and raise a family. One of his major projects is helping the Charles Wright Museum of African American History increase membership.

Strong possesses his own collection of African and African-American photographs. He also collects masks, dolls, figurines, old newspapers clippings and even has photographs dating back to Reconstruction. He shares personal photos he has taken with such notables as former President Bill Clinton, former President George Bush, Muhammad Ali, Stevie Wonder, Aretha Franklin, Michael Jackson, Rev. Jesse Jackson, Colin Powell, Tom Joyner, J. Anthony Brown, Harry Belafonte, James Brown, Steve Harvey, Billy Dee Williams, Isaac Hayes, Renee Zellweger, Reynaldo Ray, Bill Cosby and Bishop Desmond Tutu. "My favorite photo is me kissing Rosa Parks on her birthday in the Bahamas."

You can't help but wonder when Judge Strong will be given his own television show. It would surely be a hit.

Photo by Monica Morgan

Still Dancing in the Street

MARTHA REEVES

By Monica A. Morgan

Although she is known for using her voice and "Dancing in the Street," after being elected by more than 90,000 voters in November of 2005 to Detroit's city council, Martha Reeves is now using her voice in a different way.

Reeves takes pride in being a voice of the people to promote tourism, support students and teachers for a higher standard of education, help renters become homeowners, and to help entrepreneurs start and maintain new businesses in Detroit.

Although politics was a recent dream, "I knew from the time I was three and sang at my grandfather's church, Metropolitan A.M.E. in Detroit, along with my brothers Benny and Thomas, that I wanted to be a singer," shares Reeves.

Reeves has come a long way from the night she received Motown's William "Mickey" Stevenson's business card after performing with the Del-Phis at Detroit's Twenty Grand Night Club. She was invited to come to Hitsville while being told "you've got talent."

"I immediately realized that this was the company with all the new, young black artists like, The Miracles, Mary Wells, Barrett Strong, Marv Johnson, The Marvelettes and Eddie Holland," says Reeves. She arrived there the next morning only to be asked by Stevenson, "What are you doing here? We only hold auditions on the third Thursday of each month. Answer this phone, I'll be right back," and he left.

"I waited for two or three hours for his return, answering phones, meeting the producers, and became their first secretary." Berry Gordy Jr. heard Reeves' demonstration recording, which was meant for another artist, and liked her voice. The Del-Phis were hired for a recording session with Marvin Gaye. "Nine months after arriving at 2648 West Grand Boulevard, we boarded our first tour bus along with the other artists and "Come and Get These Memories" and "Stubborn Kinda Fellow" entered the top 100 charts of Billboard, Cashbox and Record World simultaneously in 1962." That same year, Marvin Gaye and the Vandellas opened for The Beach Boys.

When Martha and the Vandellas hit the stage, the crowds were already on their feet dancing wildly to the infectious beat of tunes like "Quicksand," "Livewire" and "Heat Wave."

"Dancing in the Street" had people literally jumping out of their cars and actually dancing in the street when it hit the airwaves. The song went gold and has been considered the Motown anthem, which they sang on the *Ed Sullivan Show* in 1964.

Reeves and the Vandellas went on to perform with Flip Wilson, B.B. King, Lou Rawls, The Beatles, The Rolling Stones, Richard Pryor, Bob Marley, The Who, The Doors, Chubby Checker, Bob Hope, Sam Cooke, Redd Foxx and Elvis Presley, among countless others. Reeves was later joined by her sister Lois (Sandra) who became a Vandella.

"Berry taught us stage presence and critiqued our performances, giving tips and good advice that we still apply today, and Maxine Powell was hired to turn the stars into fine, polished personalities," says Reeves who remains close with Powell.

Reeves is an inductee into The Rock and Roll Hall of Fame, the Rhythm and Blues Hall of Fame, and is in the critically acclaimed film, *Standing in the Shadows of Motown.*

Detroit's Black Bottom

Elect coleman A. Young Jr.
For Detroit

MINI-MALL

Continuing a Legacy of Service

COLEMAN A. YOUNG II

By Monica A. Morgan

I f you knew his father, you can't help but stare at him. They are truly like father, like son.

Coleman Alexander Young II closes his weekly talk television and radio show on WHPR–Channel 20/Comcast and WHPR 88.1 FM, *The Young Effect*, with, "No one cares how much you know until they know how much you care." Young is attempting to persuade the residents of Michigan's Fourth District that he cares about them and can best serve their needs as their state representative. He won the primary election and is the Democratic nominee in an overwhelmingly Democratic district.

"Even though I have name recognition, I wanted the citizens to know that I was willing to work hard for their support. So I knocked on 40 to 60 doors personally, every day. I talked to everybody. The people of the district know that I care about them and their concerns," he says.

Young believes it is God's calling on his life to serve the people of Detroit, continuing the legacy of his late father, the Honorable Coleman A. Young, the first African-American mayor of the city. Mayor Young served the citizens of Detroit for 20 years as its mayor and ten years as a state senator. A product of Detroit's Black Bottom community, Mayor Young based his life's work on the philosophy that all people were entitled to a good quality of life – a solid education, a well-paying job, a comfortable home, safe streets and family recreation.

The old saying, "The apple doesn't fall far from the tree," is proving to be true as one compares the philosophies of both father and son. Young's campaign platform proposes expanding the job market; developing affordable housing; eliminating property taxes while implementing a progressive, graduated income tax; providing health insurance for every person; capping interest rates on mortgages, loans, and credit cards; and eliminating redlining with statewide uniform insurance rates for home and auto insurance.

At 23, Young does not view limited experience as a hindrance to seeking a state representative seat. "I wanted to do this while I was young and pure at heart. When you've worked in government (for a while), it takes your passion." Young describes himself as "...passionate, energetic and willing to do whatever it takes to get the job done."

Although he organized an e-business at age 16, Young also understands the plight of minimum wage hourly workers, having been employed at Subway and Auto Zone. He was an intern for the Detroit City Council Research and Analysis Division. He attended Bible college at Azusa Pacific University and is also a student at Wayne State University majoring in communications.

Young was baptized Coleman A. Young, but his parents chose to protect him with the alias, Joel Loving. His father legally changed his birth certificate to match his baptismal record when he was 13. His mother, Annivory Calvert, instilled spiritual values in her son that permeate all areas of his life. He is now a member of St. Paul Church of God in Christ of Detroit.

Coleman A. Young II is restless. He can't wait to be sworn in as a state representative and continue to help people even more. Like father, truly like son.

MOTOWN MOMENTS

Photo by Monica Morgan

A Touchdown of Taste

SOUTHERN HOSPITALITY RESTAURANT GROUP

By Monica A. Morgan

This recipe makes Detroit a better city – Frank Taylor, Robert Porcher, and executive chef Jerry Nottage – better known as the owners who are the driving force of the Southern Hospitality Restaurant Group.

The Southern Hospitality Restaurant Group owns and operates Seldom Blues Restaurant and Jazz Super Club in Detroit's Renaissance Center; Detroit Breakfast House & Grill @ Merchant's Row in the heart of Campus Martius; and the Grand City Grille in the New Center area. The Southern Hospitality Group also operates Sweet Georgia Brown, a restaurant in the Greektown area, the Woodward Restaurant in the Compuware Building, and the food service operations and event catering for One Ford Place Café, the corporate office center for the Henry Ford Health System.

Frank Taylor is a career entertainment and food service administrator. He refined his restaurateur skills in hotel restaurants including those located in Marriott, Doubletree, and Sheraton hotels east of the Mississippi. Taylor serves the Detroit community through several organizations including The Detroit Medical Center, Detroit Economic Growth Corporation and Mayor's Time. Michigan Governor Jennifer Granholm appointed him to the Michigan Tourism and Travel Commission to represent small businesses. Taylor directly impacts metro Detroit residents by supporting St. Leo's Soup Kitchen and sponsoring an annual free Mother's Day Brunch at Seldom Blues for some of the city's most deserving mothers.

Both Frank Taylor and Robert Porcher share a belief that they must give back and create business opportunities for their adopted hometown, Detroit. Porcher, a retired defensive lineman for the National Football League's Detroit Lions, is the president of the Southern Hospitality Restaurant Group. Porcher believes that it is important to live a life of success because he has a responsibility to make his ancestors proud of what he accomplishes. He dreams big dreams and has visions of expanding the Southern Hospitality Restaurant Group into other venues, like a cooking show for Chef Jerry on the Food Network.

Executive chef Jerry Nottage is the *pièce de résistance* of the Southern Hospitality Restaurant Group. A graduate of the prestigious Culinary Institute of America (CIA), Chef Jerry is serious about the cuisine that his kitchens produce. He refers to himself as a totally different person when he is in the kitchen—driven, focused and continually raising the bar for details in excellence. He takes great pride in some of the new dishes at the Detroit Breakfast House & Grill, where he has reinvented breakfast standards into fresh and exciting faire. "Just because it's the food that people know, doesn't mean it can't be different," Chef Jerry explained when he said that you can have ten children and no two are alike. Likewise, no two dishes are exactly the same. For example, Frank Taylor's French toast is a fresh twist French toast that is pleasing to the palate.

The Southern Hospitality Restaurant Group is a winning combination recipe that produces an outstanding trio of business vision, restaurateur excellence in imaginative surroundings, and dining elegance with award-winning dishes that are pleasing for all Detroiters. It's clear that the Southern Hospitality Restaurant Group has scored a touchdown for Detroit with their recipe for fine dining success.

Simply the Best

CARMEN HARLAN

By Coire Nichols Houston

With almost three decades as a broadcast journalist, the face of Local 4 is simply the best at what she does. Consistently voted "best local anchor" from area magazines and newspapers, she was even voted as having the best hair in the industry. Carman Harlan was recently featured in *Ebony* magazine's October 2006 issue. *Ladies Home Journal* honored her as one of the top two anchorwomen in the country, and *Crain's Business Detroit* named her one of its Most Influential Women.

Carmen can be seen on NBC affiliate WDIV Local 4, Monday through Friday on the 5:30 p.m., 6:00 p.m. and 11:00 p.m. broadcasts. Our native Detroiter's interest in journalism was piqued as a result of the civil rights movement. "In the 60s and 70s television brought these historical events right into our homes and it didn't stop there. The Vietnam War was taking place and there was a movement on the part of my generation which spoke out against the war and for civil rights. That, I think, was the major hook for me, wanting that front row seat in reporting history-making events," says Harlan.

She graduated from the University of Michigan with a degree in mass communications but one of television's most beloved almost missed our screens. While studying at Michigan, Carman actually had thoughts of going into psychology. Fortunately for us, she made up her mind by going into journalism.

Very family-oriented, Carmen enjoys spending her time off with her husband, three children, two dogs, two cats and the fish. She enjoys painting and, when time permits, she loves to travel.

Carmen gravitates toward anything affiliated with children and their well-being. The Children's Center and Alternatives for Girls are organizations with whom she has worked. "We did *Focus on Families* (WDIV) for years in which we were responsible for actually placing foster children in permanent homes. Anytime it involves children, I'm there," she says.

Most recently Harlan had the opportunity to sit with the family of Margaret Mattic, a local woman who moved to New York to pursue a career in the performing arts. She was recently honored at the Fine Arts Theater in Detroit with a tribute entitled "A Little Jazz & You." Mattic was a victim of 911 and perished in the twin towers. It was during Carmen's visit that the words of Hattie Mattic, Margaret's mother, left a profound thought which still resonates with her. "She was talking about young people growing up today. She said, 'Do something valuable in life and that will guide you. To anyone who is thinking about being a terrorist or wreaking havoc on anyone, think about doing something valuable in life first.'" These are words that Harlan tries to live by.

As long as she is healthy and charged up each day, we can expect to hear her laugh, see that addictive smile, and experience the most incomparable journalism reporting for many years to come.

Photo by Monica Morgan

Missions of Compassion

WARREN C. EVANS

By Monica A. Morgan

He carefully removes photographs from the walls of the Katrina-tattered home of a New Orleans police officer, and as he caresses the frames that hold all that is left of someone else's memories, the compassion in his eyes shows that he realizes he did the right thing.

"I could look at CNN and see people dying, and I couldn't in good conscience wait for a coordinated response," says Sheriff Warren C. Evans, whose speed and effectiveness put Wayne County and Detroit in the national spotlight in a great way.

From the start of his 37-year career in criminal justice and law enforcement, Evans' mission and professional passion have always been to help create safer communities. He has lived out his mission by serving as an attorney for nearly 20 years in addition to serving in every rank in the Wayne County Sheriff's Department from police officer to undersheriff. Currently Warren has a staff of more than 1,200 and an annual operating budget of $118 million, serving over two million residents.

Although, according to the sheriff a million balls are going at once, one of his pet projects is the Missing and Exploited Children's Unit. "I really like to hear from people who have been assisted by the work that the officers in the department do," says Evans. The unit has found many, many children who were runaways... kidnapped...When you can reunite kids with their family before they've been taken advantage of or ruined for life, that's a great feeling."

An empathetic look comes across his face as he smiles and says, "It's a great feeling to know that on a regular basis you catch fugitives. If not for us catching them, they would be taking advantage of our citizens."

Since assuming the helm in 2003 of Michigan's second largest law enforcement agency, Evans has led the department in developing collaborative regional programs that have taken more than 10,000 felony fugitives off the streets, and resulted in the arrest of numerous Internet child predators with a 100 percent conviction rate. Additionally, the efforts of the Last Call Unit have resulted in a significant decrease in drunken drivers ignoring their court dates. The sheriff has also taken steps to put a major dent in auto thefts in Wayne County in hopes of ultimately convincing insurance companies to lower the insurance rates of county residents.

When he is not chasing the bad guys and inconspicuously cruising around metro Detroit in his stealth-like Charger, the sheriff trades in his urban life for a little country living and horsepower of a different kind by taking to the great open spaces with Thunder and his other horses.

At a young age, Evans started working at a stable owned by a retired African-American Buffalo Soldier who taught him the basics about horses. The experience initiated his desire to learn more and to actually own horses.

For a person who has done so many things, Evans says he wants to be remembered "for being consistent about making the county safer and serving the public, and also as a person who didn't mind doing the job."

A Provider of Compassion to the People

LOUISE GUYTON

By Coire Nichols Houston

Louise Guyton, vice president of public affairs at Comerica Bank — Detroit's only remaining hometown bank — began her career as a teller at what was then Detroit Bank and Trust. She took advantage of Comerica's education reimbursement program, majoring in business administration and psychology, and received her bachelor of science degree from the University of Detroit.

In her current position with Comerica, Guyton manages the community outreach activities and serves as Community Reinvestment Act compliance manager for the City of Detroit. The Community Reinvestment Act is a federal regulation requiring banks to give back to the community. Deeply devoted to the economic revitalization of Detroit, Guyton is honored to work with many small businesses and nonprofit organizations in the city to help them reach their goals.

In addition to her professional commitment to serve, Guyton prides herself on her personal devotion to human services. A product of the civil rights movement, while growing up in Memphis, Tennessee, Guyton witnessed firsthand the necessity for equality for blacks and humankind. As a result, she sits on the boards of many civil rights organizations including the Southern Christian Leadership Conference and the Michigan Coalition for Human Rights.

Quick to praise God at any moment, Guyton, often referred to as "the Church Lady," is privileged to work with many faith-based organizations. She is a member of Delta Sigma Theta Sorority, Inc. and a lifetime member of the NAACP. The mother of two and grandmother of six, she manages to spend quality time with all of them on a weekly basis.

Guyton is the recipient of both accolades — *Who's Who of African Americans* in 2000 (not to be confused with *Who's Who In Black Detroit*®) — and awards, including the Spirit of Detroit and Minority Achievers awards.

Guyton's maxim in life is taken from a Negro spiritual that begins, "If I can help somebody along the way, then my living shall not be in vain." She believes "if I can help somebody as I travel along, and if I close my eyes today, then I know that my living has not been in vain." In reviewing her 38 years at Comerica, Guyton feels that she has been a role model and a mentor to countless young African Americans.

Living His Dream

RALPH GILLES

By Monica A. Morgan

"I would like to be remembered simply as the leader of a great team of risk takers that helped get Chrysler's mojo back," says Ralph Gilles, 34, vice president of Jeep®/truck and component design of the Chrysler Group.

Gilles was once head of the maverick design team, Chrysler Studio 3, known for the Chrysler 300 sedan, the Dodge Magnum, and the Dodge Charger.

Gilles loves cars. "The most rewarding part of designing a car is seeing it on the road in the hands of a content customer," says Gilles." The Chrysler 300 transcends race, economic and cultural lines, it is the car of choice for corporate executives, professional athletes, as well as hip-hop artists.

Over the past 13 years, Gilles has risen from sketching interiors to overseeing the design of what some have called the freshest and most desirable products on the road today. Passionate about his craft, Gilles believes "American cars have to be about not just a great car, but also a great looking car, and an artful car – a car that says more about transportation than just getting someone from point A to B."

At age five, family members recognized Gilles' drawing ability. His drawings were clear and made sense. As a teenager, Gilles corresponded with then Chrysler chairman Lee Iacocca for advice regarding his designs. Gilles received a response from K. Neil Walling, then Chrysler's design chief, that changed his life and initiated his loyalty to DaimlerChrysler.

At the urging of his brother Max, Gilles eventually followed Walling's advice and enrolled in the transportation design program at the Center of Creative Studies (CCS) in Detroit. In 1992 Gilles combined his gift of drawing cars with his degree and began his career at DaimlerChrysler. His first design battle was the chrome ornamentation on the Jeep Liberty. After winning the battle with an impassioned plea for the pricey chrome with the marketing department, chrome is now a design element in several Chrysler models including the 300C.

Gilles stays at the top of his game by teaching part-time at CCS. He is quoted as saying, "There is nothing fresher than a kid straight off the streets who perceives the world differently from someone who's working in a corporation. Combine all that – older, experienced designers, new ones and the designers Chrysler Group gets from all over the world, and you get a nice, cultural aesthetic mix." When he is not in the design studio, one can find him on the race track with his 10-cylinder Dodge Viper.

Living his dream, Gilles shared, "I'm one of the few people who can say I pinch myself every day because this is exactly what I wanted." His parents immigrated to Canada from Haiti when he was a toddler. His formative years were spent with his parents and in New York with his Aunt Gisele, who recognized his talent early on.

What is next for the family man with a wife and two children? Well, one of his daughters may be following in his footsteps and he can't help but smile about that. "Since none of us can sit still, you will see some great, new, world-class products coming from the Chrysler Group team."

BLACK FAMILY DEVELOPMENT, INC.
EXTENDED FAMILY
COMMITMENT PLEDGE

A Call to Serve One Family at a Time

ALICE G. THOMPSON

By Coire Nichols Houston

Established in 1978, Black Family Development, Inc. (BFDI) came to fruition as a result of the visualization of some of Detroit's most prominent social service, community and business leaders: Carol Goss, Paul Hubbard, William Pickard, Gerald K. Smith, Geneva Williams, and the current CEO of BFDI, Alice G. Thompson, to name a few. As members of the Detroit chapter of the National Association of Black Social Workers, this local think tank of African-American intellects had one common goal, "To Strengthen and Preserve African American Families" in the city of Detroit.

Black Family Development, Inc. provides services to individuals and families experiencing challenges in coping with their life circumstances. Services consisting of family support, advocacy, domestic violence, abuse, neglect, mental illness, substance abuse and delinquency are available to all races and cultures, not just African Americans.

Alice G. Thompson, the staff and board members have been very aggressive and strategic in securing funding to support the mission of the organization. The organization now has a budget in excess of 20 million dollars, but it still recognizes the importance of its initial annual budget of $70,000 through support from the then Department of Social Services, New Detroit, Inc., and other local funders. The original intent of the organization's founders remains: to not only strengthen families, but to advocate for and serve the community one family at a time.

Thompson's call to serve began as a child, as she recalls having compassion to help others in spite of her own modest living conditions. "God blesses everyone with unique gifts and talents and it is our job to discover what they are and use them to help and serve others. I realized my gift as a natural helper and peacemaker."

As a graduate of Wayne State University with bachelor's and master's degrees in social work, Alice has held many positions: research assistant with the City of Detroit Model Neighborhood Program; adjunct professor with Wayne State University School of Social Work; deputy director, Diversified Youth Services, Inc.; and her current position as chief executive officer of BFDI.

In addition to her professional involvement and social and community commitments, Thompson plays a leadership role as board secretary and treasurer of New Detroit, Inc.; board president of Hope Academy; and treasurer of Communities in Schools. Likewise, she is very active with her church as the department head of Straight Gate International Church pastors' aide auxiliary.

Thompson has also served in a leadership role with the National Association of Black Social Workers (NABSW). She has authored several publications geared toward advancing the goals of NABSW.

As a recipient of many awards, both locally and nationally, she respectively says that "Everything I do has a connection, whether it's in the realm of my employment, church or community involvement, it identifies who I am. For all the accomplishments one wishes to bestow on me, it has been as a result of teamwork and support. As a leader, my success in everything has been directly attributed to those who surround me."

This is why Alice G. Thompson has been called to serve by her peers and, she believes, most importantly, by God.

Photo by Monica Morgan

The Billion Dollar Man

GREGORY JACKSON

By Coire Nichols Houston

What are the three Cs of success? Just ask automotive dealership mogul Gregory Jackson. His answer might surprise you. His three Cs — CPA (Certified Public Accountant), Cookies and Cars — are what led to Jackson's being named *Black Enterprise* magazine's 2005 Dealer of the Year in the automotive category.

Jackson, a Detroit native, attended Morris Brown College, receiving a bachelor of science degree in accounting and an MBA in finance and marketing from Atlanta University's graduate school. After graduation he worked for Arthur Anderson and later established his own accounting firm. With a college buddy, he founded the Kastleton Cookie Company, a gourmet cookie company based in Highland Park, Michigan.

What began as a manufacturing plant for the development of his original cookie dough soon evolved into a full blown cookie franchise, The Kastleton Cookie Corner. Jackson became the "Mr. Fields" of the cookie industry by selling his cookie dough, store and oven designs to Hudson's Department Stores (now Marshall Fields/Macy's) in Southeastern Michigan. While the Kastleton Company did not prove to be financially lucrative, it did provide the business management tools Jackson has come to rely on.

In 1989 Jackson was invited to join Ford Motor Company's dealership academy. After doing some research, Jackson found a similar program offered by General Motors and chose to join GM. After successfully completing the academy and working at various dealerships, Jackson became a general manager under the tutelage of Charles Harrell, chief executive officer and owner of Harrell Chevrolet.

On September 2, 1993, Jackson bought a Pontiac/Oldsmobile dealership in Mount Morris, Michigan. The dealership was financed by GM; however, Jackson bought them out within seven months. This was the genesis of Prestige Automotive.

Jackson currently owns seven dealerships in Michigan, three in Florida and one in Ohio. His dealerships sell General Motors and Ford products, and his newest dealership is Mercedes-Benz of St. Clair Shores. He is one of only four African-American Mercedes-Benz dealers in the country.

While all of this is impressive, what truly makes Jackson a Who's Who of Detroit is the fact that he is the nation's only African-American billion-dollar dealer. That's right — Jackson's automotive group has achieved a billion dollars in annual revenue. The sky is the limit for Prestige Automotive and Jackson is looking to add five more automotive entities to his holdings.

Gregory Jackson is married and the father of two, residing in Detroit. He sits on the board of the National Urban League; is a former president of the GM and the Ford Minority Dealership Associations; a staunch supporter of the United Negro College Fund (Clark Atlanta University is of one of the member schools); and is a lifetime member of the NAACP and Kappa Alpha Psi Fraternity, Inc. He is also a member of Fellowship Chapel Church.

Jackson's advice to future automotive entrepreneurs: "Save your money, establish a good credit rating, do your research and most importantly, learn every aspect of the auto industry."

Photo by Monica Morgan

Sounding the Bell for Change

CAROL A. GOSS

By Monica A. Morgan

Carol A. Goss loves children. "I feel very passionate about children," she says with her big, infectious smile. "And especially about children who don't have the same opportunities as others."

As president and CEO of The Skillman Foundation, Goss loves her job because it allows her to do what she loves best, help children.

"Family is very important to me," she says, adding that including her husband's side of the family, there are more than 30 children in their extended family.

"I come from a family where it was impressed upon us that we have to give back. If you have been blessed to have education, health, shelter and any other resources, it's really incumbent upon you to give back to others. That has been a guiding principle in my life," says Goss emphatically. She has been in social work for 18 years and in foundations for 18 years, formerly with the Kellogg Foundation and the Stuart Foundation, a family foundation that focused on children.

That guiding principle is demonstrated in the numerous organizations that Goss is involved in, including: Grantmakers for Children, Youth and Families; the Association of Black Foundation Executives; Women in Philanthropy; Detroit Area Grantmakers; the Council of Michigan Foundations; Tomorrow's Child Michigan SIDS, Inc.; the Wayne County Task Force on Foster Youth Care; Juvenile Justice Advisory Committee; The Links, Inc.; the Michigan Task Force on the Overrepresentation of Minority Children in Foster Care; Minerva Educational Development Foundation Advisory Group; the NAACP; New Detroit, Inc.; the McKinley Foundation and the Michigan Aids Fund.

In order to have balance in her life, Goss sings in the choir and is an avid runner. "Running helps me stay healthy and also helps me put things into perspective."

She and a group of friends that she met at Powerhouse six years ago run daily at Belle Isle. Although they come from various walks of life, they have become a support network. "We talk about everything and solve the world's problems," she says proudly and states that along with them, she has even participated in the *Detroit Free Press* Marathon.

In addition to being a mentor and nurturing three adult children of their own, Goss and her husband, Tom, have opened their doors to their nieces and nephews for extended periods of time so they could have other opportunities and experiences.

Goss is focused on Skillman's Good School: Sounding the Bell for Change. "A good school is only one of the many things important to the healthy development of a child. The components of a strong family and a supportive neighborhood environment are the other necessary pieces. Together the three are like the legs of a stool upon which a child might sit and feel sure and steady.

"When one leg wobbles, the whole stool becomes unsteady and precarious. For too many children, this is the story of their lives. Our goal is to create sturdy stools for all children in metropolitan Detroit from which to grow and develop into healthy, productive adults."

"If every person decided that they were going to help one family, help one child, half the problems that we now experience would be greatly reduced...particularly with children, especially children that live in poverty."

Photo by Monica Morgan

A Work in Progress

CONRAD L. MALLETT JR.

By Monica A. Morgan

There's a quiet confidence that surrounds the once chief justice of the Michigan Supreme Court who transformed Sinai-Grace Hospital, the largest hospital within the Detroit Medical Center (DMC), to generate more than $750 million a year in revenue.

Conrad L. Mallett Jr. contributes all of his success—in law, city politics, and in health career administration—to the biblical adage, "The people will perish without a vision." His vision, a commitment to excellence, deep community involvement, and an ability to engage and energize people at all levels are the core leadership attributes that have enabled Mallett to alter the face of Michigan's court system, Detroit's waterfront, and most recently, Sinai-Grace Hospital.

"My personal dedication to this community, my long history of public service and the wonderful men and women who were anxious to get the community-based leadership that I have provided, all share the certainty that it is possible to have first class service within the confines of the city of Detroit," says Mallett.

"Although Sinai-Grace is still a work in progress...we rival our suburban competitors in customer service," says Mallet, who has worked at DMC as general counsel, chief administrative officer, and later as president and CEO of Sinai in 2003.

Prior to joining DMC, Mallett had a distinguished career as a lawyer and was appointed Michigan Supreme Court justice in 1990. Two victorious statewide elections to the court were followed by Mallett being named chief justice by his colleagues, a term he served from 1996 to 1998. Always seeking to address the needs of the community, Mallett spearheaded the movement in the state legislature to completely revamp the family court system.

Mallett left the Michigan Supreme Court in 1999 briefly returning to his old law firm, Miller Canfield Paddock and Stone. Asked to join the Detroit Medical Center soon afterwards, he directed the DMC's legal department, office of federal and state government affairs, human resources, managed care and community outreach.

With the full support of the DMC board of trustees, Mallett took time away from the DMC to serve as the City of Detroit's first ever chief operating officer at the request of then newly-elected Mayor Dennis W. Archer. In this position, he managed the departments of transportation and public works, among others. More importantly, Mallett renegotiated the agreements the City of Detroit had with MGM Grand, Mandalay Bay, and Motor City Casinos, which returned control of the city's waterfront to the City of Detroit. These agreements set in motion the billion dollar development now taking place on the Detroit waterfront. With these accomplishments, Mallett returned to the DMC.

Mallett combines discipline, upbringing, training and education with hard work to accomplish great things in this community as well as the state, and values the relationships he has developed throughout his lifetime that cross racial and economic lines, providing support and counsel when needed. He holds in high esteem his father, Conrad Mallett Sr., as well as Congressman John Conyers, the Honorable Coleman Young, Malcolm Dade, Dorothy Riley, and professors Louis Brown and Leonard Rater.

Mallett, who has four degrees and seems to have done it all, says that when he retires, it will be to another job.

A New Plateau

JEROME AND DEBERA SCOTT

By Melody Moore

Jerome Scott is a businessman. He has learned to invest his money and time into developing his future. He and his wife, Debera, are the national vice presidents of AmeriPlan USA, a discount medical program. The plan, however, does not provide medical insurance, but rather offers discounts for medical services.

Scott launched a company, Nature Option, which is an international health and nutrition company. His company has since developed relationships with England, Canada, Mexico, New Zealand, Trinidad, Malaysia, Thailand and Indonesia, in addition to the United States.

Before launching his company, he worked at John Hancock and New York Life Insurance. He also taught middle, high school and college students.

In 1997 Scott began working with AmeriPlan and said it has opened tremendous doors for his family. Additionally, AmeriPlan became an alternative for him after dealing with frustrations in corporate America.

"I've always been considered as a person who is alive to opportunity, and it was time to make a decision as to where I would spend the time I had," he said. "I attended an AmeriPlan Convention, and as I sat there, the business became more and more attractive to me."

"So, I decided to get serious about it and started doing it because I saw that the rewards were so great. I made the decision to readjust my time, putting AmeriPlan as the source of where most of it was spent, and the time I spent doing that has proved that it was a wise decision." Scott added that he also became interested in AmeriPlan because he was looking for a challenge and wanted to be able to use his skills, so when the opportunity came, he decided to take it.

He earned a bachelor of arts degree in accounting and financial administration from Michigan State University and a master's degree from Wayne State University in educational leadership. While at Michigan State, Scott served as president of Phi Beta Sigma Fraternity, Inc.-Delta Kappa chapter.

He and his wife have reached the highest level of recognition in the AmeriPlan organization, and they are reaching others along the way. Scott involved his parents in AmeriPlan and they have become national sales directors in Michigan.

The Scotts are among five others inducted into this AmeriPlan USA Hall of Fame. They are also aiming to reach the $500,000 Founders Ring Club.

Currently, AmeriPlan has more than 50,000 independent business owners who participate in the program.

Inspiring a Community

REVEREND WENDELL ANTHONY

By Thomas Tennant

Reverend Wendell Anthony, senior pastor of Fellowship Chapel in Detroit and president of the Detroit Branch National Association for the Advancement of Colored People (NAACP), stands as one of Detroit's most influential community leaders. One need only look to his extensive community involvement to see just how influential Rev. Anthony has been.

He is a member of several boards and councils inside the city of Detroit, including the First Independence National Bank, the National Association of Securities Professionals-Detroit, and the Detroit Building Authority. Overseeing the construction of various building programs within the city, Rev. Anthony's influence has garnered him local and national recognition. He has also served as chair of the Detroit Police Department citizens review panel, making recommendations for new policies and procedures on the use of less-than lethal force. This panel also made various recommendations for the reform of the Detroit Police Department.

In 1995 Rev. Anthony served as co-chair for the Million Man March Committee, organizing and hosting one of the largest delegations – more than 75,000 men – during the Washington D.C. event.

A native of St. Louis, Missouri, Rev. Anthony was educated in the Detroit Public School system and graduated from Wayne State University with a bachelor's degree in political science. He received his master's degree in pastoral ministry from Marygrove College. He became the pastor of Fellowship Chapel in December of 1986, following the passing of Reverend James E. Wadsworth Jr., and was installed as senior pastor in February of 1987. During his tenure, the church has experienced the greatest growth in its 39-year history.

Rev. Anthony sites his work with the NAACP in Detroit, the largest branch in the country, as one of his greatest accomplishments. He was elected president of the Detroit Branch NAACP in 1993 and was recently reelected to an unprecedented seventh term.

During his first term, Rev. Anthony organized and led a march of more than 250,000 persons in Detroit commemorating the 30th anniversary of Dr. Martin Luther King Jr.'s march to Detroit in June of 1963. This march occurred prior to the historical march in August of that same year. It was the largest march organized for this purpose since 1963. And he has been instrumental in the continued success of the Detroit Branch NAACP's annual Fight for Freedom Fund Dinner. Launched in 1956, today the dinner is the largest sit-down dinner of its kind in the world. Serving approximately 10,000 guests with a first class meal, the dinner is known to host world-renowned keynote speakers such as Thurgood Marshall, Sammy Davis Jr., General Colin Powell, President William Clinton and many, many more.

In 2001 Rev. Anthony founded the Freedom Institute, a nonprofit, urban think tank. The Freedom Institute sponsors Freedom Weekend annually with emphasis on economic, social justice and political empowerment. Most recently, Rev. Anthony, along with several high profile community leaders, helped mediate talks between Detroit Public Schools officials and the striking Detroit Federation of Teachers.

Rich in All the Other Things

SHIRLEY STANCATO

By Monica A. Morgan

A picture of a proud Haitian girl, or aptly called "Lady in Waiting" is on her office wall. The girl is about 14 years old. Proudly dressed in a muted sky blue dress, her hair is plaited and her skin smooth and rich like a Hershey's chocolate bar. The chair is blue, old, wooden, but looks like a throne the way the young girl sits with her bare feet dangling. Her attitude says royalty.

"CEO is what I do, not who I am," says Shirley Stancato, the first woman to be elected New Detroit's President and CEO in the coalition's 39 years. She often looks at the portrait in her office that reminds her of herself. "And the 'who I am,' is all that I've gotten from my family and friends. They are my foundation."

"I am a wife, a daughter, a sister, a parent, a friend," adds the first daughter of a family of six, three boys and three girls. "The job that I have at New Detroit and the jobs that I've had before are really an opportunity to live my life and my life is all those things."

Stancato started her 30-year banking career with NBD Bank (Bank One, now Chase) going from teller to senior vice president.

"I come from a strong family. My parents were married 62 years. I go every year to my family reunion in Louisiana; it fulfills me in a way that nothing else does," says Stancato, who herself has been married almost 25 years. She is also proud to have raised a nephew who is now a junior at Michigan State.

She balances her professional life with a spiritual one. A member of Third New Hope Baptist Church, she has a family Bible study every Monday.

For more than 23 years she has been getting together with her girlfriends. "We get together at each other's houses and we share everything. We've lost parents and siblings ... we've been through a whole lot together and I wouldn't trade anything for the friendships that I have. We go on trips together, bask in the sun, shop and eat ...that's what fills up my life," she shares.

"Growing up my dad did construction work and he didn't work in the winter, but I always said we weren't poor, we just didn't have any money. I got Goodfellow boxes when I was growing up, so I know what it's like not to have a lot of money, but I also know that doesn't mean that you aren't rich in all the other things," she says with confidence, perhaps reflecting on that photograph by Emerson Matable.

Stancato believes in giving back and that doesn't always take money. She recently received a letter that touched her very deeply. It commended Stancato for her support, her leadership, and how her positive traits helped shape the individual's life who was following in her footsteps as a result.

"I really believe that to whom much is given, much is required," Stancato shares.

Photo by Allen Einstein

The Mechanic Behind the Pistons

JOE DUMARS

By Coire Nichols Houston

Many might not know that Joe Dumars, one of Detroit's "Bad Boys" (1989 and 1990 NBA Champions) and president of basketball operations for the Detroit Pistons, has an additional "love" that does not revolve around basketball. Unbeknownst to many, Detroit's recent 2006 NBA Hall of Famer also serves as a committee member of the United States Tennis Association. "I have played tennis since I was 11 years old. Because of my induction into the Hall of Fame, I was unable to travel this year, but tennis has always been a passion of mine."

Our local "Bad Boy" has proven to be a great guy to the community as a partner in the establishment of the Joe Dumars Field Houses, multi-sport complexes located in Detroit and Shelby Township, Mich. His purpose for establishing the field houses came as a result of speaking with parents 12 years ago: to provide a safe and healthy environment for the kids. Don't be surprised to see Joe at any one of the complexes, as he may drop by at any time.

As a Louisiana native, the rage of Hurricane Katrina hit Joe deeply. "This was very personal; only one of my relatives was able to survive Katrina materially. Basically my relatives lost everything, homes and cars. My mother lives only a few hours away and she had 25 relatives living with her. This was very eye opening and spoke to the lack of voice the underprivileged have in this country."

In choosing player versus president, being a player (of course basketball) is much easier. However, before heading to the office, a typical day for Dumars begins with dropping his two children off at school, remaining physically fit with a daily workout, and then on to the daily tasks at the Palace in Auburn Hills. Later he heads back home with his wife and kids.

The Detroit Pistons are recognized as a world championship basketball team. The 2005-06 regular season was considered the best in franchise history and highlighted by an Eastern Conference Championship. In 2004-05 they took the title of NBA Champions. And all of this must be attributed to Joe D who is at the helm of team development. "For the past five years we have been an elite team within the NBA, and we will be in that position this year (2006-07)," he assures with confidence.

An avid reader, Dumars considers himself to be fanatical and eclectic, particularly about world events. He admits that his spectrum is broad and that there is nothing he finds uninteresting, with the exception of, ironically, anything sports related. Joe also confessed that he is an Internet junkie.

With a 20-year career in the NBA, Dumars has been considered one of the best in the basketball league. With that said, it is only fitting that Joe Dumars was chosen to be the mechanic in charge of tuning the Pistons franchise into the champions they are.

Photo by Blake J. Discher of Firefly Studios

Ensuring Community Excellence

MICHAEL G. BICKERS

By Thomas Tennant

Michael G. Bickers is no stranger to the importance of civic involvement. Every business decision he makes as Detroit market executive for National City Corporation is touched by his desire to do what's right for his customers and community.

"I couldn't do this job without having a strong commitment to my community," says Bickers. "It just wouldn't be possible. People count on me to know the dynamics of the city I serve, and I do everything I can to follow through on that expectation."

A Detroit native, Bickers' involvement is far-reaching. He is extensively involved in the Detroit community, including participation in the Detroit Black Chamber of Commerce, Booker T. Washington Business Association, Local Initiatives Support Corporation and the Detroit Economic Club. Bickers has actively served as a panelist in forums such as the 2005 Urban and Automotive Industry Symposium and 2006 Economic Strategies for Rebuilding New Orleans. Internally at National City, he is a member of National City's Southeast Michigan Community Development Company (CDC) advisory board and charitable contributions committee.

"I've always been someone who gets involved," says Bickers, "but I've never been involved in an organization I haven't been passionate about. That's advice I'd give to anyone. Passion for a cause, a community or an industry ensures that you will do your best work. The importance of doing your best can't be understated, either, since you are representing both your company and yourself when you're interacting with the community."

Bickers joined National City's predecessor bank, First of America, in 1986 as a commercial credit analyst after graduating from Oakland University with a bachelor's degree in finance. Talent, energy and focus propelled him to his current position as market executive, a role in which he is responsible for managing the day-to-day operations and sales functions of National City's 143 Detroit area bank offices, including Southeast Michigan and the Toledo, Ohio market area, as well as the hiring and development of personnel.

To reach such levels of success, Bickers was fortunate to learn an important career lesson early on. "Don't go about it alone," he says. "You have to be part of the team. Everyone on the team will bring a different set of skills, each complementary, and you will learn a tremendous amount through your interaction with them. You also have to be a contributor to the team and be willing to take on special projects, especially those critical to your organization."

Today, Bickers applies those lessons to his work at National City, helping chart the company's direction in Detroit. It's a future in which he sees the city and the company sharing ideas and resources to create a community ready to face future challenges and capture golden opportunities.

"We truly believe we have the best people in the business, and we are continually improving National City to meet the needs of our customers and community," says Bickers. "Every day that I come to work, I look forward to strengthening our relationships with our customers and further expanding my involvement in the Detroit community. The truth is, the success of our company is dependent on the success of our community. As Detroit goes, National City goes – making it even more important that National City not only serves our community, but is an active participant and inspiring leader to our community."

Turner

Building the Future

Photo by Monica Morgan

Building on a Passion

JAMES WATKINS

By Melody Moore

James Watkins loves to build. The 41-year-old Purdue graduate is a project manager at Turner Construction Company, after transferring from Chicago.

Watkins, a Chicago native, worked at various companies prior to moving to Detroit. He has served as vice president and director of construction for other Chicago-based companies.

As project manager, Watkins oversees several multimillion dollar projects, with his most memorable being the new Renaissance High School, one of the top schools in the Detroit Public School System.

He was offered a position in Detroit and decided to accept it, after Detroit Mayor Kwame Kilpatrick was elected as the youngest mayor.

"I saw a young black mayor and I was inspired," he said. "I liked his vibrancy and I wanted to be a part of what was being done in Detroit. I worked in Chicago as project manager for Turner and I've worked in purchasing and there was an opportunity to come to Detroit and work in business development, something that I have always wanted to do."

Additionally, Watkins is working to build lives through his community service. He also serves as community affairs director for Turner, where he handles outreach and community involvement.

"Turner has a number of programs that I have been able to implement in schools and work with kids, teaching them about the construction industry," he said. "This program has been very successful in other cities."

Watkins has been instrumental in launching the Youth Force 2020 program in the metro Detroit area. This initiative is aimed toward students who are interested in a construction career. Students are able to receive scholarships and complete internships. Turner Construction Company also adopts schools to mentor the students.

Twenty years ago, Watkins realized his passion and has decided to follow it.

"I wanted to become a master builder," he said. "I've always enjoyed working in Chicago and I have always been fascinated by the big construction projects. I have always been excited about being on-site and being a part of the process."

Watkins said he has learned many valuable lessons during his career.

"I learned the importance of team work and also that you have to have a passion for it. It's drive and motivation. I have been lucky enough to find something that I love. I really have a passion for this business and I learned to respect everyone involved."

His most challenging moments have been working for small agencies where he had to fulfill a variety of tasks that were not all related to his field. Those jobs, however, opened the door for many other positions to follow.

Watkins has received numerous awards for his work and service in the construction field. He even made history with Turner Construction, receiving the first community service award.

Photo by Monica Morgan

A Dedicated Disciple of Leadership

GEORGE F. FRANCIS III

By Coire Nichols Houston

"My father told me a long time ago, 'Son, it's all a matter of timing. If you have to call someone a name, you can call them any name in the book — if you pick your time and your place, the only thing they can do is smile.'" This is advice that George F. Francis III has lived by. As senior vice president and chief administrative officer for Blue Cross Blue Shield of Michigan, time and dedication have certainly been on Francis' side.

In addition to being senior vice president and CAO of "The Blue," Francis also serves as president of the Blue Cross Foundation. This organization has close to $60 million in assets that are earmarked for funding research carried out by health care related organizations.

Born and bred in rural San Angelo, Texas, Francis came to Michigan by way of General Motors. He worked for GM in Atlanta and was transferred to Detroit. Francis has a degree in business administration from Prairie View A&M in Texas and completed a program in management development at Harvard University's Graduate School of Business.

While he considers his role at Blue Cross a continuing work-in-progress, Francis finds great satisfaction in knowing that he has served as a mentor and leadership skills teacher to many young men and women who have been promoted to the vice presidential level. He is especially pleased that these men and women come from numerous ethnicities.

Francis also feels he has been instrumental in promoting dialogue and forging partnerships between union and management leaders in exploring various health care products and services to help control health care costs.

While Francis is nearing the end of his tenure at Blue Cross, he assures us that this is only the "end point at this particular stage in my life." Francis will soon retire with 18 years of human resource and community affairs experience but plans to continue playing a role in the arena he so much enjoys — providing guidance to his many employees. Currently, Francis serves on a variety of nonprofit boards, ranging from Boy Scouts of America to the Detroit Zoological Society and The Henry Ford (museum).

After retirement, Francis wants to continue to serve in the public service field, but this time not as a boss. He wants to serve as a principle-centered leader sharing his passion for training and development of leaders, particularly up-and-coming leaders in the city of Detroit.

Married and the father of three, George F. Francis III looks forward to instilling in his three grandchildren in Texas his work ethic and passion for service.

Holding Down the Fort

ANTHONY ADAMS

By Coire Nichols Houston

Deputy Mayor Anthony Adams has one thing on his mind and that is ensuring that the residents of the city of Detroit are safe at all times. As the second chief-in-command, Adams is responsible for the public safety departments which include Detroit's fire and police departments and the administrative hearing department.

In addition to manning our public safety, the deputy mayor also oversees all activities at the Ed McNamara International Airport, water and sewage, all recreation departments, human services, public works, health, public lighting, and transportation, which includes the Detroit People Mover and municipal parking.

How can one person wear so many hats? Adams should know, as his workday begins at approximately 7:00 a.m. with a series of meetings. "I am currently working on strategic plans with public lighting, determining whether we will divest ourselves with public lighting, and also the strategic plans for the Greater Resource Recovery Authority, the city incinerator. Usually if the mayor (Kwame Kilpatrick) is unable to attend something I will sit in place for him," explains Adams.

Born in Cincinnati, Adams moved to Detroit after meeting his wife, Judge Deborah Ross Adams (Third Judicial Circuit Court of Michigan). He is a father of three and, when he is not working on restructuring the city, he enjoys golf, swimming, and chess, a game always dominated by his son. He is a serious movie buff with a collection of 600 or more in his library. One of his favorites is *The Negotiator* with Samuel L. Jackson.

Anthony Adams began his career with the City of Detroit as executive assistant to Mayor Coleman Young, working in economic development. "I initially wanted to become a city manager, but I detoured by entering into law school." Prior to joining the Young administration, Adams practiced law at the law offices of Hill Lewis (Clark Hill) as a litigator. He received his juris doctorate from Georgetown University, as well as his bachelor of science degree in urban management.

The deputy mayor loves the city of Detroit, "We are really trying to restructure the city so that it can be competitive in a very competitive world, and I am very passionate about public education."

According to Adams, because the city has been hit with so many challenges, especially in the auto industry, the city is working closely with the state in the development of the single point of entry program. This program is specifically geared to train persons who may not have the educational background for many employers by obtaining assessments, providing job training skills, and assisting them in receiving any additional services needed at one set location.

With affordable to upscale housing, attraction of new business development, continuous restructuring of the educational system and city services, and Anthony Adams at the helm of making things happen, we are certain to see a lot of things taking place to reposition our city so it will remain viable.

Giving Back is a Way of Life

TJ ADAMS

By Melody Moore

Making money pays the bills, but it is not top priority at TJ Adams & Associates.

Owner TJ Adams says he wants to affect change in people's life, well beyond job placement. "Everything we do is around the will of God, which is helping people.

"The money that we make, the prosperity that we have, we turn that back into helping the community," Adams shares. "I may never be able to place you in a job, but if you need to talk to me, I will listen."

Adams has also involved his company in prison ministries, substance abuse issues and healthcare issues to reach a broader scope of people. His company, an executive search and job placement agency, was launched in a nontraditional way.

"I had been in healthcare for 17 years and I grew to several illustrious positions," Adams said. "I held positions including the assistant director of the Michigan Department of Public Health, chief of the division of HMOs for the Department of Public Health, deputy assistant, division chief of licensing and certification, and administrative manager of cardiovascular medicine at Henry Ford Hospital. I had all this heavyweight experience in healthcare and I couldn't find a job. No one would give me an interview."

Adams searched for months, submitting at least 1,000 resumes. Finally, he was offered a position at a job placement agency, but the pay was too low, he said. He would only earn $300 a week. Months later he accepted the position so he could feed his family.

His passion to care for his family, coupled with his desire to make an impact in the lives of others fueled Adams' fire to launch his company.

The Tuskegee Institute graduate has seen his share of obstacles. Adams and his wife married while he was in college. After losing his apartment to a fire while he was in college, he rebuilt.

Years later, Adams was out of work, his family lost their house and he had a car that was barely working. He rose from his lowest point to owning a company and employing others.

Money, however, is not what makes his clock tick. It is his burning desire to provide quality service for others – after all, most of his clientele is based on relationships.

"Nothing that we do is about money," Adams said. "We are in business to make money but we do things to help someone else. When people call us, they can talk to us about anything outside of the career search. If they need to talk about other situations in their life, they can. Our goal is to make a better quality of life for our clients."

Within the past 20 years, Adams has been affiliated with a number of organizations including the National Council on Alcohol and Drug Dependency, the NAACP, the Arab-American and Chaldean Council, and the National Association of Health Service Executives.

Educational Excellence at Its Best

DR. IRVIN D. REID

By Coire Nichols Houston

Dr. Irvin Dexter Reid, president of Wayne State University, has been captivated by learning his entire life. His fascination began at age six when he was first intrigued by the pictorial in the *World Book Encyclopedia*. As he grew up on South Carolina's Pawleys Island, Reid proved to be the epitome of educational excellence.

Reid was instilled with both religious and educational values while choosing to live with his grandparents, the minister and the teacher of the isle. "I rode to school with my grandmother, who in fact, was the only teacher in a two-room school house. She not only taught the lower grades (kindergarten through fourth grade), but ran back and taught the kids in the fifth, sixth and seventh grades. I had to stay in the afternoon because the bigger kids had a longer school day, so I had a two-tiered education by doing their projects as well," says Reid.

Before coming to Michigan, Reid spent an extended period in the eastern part of the country. He received bachelor's and master's degrees in general and experimental psychology from Howard University; a master's degree and a doctorate from the Wharton School of the University of Pennsylvania, with a specialization in marketing, applied economics and business; and a certificate in educational administration from Harvard University.

A high point in his career before coming to Detroit was Reid's eight-year tenure as president of Montclair State University in New Jersey. There he worked diligently with both local and state officials to bring about Montclair State's change in status from college to university.

Since his arrival as president of Wayne State in 1997, Reid has managed to make the university an integral part of the city of Detroit. Interaction and partnering with area businesses brought about the creation of Techtown, the Wayne State University Research and Technology Park. He was also involved in bringing a Barnes & Noble bookstore to the campus, and the development of a facility to house the student services department, a new parking structure and four new residential buildings for both undergrad and graduate students.

Among the many honors bestowed upon Reid has been the 1999 Postgraduate Achievement Award from Howard University, recognition as one of "12 Outstanding Michiganians" in 2000 by the *Detroit News,* an award from the National Aeronautical and Space Administration's (NASA) Technological Utilization Office, and the 2006 Ernst & Young Entrepreneur of the Year® award.

Reid is married, a father of two and a grandfather. From his Gullah roots to university prestige, Dr. Irvin D. Reid is certain to leave a legacy of educational excellence for generations to come.

THE BEST WAY TO LEAD

(is to listen)

Only by giving full attention to the voices of our community will we become enlightened. St. John Health is dedicated to serving the health needs of all the people in southeast Michigan. It's what we call REAL MEDICINE. For more information, please call 888-440-REAL

St John
HEALTH®

www.realmedicine.org

REAL MEDICINE™

AND STILL WE RISE:
OUR JOURNEY THROUGH AFRICAN AMERICAN HISTORY AND CULTURE

This long-term exhibition is the central experience of the Charles H. Wright Museum. The 22,000 square-foot exhibition space contains more than 20 galleries that allow patrons to travel over time and across geographic boundaries.

The journey begins in prehistoric Africa, the cradle of human life. Guests then witness several ancient and early-modern civilizations that evolved on the continent. Crossing the Atlantic Ocean, they experience the tragedy of the middle passage and encounter those who resisted the horrors of bondage, emancipated themselves, and sometimes took flight by way of the Underground Railroad. Throughout this trip, the efforts of everyday men and women who built families, businesses, educational institutions, spiritual traditions, civic organizations, and a legacy of freedom and justice in past and present-day Detroit are hailed. What an awesome journey!

For information, please call your museum at (313) 494-5800, or visit us on the web at www.maah-detroit.org.
315 East Warren Avenue, Detroit, Michigan 48201

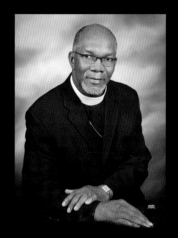

Third New Hope Baptist Church

"...A refreshing ministry for your spiritual growth"

E.L. Branch, Senior Pastor

Greetings!

As Senior Pastor of Third New Hope Baptist Church, I greet you in love and peace! We extend a special invitation for you to partner with us in ministry at Third New Hope. We are a ministry for the whole family, dedicated to the worship of God, the fellowship of believers, Christian discipleship and world evangelism.

We are preparing for a great season of worship and praise! We are committed to seeking the best of God for the cause of ministry. And in doing so, we embrace Paul's theme of victory as we "press" towards the mark for the prize of the high calling of God in Christ Jesus (Philippians 4:14)...and *we do so in the spirit of excellence.*

Please visit our web-site at www.thirdnewhope.com for detailed information regarding our many ministry services for children through adult.

Yet abiding,

Pastor E.L. Branch

WORSHIP

FELLOWSHIP

DISCIPLESHIP

EVANGELISM

As a deer longs for flowing streams, so my soul longs for you, O God.
Psalm 42:1 (NRSV)

rejoice!

WORSHIP SERVICES:

8:00 AM | 10:00 AM | 12 Noon

12850 Plymouth Road @ Steel | Detroit, MI | 48227
www.thirdnewhope.com (313) 491-7890 (Office)
(313) 491-0010 (Fax)

Comcast
Community Investment
For the connections that matter most

Using technology to bring people together is what we do at Comcast. Faster Internet and great entertainment can connect people and places in exciting new ways.

Not all networks are made of wires and switches. Networks are also made of people—families and the groups that make up a community.

Comcast is committed to keeping those networks strong. We live here too, and we're committed to keeping the lines of communication open—across your neighborhood.

1-888-COMCAST

Diversity Doesn't Just Happen...

We have 4 tools to help you succeed.

1 **DiversityInc Magazine** (12 issues)
The only business magazine focusing on diversity in the marketplace. Best practices and how-to from corporate diversity leaders.

2 **DiversityInc.com News Site**
Daily news and newsletters six days a week reported from an inclusive point of view. Hundreds of original online articles and resources to help you succeed with your diversity efforts.

3 **DiversityInc.com/Careers**
Visit the leading diversity career center on the Web that connects diverse candidates with companies committed to developing a diverse work force.

4 **DiversityInc Benchmarking**
A unique benchmarking solution that delivers the metrics needed for companies to make informed decisions around their diversity initiatives. **The DiversityInc Top 50** Companies for Diversity is also powered by this technology.

DiversityInc

Contact: Cecilia Fernandez • cfernandez@DiversityInc.com
DiversityInc • 570 Broad Street, 15th Fl. • Newark, New Jersey 07102 • 973-494-0506 • www.DiversityInc.com

Linda Thompson Adams
Dean and Professor
Oakland University
School of Nursing

D ean Linda Thompson Adams leadership has helped catapult Oakland University's School of Nursing to one of the largest schools of nursing in the country with over 1,500 students currently enrolled.

OU is the only education provider in Oakland County offering undergraduate, degree completion and masters programs in nursing accredited by the Commission on Collegiate Nursing Education.

Dean Adams, her staff and faculty work hard to meet the needs of an intense work environment by integrating clinical knowledge, communication, caring expertise and information management into programs that develop the professional skills and leadership qualities necessary for nurses of the 21st century. OU offers market-driven programs including the accelerated second degree, RN to BSN (online), RN to MSN, masters level programs in a variety of areas as well as the new Doctor of Nursing Practice degree.

Dean Adams is proud of the Oakland University / Beaumont Graduate Program of Nurse Anesthesia which was ranked sixth in the United States by U.S. News and World Report's 2004 edition of "America's Best Graduate Schools."

Oakland
UNIVERSITY

School of Nursing
Rochester, MI 48309-4401

Detroit's

MOST INFLUENTIAL

"Memories of our lives, of our works and our deeds will continue in others."

ROSA PARKS (1913-2005)

CIVIL RIGHTS ACTIVIST

MOST INFLUENTIAL

Jeanette M. Abraham
President & Chief Executive Officer
Detroit Heading, LLC

Jeanette M. Abraham is majority owner, president and chief executive officer of Detroit Heading, LLC. Detroit Heading has been ranked on *Black Enterprise*'s BE 100s list annually since 2002. Abraham was featured in *Black Enterprise* in 2003 as one of the top eight women CEOs.

Before acquiring Detroit Heading in 2000, Abraham was an executive in General Motors Worldwide Purchasing for 32 years. In 2001 she founded JMA Logistics, LLC. JMA was formed to manage all of the packaging and distribution of products manufactured by Detroit Heading.

Abraham is co-chair of the National Association of Black Automotive Suppliers' scholarship fund board, a certified member of the Michigan Minority Business Development Council, and chairman of the board for Detroit Heading.

Abraham earned her bachelor's degree from Wayne State University and her master's degree from Central Michigan University.

Abraham enjoys travel, jazz, working out, and being with friends and family. She is a member of Word of Faith International Christian Center in Southfield. A native of Detroit, Abraham resides in Farmington Hills and has an adult son, Evan.

Larry Alexander
President & Chief Executive Officer
Detroit Metro Convention &
Visitors Bureau

Larry Alexander is president and chief executive officer of the Detroit Metro Convention & Visitors Bureau (DMCVB). A 30-year veteran of the hospitality and tourism industry, Alexander has transformed the bureau into the leading organization for facilitating tourism economic development in metro Detroit. His introduction of a 10-year tourism vision for the region has led to several efforts to achieve regional beautification that are now underway; service training of hospitality industry workers; and infrastructure improvements.

Alexander efficiently runs the 50-person bureau and its $12 million budget. He leads an innovative, multi-award-winning convention sales, marketing and convention services effort that often exceeds CVB industry standards for performance.

Alexander navigated the efforts to land some of the world's most coveted sporting events, including Super Bowl XL in 2006 and the 2009 NCAA Men's Final Four. He created and leads the Detroit Metro Sports Commission, a DMCVB subsidiary responsible for landing the 2003 AAU Junior Olympic Games. He also contributed to the 2008 Women's International Bowling Congress, and the successful bid for the 2005 MLB All Star Game.

Charles E. Allen is president and chief executive officer of Graimark Realty Advisors, Inc., a real estate development company in Detroit. Prior to founding Graimark, he held various senior level positions in commercial banking and was president and CEO of First Independence National Bank of Detroit.

Allen serves on the boards of directors of the Auto Club Group, AAA Michigan, and Gartmore Mutual Funds of Nationwide Insurance Company. He was the first African-American chairman of AAA.

Allen's civic involvement includes serving on the board of directors for the Detroit Economic Club and as chairman of the Hartford Head Start Agency.

A graduate of Morehouse College, Allen received a master of business administration degree from the University of Chicago. He is a recipient of the DuSable Award from the University of Chicago, an honorary doctor of laws degree from Benedict College, the Martin Luther King Jr. Award for Distinguished Achievement in economics, the Outstanding Business Leader Award from Northwood University, and *Crain's Detroit Business* Real Estate Excellence Award.

Allen is a member of Omega Psi Phi Fraternity, Inc., Nu Omega Chapter.

Charles E. Allen
President & Chief Executive Officer
Graimark Realty Advisors, Inc.

N. Charles Anderson was reappointed president and chief executive officer of the Detroit Urban League in January of 1997. He also served in this capacity from October of 1987 to January of 1994. Anderson is the sixth and eighth person to serve as the agency's chief executive officer since its founding in 1916.

One of 100 affiliates of the National Urban League, the Detroit Urban League has an operating budget of more than $5.5 million and works to enable African Americans and other people of color to cultivate and exercise their fullest potential on par with all other Americans.

From 1994 to 1997, Anderson served as executive director of the city's department of human services, fulfilling his appointment by former Mayor Dennis W. Archer. From 1983 to 1987, Anderson was on the NAACP national staff as director of the seven-state Midwest region. He also worked for the Detroit Branch NAACP as youth director from 1981 to 1983, and he was a sales and marketing representative and district sales manager for the American Tobacco Company from 1974 to 1981.

N. Charles Anderson
President & Chief Executive Officer
Detroit Urban League

MOST INFLUENTIAL

Vernice Davis Anthony
President & Chief Executive Officer
Greater Detroit Area Health Council

Vernice Davis Anthony is the president and chief executive officer of the Greater Detroit Area Health Council (GDAHC). Leading the region's most influential healthcare coalition, she has provided leadership in developing strategies to address regional healthcare delivery through her active involvement in the creation of the Southeast Michigan Save Lives, Save Dollars initiative and the Detroit/Wayne County Health Authority. Anthony has a proven track record in developing and working with collaborative models aimed at improving healthcare quality, cost and access to care.

She serves on several boards and committees including Molina Healthcare of Michigan, the Wayne County Airport Authority, the Michigan Women's Foundation, the Governor's Council of Economic Advisors, the Detroit Economic Growth Corporation, and New Detroit. Anthony is a past president of the Western Michigan University board of trustees and is governor emeritus of the Wayne State University board of governors.

Anthony received a master of public health degree from the University of Michigan and holds an undergraduate degree in nursing from Wayne State University.

She is the proud mother of three adult children, and grandmother of three grandchildren.

Dennis Archer
Chairman
Dickinson Wright PLLC

Dennis Archer is chairman of Dickinson Wright PLLC, a Detroit-based law firm with 225 attorneys, and offices in Michigan and Washington, D.C.

Dennis served two four-year terms as mayor of the City of Detroit (1994-2001) and earned national and international respect for his success in changing Detroit's image and direction. He is currently chairman of the Detroit Regional Chamber of Commerce.

A graduate of the Detroit College of Law, Dennis has long been active in the organized bar. He was the first person of color elected president of the American Bar Association (2003-2004), as well as the State Bar of Michigan. He has also served as president of the Wolverine Bar Association and the National Bar Association. Dennis is a life member of the Fellows of the American Bar Foundation, the National Bar Association, and the Sixth Circuit Judicial Conference. He is also a fellow of the International Society of Barristers, and the College of Law Office Management.

Dennis serves on the boards of directors of Masco Corporation, Johnson Controls, Inc. and Compuware Corporation.

Born in Toledo, Ohio, but raised in Detroit, Grammy award-winning Anita Baker began singing in a Baptist church choir at age 12. Along with high school friends, she joined a band called Humanity at age 16. In 1975 Anita joined the popular Detroit group Chapter 8. After a few years the band landed a record deal with Ariola, later purchased by Arista. Following a disappointing review of her singing by Arista executives, Baker returned to Detroit and took jobs as a bar waitress and with a law firm as a receptionist.

She was approached to record a 1983 album for upstart California label Beverly Glen. The resulting album, *The Songstress*, revealed her as a developing star and attracted the attention of Elektra Records, which signed Baker to her first major label deal. Subsequent albums include *Rapture*, *Giving You the Best That I Got*, and *My Everything*, to name a few. Her music has garnered her multiple Grammys as well as American Music and NAACP Image Awards.

Anita is married to Walter Bridgeforth and the couple has two sons, Walter Baker and Edward Carlton.

Photo by Dave Hogan/Getty Images
Anita Baker
Jazz and Rhythm & Blues
Vocalist

Detroit native Don H. Barden is owner, chairman and chief executive officer of Barden Companies, Inc., the Majestic Star Casino, Waycor Development Company, and Namibia-based Barden International, Inc. His international conglomerate operates in the casino, real estate development, entertainment and automotive sales, service and manufacturing industries from the corporate headquarters in downtown Detroit.

Recognized as one of the top black entrepreneurs, he guided Barden Companies and its affiliates from earnings of $600,000 to revenues of more than $354 million, making it one of the largest African-American-owned businesses in the U.S.

Barden was the first black city councilman elected in Lorain, Ohio, and he founded the *Lorain Times*. He also spent 11 years as an on-air personality in Ohio and owned and operated five radio stations in Illinois.

A recipient of numerous honors, Barden maintains a strong commitment to Detroit through service in many organizations including, Detroit Renaissance, Inc., the Booker T. Washington Business Association, the Greater Detroit Regional Chamber and Henry Ford Health Systems.

Barden attended Central State University in Wilberforce, Ohio and holds three honorary doctor of laws degrees.

Don H. Barden
Chairman & Chief Executive Officer
Barden Companies, Inc.
Majestic Star Casino

MOST INFLUENTIAL

Jon E. Barfield, Esq.
Chairman & Chief Executive Officer
The Bartech Group, Inc.

Jon Barfield is chairman and chief executive officer of The Bartech Group, Inc. With $200 million in annual revenue and 2,700 associates, Bartech is among the largest independent human capital and professional staffing services firms in the United States, specializing in engineering, information technology and related outsourcing services and solutions. Prior to joining Bartech, Jon practiced corporate and securities law at Sidley Austin in Chicago.

Jon serves on the boards of numerous companies and nonprofit organizations, including Dow Jones & Company, National City Corporation, BMC Software, CMS Energy Corporation, Princeton University (charter trustee emeritus), The Henry Ford, Kettering University, Detroit Renaissance, and Blue Cross Blue Shield of Michigan. Jon has also served on the boards of Reading is Fundamental, the Community Foundation for Southeastern Michigan, and he is a past president of the National Technical Services Association.

Jon graduated with honors from Princeton University in 1974, and received his juris doctor degree from Harvard Law School in 1977. He is married to Norma Cassell Barfield and they have two children, Elaine and Jon.

Christine Beatty
Chief of Staff
Office of the Mayor
City of Detroit

Creating the NEXT Detroit requires capable leadership that knows how to manage people, build coalitions and put the citizens of Detroit first. As chief of staff, Christine Beatty has a solid "can do" reputation. With direct oversight of human resources, the Detroit Building Authority, Office of the Mayor, Neighborhood City Halls and Senior Citizens Department, Beatty has served in this important cabinet post since 2002.

Named one of Michigan's Most Influential Women by *Crain's Detroit Business*, Beatty's relentless commitment has produced solid results for the Kilpatrick administration. From successfully negotiating open labor contracts to playing a key role in creating the Detroit Wayne County Health Authority, Beatty has helped to bring about several victories for the city of Detroit.

For more than ten years, Beatty's commitment to public service has benefited Detroit, first serving as legislative aide for then-State Representative Kwame Kilpatrick. While Kilpatrick was House Democratic leader, Beatty was his district director in Detroit. Prior to working in state government, Beatty worked in the social services field, where she gained experience that has helped her contribute to public policy in Detroit.

M arvin Beatty has shareholder interest in Greektown Casino and is secretary of the Greektown Casino management board. He represents the casino and its community relations committee.

Beatty served with the Detroit Fire Department for more than 22 years. In 1994 he retired as Detroit's first African-American deputy fire commissioner. He served as executive director at the Wadsworth Community Center in Detroit. In 1995 the Detroit City Council appointed him to the Board of Zoning Appeals, on which he still serves. Beatty's "Women in the Fire Service" was included in an NFPA publication.

Beatty attended Osborn High School, and earned a bachelor of arts degree in urban management at California Coast University. He completed the National Fire Academy executive development program.

He serves on boards for the NAACP, the Detroit area council of the Boy Scouts of America, Boys Hope Girls Hope, the Coleman A. Young Foundation and the Downtown Detroit Partnership, among other nonprofits.

Beatty and his wife, Maxine, formed New Millenium Consultants. They live in Detroit and have two children and three grandchildren. Beatty's hobbies include golf and travel.

Marvin Beatty
Owner & Manager
Greektown Casino

C harles Beckham has been called to serve the City of Detroit more than once in the past 35 years. Beginning in 1974 as part of the Coleman A. Young administration, he served for ten years. He held numerous positions, including vice president of the public lighting commission, president of the water board, director of the Water and Sewerage Department and executive assistant to the mayor.

As part of the NEXT Detroit leadership team under Mayor Kilpatrick, Beckham brings tremendous experience and past success to the newly created Department of General Services. As chief operating officer, his talents for organization will be greatly utilized in shaping a modern government for Detroit.

His non-governmental achievements include founding BEnterprises in 1984, a technical management consulting firm in Detroit. A graduate of the University of Michigan, Beckham is president of the African American Alumni Council for the university. He has served on numerous boards and is a lifelong supporter of families, economic access and business in the African-American community.

Charles Beckham
Chief Operating Officer
Director, General Services Department
City of Detroit

MOST INFLUENTIAL

The Honorable Alisha Bell
County Commissioner
Wayne County

Alisha Bell is the youngest African-American woman to serve as a county commissioner in the nation. Bell was elected to the Wayne County Commission in November of 2002. She is the chair of the committee on health and human services and the special committee on women in government and business. She is also a member of the committee on economic development and the committee on ways and means.

As an active member of the community, Bell serves on the board of Planned Parenthood of Southeast Michigan, the National Council on Alcohol and Drug Dependence, the Salvation Army Southeastern advisory board, the Women's Informal Network and the Detroit Recovery Project. Moreover, she is a proud member of Delta Sigma Theta Sorority, Inc.

Bell is a native Detroiter. She grew up in the 8th District of Wayne County. A graduate of Cass Technical High School, Bell received her bachelor's degree in business administration from Florida A&M University. She received a master's degree in education from the University of Nevada, Las Vegas.

Alisha was married in November of 2004 to Mr. Kranston Young.

Dwight Belyue
President
Belmar Development, LLC

With over 24 years of experience as a licensed realtor and builder, Dwight Belyue is involved in real estate development and construction management. Building on experience from General Motors Corporation, he has managed and supervised more than $1.5 billion of construction and development projects. He is an expert in building design, contract negotiation, estimating, acquisition, construction management and financing.

Belyue is responsible for the development and management of several hundred thousand square feet of commercial space. He owns and manages Belmar Development, LLC, Belyue Enterprises, Bonnie Bridge Villas, 3100 Woodward, Condos @ 75, Central Brush Park and @water Lofts. He has also served on housing and nonprofits boards as a consultant and expert on affordable urban redevelopment.

Belyue aided in building an automotive processing center in Africa and the Majestic Star Casino Development at Buffington Harbor in Indiana.

Dwight is married and has two children. He and his family are devoted members of Word of Faith International Christian Center. He also volunteers his free time at the Detroit branch of the national Christian mentoring group, Young Life.

Dr. Melba Joyce Boyd is the distinguished professor and chair of Africana studies at Wayne State University. Poet, biographer, filmmaker, essayist and Fulbright Scholar, Boyd is the author of 50 essays and 11 books, seven of which are poetry. Her most recent books are *Blues Music Sky of Mourning: the German Poems*, *The Province of Literary Cats*, and *Wrestling with the Muse: Dudley Randall and the Broadside Press*, which received the 2005 Honor Award for Nonfiction from the Black Caucus of the American Library Association, Inc.

In 1980 Boyd received a Michigan Council for the Arts Individual Artist Award. In 1997 her work, "This Museum Was Once a Dream," was inscribed in the Wright Museum of African American History. Lines from "We Want Our City Back," appear in the downtown sculpture, *Transcending: Michigan's Tribute to Labor*. Additionally, Boyd's documentary film, *The Black Unicorn*, has been widely distributed and broadcasted.

Boyd has a bachelor of arts degree and a master of arts degree from Western Michigan University and a doctor of arts degree in English from the University of Michigan.

Dr. Melba Joyce Boyd
Distinguished Professor and Chair
Department of Africana Studies

Bill Brooks is chairman, president and chief executive officer of United American Healthcare Corporation. He is a member of the board of directors of Covansys, Inc.

Brooks is a retired U.S. Air Force officer and a retired vice president of General Motors Corporation. He is a former member of the board of directors of Louisiana Pacific Corporation and DTE Energy. He has served as chairman of the board of the Detroit Regional Chamber of Commerce and chairman of Detroit Public Schools Board of Education.

Brooks was nominated by President Bill Clinton on August 10, 1995, and was confirmed by the U.S. Senate, to serve as a member of the social security advisory board. He was nominated by President George Bush on June 8, 1989, and confirmed by the U.S. Senate, to be the assistant secretary of labor for the Employment Standards Administration, the largest agency in the Department of Labor.

In May of 1987, Brooks was the commencement speaker at Florida A&M University and was awarded an honorary doctor of humane letters.

William C. Brooks
Chairman, President &
Chief Executive Officer
United American Healthcare
Corporation

Ella Bully-Cummings
Chief of Police
City of Detroit

Ella M. Bully-Cummings is chief of police for the City of Detroit. When the Honorable Mayor Kwame M. Kilpatrick appointed her on November 3, 2003, she became the Detroit Police Department's first female chief in its 138-year history. Leading more than 4,700 sworn officers and civilian employees, Bully-Cummings commands the tenth-largest police department in the nation. Throughout her stellar career, she has always held issues affecting Detroit citizens in the highest regard.

Bully-Cummings received a bachelor's degree with honors in public administration from Madonna University and earned a law degree, cum laude, from the Detroit College of Law at Michigan State University. She was sworn in to the State Bar of Michigan in 1998.

Bully-Cummings also belongs to the National Bar Association, the Wolverine Bar Association, the International Association of Chiefs of Police, the National Organization of Black Law Enforcement Executives, and the Michigan Association of Chiefs of Police. She is a graduate of Detroit Leadership XX.

She resides in Detroit with her husband, William Cummings, a retired Detroit Police Department commander.

Craig A. Burres
Senior Vice President &
Internal Auditor
Flagstar Bank

Craig A. Burres, senior vice president and internal auditor of Flagstar Bank, has more than 20 years of experience in commercial banking. He is currently responsible for the bank's internal audit function and oversees its staff of 11 auditors. Previous to his current position, Craig served as a commissioned national bank examiner for the Comptroller of the Currency and as head of internal loan review at a local community bank.

Graduating from Cass Technical High School in Detroit, Craig received a bachelor of business administration degree from Western Michigan University in Kalamazoo, Michigan.

Craig is currently the treasurer and board member of Don Bosco Hall, a nonprofit organization in Detroit. He is also involved with the Boy Scouts of America and various booster and support groups at his sons' high school.

A Detroit native, he is an avid golfer who also enjoys traveling and photography. Craig's family includes his wife of more than 20 years, Roselini, and sons, Kyle and Cory.

State Senator Irma Clark-Coleman lives life with a purpose. Born in rural Georgia, she migrated to Detroit as a child. In 2006 she won a second term in the Michigan Senate. She serves on the banking and financial institutions, education, families and human services, and senior citizens and veterans affairs committees.

Clark-Coleman's public service began in 1967, when she joined the Wayne County Road Commission. For seven of her 31 years with the county, she served on the Detroit School Board, three of which she was elected president. In 1998 she retired from the county and ended her tenure on the board. That same year she was elected to the Michigan House of Representatives.

Clark-Coleman's honors include the Women of Wayne State University Alumni Association's 1997 Headliner Award, and the 150 Most Influential Black Women in Metro Detroit, 1997. She is involved in the community with the NAACP, God Land Unity Church, Alpha Kappa Alpha Sorority, Inc., and the United Way.

She earned her bachelor of arts and master of arts degrees in communications at Wayne State University.

The Honorable
Irma Clark-Coleman
State Senator, 3rd District
Michigan Senate

Representative John Conyers Jr. serves the 14th Congressional District in Michigan. His district covers large portions of Detroit and Dearborn, as well as Highland Park, Hamtramck and the down-river communities of Melvindale, Allen Park, Southgate, Riverview, Trenton, Gibraltar and Grosse Ile.

Elected to Congress for the first time in 1964, Conyers is the second-most senior member of the House of Representatives. He served as the chairman of the House Committee on Government Reform for five years and is currently the ranking member of the powerful Judiciary Committee.

During his tenure, Conyers has authored numerous seminal pieces of legislation, including the Martin Luther King Holiday Act, the Motor Voter Bill, the Alcohol Warning Label Act and the Jazz Preservation Act.

Conyers holds the distinction of being the only member of the Judiciary Committee to have participated in both the Watergate impeachment and the Clinton impeachment inquiry. He is a founding member of the Congressional Black Caucus and serves as the dean of that organization.

The Honorable
John Conyers Jr.
State Representative
14th District of Michigan

MOST INFLUENTIAL

Nathan G. Conyers
President
Jaguar of Novi

Nathan G. Conyers is president of Jaguar of Novi. He has the unique distinction of being the second longest tenured African-American retail vehicle dealer in the industry.

Born in Detroit, Conyers received his law degree from Wayne State University in 1959 and began a civil rights law practice. In 1970 he decided to pursue a family dream of becoming a successful entrepreneur and opened a Ford dealership. He became involved in the formation of and held leadership positions in several minority dealer organizations in the 1970s and 1980s. An advocate for equity and parity for African-American dealers, Conyers continues to remain an active voice as the "Dean of African-American dealers."

In 2002 Conyers opened the third African-American-owned Jaguar dealership in the country. Jaguar of Novi has received the prestigious Pride of Jaguar award for sales and service excellence for three consecutive years.

Conyers has been married to Diana for 50 years, and has five adult children and ten grandchildren.

Tyrone M. Davenport
Chief Operating Officer
Charles H. Wright Museum of
African American History

Tyrone M. Davenport is chief operating officer of the Charles H. Wright Museum of African American History. He joined the staff in April of 2002. Davenport retired from Bank One Corporation as senior vice president of technology risk management after 35 years of service. Before retiring, he held numerous senior management positions in the technology field for NBD Bank, First Chicago NBD and Bank One.

A Detroit native and product of Detroit Public Schools, Davenport received his B.S. degree in accounting from Wayne State University in 1968. He also graduated from the School of Bank Administration at the University of Wisconsin in 1978.

Davenport serves on the boards of the Detroit Omega Foundation and the board of visitors of the School of Pharmacy at Wayne State University. Previously, he served as chairman of the Michigan Automated Clearinghouse and vice chairman of the board of the Detroit Urban League.

Davenport resides in Detroit with his wife, Linda D. Forte; two daughters, Lynette P. Davenport, M.D. and Simone N. Perry, a Detroit public school teacher; and two granddaughters, Angela and Aurianna.

Donald Davis is chairman of First Independence Bank, Michigan's oldest African-American-owned commercial bank. He leads a bank with more than $220 million in assets, making it the 12th-largest black bank in the U.S., according to *Black Enterprise*.

A lifelong entrepreneur, Davis has been acknowledged as a leader in Detroit's business community for four decades. He is known for pioneering efforts in the music industry, as a proponent of community development through housing and banking, and as an innovative supplier of services to major corporations.

His success in financial and business ventures followed his departure from the music industry two decades ago, where he enjoyed an exceptional career as a music publisher, three-time Grammy winner and record producer.

A native Detroiter, Davis attended Central High School, where his love of music was nurtured.

An active patron of the arts and advocate of charitable organizations, Davis serves on the boards of Detroit Renaissance, the Detroit Economic Club and the Booker T. Washington Business Association.

Davis and his wife, Kiko, are the proud parents of one daughter.

Donald Davis
Chairman
First Independence Bank

Linda D. Forte is senior vice president of business affairs for Comerica Incorporated and a member of Comerica's management council. Forte is responsible for defining and driving business strategies that establish Comerica as a leader in diversity and work life practices. She also oversees the Comerica Charitable Foundation, corporate contributions and civic affairs.

Forte began her banking career with Comerica in 1974. She has held management positions in Comerica's small business, U.S. banking and loan administration groups, as well as positions in human resources and branch administration.

Forte serves as a director of the Economic Development Corporation of the City of Detroit, the Neighborhood Development Corporation of the City of Detroit, City Year Detroit, and the Women's Caring Program. She is a board member and chair of the Local Development Finance Authority, and chair-elect of the Michigan Women's Foundation.

In 2005 Forte received the YMCA's John Copeland Community Leadership Legacy Award. She holds a bachelor's degree from Bowling Green State University and an MBA in finance from the University of Michigan.

Linda D. Forte
Senior Vice President
Business Affairs
Comerica Incorporated

MOST INFLUENTIAL

Bellandra B. Foster, Ph.D., P.E.
President & Principal Engineer
BBF Engineering Services, PC

Bellandra Foster is founder and president of BBF Engineering Services, PC. The company is a civil and transportation engineering consulting firm founded in 1994 in the State of Michigan. The firm specializes in road and bridge construction inspection, transportation engineering, utility engineering, permit engineering and project management.

In 1999 Bellandra earned her doctorate degree in civil and environmental engineering from Michigan State University (MSU). She previously received her bachelor of science degree in civil and environmental engineering from MSU and a master of science degree in civil engineering from Wayne State University.

The achievements of BBF Engineering Services have gained regional and national recognition, having received the Federal Highway Administration's Minority Business Enterprise of the Year award. In 2004 the company was profiled in *Black Enterprise* magazine and in *Essence* magazine in 2005.

Bellandra enjoys being a wife and mother and shares her experiences, challenges and successes in combining these roles with being an engineer and entrepreneur.

A Michigan native, Bellandra is the wife of Michael Foster and the mother of two sons.

Harold Gardner
Senior Vice President, Gas Operations
Michigan Consolidated Gas Company

Harold Gardner is senior vice president of gas operations for DTE Energy subsidiary Michigan Consolidated Gas Company (MichCon), a natural gas utility company serving 1.3 million customers in Michigan. He is responsible for managing the operation of MichCon's transmission, distribution and gas storage systems.

Gardner previously served as DTE Energy's senior vice president of corporate services, and as MichCon's vice president of marketing, sales and regulatory affairs. Prior to joining MichCon, he was director of finance for the Detroit Science Center and a senior financial analyst for Ford Motor Credit Company.

Gardner earned a bachelor of arts degree in industrial management from Michigan State University and a master's degree in business administration from Harvard Business School.

He serves on the board of trustees for Leader Dogs for the Blind and has been a board member of numerous Detroit-area nonprofit organizations, including the American Red Cross Southeastern Michigan Chapter, Matrix Human Services and Adult Well-Being Services.

An entrepreneur and longtime business and civic leader, Ronald E. Hall is the president and chief executive officer of Bridgewater Interiors and Renaissance Alliance. He is also chairman and chief executive officer of New Center Stamping.

Hall is known for turning the Michigan Minority Business Development Council into one of the premier minority business organizations in the country, more than doubling its minority business and corporate memberships.

Maintaining board involvement in the Amateur Athletic Union (AAU) and Boy Scouts of America, Hall is very active in youth organizations. He serves as an AAU boy's national basketball commissioner, donating time during the summer to conduct national tournaments. Additionally, Hall is a national board member for the American Diabetes Association (ADA). He also serves as the chairman of the ADA of Michigan. Hall was elected to serve as a delegate at the White House Conference on Small Business.

Earning a bachelor of science degree in mathematics from Western Michigan University, Hall earned a master of business administration degree from Wayne State University.

Ronald E. Hall
President and Chief Executive Officer
Bridgewater Interiors

Kenneth L. Harris is the founder, president and chief executive officer of International Detroit Black Expo, Inc., an economic empowerment agent for African-American businesses in the state of Michigan. Founded in 2004, IDBE has grown to more than 10,000 businesses, the largest African-American business organization in Michigan. In May of 2007, IDBE will host the largest African-American consumer expo in the country, Detroit Black Expo Buy Black Weekend, at the Cobo Convention Center.

Kenneth has achieved numerous accomplishments at the age of 32. He earned a bachelor of arts degree in psychology, and a master of arts degree in counseling psychology from Clark Atlanta University, and is currently a candidate for an educational specialist degree at Wayne State University.

Kenneth made landmark accomplishments as the first African-American chief of staff and executive assistant to Mayor Brenda L. Lawrence of Southfield, Michigan, and the first African-American director of Greek affairs at Wayne State University. He is also a member of Omega Psi Phi Fraternity, Inc., Prince Hall Masonry and the Detroit Regional Chamber of Commerce.

Kenneth L. Harris
Founder, President &
Chief Executive Officer
International Detroit Black Expo, Inc.

MOST INFLUENTIAL

Joyce Hayes-Giles
Senior Vice President
Detroit Edison and Michigan
Consolidated Gas Company

Joyce Hayes-Giles is senior vice president of customer service for DTE Energy subsidiaries Detroit Edison and Michigan Consolidated Gas Company. She has held several leadership positions with the company, including vice president of corporate resources at MCN Energy Group. Previously, she was employed at the Automobile Club of Michigan and Chrysler Corp.

Hayes-Giles earned a bachelor's degree in psychology from Knoxville College, a master's degree in business from the University of Detroit, and a law degree from Wayne State University.

Hayes-Giles was elected to the Detroit School Board in 2005 and serves as its vice president. She was recently appointed to the Mentor Michigan Leadership Council by Governor Jennifer Granholm. She serves on numerous boards, including Marygrove College, Music Hall, THAW and Oakwood Healthcare, Inc. She is an active member of the NAACP, the Urban League, and she belongs to Delta Sigma Theta Sorority, Inc. and The Links, Inc. She was recognized by *Crain's Detroit Business* as one of Metro Detroit's Most Influential Black Business Leaders, and by *Corp! Magazine* as one of Michigan's Extraordinary African American Achievers.

Willie Horton
Executive Advisor &
Special Assistant to President
The Detroit Tigers

Willie Horton's civic and philanthropic commitment to the city of Detroit spans more than 45 years. Joining the Tigers' front office in 2001 at the request of owner Michael Ilitch, Horton is the highest-ranking African American in Detroit Tigers baseball operations.

An 18-year veteran of major league baseball, Horton produced nearly 2000 hits and 325 home runs. Horton is most noted for throwing out Lou Brock at home plate in Game Five of the 1968 World Series.

In 2000 the Detroit Tigers retired Horton's jersey, No. 23, and unveiled a statue in his honor, making him only the fifth Tigers player to receive this distinction. Governor Jennifer Granholm signed House Bill 5200, officially designating Horton's birthday, October 18, as Willie Horton Day in the state of Michigan. Known as the man who left Tiger Stadium in uniform after a game in 1967 in a desperate attempt to quell rioting in Detroit, Horton will forever be Detroit's hometown hero.

Horton and his wife, Gloria, reside in metro Detroit and have seven children, 19 grandchildren and four great-grandchildren.

Since serving as the fifth president of New Detroit, Inc., Paul Hubbard has held several management and community positions.

Hubbard is a life member of the NAACP. He is the past national vice president of the Association of Black Social Workers. Hubbard serves on several boards including Diversified Youth Services, Franklin-Wright Settlements, Goodwill Industries, the Detroit Science Center, Marygrove College, Grand Valley State University, WTVS Channel 56, the executive board of the Boy Scouts of America, Harper Hospital, and the National Urban League.

Hubbard has written several editorials for the *Detroit News*, the *Detroit Free Press*, *Crain's Detroit Business* and the *Michigan Chronicle*. He has received more than 100 awards, plaques and honors in recognition for his achievements in the community and civic service.

Currently, Hubbard is chairman of Alpha Restaurant Group, owners of Captain D's Seafood in Detroit.

Paul Hubbard
Chairman
Alpha Restaurant Group

Tupac A. Hunter was first elected to the Michigan House of Representatives in 2002. He serves as the ranking Democrat on both the banking and financial services committee and the insurance committee. He has led the effort to protect Michigan consumers from predatory lending practices and to address the high cost of home and auto insurance.

Hunter has also been a leader in the effort to increase youth literacy. He regularly speaks at Detroit public schools, and has donated more than 10,000 books to children across the metro area through his Leaders Are Readers program.

In August of 2006, Hunter won the Democratic nomination for state senator of the Fifth District, which includes northwest Detroit, Dearborn Heights and Inkster. He will become the first African American ever to represent this district in the State Senate.

Hunter earned a bachelor of arts degree in urban studies and public policy from Morehouse College in Atlanta, Georgia.

A native of northwest Detroit, Hunter is engaged to marry RaShawn Rushing and is the proud father of one son, Jalen.

Tupac A. Hunter
State Representative, Ninth District
Michigan House of Representatives

MOST INFLUENTIAL

George Jackson Jr.
Chief Development Officer
City of Detroit

The NEXT Detroit requires strong and aggressive economic development leadership that will do what is necessary to create a global destination through increased economic and development activity. In January of 2006, Mayor Kilpatrick named George Jackson Jr. as the city's chief development officer to continue the economic progress Detroit has made in the past four years.

As chief development officer, Jackson will be responsible for coordinating all economic development activity within the city. With an extensive professional background and deep-rooted ties to the community, Jackson is uniquely qualified to serve in this critical cabinet position.

In 2002 Jackson was elected president and chief executive officer of the Detroit Economic Growth Corporation. In this role, Jackson led efforts to transform Detroit by completing monumental revitalization projects such as the Lower Woodward Improvement Program, which redefined the city's decades-old central business district. Playing such an integral role in Detroit's economic momentum over the past four years, Jackson is sure to help continue the transformation of Detroit, neighborhood by neighborhood.

John A. James
Chairman
James Group International

John A. James is chairman and chief executive officer of James Group International (JGI) in Detroit. JGI offers international supply chain services including consolidation, deconsolidation, sub-assembly, inventory management, warehousing, distribution and transportation. His first business venture was O-J Transport, which he founded with his uncle, Calvin Outlaw, in 1971.

James' pioneering efforts in the transportation industry include taking his case for transportation authority to the U.S. Supreme Court in 1975. *O-J Transport v. United States* contributed greatly to the inclusion of African Americans in national transportation policy. He was the first African American in the U.S. to be issued broad operating authority to transport automotive parts and other commodities in interstate and foreign commerce. O-J Transport evolved into the group of five companies that comprise JGI.

A native of Starkville, Mississippi, James received a bachelor of science degree in sociology from Mississippi Valley State University in 1964. He is a former commissioned officer of the Corps of Engineers.

James is married to the former Sharon Nicks, also of Starkville, Mississippi, and they have three children, John, Lorron and Keri.

Placing great emphasis on the need to assemble the best legal minds to address challenges in creating the NEXT Detroit, Mayor Kilpatrick appointed John E. Johnson Jr. as corporation counsel for the City of Detroit. Johnson brings more than 25 years of legal expertise to the Kilpatrick administration along with a career that exemplifies legal advocacy on behalf of the public.

Having spent most of his legal career representing the indigent and middle class, Johnson is perfectly qualified to protect and represent the best interests of the citizens of Detroit. Serving as both corporation counsel and director of the law department, Johnson is responsible for helping manage the city's legal matters, while reducing its caseload.

Johnson's background in the legal arena and civic and community affairs has uniquely qualified him for his role in Mayor Kilpatrick's cabinet team. From running one of the nation's largest legal aid programs, to serving as past president of both the Michigan Coalition for Human Rights and the Wolverine Bar Association, Johnson is a respected legal mind and civic activist in Detroit.

John E. Johnson Jr.
Corporation Counsel
City of Detroit

The Honorable Brenda Jones is a member of the Detroit City Council. There, she is committed to improving the safety of neighborhoods and schools, as well as preserving the character of residential neighborhoods, creating affordable living and exhibition space, and fostering an atmosphere of responsible development.

Jones is the former president of Communications Workers of America, Local Union 4004. She also serves as secretary for the CWA International Union Minority Caucus. She is a trustee of Michigan Minority Networking Women – Detroit chapter, and a trustee of Friends of Black Men in Unions.

Jones is a precinct delegate of the City of Detroit and vice president of the A. Philip Randolph Institute – Detroit chapter. She is a member of the Coalition of Black Trade Unionists, the Trade Union Leadership Council and the NAACP. She is the NEB delegate of the Coalition of Labor Union Women.

A graduate of Wayne State University's Labor School, Jones is a native of Detroit.

The Honorable Brenda Jones
Council Member
City of Detroit

MOST INFLUENTIAL

Diana C. Jones
Vice President, Community Affairs
Blue Cross Blue Shield of Michigan

Diana C. Jones is vice president of community affairs for Blue Cross Blue Shield of Michigan. She is responsible for corporate giving and community outreach events statewide. She joined Blue Cross Blue Shield in 1974 and has since held positions as senior community relations representative, coordinator of case management and manager of GM managed care.

Diana holds a juris doctorate from the University of Detroit Mercy School of Law; and a master's degree in speech communications and a bachelor's degree in psychology and speech from Wayne State University. She is a member of the American College of Medical Quality, and received advanced certification in corporate community relations and social responsibility at Boston College.

Diana serves on the boards of the American Heart Association, Central Michigan University president's advisory council, the Visiting Nurses Association, and the Elder Law of Michigan, Inc. She is a trustee of the Downtown Detroit Partnership and was appointed to the Governor's Taskforce on Elder Abuse.

Born in Detroit, Diana is a member of The Links, Inc., Renaissance chapter, and the State Bar of Michigan.

Theresa C. Jones
President & Owner
Northwestern Dodge, Inc.

Theresa Jones is president and owner of Northwestern Dodge, Inc. In this position, she oversees the day-to-day management and major decisions for the automobile dealership. She currently has 70 employees in departments including new cars, used cars, service, parts and body shop. She is the only African-American female Dodge dealer in Michigan.

Theresa was named the first woman president of the Daimler Chrysler Minority Dealer Association in 1994. She currently serves on their board of directors – council of presidents. She has received numerous awards with the association.

Theresa received her bachelor of arts degree from St. Mary's College in Leavenworth, Kansas, and her master's degree from Wayne State University. She is currently in the process of defending for her doctor of philosophy degree.

A native of Kansas City, Kansas, Theresa is the widow of Jesse Jones since 1990, and the proud mother of three children, Michelle, Jason and Joseph.

Aaron E. Jordan is president and chief executive officer of Diversified Fuel Group, Inc., an ExxonMobil distributor specializing in customized fuel management solutions throughout the Midwest.

With more than 15 years of petroleum experience, Jordan has enjoyed a successful career with ExxonMobil that ultimately led to his majority ownership of Diversified Fuel Group, Inc., a minority-owned-and-operated distributorship.

Soon after joining the Quaker Oats Company immediately following college, Jordan began a career with Mobil Oil Corporation.

At Mobil, he acquired extensive knowledge in business management including retail operations in corporate and dealer stores, real estate, fleet operations and marketing. He held key leadership positions for both Mobil and ExxonMobil in Chicago, Detroit, Phoenix, the Los Angeles Basin, San Diego and Fairfax. As diversity marketing manager, Jordan led a multi-market initiative to build business, brand awareness and community relations within the African American and Hispanic segments.

Aaron is president of the ExxonMobil Distributor Council and a member of the Michigan Petroleum Association and the Detroit Oilman Club. He is also a lifetime member of Alpha Phi Alpha Fraternity, Inc. and the NAACP.

Aaron E. Jordan
President & Chief Executive Officer
Diversified Fuel Group, Inc.

Currently serving as president of the Southfield City Council, Sylvia Jordan was elected to council in 1997. She and her husband are also founders of the Family Victory Fellowship Church located in Southfield.

Jordan is actively involved in the National League of Cities (NLC) serving as a panelist and workshop moderator. She received a NLC Leadership Training Award - "Foundations of Leadership: Building Character, Courage & Credibility." She also serves on the board of directors for Inform Yourself, Inc., which teaches youth entrepreneurship skills.

The author two books, *Seven Great Women Who Changed the Course of History* and *Turning Your Dreams Into Reality*, Jordan has traveled to Cape Town and Johannesburg, South Africa. Her recent trip to South Africa was documented, receiving a Telly Award for the humanitarian work performed.

A graduate of Cass Technical High School, Jordan holds a bachelor's degree in urban studies from Michigan State University and performed graduate studies at Oakland University.

The acclaimed author, entrepreneur and public speaker is married to Pastor Larry T. Jordan and the proud mother of two young adults.

The Honorable Sylvia Jordan
President
Southfield City Council

MOST INFLUENTIAL

**The Honorable
Carolyn Cheeks Kilpatrick**
U.S. Representative
13th Congressional District of Michigan

The Honorable Carolyn Cheeks Kilpatrick was elected to the U.S. House of Representatives in 1996. A member of the powerful House Appropriations Committee, she has secured more than a half billion dollars to revitalize Michigan.

Kilpatrick has fought for affordable health care and secured $18 million in home mortgages for moderate-income families. She obtained a presidential executive order increasing federal contracting opportunities for minority businesses.

A native Detroiter, Kilpatrick earned a bachelor's degree from Western Michigan University and a master's degree from the University of Michigan. She taught business education in the Detroit Public Schools before being elected to the Michigan House of Representatives. There, she served 18 years and became the first African-American woman on the Michigan House Appropriations Committee.

Kilpatrick is second vice chair of the Congressional Black Caucus. She is the first African-American member of Congress to serve on the Air Force Academy Board.

Kilpatrick is the proud mother of a son, Kwame, who is serving his second term as mayor of Detroit, and, a daughter, Ayanna. She is grandmother to five grandsons, including two sets of twins.

**The Honorable
Kwame M. Kilpatrick**
Mayor
City of Detroit

In 2002, at 31, Kwame M. Kilpatrick became the youngest mayor of any major U.S. city. Now in his second term as mayor of Detroit, Kilpatrick has revitalized America's 11th-largest city.

As mayor, Kilpatrick has successfully handled an oil spill, a blackout and a sluggish economy. He led Detroit to the largest residential, commercial and economic boom in 50 years. In 2006 Detroit was named the top city in Michigan's southeast region in terms of new development.

Prior to his election as mayor, Kilpatrick was the first African American and the youngest person elected as the leader of any party in the history of the Michigan legislature. As a state representative, he helped to design the Clean Michigan Initiative.

A lifelong resident of Detroit, Kilpatrick graduated from Cass Technical High School. He earned his bachelor of science degree in political science from Florida A&M University, and his law degree from the Detroit College of Law at Michigan State University.

He and his wife, Carlita, have twin ten-year-old boys, Jelani and Jalil, and a four-year-old son, Jonas.

Brenda L. Lawrence was elected mayor of the City of Southfield in November of 2001. She is the first African American and first woman mayor of Southfield. The city has a resident population of 78,300, a city budget of $118 million, and 833 city employees. Lawrence is committed to diversity, fiscal responsibility, education, and keeping a clean and safe city.

Since becoming mayor, Lawrence has initiated the following community programs: The Mayor's Walk community health program; the Mayor's Roundtable, a citizen-driven forum where residents can have one-on-one discussions on topics of concern; Annual Flower Day; a citywide blood drive; and *Today's Woman*, a cable show featuring respected women in and around Southfield.

Lawrence is a member of the Oakland County Chapter of the NAACP, the Michigan Association of Mayors board of directors, the U.S. Conference of Mayors advisory board, and the Southfield-Lathrup Optimist Club.

Lawrence and her husband, McArthur Lawrence, are the proud parents of Michael and Michelle, and they have a granddaughter, Asya.

**The Honorable
Brenda L. Lawrence**
Mayor
City of Southfield

Aubrey W. Lee earned his first degree at age 20 from West Virginia State College and his master's degree from Marshall University at age 21. He has since been a trailblazer in the banking industry both locally and nationally. He is an advisor for Fifth Third Bank of Eastern Michigan where he reports to the president and CEO, and also serves on the board of directors for Beaumont Hospitals.

In 1972 Aubrey became one of the first African-American vice presidents of a major United States bank and in 1980 he was appointed chairman, president and CEO at NBD's Troy Bank. He became regional director for regional banking in 1983, and was responsible for all lending and branch operations for half of the city of Detroit. He retired as senior vice president of NBD/Bank One.

In 1982 Aubrey was elected to Beaumont Hospital's board of directors and is the immediate past chairman of the board. He has played a critical role in the success of Beaumont's diversity initiatives.

Aubrey has been recognized with more than 20 state, local and national awards.

Aubrey W. Lee
Board Member
Beaumont Hospitals

Elaine Lewis
Vice President
Public Affairs and Strategic Planning
Detroit Tigers, Inc.

Elaine Lewis, the highest-ranking African American and woman in Detroit Tigers business operations, is avidly committed to community service and the empowerment of youth. Elaine plays a pivotal role in developing programs that encourage Detroit's youth to embrace the game of baseball. Under her leadership, the Tigers Fields of Champions program has renovated numerous inner city fields including the Willie Horton baseball and softball diamonds at Horton's alma mater, Northwestern High School in Detroit.

Elaine's accomplishments include the establishment of the Detroit Tigers Foundation, Negro Leagues Weekend community events, the Community Ticket Program, and the Detroit Tigers Speakers Bureau. She oversees the Tigers Diverse Business Partners Program, which is one of the most successful in Major League Baseball.

Elaine earned a bachelor's degree from Wayne State University and a master's degree from Central Michigan University. She serves on the boards of Ilitch Charities for Children, the Michigan Sports Hall of Fame, the University of Detroit High School and CATCH.

A member of Delta Sigma Theta Sorority, Inc., Elaine currently resides in northwest Detroit with her husband and two children.

Samuel Logan
Publisher
Michigan Chronicle

Samuel Logan is publisher of the *Michigan Chronicle* and one of the owners of Real Time LLC, which includes the *Michigan Chronicle, The Michigan FrontPAGE, Chicago Defender, New Pittsburgh Courier* and *Memphis Tri-State Defender*.

A graduate of the High School of Commerce in Detroit, Logan earned a bachelor of business administration degree in marketing at the University of Detroit. He also received an honorary doctor of public service from Central Michigan University.

Logan served in the Paratrooper Division of the U.S. Army. He is a member of the Detroit Urban League, the Booker T. Washington Business Association, the Detroit Chamber of Commerce, and a life member of the NAACP. Some of his current board memberships include the Michigan Historical Commission, New Detroit, Inc., the Detroit Historical Society and the Communicating Arts Credit Union.

A man of great distinction and accomplishment, Logan has been honored by numerous organizations and government entities, including the State of Michigan, Wayne County, the City of Detroit, the Michigan Department of Public Health, Detroit Public Schools, the Metro Youth Foundation, and Omega Psi Phi Fraternity, Inc.

Karen Love is chief operating officer of the *Michigan Chronicle* and chief operating officer/publisher of *The Michigan FrontPAGE*. As chief operating officer, Karen is responsible for local and national advertising sales and is the liaison to other African-American newspapers and related organizations across the country. She has been responsible for overseeing the daily operations of the company since 1989.

With more than 30 years of newspaper experience, Karen's awards are too lengthy to list. They include the *Chicago Tribune* Black Achiever Award, the National Political Congress of Black Women (Detroit) Woman of the Year, the American Diabetes Association Awareness Award, and the 2004 Pillar Awards of Excellence from MPRO and the Michigan Department of Community Health. The Michigan State Senate presented her with a proclamation recognizing her as one of Detroit's outstanding leaders. She is also founder of Project LoveSHARE and serves on numerous boards.

Karen graduated with honors with a bachelor's degree in Christian education from Eastern North Carolina Theological Institute in 2004, and she is a graduate of Wayne County Community College.

Karen Love
Chief Operating Officer
Michigan Chronicle

George Mathews is currently the president of WGPR Inc. and supreme president of the International Free and Accepted Modern Masons, a black Masonic organization with 350,000 members.

A native of Montgomery, Alabama, Mathews is a graduate of Buffalo State College with a degree in accounting. He served in the U.S. Navy and began his career at Union Carbide Corporation as a benefit plans administrator, retiring after 32 years of service.

Mathews is a board member of the Rotary Club of Niagara, a chairman of the Commission of Civil Service, and a planning board chairman of the City of Niagara Falls. He is involved with the Casino Gambling Commissioner Study Group, the Urban Renewal Agency of Niagara Falls, the Niagara Political Action Committee, the Black Achievers Committee, and the Human Rights Commission. A member of the NAACP, Mathews also serves the United Way of Niagara, the Salvation Army, Boys and Girls Club of Niagara, and the Industrial Management Club. Mathews is the recipient of the honored Top Hat Award from WHLD radio.

Mathews is married to Alline, and father to Patricia.

George Mathews
President & General Manager
WGPR Inc.

MOST INFLUENTIAL

Cassandra McKinney
Senior Vice President &
National Product and
Sales Management Director
Comerica Bank

Cassandra McKinney is senior vice president and national product and sales management director for the Detroit-based Comerica Bank. She leads the development/management and integration of products for small business and personal banking relationships; manages a $22.7 billion product portfolio for growth and profitability; and provides training and sales support for teammates across the franchise.

McKinney has 22 years of experience in sales, marketing and strategy. Prior to joining Comerica Bank, she served at Bank of America, leading key lines of businesses, as well as providing strategic, planning and technical support. She started her career at IBM where she gained critical leadership and sales skills, providing client support for Fortune 100 accounts.

McKinney holds bachelor's degrees from the Columbia University School of Engineering and Applied Science, and Dillard University.

McKinney serves on the board of directors for YMCA of Metropolitan Detroit and is a member of the United Way Tocqueville Society.

Maurice McMurray, Esq.
Senior Vice President &
General Counsel
Health Alliance Plan

Maurice McMurray is senior vice president and general counsel for Health Alliance Plan (HAP), one of Michigan's largest, most experienced health plans. Maurice oversees HAP's team of corporate lawyers and serves as the secretary for the board of directors.

Maurice has more than 20 years of legal experience in the Detroit area as in-house counsel. He came to HAP in 1994 from Henry Ford Health System, HAP's parent organization. He was previously an attorney for General Motors.

Active in civic organizations, Maurice is making an impact on Detroit. He is a charter member of 100 Black Men of Greater Detroit, an organization that improves the lives of African-American youth. Maurice also spent six years as commissioner of The Greening of Detroit, which guides the reforestation of Detroit through tree planting and educational programs.

Maurice graduated magna cum laude from the Detroit College of Law with a juris doctor degree, and earned a bachelor's degree from Wayne State University. He holds a master's degree from the University of Michigan, and is a graduate of the prestigious Leadership Detroit and Leadership Michigan.

L egal expertise will play a critical role in creating the NEXT Detroit. Understanding the fundamental need to assemble some of the best and brightest legal minds, Mayor Kilpatrick appointed former city council member Sharon McPhail as general counsel in the Office of the Mayor. McPhail's 30-plus years practicing law and her extensive knowledge of city government makes her uniquely qualified for this important cabinet post.

McPhail's portfolio includes law, human rights and the workforce planning and development departments. These departments will be critical to helping improve antiquated systems and outdated work processes that have challenged city government for decades. Her expertise in practicing law includes work as a trial lawyer, an assistant United States attorney, a division chief in the Wayne County Prosecutor's Office, corporate counsel with Ford Motor Company and partner in a local law firm.

McPhail has also served in several quasi-judicial capacities including that of hearing officer for the Michigan Civil Rights Commission, and arbitrator and mediator in both Wayne and Oakland Counties.

Sharon McPhail
General Counsel
City of Detroit

I n 2001 Derrick Miller was appointed deputy chief of staff under the first African-American democratic leader in the Michigan House of Representatives, Kwame M. Kilpatrick. In this role, Derrick was responsible for developing the Democratic caucus agenda and he worked closely with members of each branch of government.

In 2002 Kilpatrick was elected mayor of Detroit and appointed Derrick the chief administrative officer. There, Derrick served as senior advisor to the mayor, provided strategic oversight of key large-scale initiatives and coordinated the enterprise-wide processes for the City of Detroit.

Derrick was appointed chief information officer in 2006. He leads the city's information technology systems and is currently working on plans to make Detroit a completely wireless community in 2008.

Derrick serves as co-chair for the Detroit East Riverfront Development Conservancy, vice chair for the Wayne State University Research and Tech Park Board, and co-chair for the Detroit Area Regional Transportation Authority. He serves on the boards of the Detroit 300, the Detroit Economic Development Corporation, the Greater Downtown Partnership Committee, Next Detroit and Next Energy.

Derrick Miller
Chief Information Officer
City of Detroit

MOST INFLUENTIAL

Kandia Milton
Mayor's Office Liaison to City Council
City of Detroit

Creating the NEXT Detroit requires capable leadership that can work closely with the legislative branch of city government to improve the overall quality of life for the citizens of Detroit. As the Mayor's Office liaison to City Council, Kandia Milton has helped to forge a more cooperative relationship between the executive and legislative branches of city government to implement progressive policy that will help create the NEXT Detroit.

For more than two years, Milton has worked daily with the Detroit City Council and their staff on several initiatives and policies to help improve the city. He has worked tirelessly to help pass initiatives such as the Lower Eastside Development Plan, the creation of the Department of Administrative Hearings, and four important capital improvement bonds worth millions in infrastructural enhancements in neighborhoods across Detroit.

Joining the Kilpatrick administration in 2002, Milton has developed a strong grasp on the inner workings of city government, an invaluable asset in his continued efforts to move the administration's various policies and initiatives to enhance Detroit, neighborhood by neighborhood.

Rodney O'Neal
President & Chief Operating Officer
Delphi Corporation

Rodney O'Neal is president and chief operating officer of Delphi Corporation, a leading maker of automotive and transportation electronics and systems. He is a member of the Delphi strategy board, the company's top policy-making group.

O'Neal has also held numerous positions at General Motors, including a number of engineering and manufacturing positions in Dayton, Portugal and Canada. In 1997 he was elected a GM vice president. In 1998 he was elected a Delphi vice president, and in 2003 he was named president of the dynamics, propulsion, thermal and interior sector.

O'Neal earned a bachelor's degree from Kettering University and a master's degree from Stanford University. He is a member of the Executive Leadership Council and sits on the board of directors for the Goodyear Tire and Rubber Company. He is a former member of the board of directors for INROADS, Inc., the Michigan Manufacturers Association and the Woodward Governor Company, as well as the advisory board for Focus: HOPE.

Linda V. Parker was appointed director of the Michigan Department of Civil Rights in November of 2003. A native Detroiter, she is a former partner at the Detroit-based law firm of Dickinson Wright, PLC. Parker was the first executive assistant U.S. attorney for the Eastern District of Michigan under the leadership of former United States attorney Saul A. Green from 1994 to 2000. Additionally, she served as the director of development at the Detroit Institute of Arts.

Parker is a University of Michigan graduate with a juris doctorate from the National Law Center at George Washington University in Washington, D.C. She is past president of the Wolverine Bar Association and has served as chair of New Steps. Currently, Parker is a member of the Michigan Board of Law Examiners, a fellow of the Michigan State Bar Foundation, and a board member of Boys Hope Girls Hope and the National Conference for Community and Justice.

She is a recipient of the 2006 Anti-Defamation League Women of Achievement Award and the 2005 Damon J. Keith Community Spirit Award.

Linda V. Parker
Director
Michigan Department of Civil Rights

Randi Payton, president and chief executive officer of OnWheels, Inc., founded the only multimedia automotive communications company for African Americans, Latinos and Asians, in July of 1995. *African Americans OnWheels*, circulates 750,000 magazines, bi-monthly in 40 black and four mainstream daily newspapers. Serving second and third generation ethnic minorities, *Latinos OnWheels* has a quarterly circulation of 400,000 in 37 newspapers, and *Asians OnWheels* will distribute 137,000 copies bi-annually.

OnWheels launched its Web site in July of 1995, opening doors for all minority media and agencies when it became the first to secure luxury vehicle advertisements.

The annual Urban Wheel Awards is the only multicultural event held in conjunction with the North American International Auto Show. Payton also founded the Edward Davis Education Foundation to provide scholarships, internships, and mentoring to minority youth pursuing careers in the auto industry and communications.

Randi Payton
President & Chief Executive Officer
OnWheels, Inc.

Payton was awarded the 2006 National Minority Media Cornerstone of the Year Award from the U.S. Minority Business Development Agency, and was selected by *Folio* magazine as one of the Top 40 Industry Influencers who are shaping the magazine business.

MOST INFLUENTIAL

Glenda D. Price, Ph. D.
Retired President
Marygrove College

Glenda D. Price, Ph.D. assumed the presidency of Marygrove College on July 1, 1998. She was the college's seventh president and the first African-American female to hold the position. She retired on June 30, 2006.

A native of Pennsylvania, Price attended Temple University. She earned a bachelor's degree in medical technology, a master's degree in educational media, and a doctorate in educational psychology. She also completed the management development and New President's Institute programs at Harvard University.

Prior to coming to Detroit, Price served as provost at Spelman College. She has held positions as dean of the School of Allied Health Professions at the University of Connecticut, and professor and assistant dean of the College of Allied Health Professions at Temple University.

Price is involved in numerous community organizations in Detroit. She serves on the boards of Alma College, ArtServe Michigan, LaSalle Bank, Compuware Corp., the Detroit Receiving Hospital, the Mercy Education Project, the Detroit Symphony Orchestra, the Detroit Institute of Arts and the Michigan Colleges Foundation.

Price resides in Detroit and enjoys gourmet cooking, reading and international travel.

George L. Richards Jr.
Senior Vice President
Southeast Michigan Retail Banking
Center Administration, Comerica Bank

George L. Richards Jr. is senior vice president for Comerica Bank's southeast Michigan retail banking center administration, which includes Comerica's 161 banking centers in and around the Detroit metropolitan area.

Richards began his banking career in 1973 when he joined Comerica's branch management training program. He has held positions in branch management, branch operations, regulatory compliance and corporate communications.

Richards earned a bachelor's degree from Fisk University and is a graduate of Leadership Detroit.

After receiving her master of business administration degree from Duke University in 1983, Pamela Rodgers returned to her hometown of Detroit, where she joined Ford Motor Company as a financial analyst.

Rodgers launched her career in automotive sales, working as a sales person at several dealerships where she gained invaluable experience in all aspects of dealership operations. She applied and was admitted to Ford's minority dealer development program in 1988, making her one of only a handful of women granted this opportunity.

In early 1993 she took over the Flat Rock dealership in Detroit, managing to increase sales to $18 million. In 1995 it became number one in service satisfaction for the Detroit area. Unfortunately, GM closed the Flat Rock facility, so Rodgers purchased the neighboring dealership in Woodhaven, and named it Rodgers Chevrolet, which she has operated since 1996.

Rodgers Chevrolet has grown from 40 units per month to 210 units. In 1996 the dealership generated revenues of $37 million. By 2001, sales were more than $80 million and continue to average more than $75 million.

Pamela E. Rodgers
Owner
Rodgers Chevrolet

Creating the NEXT Detroit will require sound knowledge of the city's fiscal and budgetary functions. Having served as the deputy budget director, Pamela Scales has more than 19 years of service with the City of Detroit. She brings extensive experience in dealing with the specific challenges of managing the city's budget to her newly appointed post of budget director.

During her tenure as deputy budget director, the City of Detroit has been awarded nine Distinguished Budget Awards from the Government Finance Officers Association. A faculty member with University of Phoenix, Scales teaches graduate and undergraduate finance courses. Her invaluable knowledge of the inner workings of budgetary functions, coupled with her commitment to the citizens of Detroit and demonstrated service will help strengthen fiscal operations as they create the NEXT Detroit.

Pamela Scales
Budget Director
City of Detroit

MOST INFLUENTIAL

**The Honorable
Martha G. Scott**
Senator, 2nd District
Michigan State Senate

State Senator Martha G. Scott, a Democrat from Highland Park, represents Michigan's 2nd District, which includes portions of Detroit, Hamtramck, Highland Park, Harper Woods and the Grosse Pointes. Elected to the Senate in 2001, she serves on the Senate Appropriations Committee.

Scott began her public service career in 1972 as a precinct delegate. In 1977 she was appointed to the Wayne County Board of Commissioners, serving as vice chair of the Wayne County Civil Service Commission in 1979. From 1984 to 1987, Scott was president of the Highland Park City Council. She was elected mayor of Highland Park in 1988. From 1998-2000, she served as state representative of the 6th House District, representing Highland Park, Hamtramck and portions of Detroit.

Scott is a South Carolina native and graduate of Highland Park Public Schools and Highland Park Junior College. She has honorary doctorate degrees from the Urban Bible Institute of Detroit and the Tennessee School of Religion. Scott retired from Michigan Bell in 1986 after 26 years of service. She has two children and two granddaughters.

Nettie H. Seabrooks
Chief Operating Officer
Detroit Institute of Arts

Nettie H. Seabrooks was named Detroit Institute of Arts (DIA) chief operating officer on September 19, 2002, after having joined the museum in February of 2002 as senior associate to the director.

Prior to joining the DIA, Seabrooks was the chief operating officer and chief of staff for Detroit Mayor Dennis W. Archer. Appointed to this position on January 1, 1998, Seabrooks also served as Mayor Archer's deputy mayor and chief administrative officer during his first four-year term in office. At the time of her appointment by Mayor Archer in 1994, Seabrooks was director of government relations for General Motors Corporation's North American Operations, and had been with GM for 31 years.

Seabrooks has a bachelor of science degree in chemistry from Marygrove College and a master of arts degree in library science from the University of Michigan. She also earned a master of arts degree in art history from Wayne State University, and received honorary doctor of humane letters degrees from Marygrove College and the University of Detroit-Mercy.

Creating the NEXT Detroit requires strong and experienced fiscal stewardship. As the director of the city's budget department and former city auditor general, Mayor Kilpatrick appointed Roger Short as chief financial officer to lead the effort to improve the city's financial condition. As a part of the mayor's cabinet team, Short is responsible for overseeing the daily financial matters of the city. His portfolio includes the finance, budget and purchasing departments.

As a certified public accountant with more than 20 years of accounting and financial management expertise within city government, in addition to seven years in the public accounting sector, Short is uniquely qualified to help develop the necessary strategies to deal with the city's financial challenges, and ultimately help to put Detroit on solid financial ground.

Roger Short
Chief Financial Officer
City of Detroit

Born in Detroit, Marjorie Ann Staten is a graduate of the University of Detroit Mercy and the University of Detroit School of Law. For nine years, she worked at the country's largest minority-owned law firm, Lewis & Munday, P.C.

Staten serves as executive director of the General Motors Minority Dealers Association. In the past five years, she has helped the GMMDA to increase membership, and develop and implement benefits, programs and initiatives. Staten was a key player in a major research project to develop the first private investment fund with a group of minority investors.

Staten is involved with numerous civic and professional organizations. She serves on the boards of the National Association of Minority Automobile Dealers and the Student Mentor Partners Program. A member of the State Bar of Michigan and the Wolverine Bar Association, she was awarded the WAAI's 2004 Spirit of Leadership Award and was honored as one of the 25 Influential Black Women in Business by *The Network Journal*.

An active member of St. Mary's of Redford Church, Staten is the mother of one son, Martin.

Marjorie Ann Staten
Executive Director
General Motors Minority
Dealers Association

MOST INFLUENTIAL

Emanuel Steward
Manager & Trainer
Kronk Gym

Emanuel Steward has guided some of the greatest boxers of the past three decades to world championships, and has helped many regain lost championships. He transformed Kronk Gym in Detroit from a neighborhood recreation center to the most famous boxing gym in the world. In addition to managing and training, Steward is also a member of the HBO broadcast team and is director of coaching for USA Boxing.

Steward began boxing at the age of eight in the Detroit parks and recreation programs. He won numerous junior and local amateur titles before winning the 1963 National Golden Gloves title. In 1961 he began training other boxers.

In the 1980s Steward was the only manager to be honored twice as Manager of the Year by the Boxing Writers of America Association. He has also been named Trainer of the Year three times. In 1996 he was inducted into the International Boxing Hall of Fame and in 2001 he was inducted into the World Boxing Hall of Fame as a manager and trainer.

Steward lives in Detroit and has two daughters, Sylvia and Sylvette.

O'Neil D. Swanson
Founder & President
Swanson Funeral Home

O'Neil D. Swanson is the founder and president of Swanson Funeral Home in Detroit. He has served as the director of the National Funeral Directors and Morticians Association and is currently a board trustee of the National Foundation of Funeral Services.

A graduate of Central State University in Ohio, Swanson attended the Cincinnati College of Mortuary Science. He established The Swanson Foundation to support education and civic life, providing scholarships for minority students and support for higher education. Swanson is the recipient of honorary doctorate degrees from Central State University, Shaw College, and the Urban Bible Institute.

Swanson has been an active member of numerous organizations, including Alpha Phi Alpha Fraternity, Inc., the People's Community Civic League, the Booker T. Washington Business Association, the Detroit Better Business Bureau, Boy Scouts of America, the Michigan Department of Commerce, and many more.

A lifetime member of the NAACP, Swanson was awarded the Freedom and Justice Award, honoring his civic leadership and lifetime commitment to the NAACP in Detroit.

A veteran of the U.S. Army, Swanson belongs to Mt. Zion Baptist Church.

Throughout her career, Dr. Iris A. Taylor has served as a practitioner, educator, consultant and administrator. Having dedicated most of her career to patient care, Taylor spent more than 20 years in various leadership positions at Detroit Receiving Hospital. In 1999 she was appointed chief nursing officer at Detroit Medical Center (DMC), where she was responsible for nursing and patient care services. In 2002 she was named president of Harper University Hospital and Hutzel Women's Hospital, where she served until 2004, when she rejoined Detroit Receiving Hospital as president. Taylor continues to serve as one of DMC's leaders on key issues.

Taylor received her bachelor's and master's degrees in nursing, as well as a doctorate of philosophy, from Wayne State University. She completed her management fellowship at the Wharton School of Business.

Taylor is an adjunct professor at Wayne State University's College of Nursing and School of Medicine. She has held seats on the boards of many organizations, including the Merrill-Palmer Institute, Detroit Central City Community Mental Health, Neighborhood Service Organization and Eastern Michigan University's School of Nursing curriculum advisory board.

Iris A. Taylor, Ph.D., R.N.
President
Detroit Receiving Hospital

Roxane Whitter Thomas is the president of Whitter Interiors in Detroit, formerly at the Michigan Design Center. In 2001 *Architectural Digest* named her an Outstanding Interior Designer of Michigan. In 2005 Detroit's own *Metro Exposure* hailed her one of the best interior designers.

Locally, some of Roxane's work includes Sweet Georgia Brown, a prototype McDonald's and the Detroit Metro Airport. She was the first woman and African American commissioned to redesign the Manoogian Mansion. She is a member of the American Society of Interior Designers and president-elect of the International Furnishings and Design Association of Michigan.

Some of Roxane's proudest accomplishments stem from working with the United Nations as a delegate to their Conference on Racism in South Africa, and helping minority designers with her colleagues from Harvard's Graduate School of Design. She is vice president of legislative affairs on the national board of the Black Women's Agenda in Washington, D.C. She also serves on the Friends of African and African American Art board at the Detroit Institute of Arts and is a member of the 108-year-old Detroit Study Club.

Roxane Whitter Thomas
President
Whitter Interiors

MOST INFLUENTIAL

The Honorable
Samuel "Buzz" Thomas III
Senator, 4th District
Michigan State Senate

Senator Buzz Thomas has been called "A Rising Star" by both the *Detroit News* and *The Hotline*, one of Michigan's five "Key Technology Leaders" by the *Detroit Free Press*, and an "Under-40 Political 'Buzz' Saw" by the *Michigan Front Page*. He was also recognized as one of four "Up-And-Coming Leaders" by *Savoy* magazine. Thomas, D-Detroit, is known not only as a political force, but also as a dynamic legislative leader.

One hundred and four years after Michigan's first African American, William Web Ferguson, was elected to the state legislature, his great-grandnephew, Thomas, was elected to the Michigan House of Representatives. In 2002 Thomas was unanimously voted as the Michigan House Democratic Leader.

Thomas is a leader in the fields of energy and technology, health policy and urban development. He is also an avid supporter of the arts and culture community.

Thomas continues his activism by donating his state salary adjustments to several community, civic and cultural organizations. He serves on several community boards, including the Diabetes Association of Michigan, Independent Policy Group, Matthew NcNeely Neighborhood Foundation and Plowshares Theater.

Terence A. Thomas Sr.
Senior Vice President
Advocacy and Corporate Responsibility
St. John Health

Terence Thomas is senior vice president of advocacy and corporate responsibility for St. John Health. He oversees legal, government affairs, advocacy and corporate responsibility.

Before joining SJH, Thomas was a principal at the law firm Miller, Canfield, Paddock and Stone, PLC, and served as a judicial clerk to Michigan Supreme Court Justice Conrad L. Mallet Jr. Thomas' practice areas included commercial and intellectual property litigation and emerging business development.

Thomas is a member of the American Bar Association, the State Bar of Michigan, the Wisconsin Bar Association and the Wolverine Bar Association. He is a member of the board, executive committee and audit committee of the Detroit Economic Growth Corporation. Thomas is also a trustee and strategic planning committee member of the Detroit Historical Society, a board member of Think Detroit PAL, and Matrix Human Services, and a member of the Leadership Detroit Class of XXI. He also serves on the Focus Macomb economic development subcommittee.

Thomas earned a bachelor's degree from Albion College and a law degree from the University of Wisconsin Law School.

Kim Trent is one of Detroit's most outspoken political activists, using her talents as a communicator to forward a progressive agenda. A former newspaper reporter and Congressional press secretary, Trent now serves as Detroit regional manager for U.S. Senator Debbie Stabenow. Trent is Stabenow's link to Detroit's political, business and grassroots leadership.

Trent is a graduate of Leadership Detroit and has completed fellowships with the American Political Science Association and the Michigan Political Leadership Program. She holds bachelor's and master's degrees from Wayne State University.

She serves on many boards, including the Rosa Parks Scholarship Foundation, Detroit Institute of Arts' Friends of African and African-American Art, and the Michigan State Council of Delta Sigma Theta Sorority, Inc. Trent's social activism has garnered her many awards, including the State Bar of Michigan's Liberty Bell Award, the Michigan Democratic Party's Martin Luther King Freedom Award, the YWCA of Western Wayne County's Woman of Achievement Award, the Michigan Women's Political Caucus' Millie Award, and the Detroit Chapter of NOW's Harriet Tubman Award.

Trent and her husband, Kenneth Coleman, live in downtown Detroit.

Kim Trent
Detroit Regional Manager
U.S. Senator Debbie Stabenow

The NEXT Detroit will require strong legislative and advocacy leadership. As Detroit's chief administrative officer, Lucius A. Vassar brings an extensive background in legislative and relationship management to this important cabinet post. As chief administrative officer, Vassar is responsible for managing all inter-governmental and international affairs, as well as local policy-making that impacts the city. In addition, he is responsible for building and managing strategic partnerships with the city's corporate, civic and philanthropic communities.

Vassar joined the Kilpatrick administration in 2002 as director of corporate and civic affairs, where he worked daily with the business and civic community. In that role, Vassar led the effort to retain a $1 billion company in Detroit, keeping the city as its headquarters for years to come. Having previously served in both the public and private sectors, Vassar brings a well-balanced approach to helping bring a new result-driven culture to city government. Addressing key issues such as property taxes and business retention, his advocacy and commitment to Detroit are sure to continue to bring about a positive transformation.

Lucius Vassar
Chief Administrative Officer
City of Detroit

MOST INFLUENTIAL

Randy Walker
President
100 Black Men of Greater Detroit, Inc.

R andy Walker is vice president of health management services for Health Alliance Plan (HAP) in Detroit. Hard work and perseverance have guided Randy through his 28-year career with the Henry Ford Health System. He began in college as a dishwasher at Henry Ford Hospital and worked his way up the ranks at Henry Ford and HAP.

Randy has a diverse leadership background in healthcare. He has served as member services supervisor, director of provider contracting and associate vice president of corporate alliances.

His true passion is mentoring African-American youth. Randy has devoted 4,000 hours to providing unconditional love, educational support and a listening ear. He is president of 100 Black Men of Greater Detroit Inc., and board member of Black Family Development and the University of Detroit Jesuit High School.

Randy was honored with the 2006 Michigan Governor's Service Award, *Crain's Detroit Business* 40 Under 40, and the YMCA Minority Achiever of the Year Award.

Randy earned a bachelor's degree and master of business administration degree from Wayne State University. He lives in Southfield with his wife and two sons.

Carolynn Walton, CPA
Vice President & Treasurer
Blue Cross Blue Shield of Michigan

C arolynn Walton is vice president and treasurer at Blue Cross Blue Shield of Michigan (The Blues). She is responsible for managing the company's investment portfolios, financing and investment options for the company's pension, 401(k) and deferred compensation plans. Additionally, she is responsible for risk management and business continuity planning functions and income securities for The Blues and Accident Fund Insurance Company of America.

Previous to this position, Walton served as director of treasury services. Prior to joining The Blues, she was manager of benefits and trust administration for the Kellogg Company.

A Detroit native, Walton received a master of business administration degree from Western Michigan University and a bachelor 's degree from the University of Michigan.

She is a member of both the Michigan and American Institute Associations of Certified Public Accountants, the National Association of Black Accountants, and the Michigan Women's Foundation's investment committee. She also serves on the board of directors of the Michigan Chamber of Commerce and Executive International Detroit.

Carolynn is the wife of John Andrews and the proud mother of two children, Crystal and John.

Jewel Ware has been a Wayne County commissioner since 1995. She became chair of the Wayne County Commission in 2003. As chair, she provides fiscal and legislative oversight of Wayne County's $2.4 billion annual budget. She was the first African-American female to be elected chair of the Commission.

A social worker by trade, Ware is a forceful advocate for the underserved of Detroit and Wayne County. In Wayne County, she has worked to develop new programs to better serve senior citizens, underprivileged children, the mentally ill and the developmentally disabled. During her tenure, Wayne County has developed novel health care programs that serve the working poor.

Ware received her bachelor's and master's degrees from the University of Detroit. She is a member of numerous civic and community organizations, including Mack Alive, the NAACP, the National Black Caucus on Aging, the Coalition of Labor Union Women, the Pittman Memorial Housing Development, HOPE (Helping Our Prisoners Elevate), the Warren-Conner Development Coalition, and Genesis Lutheran Church. Ware is also the chair and founder of the Mattie Ware Community Fund.

Jewel Ware
Chairwoman
Wayne County Commission

Glenn Edward Wash is an entrepreneur, a developer and a construction contractor. He began the journey of entrepreneurship at an early age, building and selling birdhouses, and even shining shoes.

Wash attended the University of Detroit, where he studied architectural engineering, before serving as a builder in the Navy. He worked in construction for companies including H.L. Vokes, Practical Homes, A.J. Etkin, many Detroit firms, and H.L. Vokes of Cleveland, Ohio.

G.E. Wash Construction was founded in 1967. In 1977 the company was renamed Glenn E. Wash & Associates, becoming one of the first black multimillion dollar construction companies in the country. Among the company's clients are Ford Motor Company, the City of Detroit, Michigan Bell, General Motors, the State of Michigan, and Chrysler. Wash currently operates in the areas of developing, constructing and managing. His properties include Livernois Square and Association, Meyers Court Apartments, Schaefer Lyndon Self Storage in Detroit, as well as other projects in the development stage.

Glenn Edward Wash
Chief Executive Officer
Glenn E. Wash & Associates

MOST INFLUENTIAL

**The Honorable
Mary D. Waters**
State Representative
Michigan House of Representatives

Mary D. Waters is serving her third term as the state representative for Michigan's 4th District, and her second term as the Democratic floor leader in the Michigan House of Representatives.

Mary has served on several committees and task force groups, working to improve the quality of life for citizens in her community. Her recent activities include working on the transition team for Detroit Public Schools and promoting literacy programs in Michigan. She also works diligently to ensure services for seniors and low-income residents. She annually sponsors Operation Dental Flush, a program that provides free teeth cleanings.

Mary's numerous memberships include the Detroit NAACP, Spanish Speaking Democrats, the Trade Union Leadership Council, the National Political Congress of Black Women, and Women's Action for New Directions (WAND).

A true advocate for the rights of all people, Mary is dedicated to representing the needs and concerns of her constituency.

RJ Watkins
Chief Executive Officer & Founder
WHPR & TV 33

RJ Watkins is the chief executive officer and founder of the Highland Park/Detroit-based media outlet whose flagship stations include WHPR radio and TV 33. RJ inherited the entrepreneurial drive from his father, the late Willie Watkins, who owned a gas station and a party store.

In 1973 Watkins was awarded the opportunity as an independent contractor at WGPR radio and television. He honed his skills as a producer, ultimately working under the direction of Nat Morris on the popular dance show, *The Scene*. He secured a contract from Channel 62 to produce *Late Night Entertainment*, thus launching his career to produce *The New Dance Show*, which, at its apex, tripled the ratings of *Soul Train*. In November of 1993, RJ moved his entertainment operation to Highland Park, Michigan.

Watkins' Broadcasting, *The New Dance Show*, *Late Night Entertainment*, WHPR radio and TV 33 all represent jewels in the crown of a true icon in this Detroit metropolitan community.

Watkins provides a continuous voice for the needs, desires and priorities of Detroit's people.

Dr. JoAnn Watson is serving her second term as a member of the Detroit City Council. Watson is a native Detroiter and an award-winning journalist for both electronic and print media. She is the only woman to serve as the executive director of the Detroit Branch NAACP. She has served as vice chair of the Detroit Human Rights Commission; chair of Women's Equality Day for a decade; and as a local and national executive of the YWCA.

Prior to her election, Watson was public policy liaison for Congressman John Conyers, and was a co-founder of the Coalition for Health Care Equity, Inc.

Watson earned a journalism degree from the University of Michigan where she co-founded the Black Action Movement. Currently, she is a board member for numerous organizations including the ACLU, the NAACP, the National Anti-Klan Network, and the YWCA.

Watson is the mother of four and has garnered more than 125 awards during 30 years of professional service.

The Honorable JoAnn Watson
Council Member
City of Detroit

Janice M. Winfrey is a public administrator and educator who has been serving Detroiters for more than a decade. She began her professional career as deputy director for New Detroit Inc. Today, she is serving her first term as city clerk where she and her staff have adopted the philosophy of "One team, one goal."

Before her election to city clerk, Winfrey was a math specialist with Detroit Public Schools. A committed public servant, she views public office as the most effective way to influence public policy and ensure efficiency and accountability in local government.

A native Detroiter, Winfrey graduated from Eastern Michigan University and Cass Technical High School, where she was recognized as a distinguished alumna.

Winfrey is a member of the Detroit Federation of Teachers; the Association of Wayne County Clerks; the Michigan Municipal Clerks Association; the International Association of Clerks, Recorders, and Election Officials and Treasurers; the NAACP; and Alpha Kappa Alpha Sorority, Inc.

Winfrey and her husband of 19 years live in Detroit with their three children. They are members of Greater Grace Temple of the Apostolic Faith.

The Honorable
Janice M. Winfrey
City Clerk
City of Detroit

**The Reverend
Jimmy Womack, M.D.**
President
Detroit Public Schools
Board of Education

Minister, physician, philanthropist and public servant, Dr. Jimmy Womack works to make a positive impact on the people he meets. He shows his deep concern for others by working with young people and serving on numerous boards, including president of the Detroit Public Schools Board of Education. He also keeps the community informed through venues like *The Dr. Jimmy Womack Show*, sponsored by the Detroit Medical Center.

Womack has mentored young African-American males, opened his home to several and helped them with judicial issues. His philanthropy is expressed primarily through the Coalition Inc. (Circle Of Hope) a nonprofit created by Womack and his wife, Dr. Sophie Womack, to reduce morbidity and mortality in the community.

A retired anesthesiologist, Womack earned a master of divinity degree and is an ordained minister serving Plymouth United Church of Christ and St. Luke United Church of Christ. Womack triumphed over attention deficit disorder (ADD) to reach his goals and serves as a role model for others with learning disabilities.

He and his wife have two daughters in college, Brandi and Ashley.

Sophie J. Womack, M.D.
Vice President, Medical Affairs
Harper University Hospital

Dr. Sophie J. Womack is vice president of medical affairs at Detroit Medical Center's Harper University Hospital and Hutzel Women's Hospital. She is an associate clinical professor in pediatrics at Wayne State University.

Previously, Womack was the division chief of neonatology at Sinai-Grace Hospital. There, she was elected the first African-American and female president of DMC, a position she held from 2004 to 2006.

Womack is the former board chair of Tomorrow's Child/Michigan SIDS, which promoted the Back to Sleep campaign. With her husband, she formed The Coalition Inc. – Circle of Hope, which promotes childhood health and wellbeing, and helped to raise more than $1 million for the organization's community efforts.

In May of 2006 Womack was the first African-American female to be elected president of the Wayne County Medical Society of Southeast Michigan.

A graduate of Howard University, Womack earned her medical degree from Meharry Medical College. She received a master of business administration degree from the University of Tennessee at Knoxville. A mother of two, Womack resides in Detroit with her husband, Rev. Jimmy Womack.

DAIMLERCHRYSLER

DaimlerChrysler Financial Services

CORPORATE SPOTLIGHT

DAIMLERCHRYSLER

DaimlerChrysler Financial Services

DaimlerChrysler Financial Services Americas is part of the global automotive finance services company of DaimlerChrysler AG. We provide an array of financial solutions, from leasing vehicles to financing retail and commercial sales, financing and managing passenger and commercial fleets, and offering financial support and insurance to dealers. Our business policies and practices place the highest priority on customer service and satisfaction through innovative products and services.

Headquartered in Farmington Hills, MI, we represent the largest subisidiary within the financial services division. Established more than 40 years ago, the company provides flexible financial solutions and products to more than 5,000 DaimlerChrysler passenger car and commerical vehicle dealerships and their customers throughout the Americas. DaimlerChrysler Financial Services employs more than 5,600 professionals, who manage a portfolio of approximately $107 billion and services close to five million contracts. We are committed to an inclusive work environment, respectful of the differing lifestyles, backgrounds, perspectives, skills and talents of our employees.

We work hard to take part in activities that build productive relationships, transfer knowledge and create opportunities for development and independence. DaimlerChrysler Financial Services is an ongoing participant in charitable, educational and cultural events in the communities in which we do business.

DaimlerChrysler Financial Services provides innovative, financial solutions through four strong brands – Chrysler Financial, Mercedes-Benz Financial, DaimlerChrysler Truck Financial and DaimlerChrysler Insurance Company - with global operations in 39 countries around the world including the United States, Canada, Mexico, South America, Puerto Rico and more.

For more information, visit us at:
www.daimlerchryslerfinancialservices.com/na

DaimlerChrysler Corporation

The Chrysler Group is one of the world's largest manufacturers of passenger vehicles and heavy-duty trucks. Headquartered in Auburn Hills, MI, we are the North American-based unit of DaimlerChrysler AG. The Chrysler Group designs, manufactures and sells vehicles under the Chrysler, Jeep® and Dodge brand names. Through our fourth brand, Mopar, we offer original equipment and performance quality parts and accessories.

The Chrysler Group produces approximately 2-dozen passenger vehicles and has 14 assembly, 11 powertrain, five stamping and two components plants in North America, as well as dozens of administrative centers, business and sales offices and 28 parts distribution centers. In addition, we are located in nearly every state and province in the United States, Canada and Mexico, and there are offices and facilities in more than 120 countries around the world.

With over 90,000 employees, we know that it takes great people working together to produce great cars and trucks. An inclusive workforce is what drives smart solutions and innovative products needed to win in the highly competitive global marketplace. Our company policies and practices enforce dignity and respect. The diversity in our workforce creates unlimited potential, infinite possibilities and immeasurable success.

Diversity is integrated in all aspects of our business – from our supplier and dealer base to our community support to our internal business processes and identification of top talent. Embracing the rapidly changing global demographics and leveraging its impact on the workplace and marketplace is a top leadership priority and part of our overall business strategy.

For more information, visit us at:
www.daimlerchrysler.com
About careers: career.chrysler-group.com

Monica E. Emerson
Executive Director, Corporate Diversity Office
DaimlerChrysler Corporation
Chrysler Group

W. Frank Fountain
Senior Vice President
External Affairs and Public Policy
DaimlerChrysler Corporation

Monica is responsible for the design, development and deployment of DaimlerChrysler's corporate diversity strategies, work-life policies and programs, and equal employment opportunity compliance and governance.

Monica received the Presidential Diversity Award from the National Association of Women Business Owners - Greater Detroit Chapter, and Career Communication Group's Leadership in Diversity Award. She has presented nationally and internationally on the subject of diversity and inclusion in the workplace to private industry, government and educational institutions.

Monica actively participates on national and local boards, including Catalyst's board of advisors, the National Coalition of 100 Black Women, Focus: HOPE, and *Working Mother Media*'s "Best Companies for Women of Color." She is a member of Inforum, formerly Women's Economic Club and a founding member of the DaimlerChrysler African American Network (DCAAN) where she serves on the board of directors. She also mentors young professionals in the company and community.

A native Detroiter, Monica received her bachelor's degree from Oakland University, a master's degree in guidance and counseling from Wayne State University and a professional development in management degree from University of Michigan.

Frank Fountain is responsible for maintaining and coordinating DaimlerChrysler's interface with state and local governments across the country. He directs a staff of government affairs specialists who are responsible for analyzing, developing, and presenting to these units of government all issues that are important to DaimlerChrysler and the auto industry. He also develops strategies and initiatives to address common interests across domestic auto industry manufacturers.

Additionally, Fountain is responsible for DaimlerChrysler's community relations, national education programs, and the DaimlerChrysler Corporation Fund, the company's philanthropic organization, where he serves as president.

Since joining the Chrysler Corporation in 1973 as an investment analyst, Fountain has held numerous positions of increasing responsibility in Chrysler's corporate controller's office, treasurer's office and government affairs office in Washington, D.C.

Frank is a member of many business and professional organizations and serves on numerous boards. He holds a bachelor's degree in history and political science from Hampton University, a master of business administration degree from the University of Pennsylvania's Wharton School, and an honorary doctorate of public service degree from Central Michigan University.

Byron M. Green
**Vice President, Truck & Activity
Vehicle Assembly Operations
Chrysler Group**

Darryl R. Jackson
**Vice President, Great Lakes Business Center
Sales & Marketing
Chrysler Group**

A trailblazer for the African-American community in the automotive industry, Byron M. Green has set the course for younger generations of African Americans to follow. Green joined the Chrysler Group in February of 1998 as a senior manager of paint operations at the St. Louis North Assembly Plant. In 2002 Green became the first African American to reach the level of vice president in manufacturing at DaimlerChrysler Corp.

Currently responsible for an organization with more than 16,000 employees and an annual budget of $1.8 billion, Green oversees five of DaimlerChrysler's most important vehicle assembly operations. He leads production of four active vehicle plants that build the Jeep® Grand Cherokee, Liberty, Wrangler, Wrangler Unlimited and the Dodge Durango. In addition, he oversees two plants that assemble the Dodge Ram and the Dodge Dakota pickup truck.

Green received a bachelor of science degree in electrical engineering from General Motors Institute in 1986 and a master of science degree in engineering management from the University of Detroit Mercy in 1989.

Darryl Jackson is responsible for business operations of the Great Lakes Business Center, which represents nearly 500 Chrysler/Jeep® and Dodge dealers in Michigan, Ohio, Indiana and Kentucky. In this role, he leads a staff of more than 100 professionals focused on sales, service and marketing of Chrysler Group products and services in the Great Lakes area. Representing $6.8 billion in vehicle sales, this would make them No. 307 on the Fortune 500 list of companies.

Two words are key to Jackson's success, "listen" and "silent." He recommends that all take them to heart. "Both words are spelled with the same letters, and if you do both, you will always know where you are going and how to get there."

Jackson holds a bachelor's degree in accounting from Central Michigan University and a master of business administration degree from Harvard University. Additionally, he is a certified public accountant and a member of the Central Michigan University Development Board.

Kim Harris Jones
Vice President
Product, Procurement & Cost Management Finance
Chrysler Group

In 2004 Kim Harris Jones became the first African-American woman to be named vice president at DaimlerChrysler. In this position, Kim is responsible for managing the development costs of new vehicles and costs that impact the style, features and profit margins of products sold in North American and international markets. She also ensures that vehicles produced and sold by the Chrysler Group meet financial requirements. Additionally, Kim oversees engineering, research and development budgets, and capital expenditure investment strategies.

Kim volunteers her time to support company and community initiatives. She is co-chair of DaimlerChrysler's affinity group and the African American Network (DCAAN). She is on the board of directors for Beijing Benz DaimlerChrysler Corp., the company's joint venture in China. Kim also serves as president of the board for the Boys & Girls Republic youth home.

Serving as mentor to up-and-coming professionals, Kim encourages her mentees to serve as mentors to others. She believes that each one *can* reach one.

Kim received a bachelor's degree in accounting and a master of business administration degree in finance from the University of Michigan.

William F. Jones Jr.
Vice President
Chrysler Financial
DaimlerChrysler Financial Services Americas

William F. Jones Jr. is vice president of Chrysler Financial for DaimlerChrysler Financial Services Americas. William began his automotive career with DaimlerChrysler Corporation as a corporate analyst in 1981. He was promoted to several management positions in the company and gained experience in all areas of finance and controlling.

In 2004 William transferred to his current position. He directs all of Chrysler's financial activities supporting more than 4,000 Chrysler, Jeep® and Dodge dealers and their customers. Prior to this position, he was vice president of Corporate Financial Control for Chrysler Group.

Before joining DaimlerChrysler Corporation, William worked as a management consultant for Metropolitan Life and a financial analyst for W.R. Grace and Company in New York. While in New York, he earned a bachelor's degree in psychology and a master of business administration degree in finance from Columbia University.

William is a volunteer on the board of Focus: HOPE in Detroit and Walsh College board of directors. He is an avid spokesperson for financial education. William is married to Marion Jones and is the proud parent of three wonderful boys.

Jethro Joseph
Senior Manager
Diversity Supplier Development
DaimlerChrysler Corporation

Byron A. Kearney
Vice President, Product Development Core
Components & Process
Chrysler Group

As senior manager of diversity supplier development, Jethro Joseph identifies qualified minority suppliers, develops existing minority suppliers, verifies credentials, and expands minority suppliers through first-tier opportunities. Encouraging minority subcontracting with first-tier suppliers, he also monitors progress toward annual minority supplier participation goals and provides minority suppliers access to DaimlerChrysler's procurement and supply community. In addition, he monitors second-tier participation and interfaces with the community.

Joseph was honored, on two occasions, as the Minority Business Enterprise Coordinator of the Year by the National Minority Supplier Development Council. He serves on the board of directors for the Michigan Minority Business Development Council and the National Minority Supplier Development Council. Additionally, he is a member of the National Association of Purchasing Managers, The Michigan Association of CPAs and the Detroit Inter Alumni Council.

Previously, Joseph was a financial controller at three DaimlerChrysler facilities. He has also operated a Dodge dealership.

Joseph holds a bachelor's degree from Morris Brown College and a master of business administration degree from Wayne State University. He has done further studies at the University of Michigan and Walsh College.

Byron Kearney leads the focus on designing and developing common components and best practices across all DaimlerChrysler product lines. This includes Chrysler, Dodge, Jeep® and Mercedes. Byron is responsible for the body-in-white exterior, chassis, interior components, quality metrics, modularity and resource balancing of products. He is also responsible for product development processes and process quality.

Byron leads a team across global business units and organizations to identify commonalities in parts and processes, resulting in immense cost reductions and improved efficiencies. A huge undertaking, Byron's proactive approach is pioneering the way in which DaimlerChrysler Corporation designs, develops and creates its world-class products. Furthermore, building the critical global links to remain successful in the highly competitive and global manufacturing industry.

His words of wisdom to up-and-coming professionals, "Life is full of opportunities, don't miss yours," and "Someone has to be first, why not you?"

Byron holds a bachelor's degree in mechanical engineering from North Carolina A&T State University and completed the Carnegie Mellon University Graduate School of Industrial Administration executive education program in 1994.

DAIMLERCHRYSLER
DaimlerChrysler Financial Services

Janet E. Marzett
Vice President
Human Resources & Administrative Services
DaimlerChrysler Financial Services Americas

Karla E. Middlebrooks
Vice President
Finance and Controlling Americas
DaimlerChrysler Financial Services Americas

Janet E. Marzett is vice president of human resources and administrative services in Farmington Hills, Michigan and Mercedes-Benz USA in New Jersey. Prior to this position, she was senior manager at Dallas Customer Contact Center, the largest DaimlerChrysler customer service center in the U.S. Janet joined DaimlerChrysler in 1980 as a retail credit investigator in Dallas. She was promoted to several retail credit, dealer credit, sales and customer contact management positions.

In 2004 Janet was given the opportunity to move to Detroit. Her work-related responsibilities include employee relations, diversity, employment, compensation and benefits, personnel development and training, and organization planning and facilities services.

To Janet, being an employer of choice means creating an environment of openness, providing an inclusive work environment, and celebrating and respecting differing cultures, lifestyles, backgrounds and perspectives.

Janet received a bachelor's degree in business marketing at the University of Texas. Janet enjoys spending time with her husband Kelly, daughter Kelli and son Dayton. She is known for her philosophy on mentoring, "Don't limit your mentors to people who walk, talk and look like you."

Karla E. Middlebrooks is the vice president of financial reporting and corporate controlling for DaimlerChrysler Financial Services Americas. In this position she is responsible for directing all accounting and financial reporting for DaimlerChrysler Financial Services Americas.

Previously, Karla was director of capital investment financial control. In August of 1984, Karla joined DaimlerChrysler as a financial analyst. Additionally, she has served in various areas of financial and controlling management, including competitive analysis, marketing cost analysis, Mopar Parts, product finance, and procurement and supply.

Karla is a member of the Detroit chapter of The Links, Inc. She was also the 2001 recipient of the National Eagle Leadership Institute Award.

Karla received her master of business administration degree from Harvard Graduate School of Business in June of 1984 and her bachelor's degree in industrial engineering from Northwestern University in 1980.

A native of Detroit, Michigan, Karla resides in West Bloomfield with her husband Bill and two sons, Arthur and Andrew.

THE INTERNATIONAL DETROIT BLACK EXPO, INC.

presents

Buy Black Weekend

May 25-28, 2007 • Cobo Convention Center

FEATURING OVER 1,000 AFRICAN AMERICAN BUSINESSES!

PRESENTED BY

  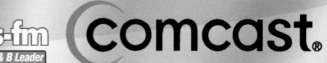

Register your business today for the Largest African American Consumer Expo in the Country.

(313) 309-3215

"For the People, By the People, To Empower the People"

www.DetroitBlackExpo.com

REGISTER TODAY!

BLACK WEEKEND HIGHLIGHTS

Black Bottom Music Festival
Entrepreneurship Conference
Health Disparities Fair
Black Marketplace Pavilions
Collegiate Employment Fair
Celebrity Entrepreneur Weekend
Emerging Entrepreneurs Boot-camp
Corporations, Small Businesses, Franchises

AND MUCH MORE!

FOR MORE INFORMATION CONTACT:

The International Detroit Black Expo, Inc. • 65 Cadillac Square, Suite 2200 • Detroit, Michigan 48226 • (313) 309-3215 Office • (313) 961-6769 Fc
Email: info@DetroitBlackExpo.com • Website: www.DetroitBlackExpo.com

Fifth Third Bank
Working Hard To Be The Only Bank You'll Ever Need.

CORPORATE SPOTLIGHT

Karl I. Bell
Senior Managing Director
Public Funds and Healthcare Groups
Fifth Third Bank

Karl I. Bell is the senior managing director of the public funds and healthcare groups at Fifth Third Bank, Eastern Michigan. Previously, he worked as a credit analyst and in various commercial lending positions. Karl graduated from the Graduate School of Banking at the University of Wisconsin in 1997. In 1999 he assisted in the development of a private banking/wealth management group within the relatively new commercial banking division. Karl received his consortium-dual master of business administration degree in marketing and finance from the University of Wisconsin, and his bachelor's degree in marketing and finance from Morehouse College.

Karl serves his community with New Detroit, Inc., Mayor Archer's Small Business Economic Development Task Force, the Southfield Symphony Orchestra, the Hartford Men's Choir, the Girl Scouts of America, the Urban Banker's Forum, the Detroit Youth Sports and Recreation Commission, the Coalition On Temporary Shelter, the Michigan Monarchs AAU Basketball Club, and the Michigan advisory board for Business Professionals of America. He is a career day speaker for Detroit Public Schools.

A native of Atlanta, Georgia, Karl is married with three children.

Byna Elliott
Vice President & Director
Community Development
Fifth Third Bank

Byna Elliott is a community reinvestment professional with more than 13 years of experience, including five years of administering all aspects of consumer compliance programs and Community Reinvestment Act initiatives. She began her career at the Office of the Comptroller of the Currency in 1993, moved into the financial services industry in 1998, and currently serves as vice president and director of Fifth Third Bank's community development department.

Elliott is involved with numerous organizations, including Habitat for Humanity-State of Michigan, Detroit Neighborhood Housing Services, the Local Initiatives Support Corporation loan committee, the Detroit Community Initiative, the Macomb County and Oakland County CRA Associations, the Michigan Compliance Officers Association and Delta Sigma Theta Sorority, Inc.

Elliott's vision for the city of Detroit includes a diverse community where people are proud to live in quality housing and safe neighborhoods. She continues to build strategic partnerships with successful nonprofit developers and established organizations to help small businesses in Detroit. Elliott believes that by thinking outside the box to utilize all available resources, government, corporations and community organizations can make a difference together.

J ohn Hale III joined Fifth Third Bank, Eastern Michigan, in 2005 as a vice president of middle market banking. He started his banking career as a credit analyst. John briefly left the banking industry to work as a consultant at BBK (a local turnaround consulting firm). He completed his bachelor's degree in political science at the University of Michigan and his master's degree in finance from Carnegie Mellon University.

John's community organization and association memberships include the following: treasurer of the Founder's Junior Council of the Detroit Institute of Arts, board member of the American Heart Association, board member of the Michigan State Board of Nursing, congregation member of Tabernacle Missionary Baptist Church, and member of Alpha Phi Alpha Fraternity, Inc.

In his spare time, John enjoys golfing, reading biographical literature, and his favorite movie is *The Godfather* trilogy.

John Hale III
Vice President
Middle Market Banking
Fifth Third Bank

C olette Rush is vice president and team lead in the treasury management division at Fifth Third Bank. She is responsible for leading a team of treasury professionals that support the southeastern Michigan market.

Colette has twenty-plus years of banking experience, working primarily with organizations and businesses to develop and enhance treasury operations. She received her bachelor of science degree in economics from the University of Michigan.

She is a member of the following organizations: the Association of Financial Professionals, the Detroit Treasury Management Association, and Second Baptist Church in Ann Arbor, Michigan.

Colette is married and has two college-age children.

Colette Rush
Vice President & Team Lead
Treasury Management Division
Fifth Third Bank

Russell Simmons
Vice President, Public Funds
Fifth Third Bank

Russell Simmons came to Fifth Third more than a year ago with 25 years of banking experience. He started his career as a teller and worked in various banking capacities including commercial field examiner, lobbyist and treasury management sales. He is vice president and director of public funds banking, and is responsible for directing public funds banking activities in Wayne, Macomb, and Genesee Counties and Taft-Hartley (union) organizations.

He holds a bachelor's degree from Wayne State University with a major in corporate finance.

Simmons is a member of the Wayne County Treasurers Association, Michigan Municipal Treasurers Association, Michigan Association of Public Employees Retirement System, Detroit Treasury Management Association, Urban Financial Services Coalition, Wayne State Alumni Association, Wayne State University Organization of Black Alumni, and the Institute for Black Family Development.

He is married with two children and enjoys outdoor activities, especially golf. Simmons feels a great sense of satisfaction when representing Fifth Third Bank.

His favorite quote came from his grandfather after the death of a family friend, "A person's life is represented by the hyphen between the years."

Dolores Sturdivant
Vice President & Regional Manager
Detroit/Macomb Business Banking
Fifth Third Bank

Dolores Sturdivant is vice president and regional manager of the Detroit/Macomb business banking group. She has been in banking for 35 years, with a background in commercial lending, small business lending and international banking. Dolores received her bachelor's degree from Wayne State University, and her liberal arts MBA in finance from the University of Detroit Mercy.

She is involved in many organizations and currently serves as a board member for the Youth Sports and Recreation Commission. Dolores is board president of the NAWBO/Excel - Girlbiz; secretary of the People First Community Outreach & Non-Profit Housing Corporation; a member of the Michigan Women's Business Council's certification board; and a board member of the Detroit Entrepreneurship Institute. She is also a microloan program partner for the Booker T. Washington Business Association, a member of the Leadership Detroit Class XIII, Detroit site coordinator for the March of Dimes, Fifth Third Bank Detroit site coordinator, and a member of the Urban Financial Services and the Women's Economic Club.

Dolores is actively involved in her church and the community. She is married with two sons.

Fifth Third Bank
Working Hard To Be The Only Bank You'll Ever Need

Anthony Weekly is a vice president and affiliate sales manager for the mortgage division at Fifth Third Bank. He manages a mortgage sales force that covers Wayne, Washtenaw and Livingston Counties, and a construction lending group that covers southeastern Michigan.

Weekly has more than 19 years of banking experience in various positions and capacities, and has been in the mortgage line of business for 15 of the 19 years. He received his bachelor of science degree in management, cum laude, from the University of Detroit, and his certificate of management from the Bank One Managerial Supervisory College.

Anthony is a member of the Fannie Mae Michigan Advisory Council and is active in youth sporting activities. He enjoys spending quality time with family and collecting miniature lighthouses. Anthony's personal motto is: "Perseverance-the difference between a successful person and others is not a lack of strength, not a lack of knowledge, but rather a lack of will."

Anthony Weekly
Vice President &
Affiliate Sales Manager
Mortgage Division
Fifth Third Bank

Currently, Aleta Young oversees two financial centers located in Southfield, Michigan for Fifth Third Bank. She has more than 14 years in the retail banking industry. Aleta assists consumers and small business clients in obtaining a variety of full-service financial products and services in the retail market. Her primary products of focus are consumer deposits, loans and investment vehicles. She also services small businesses in the market for both deposit and loan needs.

Aleta is listed as one of the founding members of the Women's Coalition for the Southfield Community Foundation. She is an active member of the African-American Network of Fifth Third Bank. Aleta previously served on the City of Pontiac's economic development board for six years and held the acting chair seat of the Pontiac Business Development Center for two years. Her hobbies include reading and walking.

Aleta Young
Vice President, Retail Banking
Fifth Third Bank

Community Development

Community Development is a core value at Fifth Third Bank. Our team of dedicated professionals is committed to making a difference in our communities where we live and work. Our bank's philosophy is to give back through our charitable giving but also through our employees' volunteer efforts. In 2005, we gave back approximately $2 million to the communities in Southeast Michigan. Our employees volunteered over 3,500 hours assisting families with financial education, small business technical assistance, homeownership education, and nonprofit technical assistance. Additionally, our team is involved in supporting organizations such as, the Special Olympics of Michigan, Charles H. Wright Museum of African American History, the Arab-American Chaldean Council and Habitat for Humanity.

The bank also believes that building a better community starts with helping our customers. Over the past two years the bank has provided, in partnership with local and federal government programs, over $1 million dollars to assist our low wealth customers become first-time homebuyers. Additionally, we have provided over $400,000 to assist current homeowners with home repair grants.

The efforts and commitment do not happen by chance. A group of dedicated professionals at the bank are focused on our community every day! This page highlights the team that is in your community "Working Hard to be the Only Bank the Community Needs!"

Fifth Third Bank
Working Hard To Be The Only Bank You'll Ever Need.

COMMUNITY DEVELOPMENT

Angela Hudson
Assistant Vice President
Community Development
Fifth Third Bank

Angela Hudson is assistant vice president of community development at Fifth Third Bank, Eastern Michigan. Angela has more than 11 years of experience in the banking industry with a background in business and litigation law, consumer regulatory compliance and Community Reinvestment Act/community development. She is responsible for ensuring that the bank complies with the Community Reinvestment Act. Angela's primary areas of focus are working within the community, reporting the bank's performance in areas of lending, investment and service, and the oversight of charitable gifts.

She attended Wayne State University and Central Michigan University to work on her bachelor of science degree in business administration and plans to complete her master's degree in economics.

Angela's board/committee memberships include Rebuilding Together Detroit, Central Detroit Christian Community Development Corporation, the Financial Institutions Conference Forum, Community Development Advocates of Detroit (CDAD), Young Detroit Builder, and the Detroit Homeownership Preservation Taskforce.

Angela enjoys spending her spare time with her two children, Jasmine and Truman. She also takes pleasure in listening to jazz and classical music, cooking, attending spoken word venues, and skiing.

Brenda Massey
Community Reinvestment Act Analyst
Fifth Third Bank

Brenda Massey currently works in the community development department as a Community Reinvestment Act analyst with Fifth Third Bank. She is responsible for all specialty programs including the economic empowerment program, which is committed to helping people in Detroit achieve their financial success with unique business and home loan opportunities. Additionally, Brenda oversees more than $1.5 million in down payment assistance programs for first-time homebuyers in Michigan, Indiana, Kentucky, Florida, and Illinois.

Brenda received her bachelor of business degree from Marygrove College. She is a Girl Scout troop leader and very involved with the parent teacher organization at her daughter's school. She is also very active in volunteerism opportunities at Fifth Third.

There are three passions in Brenda's life. The first is family. She enjoys spending time with her daughter and extended family. Secondly, Brenda loves helping others. In her current job, she has the privilege of assisting families achieve their dream of homeownership. Lastly, she has a passion for excellence and strongly believes in doing things right.

Because we believe in our community

Here at the Blues, we define corporate citizenship as the business strategy that shapes the values behind our mission. These values shape the choices made each day by our executives, our unions, and our employees.

As a committed, engaged corporate citizen, we believe that corporate giving alone is not enough. That's why we actively build partnerships and provide resources to organizations that share our vision of a healthier Michigan. And, it's why we're so very proud of our employees, who continually volunteer their time, resources and talents through our employee volunteer program.

We have developed programs such as Walking Works℠ to help improve the health of our employees as well as the communities in which we live and work. Through our partnership schools, we offer opportunities for employees to make classroom presentations at career days and participate in mentoring programs such as Lunch Buddies. And, with our financial and human resources, we continue our commitment to our youth and our seniors.

**Blue Cross
Blue Shield
of Michigan**

A nonprofit corporation and independent licensee of the Blue Cross and Blue Shield Association

Detroit's
CORPORATE BRASS

"If you have achieved any level of success, then pour it into someone else. Success is not success without a successor."

BISHOP T. D. JAKES

CORPORATE BRASS

James Adams
Director of Food and Beverage
Greektown Casino

Pamela G. Alexander
Director of Community Development
Ford Motor Company Fund

James Adams is director of food and beverage at Greektown Casino. His responsibilities include directing the operation of activities including banquets, employee dining, the VIP Pantheon Lounge and Greektown Casino's two restaurants, the upscale Alley Grille Steakhouse and the casual dining Grapevine Café.

James completed a successful career in the U.S. Air Force, specializing in computer operations, guidance system engineering on the Titan ICBM, weapons systems deficiency analysis and club operations. He received service awards including the Air Force Meritorious Service Medal, the Club Operation Director Award and the Outstanding Achiever Award.

The second phase of his career began in Phoenix, Arizona nine years ago, when James began working in the casino industry. He managed the food and beverage department for the largest casino enterprise in Arizona, consisting of three casinos.

James received a bachelor of science degree in management from Park University in Missouri, and an associate degree in hotel restaurant management from the CCAF.

James recently relocated to Michigan from Phoenix, Arizona. He is the proud father of one daughter and two sons.

Pamela Alexander is director of community development and fund operations for Ford Motor Company Fund. In this position she is responsible for Ford Fund's community development and outreach initiatives with key communities and organizations throughout the U.S. Pamela also oversees the business operations of Ford Motor Company Fund. In 2005 Ford Fund dedicated almost $80 million to educational initiatives, cultural sponsorships and performing arts programs across the nation.

Pamela joined Ford in 1990 and began her career in the controller's office. Prior to her appointment to the Ford Fund, she held a variety of positions in Ford Motor Company's governmental affairs office. Her experience includes policy development, legislative and community interaction, and managing the company's PAC and grassroots activities.

A native Michigander, Pamela holds a bachelor's degree from Georgetown University and a master's degree from Columbia University.

Pamela has dedicated her time to serve on various nonprofit boards and has been featured in *Ebony* magazine's "Speaking of People" column and *African Americans On Wheels* as one of the auto industry's most influential African-American women.

David Bangura
General Sales Manager
WMYD-TV20 Detroit

Charles Briggs
Vice President
Marsh USA, Inc.

Since March of 2005 when David Bangura was elevated to the position of general sales manager for WMYD-TV20 Detroit, he has been leading the station's sales team. With his forward-thinking strategies, he is strengthening TV20's position in the advertising and business community and taking the station to the next level.

Bangura previously served as local sales manager, and later as national sales manager, for TV20. He then joined WKBD-TV as general station manager before returning home to TV20.

Prior to joining the staff at TV20, David worked for five years as a senior account executive at WJBK-TV Fox 2 Detroit. His extensive background includes experience in investment finance.

Bangura holds a degree in business administration from Wayne State University. He is a member of the Adcrafter Club and is involved in various youth education projects in the Detroit community.

Bangura was born and raised in Dublin, Ireland until age ten, when his family moved back to Sierra Leone, West Africa. Later, he spent two years in Berlin, Germany before coming to Michigan. He is fluent in German and Creole.

Charles Briggs is a vice president and senior consultant at Marsh USA, Inc., providing client-consulting services. His clients are in various fields such as construction, public entity, higher education, government, manufacturing and healthcare.

Charles is the current president of the Michigan chapter of the National African American Insurance Association (NAAIA). Their mission is to enhance the position and strengthen the careers of minority professionals in the insurance and related industries in order to benefit the companies they represent and the multicultural communities they serve.

Charles serves as a board member and is the current treasurer of the Detroit Hispanic Development Corporation (DHDC), a nonprofit organization that provides bilingual information and direct services to individuals through programs centered in the community.

He is a partner at the Rhino restaurant and nightclub at Harmonie Park in Detroit.

A graduate of Moravian College in Pennsylvania, Charles received his law degree from Howard University School of Law in Washington, D.C.

CORPORATE BRASS

Harriet Carter
Director of Bureau Services
Detroit Metro Convention &
Visitors Bureau

Joseph Cazeno Jr.
Regional Manager
Corporate & Government Affairs
DTE Energy

Harriet Carter is director of bureau services for the Detroit Metro Convention & Visitors Bureau (DMCVB). Carter began her career with the DMCVB in 1989 as a sales account executive.

In her current role, Carter is responsible for developing customer service and membership programs and initiatives. Her position is critical in developing and maintaining relationships with customers such as the Society of Automotive Engineers, Alpha Kappa Alpha, the National Urban League and the National Baptist Convention, USA, whose choice of Detroit as a meeting destination brought considerable economic impact to the Detroit economy.

Carter has received several awards for her efforts in bringing major conventions to Detroit. She has been featured in several national publications, such as *Meetings & Conventions* magazine and "Who's Who in the Travel Industry" in *Dollars & Sense* magazine.

A graduate of Michigan State University, Carter has a bachelor of arts degree in international relations. She also earned two professional designations, Certified Meeting Planner (CMP) and Certified Hospitality Sales Professional (CHSP).

Joseph Cazeno Jr. is regional manager of corporate and government affairs for DTE Energy, the largest utility supplier in Michigan. In this position, he serve as the company's lobbyist regarding local legislation in counties, cities, townships and villages, and assists the company's state and federal lobbying efforts. He guides the decision- making process on behalf of DTE Energy at government meetings throughout the metropolitan community. Joseph promotes DTE Energy's interests in the areas of electric power generation and transmission, gas production and distribution, nuclear operations, environmental concerns, taxes, media and public relations.

Joseph is a civic leader in the Detroit area, serving on 11 business boards, including the Downtown Detroit Partnership and the Booker T. Washington Business Association. Joseph also works to raise the awareness of organizations that serve and promote diversity and leadership.

Joseph received a bachelor of science degree from Lawrence Technological University in Southfield, Michigan.

A native of Detroit, Joseph is the husband of Ardis Cazeno, and the proud father of two sons, Andre and Joseph.

Andrea M. Cole
Treasurer, Director of Finance
The Skillman Foundation

Nancy L. Conyers
Customer Relations Manager &
Vice President
Jaguar of Novi

Andrea Cole is treasurer and director of finance of the Skillman Foundation. In this role, she serves as the chief financial officer of the Foundation and is responsible for all financial operations including oversight of budget, tax, audit, benefit and operational functions. Andrea is the first African-American appointed chief financial officer of the organization.

Andrea received both her master's degree and bachelor of science degree in finance from Wayne State University. She is actively involved in her community and serves on several boards. She is also a member of the National Black MBA Association, the Institute of Management Accountants, the Foundation Financial Officers' Group, the Association of Black Foundation Executives and Women in Philanthropy.

Andrea is the wife of Kelvin Cole and the proud mother of two sons, Brandon and Christopher.

Nancy L. Conyers is the customer relations manager and a vice president of Jaguar of Novi, a Jaguar dealership, located in a western suburb of Detroit, Michigan.

As a result of her efforts and maintaining customer satisfaction scores in the top 10 percent of all Jaguar dealers in the U.S., Jaguar of Novi has received the prestigious Pride of Jaguar Dealer Excellence Award every year since the dealership's inception in 2002.

A graduate of the University of Michigan, with a degree in communications, Conyers has honed her skills for over 25 years in the automotive industry. She has served the industry in various capacities, including as secretary-treasurer, business manager and instructor. As an instructor, Conyers taught employees the customer relationship standards she implemented in numerous dealerships throughout the years.

She has been recognized by the Ford Motor Company and sought after for speaking engagements nationwide to promote the advancement of minority, female participation within the retail automotive sector.

A native Detroiter, Conyers is the single parent of two school-age children.

CORPORATE BRASS

Nicole Cook
Managing Director
INROADS Metropolitan Detroit, Inc.
North Central Region

Nicole Cook is the managing director and national account manager for INROADS Metropolitan Detroit, North Central Region. In this role, she provides career development and training to talented minority students. Nicole's territory includes service to southwest Michigan and metropolitan Detroit.

Among Nicole's past and current clients are GM, Kelly Services, Cintas, EDS, Pfizer, Deloitte, Masco, LaSalle Bank, Ernst & Young and the Lansing Board of Water and Light.

Nicole's accomplishments in the community include serving as an advisory board member for both the Skillman Foundation and the Workforce Development Council for the City of Detroit. Nicole is currently the education department director for her place of worship, Perfecting Church, in Detroit.

A native Detroiter, Nicole received a bachelor of science degree in human resources from the University of Detroit and is a member of Zeta Phi Beta Sorority, Inc.

The second of three siblings, Nicole's niche is in educating and developing young leaders through Christian principles and coaching.

Glenn A. Croxton, C.P.M.
Director
Vendor, Compliance & Management
Henry Ford Health System

Glenn Croxton was born and raised in Detroit, Michigan. He attended Detroit Public Schools and later received his bachelor of arts degree from Ferris State University in Big Rapids, Michigan, in 1974.

Glenn began his professional career as deputy purchasing agent for Highland Park General Hospital in 1974. He enrolled as a graduate student at Central Michigan University in 1978 and received his master of arts degree in management and supervision with a concentration in public administration in 1980.

In 1989 Glenn embarked upon an intensive self-study academic program administered by the National Association of Purchasing Management (NAPM) and received his certified purchasing manager (C.P.M.) designation in 1991.

He joined his current employer, Henry Ford Health System, in December of 2002 and is currently the director of vendor compliance and management. In 2004 Henry Ford Health System honored Glenn with its Focus on People achievement award for outstanding contributions to the workplace and community.

Glenn is currently pursuing his doctorate in health administration degree at Central Michigan University.

Olisaeloka I. Dallah
Vice President
Compliance and Security
Greektown Casino

Olisaeloka I. Dallah's tenure at Greektown Casino began in April of 1999 as the manager of compliance. He was promoted to director and then to vice president of compliance and internal audit. In 2004 he was promoted to vice president of compliance and security. Dallah's responsibilities include developing, administering and interpreting administrative rules from and with the Michigan Gaming Control Board and other licensing and regulation agencies. He also oversees the completion of all operational compliance reviews and all regulatory divisions.

A Michigan native, Dallah is a graduate of the University of Michigan. He earned dual bachelor's degrees in economics and sociology with an emphasis in finance, business and social welfare.

Dallah's career began at Thyssen Steel Group in the finance and accounting departments. In this capacity, he compiled capital expenditures and corporate investments for the coming fiscal years, reported quarterly to the chief financial officer on capital budget spending for all divisions, and co-managed inspections within the processing center for accreditation.

Dallah enjoys surfing the Internet, building Web pages, and assisting family and friends with financial planning.

Donald M. Davis Jr.
Vice President
Human Resources & Customer Relations
Health Alliance Plan

Donald M. Davis Jr. is vice president of human resources and customer relations at Health Alliance Plan (HAP), one of Michigan's largest, most experienced health plans.

Don's expertise extends more than 30 years across all areas of human resources and includes pioneering efforts to measure the effectiveness of HR. Don specializes in organization effectiveness, strategic planning, performance management and leadership development.

Don is active in the HR field locally and nationally. He serves as a national panel member with the Society for Human Resources Management and as a board member for the American Society of Employers.

A trusted community leader, Don is secretary of the board for Detroit Commerce Bank and co-founder and chairman for the Detroit chapter of the National Association of African Americans in Human Resources. Don is also a charter member of 100 Black Men of Greater Detroit and an advisory board member at Eastern Michigan University. He served as deputy CEO for human resources at Detroit Public Schools from December of 2000 to March of 2001.

Don and his wife, Dolores, have one daughter, Dana.

CORPORATE BRASS

Pamela Dover
Regional Director, Public Affairs
Comcast Detroit

Jerome Espy
Director of Communications
Michigan Region
Comcast Cable Communications, Inc.

Pamela Dover is a marketing and public relations professional with more than 20 years of experience in the Detroit area.

In 1991 she established Dover Harrison Advertising & Communications, a full-service media and communications company. Her clients included the U.S. Postal Service, the State of Michigan, Rally's and Avis Ford. In 1994 Dover was hired by Comcast as an account executive. Within six months, she was promoted to marketing manager for Comcast Detroit. Throughout her tenure in marketing, she demonstrated the ability to produce immediate results and handle difficult situations with poise and composure.

Later, when assigned to develop a comprehensive public affairs strategy for Comcast Detroit, Dover developed strong relationships with city officials and community leaders. This helped change the negative perception of the company through creative community efforts and strategic relationship building.

Currently, as regional director of public affairs for Michigan, Dover creates and executes public affairs programs across the state. She actively works to ensure that Comcast community investment strategies are implemented. Dover also serves as a mentor/coach for other corporate affairs personnel nationally.

Jerome Espy is director of communications for Comcast's Michigan region, where he is responsible for directing public relations and communications initiatives. The Michigan region serves nearly 1.4 million Comcast customers throughout the state.

Espy joined Comcast in March of 2003, bringing more than 20 years of experience in public relations, journalism and communications to the company. Prior to joining Comcast, he served as an account supervisor for Marx Layne and Company, where his responsibilities included the development and implementation of strategic public relations programs for corporate and nonprofit clients.

Espy earned a bachelor of arts degree in communications from Western Michigan University and is currently pursuing a master's degree in business administration. An active community advocate, he is the Michigan president of the National Association of Multi-Ethnicity in Communications. He serves on the boards of several organizations, including the National Black Public Relations Society and Cyber Seniors, a nonprofit group that uses elementary children to teach computer skills to senior citizens.

Espy resides in Oak Park, Michigan with his family.

Paula Green-Smith
Director of Training and Development
Greektown Casino

Carolyn Hampton
Vice President, Human Resources
Detroit Heading, LLC

Paula Green-Smith manages the training academy and team member morale programs at Greektown Casino. She joined their executive team in December of 2000, after six years of providing training and mediation services through her consulting firm, The Green-Smith Group. She also spent more than 11 years in community college administration, last serving as associate dean in charge of services for special needs students at Oakland Community College.

Paula has provided training for small businesses and Fortune 500 corporations alike. She also mediated and counseled equal employment opportunity claims for the U.S. Postal Service and the U.S. Army TACOM base in Warren, Michigan. She received a bachelor of science degree from Bowling Green State University, and a master of arts degree in education leadership from Eastern Michigan University.

A former classical and ethnic dancer, Paula espouses the concept of "edu-training," combining tenets of education and entertainment to the mission of training. She incorporates her innate desire to entertain in developing innovative approaches to train all learning styles.

Paula is a proud Detroiter and the mother of one daughter, Taryn Smith.

Carolyn Hampton is vice president of human resources at Detroit Heading, LLC. Located in Detroit, it was featured in *Black Enterprise* as a BE 100s Company. Hampton directs the development, implementation and coordination of policies and programs encompassing all aspects of personnel, training and development, and employee relations issues. Reporting directly to the CEO, she negotiates with elected union representatives and executes policy interpretation and implementation.

Before joining Detroit Heading in 2000, Hampton served as equal employment opportunity (EEO) compliance manager for AAA Michigan, located in Dearborn. Her responsibilities included managing the reporting for all EEO processes, handling state and federal compliance issues relating to employment, and investigating and responding to internal/external litigation requests.

Hampton is a member of the Society for Human Resource Management (SHRM), and a board member of Detroit Heading, LLC. She earned her master's degree in human resources from Central Michigan University, and her bachelor's degree from Wayne State University.

Hampton's hobbies include interior design and traveling. Active members of Hartford Memorial Baptist Church, she and her husband, Clifton, reside in West Bloomfield.

CORPORATE BRASS

Audrey J. Harvey
Vice President of Corporate Services
Blue Cross Blue Shield of Michigan

Marilyn French Hubbard, Ph.D.
Corporate Vice President
Organization & Community Partnerships
Henry Ford Health System

Audrey J. Harvey is vice president of corporate services for Blue Cross Blue Shield of Michigan, the state's largest health insurance provider. She provides leadership for facilities management, enterprise security, corporate procurement and communication support services.

Audrey has a track record of improving operations and processes and developing successful cost-saving strategies in several departments within Blue Cross Blue Shield. She received the Outstanding Achievement Award from the Detroit chapter of the National Association of Black Accountants and the designation of Certified Healthcare Insurance Executive from America's Health Insurance Plans.

Audrey received a bachelor of science degree in accounting from Wayne State University and a juris doctor degree and master of laws in taxation degree from the Wayne State University School of Law. She is a certified public accountant in Michigan and a licensed attorney in Michigan and Illinois.

She is currently serving on several community boards and is the chairperson of the Accounting Aid Society in Detroit. A native Detroiter, Audrey is married to Jerome Harvey and enjoys being a mentor, gardening and traveling.

Dr. Hubbard believes there is a link between health, wealth and spirituality and that true leaders are those who lead by serving others. She is committed to helping individuals and organizations create the futures they desire. She is on the senior leadership team at Henry Ford Health System. She is accountable for aligning the system's vision, mission and values with its commitment to public responsibility, diversity, community health and advocacy.

Hubbard has earned three business degrees and is a graduate of Ferris State University, the University of Detroit Mercy, Central Michigan University and the American Institute. She is a master certified coach (MCC), spokesperson, author and international speaker. She is the founder of the National Association of Black Women Entrepreneurs, Inc. and the author of the business book, *Sisters Are Cashing In* (Penguin Putnam, 2000), published in English and Chinese.

Hubbard serves on numerous boards and committees. She has received numerous awards and recognition for her outstanding leadership ability and passion for improving the economic status, health, wellbeing and quality of life for women, their families and their communities.

Chacona Winters Johnson
Associate Vice President for Development
University of Michigan

Tish King
Vice President of Human Resources
Greektown Casino

Chacona Winters Johnson is associate vice president for development at the University of Michigan where she is part of the fundraising management team, currently undertaking a $2.5 billion campaign. Johnson is responsible for cultivating, soliciting and stewarding leadership gifts. She works closely with the president, vice president for development and campaign chair, coordinating itineraries and special activities. She also oversees the president's advisory group activities, and serves as special counsel to a number of deans and directors.

Johnson has received awards from the Detroit Metro Girl Scout Council, the Metropolitan Detroit Teen Conference, as well as the Brotherhood Award from Bethel AME Church. A board member of the Mosaic Youth Theatre Group, Johnson is also involved with the UM Ginsberg Center for Community Service learning advisory board, the Detroit Riverfront Conservancy, the advancement and membership committee, the Detroit Study Club, the Greater Wayne County Chapter of The Links, Inc., and the Detroit chapters of Chums, Inc. and Girlfriends, Inc.

Johnson earned her bachelor of arts degree from Saint Augustine's College, and her master's degree in public administration from The Ohio State University.

Tish King joined Greektown Casino's opening team in 1999. As vice president of human resources, Tish oversees all human resource activities and a multi-million dollar departmental budget. These activities include recruitment, benefits administration, employee relations, labor negotiations, training and risk management.

A member of the National Political Congress of Black Women, Tish's career began in municipal government. She is a past recipient of the Shirley Chisholm Woman of the Year Award.

Tish earned a bachelor of arts degree in public affairs management from Michigan State University and a master of arts degree in industrial relations from Wayne State University. Certified by the Society of Human Resources Management, she is a member of several professional organizations and boards working to impact the community and the HR profession. She is a policy board member of the Detroit Plan to End Homelessness, and a member of the HAP customer advisory board. She is a lifetime NAACP member.

A native Detroiter, Tish lives in the Detroit area with her husband, Edward, and their dog, Tia. She is a member of Oak Grove AME Church.

CORPORATE BRASS

William E. Langford
Director, Urban Market Development
PepsiCo

Gerald F. Latham
Assistant Vice President &
CRA Officer
Flagstar Bank

William Langford is director of urban market development for PepsiCo, the third-largest food and beverage company in the world. He is responsible for developing integrated sales and marketing programs for Frito Lay, Pepsi and Quaker Oats. William is also responsible for developing and managing relationships with key customers and community partners.

Prior to joining PepsiCo, William spent eight years with Philip Morris, where he held various sales positions in Detroit, New York and Cleveland.

William is a native Detroiter and a graduate of Cass Technical High School. He attended Michigan State University where he received a bachelor of science degree in food systems economics and management. William is a member of Kappa Alpha Psi Fraternity, Inc., the board of directors for the Salvation Army, and the Arts League of Michigan community advisory board.

William and his wife, Karen, are the proud parents of three children, Autumn, Julian and Tanner. He and his family are members of Hope United Methodist Church.

Gerald Latham is an assistant vice president in Flagstar Bank's Community Reinvestment Act (CRA) department. In this position, he is responsible for managing the bank's efforts to comply with this federal regulation.

Gerald has more than 30 years of experience in the banking industry and has been with Flagstar for over six years. As CRA officer, Gerald is very involved in the community. He has served in various capacities on boards and committees of several community organizations, including New Hope Non-Profit Housing Corp. and Detroit Neighborhood Housing Services. He also serves as a trustee for King of Kings Missionary Baptist Church.

A graduate of Cass Technical High School, Gerald is a past recipient of the YMCA Minority Achievers Award and the National Association of Urban Bankers, Detroit chapter, Banker of the Year Award. He received a bachelor of science degree in business management from Wayne State University.

Gerald enjoys sports and traveling with his wife of 25 years, Minner.

CORPORATE BRASS

Barbara J. Mahone
Executive Director, Human Resources
Global Product Development
General Motors Corporation

Allison Wheatley Martin
Director of Quality Improvement
Sinai-Grace Hospital

Barbara Mahone is executive director of human resources for General Motors Corporation Global Product Development. In this position, she is responsible for providing strategic human resource leadership for GM's global product development functions worldwide.

A member of Beaumont Hospitals' board of directors, Barbara is a founder and former president of the National Black MBA Association – Detroit Chapter. She has received many honors and awards including *Crain's Detroit Business* Most Influential Women; *Ebony* magazine's Women at the Top in Corporate America; *Dollars & Sense Magazine*'s honoree for America's Best and Brightest Business and Professional Men and Women; and the Mary McLeod Bethune Award. The Pimlico Elementary School library in Baltimore, Maryland, was renamed the Barbara J. Mahone Multi-Cultural Learning Center, honoring her commitment and dedication to youth education.

Barbara earned a bachelor of science degree from The Ohio State University and a master of business administration degree from the University of Michigan. She completed the Harvard University Management Development Program.

A native of Notasulga, Alabama, Barbara was raised in Cleveland, Ohio and is the youngest of ten children.

Allison Wheatley Martin is the director of quality improvement at Sinai-Grace Hospital. She is responsible for leading hospital-wide quality improvement, regulatory compliance, ISO registration, and overseeing the epidemiology department.

Her background includes over 15 years of combined leadership experience in operations analysis, process improvement and program development. She has widespread experience in project management, streamlining operations and developing business metrics. Prior to her current position, Allison was a director of quality improvement within the St. John Health System. She also has manufacturing experience from Westinghouse Electric Corporation.

Allison obtained a bachelor of science degree in industrial engineering from the University of Michigan and a master of science degree in industrial engineering from Wayne State University.

An active participant in community service organizations, Allison is the president of the Detroit chapter of The Links, Inc. She is a member of the Detroit chapter of Girl Friends, Inc., the Oakland County chapter of Jack and Jill of America, Inc., and Delta Sigma Theta Sorority, Inc.

A Detroit native, Allison is the mother of one son, Harold Michael, and is married to Harold Martin.

CORPORATE BRASS

Nicolle McCarty
Director, Mid Central Urban Promotions
Def Jam Records

Angela Mitchell
Vice President
National Wholesale Lending & Emerging Markets
Flagstar Bank

Nicolle McCarty presents music and promotions for Def Jam and Island Records to radio stations and disc jockeys. She has worked with artists including Kanye West, LL Cool J, Lionel Richie and Ne-Yo. Nicolle travels to urban stations in Michigan, Ohio and Pittsburgh, Pennsylvania. She was nominated as Regional of the Year 2006 in *R&R* magazine.

Nicolle is a witness that with faith, perseverance and hard work, you can do anything. A graduate of Michigan State University with a bachelor of arts degree in marketing, her career began in college as an intern for General Mills. After graduating, Nicolle discovered her dream and eventually landed a promotions job with jazz label GRP, and later RCA Records. After holding various positions with Specs Howard and Johnson and Johnson, she returned to her passion and found her way back to the music industry with Def Jam Records.

Raised in Muskegon, Nicolle is the eldest born to Ossie and Carol McCarty in Flint, Michigan. Her sister, Shawn, lives in Nashville, Tennessee, and her brother, Tory, lives in Phoenix, Arizona.

Angela Mitchell has over 13 years of mortgage banking experience. She currently holds the position of vice president of national wholesale lending and emerging markets at Flagstar Bank. Flagstar is one of the nation's leading originators and wholesalers of residential mortgage loans.

Angela also manages the bank's emerging markets division. In this capacity, she identifies emerging markets as potential customers for wholesale and retail home financing, builds relationships with community leaders to help identify emerging market needs, and creates products targeted to these markets.

Angela is highly active in the community, providing homebuyer education to prospective homeowners. She also serves on the board of Izak's House, a nonprofit organization where she is director of homebuyer education and financial literacy. She has a strong passion for working with single mothers and helping them to realize their goal of homeownership.

Angela graduated from Oakland University with a degree in business administration and a concentration in marketing. She is married to Dwayne Mitchell and has two children, Dijone and Xavier.

Melanie C. Odom
Vice President & Civic Affairs Manager
Comerica Bank

Karen Payton
Vice President
OnWheels, Inc.

Joining the bank in 1996, Melanie C. Odom is vice president and civic affairs manager at Comerica Bank. Odom is responsible for promoting Comerica as a good corporate citizen. As civic affairs manager, she assists the bank in setting the strategic agenda for relationships with major civic organizations. She also manages, tracks and reports on the bank's community involvement and financial education programs. Odom manages Comerica sections in the *Michigan Chronicle* and *Michigan Front Page* publications.

With more than 20 years of experience in financial services, Odom has worked in investment banking, trust, insurance and treasury departments and served as chief financial officer for a NASD member firm.

A native Detroiter, Odom graduated from Cass Technical High School and earned a bachelor's degree in accounting from Western Michigan University.

Odom is involved with several civic and professional organizations. She attends St. Stephen AME Church and is a member of Delta Sigma Theta Sorority, Inc., the Jim Dandy Ski Club, and the North Rosedale Park Civic Association. A resident of Detroit, she is the proud mother to 2-year-old Ayana Grace.

As vice president of OnWheels, Inc., Karen Payton utilizes the skills she honed during her career in the pharmaceutical industry in day-to-day operations at OWI. She builds relationships with key decision-makers inside and outside the auto industry.

Payton's career highlights include expansion of OWI's advertorial strategy, and production of the popular special editions of *African Americans OnWheels Magazine*, noting top executives. She has emerged as a powerful force, attracting commitments from nontraditional accounts and expanding OWI's base.

Payton's ingenuity and dedication has not gone unnoticed. She made history when she was selected as the first African American to join the board of the Women's Automotive Association International. Named director of diversity, her mission is to recognize mentors and role models in the auto industry.

Payton brought the mission of mentorship to life with her own women's forum. In April of 2006 she launched *Fifty & Fabulous*, celebrating top women and improving OnWheels' presence with marketers and in politics. It provided powerful networking and served as a fundraiser for the Ed Davis Scholarship Foundation.

CORPORATE BRASS

Gail Perry-Mason
First Vice President, Investments
Oppenheimer & Co. Inc.

Violet Ponders, Ph.D.
Chief Operating Officer
Lewis College of Business

Gail Perry-Mason is well known in the securities industry where she climbed the corporate ladder from receptionist to first vice president of investments of Oppenheimer & Co. Inc. Service, education and economic empowerment are first and foremost for her clients. Gail assists nonprofit and for-profit organizations and families in their efforts to achieve long-term financial goals. She organized and sponsored several trips to annual shareholders' meetings of companies that her clients hold to educate them about the right to vote by owning stock.

Gail founded and directed the first youth investment club through the National Association of Insurance Commissioners, along with the original money camp for teens called Money Matters. Money Matters has instructed more than 1,500 youth in the Detroit metropolitan area.

Gail's affiliation and membership extends to many organizations. She serves on six nonprofit boards that assist children, seniors and the homeless. She is also an honorary member of Elliottorian Business Women's Club, and co-author of a bestselling book.

The third generation in her family to serve the Detroit community, Violet Ponders, Ph.D., is currently chief operating officer of Lewis College of Business (LCB). She shares her first name and passions with her late grandmother, Dr. Violet T. Lewis, the founder of Lewis Business College, Michigan's only HBCU. She has served in various roles at the college including vice president of enrollment services, vice president of special projects, financial aid and Title III director.

In these roles, Violet has supervised admissions, financial aid, counseling and student records departments. She has administered federal, state and institutional financial aid programs that generate 95 percent of LCB's annual budget. Violet has researched, written and managed several federal and state proposals. She has also developed and managed the federal Title III program since 1987, bringing more than $7 million to the college.

Violet serves on the board of directors for the eastern region of the March of Dimes and Catholic Social Services of Wayne County. She is a member of Plymouth Congregational United Church of Christ and Gamma Phi Delta Sorority, Inc.

Michael C. Porter
**Vice President, Corporate Communications
DTE Energy**

Adrienne Redden
**Director of Government &
Community Affairs
Sinai-Grace Hospital**

Michael C. Porter is vice president of corporate communications at DTE Energy, a $9 billion diversified energy company involved in the development and management of energy-related businesses and services nationwide. He is responsible for internal and external corporate brand stewardship, including advertising and sponsorships, employee communications, media relations and public information.

Prior to joining DTE Energy, Porter held senior vice president posts in account management and strategic planning at the McCann-Erickson advertising agency. Previously, he was vice president of marketing at Stroh Brewery Company, after beginning his career at American Motors Corporation.

Porter earned a bachelor of business administration degree from the University of Michigan-Dearborn, and a master of business administration degree from the University of Detroit.

He serves on the boards of trustees of the DTE Energy Foundation and the Children's Hospital of Michigan, and the board of directors of Detroit Public Television and the University of Detroit Jesuit High School. He is a member of the University of Michigan-Dearborn's citizens advisory council and is chairman of the U of M-Dearborn School of Management Dean's advisory council.

In addition to government skills gained as a project manager in the office of Mayor Kwame M. Kilpatrick, Adrienne Redden has many years of valuable experience in the healthcare industry gained through the Detroit Medical Center. This includes community outreach management at Sinai-Grace Hospital, public relations and marketing at Harper University Hospital and corporate procurement. All of these experiences aid in her current position as director of government/community affairs at Sinai-Grace.

In this position, Adrienne's major responsibilities are community outreach and satisfaction. She directs and coordinates business/legislative activities consistent with the goals, objectives and priorities of Sinai-Grace Hospital. In addition, she maintains ongoing external relationships and manages efforts to inform and engage citizens, constituent groups and organizations to actively seek their input and perspectives as policies and programs are discussed and implemented.

Adrienne holds a bachelor's degree from the Detroit College of Business and a master's degree in business administration, with an emphasis in strategic management, from Davenport University. She is married to Charles Redden and they have two children.

Michele A. Samuels
Vice President & General Auditor
Blue Cross Blue Shield of Michigan

Sharon Seaward
Key Account Manager
Food Service Sales
The Pepsi Bottling Group

Michele A. Samuels is vice president and general auditor for Blue Cross Blue Shield of Michigan (BCBSM). There, she oversees the corporate internal audit and quality functions. Samuels started her career at the public accounting firm of KPMG. She has held various positions at BCBSM, including audit, accounting and management information.

She earned an executive master of business administration degree from Michigan State University and a bachelor's degree in business from the University of Windsor, Canada.

A certified public accountant, Samuels is active in the community for the betterment of youth and is a board member and past chair of Big Brothers Big Sisters of Metropolitan Detroit. She is co-chair of the BCBSM physical activity and nutrition committee, which aims to reduce obesity and related chronic medical ailments in Michigan. She also serves on the board of directors of the Greater Detroit Area Health Council and chairs their community health improvement committee.

A native of Windsor, Ontario, Samuels is the wife of Paul and the proud mother of two daughters, Tosh and Cheryl, and one son, Parker.

A Detroit native, Sharon Seaward is a key account manager for The Pepsi Bottling Group. In this position she manages over 20 key and chain accounts in sales, promotions and marketing while supervising representatives in new business sales. During her 25-year career in sales and sales management, Sharon has received several awards, including the President's Award.

Sharon received a bachelor of arts degree from Michigan State University, a master of science degree from Central Michigan University, and is currently pursuing a second master's degree in management.

For the past sixteen years, Sharon has enjoyed mentoring young females as a cheer coach through various community leagues. As owner and founder of All Events Etc, she developed a job-readiness and employability-skills program for teens. This program is presented at community, church and college workshops. Sharon is the current Detroit chapter president of National Sales Network, and also enjoys mentoring young adults in making career choices.

Sharon is a single mother of a teen daughter, Shelby, and an active member of Liberty Temple Baptist Church.

Gerald W. Smith
Area Director, Corporate Affairs
Comcast Cable Communications, Inc.

Jennifer R. Smith
Director of Community Relations
Pepsi Bottling Group-Detroit

Gerald W. Smith is the area director of corporate affairs for Comcast Cable Communications, Inc., in Detroit. He oversees government relations, community relations, media relations and employee communications in Detroit and Hamtramck.

Before joining Comcast, Smith was director of community and project development at Channel 56 Detroit Public Television for 14 years. He is best known for his role as co-host on *Back-To-Back*. He currently hosts a talk show on Detroit Public TV, *Good Schools: Making the Grade*.

Smith serves on the faculty of Wayne State University in the department of Africana studies and was named 1990 United States Peace Corps Black Educator of the Year.

A native Detroiter and a graduate of the University of Detroit, he is the recipient of more than 60 community service awards, including public television's 1993 Gold Award for Local Programming and Community Outreach, four Spirit of Detroit Awards and Comcast Cable's inaugural Community Star Award.

Some of his board memberships include the Michigan chapters of the Southern Christian Leadership Conference, the National Television Academy and the Governor's Transition Team for Detroit Public Schools.

Jennifer Smith is director of community relations for Pepsi Bottling Group (PBG), the world's largest manufacturer, seller and distributor of Pepsi-Cola beverages. Jennifer is committed to building a culture of giving through effective community programming and employee volunteerism in the Detroit community.

Prior to joining PBG, Jennifer welcomed the world to Detroit for Super Bowl XL, serving as community relations manager for the Detroit Super Bowl XL host committee.

Previously, Jennifer was the director of programs and operations for Why Not Sports, Inc., an Atlanta nonprofit organization with the mission of educating youth on alternative careers within the sports industry.

A native of Detroit, Jennifer is a proud alumna of Grambling State University, where she received a bachelor of arts degree in mass communication-public relations. She also holds a master of science degree in sports management from Georgia State University.

Jennifer contributes to various community organizations in the metropolitan Detroit area and is a big sister through Big Brothers Big Sisters of Metropolitan Detroit. She is also a member of Delta Sigma Theta Sorority, Inc.

CORPORATE BRASS

Loretta Gary Smith
**Vice President & Community
Reinvestment Market Manager
Comerica Inc.**

Larry E. Steward
**Vice President of Human Resources
DTE Energy**

Loretta Gary Smith is vice president/community reinvestment market manager for Michigan in the community affairs division of the public affairs department for Comerica Inc. She works with community-based organizations to offer bank products and services to businesses and residents in Michigan. She also assists with development and funding for community/economic development programs that enhance the quality of life for its residents.

Smith is dedicated to programs that benefit children and education. A lifetime member of the NAACP, Smith is actively involved with the Plymouth Educational Center, Pro-Literacy Detroit, the Knight Foundation and the James Tatum Foundation for the Arts.

Married to a minister, Smith and her family are devoted members of New Mt. Hermon Baptist Church, where she serves as the youth department director.

Smith was featured in the *Detroit News* as one of the Influential Women helping to shape Detroit. Over the years, she has received many awards and acknowledgments.

A native Detroiter, Smith attended Detroit Public Schools and the University of Detroit-Mercy. She is married to William Smith, and is the mother of three adult daughters, Stacey, Stephanie and Ashley.

Larry E. Steward is vice president of human resources for DTE Energy, a $9 billion diversified energy company involved in the development and management of energy-related businesses and services nationwide. Steward is responsible for delivering an integrated human resource strategy that aligns the company's human resource programs and practices with a business strategy focused on aggressive growth.

Prior to joining DTE Energy, Steward was vice president of human resources at Invacare Corporation in Elyria, Ohio. He previously held leadership positions in human resources, labor relations and employee relations at LTV Steel Company in Cleveland, and Mellon Bank Corporation in Pittsburgh. Steward also served as deputy attorney general for the Pennsylvania Department of Justice.

He earned a bachelor of arts degree from Antioch College, and a law degree from the University of Toledo College of Law.

Steward is a board member of the Detroit Youth Foundation and the American Society of Employers. He is vice chair of the American Bar Association's section of public utility, communications and transportation law, and a member of the HR Policy Association board of directors.

Kevin Sweeney
Vice President, Public Funds
Fifth Third Bank

Cynthia Taueg
Vice President
Community Health and Senior Services
St. John Health

Kevin Sweeney, vice president of public funds, is a relationship manager and commercial loan officer with Fifth Third Bank. He is responsible for developing and managing commercial loan relationships with nonprofit and faith-based institutions as well as charter schools operating within Fifth Third's southeastern Michigan affiliate footprint.

He is a member of the Urban Financial Services Coalition, Hartford Memorial Baptist Church, and Omega Psi Phi Fraternity, Inc.

Sweeney holds a bachelor of arts degree from Morehouse College in Atlanta and a master of business administration degree from Atlanta University.

Cynthia Taueg is vice president of the community health division and the senior services operations of St. John Health, the largest health system in southeastern Michigan. Under Taueg's direction, the community health division has grown to offer and operate 13 school-based health clinics, parish nursing programs, HIV-AIDS clinics, community health centers, health education and screenings, and a grieving children's program.

Taueg also spent more than 20 years in public health, with the Detroit and Wayne County Health Departments. A devoted community servant, she serves on many boards including the Detroit Wayne County Health Authority, the Greater Detroit Area Health Council, the Michigan Primary Care Association and the Women Healthcare Leaders Organization. Her awards include being named as one of the 100 Most Influential African Americans, and the American Medical Association's Nathan Davis Award.

Taueg earned a bachelor of science degree in nursing from Wayne State University and a master's degree in public health from the University of Michigan in Ann Arbor.

CORPORATE BRASS

Stephen E. Thomas is the vice president and general manager for Comcast Cable's Detroit systems. This includes Detroit and Hamtramck, and encompasses approximately 115,00 customers. He assumed this role in April of 2003. Previously, he worked as a general manager for Comcast's system in Flint, Michigan.

Thomas joined Comcast in 1987 as a cable installer. He has more than 16 years of engineering and operations experience in the cable industry, and has spent the majority of those years as a supervisor, engineer, manager and training director.

Thomas holds a bachelor's degree from Siena Heights University and is pursuing a master's degree at Central Michigan University.

Stephen E. Thomas
Vice President & General Manager
Midwest Division
Comcast Cable Communications, Inc.

LaSalle Bank
ABN AMRO

CORPORATE SPOTLIGHT

Simone Charter-Harris
First Vice President &
Audit Manager
LaSalle Bank

S imone Charter-Harris is first vice president and audit manager for LaSalle Bank. In this role, she manages audits with a focus on Sarbanes-Oxley compliance.

Simone joined Michigan National Bank, which merged with Standard Federal Bank in 2001 and became LaSalle Bank in 2005, in 1992 as a senior internal audit consultant. She was promoted to assistant vice president and audit supervisor in 1995, vice president in 1998 and first vice president in 2006.

Prior to joining Michigan National, Simone was with Chemical Bank, formerly Manufacturers Hanover Trust, in New York City from 1987 to 1992. She worked for the New York City Controller's Office from 1983 to 1987.

In 1989 Simone earned a master of business administration degree from Baruch College in New York and a bachelor's degree in accounting from Queens College in New York in 1983. She is a member of the American Institute of Certified Public Accountants (AICPA), The Institute of Internal Auditors (IIA) and The Fiduciary & Investment Risk Management Association, Inc.

Simone lives in Novi with her husband and two children.

Sonya Delley
Senior Vice President & Division Head
Urban & Community
Real Estate Lending
LaSalle Bank

S onya Delley is a senior vice president and division head for urban and community real estate lending at LaSalle Bank. Delley joined LaSalle in 2003 to assist in creating this urban-focused division of LaSalle's commercial real estate department.

Prior to joining LaSalle Bank, Delley worked for four years as a vice president and community development manager for National City Community Development Corporation. Before joining National City, she was a vice president at Bank One CDC.

Delley earned her bachelor's degree in business administration from Florida A & M University in Tallahassee, Florida.

She serves on the boards of the Detroit Economic Growth Corporation, Downtown Development Authority, Detroit Investment Fund, Vanguard Community Development Corporation, Orchards Children Services and The Local Initiatives Support Corporation's (LISC) advisory board. She is also a loan committee member for the Lower Woodward Corridor Housing Fund and Detroit Renaissance.

Delley lives in Detroit's midtown community.

LaSalle Bank
ABN AMRO

Walter Elliott is senior vice president and director of targeted business development for LaSalle Bank. In this role, he oversees the group in the bank's commercial lending division that is responsible for serving women-owned and minority-owned businesses.

Elliott joined Michigan National Bank, which merged with Standard Federal and subsequently became LaSalle Bank, in 1970 as a management trainee. Over the years, he earned numerous promotions, including vice president in 1987, first vice president in 1988 and his current title in 2002.

Elliott is a board member of the Rivertown Business Association, Detroit Institute of Children and the Michigan Hispanic Chamber of Commerce. He is a loan advisory board member for the Detroit Economic Growth Corp and HP Devco. Elliott also serves on the foster care advisory board for the Children's Center of Detroit and belongs to several other Detroit-area organizations. He is a past president of the Detroit Golf Club.

A resident of Beverly Hills, Elliott and his wife have four children.

Walter C. Elliott Jr.
Senior Vice President &
Director of Targeted
Business Development
LaSalle Bank

Valda Strong Glenn is first vice president and senior human resources advisor for LaSalle Bank Midwest, formerly Standard Federal Bank. In this role, she provides consulting services on recruiting, employee relations and other human resources issues.

Prior to joining LaSalle, she was human resources director for Michigan National Bank, which merged with Standard Federal Bank in 2001. Glenn joined Michigan National in 1989 as a staffing director.

Glenn has more than 24 years of experience in human resources. She earned her bachelor's degree in marketing from The Ohio State University. She currently resides in West Bloomfield, Michigan.

Valda Strong Glenn
First Vice President &
Senior Human Resources Advisor
LaSalle Bank

Sandra R. Glover
Senior Vice President &
Division Manager
Treasury Advisory & Global Trade
Services Sales Group
LaSalle Bank

Sandra Glover is senior vice president and division manager for the LaSalle Bank's treasury advisory and global trade services sales group. She joined LaSalle Bank as a vice president and sales representative in the commercial lending division in November of 1998. She was promoted to first vice president in October of 2002 and senior vice president in March of 2006.

Glover began her banking career in 1974 at National Bank of Detroit, which is now Chase Bank. In 1990 she was promoted to treasury cash management sales representative, where she maintained a national calling market responsible for selling treasury services to Fortune 500 companies.

Glover earned a bachelor's degree in business administration from Sienna Heights College in 1988. She is a Certified Treasury Professional (CTP) and holds Series 6 and 63 securities licenses.

Glover serves on the board of directors for Firm Foundation Church and Deliverance Temple Church. She earned the Minority Achievers Award from the YMCA of Metropolitan Detroit and was the honorary chairperson for WINGS (Women in Need of Guidance) in 2002.

Glover lives in suburban Detroit.

Carol L. Guyton
Senior Vice President
Commercial Lending Services
LaSalle Bank

Carol Guyton is senior vice president in commercial lending services for LaSalle Bank. In this role, she is operationally accountable for commercial and real estate loan portfolios exceeding $32 billion. She manages a department with more than 60 employees in Michigan and Illinois.

Guyton joined Michigan National Bank, which merged with Standard Federal Bank and LaSalle Bank, as a collections supervisor in 1984. In 1989 she was promoted to operations supervisor in the bank's marketing department. She was elected assistant vice president in 1991, vice president in 1996, and first vice president in 2002.

Guyton earned a bachelor's degree from Madonna University in Livonia, Michigan in 2003. She is a member of the LaSalle Bank Black Leadership Council.

A resident of Bloomfield Hills, Guyton is married with one child.

Lawrence S. Jones is senior vice president and chief administrative officer for commercial banking at LaSalle Bank. He joined Michigan National Bank's commercial lending division in 1992. While with Michigan National, Jones held the position of senior vice president where he was responsible for all commercial activities in the state of Michigan. In 1996 he was named director of Greater Michigan and became responsible for all out-of-state commercial activities.

Prior to Jones' tenure with Michigan National Bank, he was president of First Independence Bank of Detroit. Previously he held positions with Meritor Savings Bank, Princeton Bank and Mellon Bank.

Jones serves as chairman of the board for St. John Detroit Riverview and as board director for the Winans Academy of Performing Arts, National Conference for Community and Justice, Michigan Opera Theatre, Michigan Minority Business Development Council, American Diabetes Foundation and the Detroit Urban League.

He received his bachelor's degree in business management from Rutgers University in 1974. He earned a master of business administration degree from LaSalle University in Philadelphia in 1988.

Lawrence S. Jones
Senior Vice President &
Chief Administrative Officer
Commercial Banking
LaSalle Bank

Mark S. Lee is senior vice president of marketing and corporate communications for ABN AMRO Mortgage Group, Inc. (AAMG), a wholly-owned subsidiary of LaSalle Bank. Prior to joining AAMG in 2004, he held senior-level positions at various consumer marketing and financial organizations. Most recently, Lee served as head of marketing for the Auto Club Group (AAA of Michigan). He has more than 20 years of experience at various blue chip organizations, including Pillsbury and PepsiCo.

Lee earned a bachelor's degree in business administration from Eastern Michigan University in Ypsilanti, Michigan and a master of business administration degree from Northwestern University's Kellogg Graduate School of Management in Evanston, Illinois. In 1982 Lee was one of 15 individuals selected from a field of 3,000 applicants for the Johnson & Johnson Fellowship program. This program provides full-ride scholarships to minority students based upon their leadership skills.

Lee sits on numerous local boards, including Operation Able, the President's advisory council for Walsh College, and the marketing advisory board for Eastern Michigan University.

A Detroit native, Lee lives in Plymouth, Michigan.

Mark S. Lee
Senior Vice President of Marketing &
Corporate Communications
ABN AMRO Mortgage Group, Inc.

Larry L. Mann
First Vice President &
Division Manager
LaSalle Bank

L arry Mann is first vice president and division manager for LaSalle Bank Midwest, a position he has held since 2006. In this role, he is responsible for overseeing branch personnel and operations for 11 LaSalle Bank branches.

Mann joined Standard Federal Bank, which became LaSalle Bank in 2005, as a vice president and relationship manager in 2000. In 2002 he was promoted to senior lender in the commercial banking division.

Prior to joining Standard Federal, Mann was an assistant vice president with Key Bank from 1997 to 2000. He began his banking career with National City Bank in 1995.

In 1991 Mann earned a bachelor's degree in business administration from Central State University in Wilberforce, Ohio.

A resident of Sterling Heights, Michigan he is married and has three daughters. Mann is also the senior pastor of New Vision Christian Fellowship Church in Roseville, Michigan.

Sharon Thomas-Hardin
First Vice President &
Division Manager
Personal Financial Services Group
LaSalle Bank

S haron Thomas-Hardin is a first vice president and division manager for the personal financial services group of LaSalle Bank. In this role, she oversees branch staff, budgets, sales and operations for 11 branch offices located in Detroit.

She has worked in retail banking for 16 years, with 12 of those years in management. Sharon joined Standard Federal Bank, which became LaSalle Bank in 2005, as a branch manager in 2000. Prior to joining LaSalle, Sharon was with the American Lung Association, where she served as regional manager for Metropolitan Detroit. She also worked with First Federal/Charter One Bank for nine and a half years in various capacities, most recently as a branch manager.

Earning a bachelor's degree from the University of Detroit in 1994, Thomas-Hardin earned a master's degree in administration from Central Michigan University in 2000.

She is a member of LaSalle Bank's Black Leadership Council and the Caleidoscope of Culture Foundation. A resident of Pontiac, Michigan, Sharon and her husband have one daughter.

Detroit Lions

Martin Mayhew
Senior Vice President &
Assistant General Manager
Detroit Lions

Donnie Henderson
Defensive Coordinator
Detroit Lions

Martin Mayhew coordinates the team's salary-cap objectives, player contract negotiations, football operations, football-related legal issues and human resources. He also assists with NFL Collective Bargaining Agreement issues and NFL policies and procedures.

Previously, Mayhew was director of football administration for the XFL where he developed policies and procedures and supervised team activities.

Mayhew earned his law degree from Georgetown University Law Center in 2000. While attending law school, he served internships with the Washington Redskins professional personnel department and the NFL's labor operations and legal departments.

Mayhew played cornerback for the Buffalo Bills (1988), Washington Redskins (1989-92) and Tampa Bay Buccaneers (1993-96). He was a starter on the Redskins' Super Bowl XXVI championship team.

Mayhew entered the league after graduating from Florida State with a bachelor's degree in business management. He lettered on the football and track teams. Mayhew is a member of the American Bar Association, the Florida Bar and the Sports Lawyers Association.

He and his wife, Sabrina, have a daughter, Sierra, and two sons, Ryan and Justin.

Donnie Henderson joins the Lions' staff after serving two seasons as the New York Jets defensive coordinator. Prior to joining the Jets, Henderson spent five seasons coaching defensive backs with the Baltimore Ravens, and was part of the franchise's Super Bowl XXXV championship team.

Before coaching in the NFL, Henderson was defensive backs and assistant head coach at the University of Houston in 1998. He spent 1992-97 with Arizona State, coaching safeties from 1992 to 1994 and defensive backs from 1995 to 1997. He also coached at the University of California from 1983 to 1991.

Henderson's coaching career began at his alma mater, Utah State, in 1983 as a graduate assistant. He took over the Aggies' linebackers in 1986 and was an assistant coach from 1983 to 1988.

Henderson played two seasons at Santa Monica Junior College before transferring to Utah State, where he earned first team All-PCAA honors as a senior cornerback. He was selected by the Detroit Lions in the 1980 NFL draft.

Born in Baltimore, Maryland, Henderson attended Locke High School in Los Angeles, California.

Malcolm Blacken
Strength & Conditioning Coach
Detroit Lions

Kippy Brown
Wide Receivers Coach
Detroit Lions

Malcolm Blacken, the Lions' strength and conditioning coach, enters his sixth year with Detroit. Blacken has been instrumental in the team's transition to their new weight and conditioning facilities, as well as with the instruction of new strength and conditioning programs. Previously, he spent five seasons as a strength and conditioning assistant with the Washington Redskins.

Blacken began coaching at the University of South Carolina in 1990, serving as their assistant strength and conditioning coach. From 1992 to 1994, he was the head strength and conditioning coach for George Mason University and oversaw strength and conditioning programs for all varsity sports.

In 1995 he became the strength assistant coach for the University of Virginia's football program and worked with all other sports in the Cavaliers' athletic department.

Blacken graduated from Virginia Tech with a bachelor's degrees in art and physical education. He was a running back from 1984 to 1988 and won the Super Iron Hokie Award for being the strongest player in 1987 and '88.

He and his wife, Marcy, have two children, Maya, 7, and Bo, 5.

Kippy Brown joins Detroit this year after serving four seasons as the Houston Texans' wide receivers coach. Before the Texans, Brown was head coach of the XFL's Memphis Maniax, and served as the Green Bay Packers running backs coach in 2000.

Brown's coaching career began at Memphis State, where he coached wide receivers in 1979-80 and running backs in 1978. He went on to serve two stints at the University of Tennessee as wide receivers coach 1983-89, and as the assistant head coach and wide receivers coach 1993-94. Prior to Tennessee, he was wide receivers coach at Louisville.

Brown's first NFL coaching position was with the New York Jets as running backs coach from 1990 to 1992. In 1995 he became the running backs coach for the Tampa Bay Buccaneers and from 1996 to 1999, the offensive coordinator and running backs coach for the Miami Dolphins.

Brown played quarterback at Memphis State where he graduated with a bachelor's degree in communications. Brown and his wife, Deon, have two children, Jerome and Jennifer.

Pat Carter
Tight Ends Coach
Detroit Lions

Shawn Jefferson
Offensive Assistant Coach
Detroit Lions

Pat Carter returns to Detroit as the Lions' tight ends coach. He was originally drafted as a tight end out of Florida State by the Lions in the second round of the 1988 NFL Draft. Carter went 32nd overall. Last season, Carter served as an offensive assistant for Lions' offensive coordinator Mike Martz's coaching staff in St. Louis after working as a coaching intern for the Rams in 2004.

After playing his rookie season with the Lions in 1988, Carter moved on to spend the bulk of his professional career with the Rams (1989-93, 1995). He also played one season with the Houston Oilers (1994) and finished his ten-year career with Arizona (1996-97).

Carter played in 154 NFL games and had 107 career receptions for 1,117 yards and nine touchdowns. His best professional season was in 1996 when he registered 26 receptions for 329 yards and a touchdown with the Arizona Cardinals.

Carter and his wife, Charlene, have a son, Jamelle, and a daughter, Alec.

Shawn Jefferson, who spent the 2003 season with the Lions as a player, began working with the Lions' wide receivers unit in 2005. Jefferson brings 13 years of NFL playing experience to the club. In addition to his year as a Lion, Jefferson spent five seasons with San Diego, four with New England and three with Atlanta. Accumulating over 7,000 yards receiving and 29 touchdowns, Jefferson also played in Super Bowl XXIX with the Chargers and Super Bowl XXXI with the Patriots.

Following his playing career, Jefferson spent the 2004 season as a volunteer coach with his high school alma mater, William Raines, and spent a month with the Jacksonville Jaguars as part of the team's scouting seminar.

Between 1988 and 1990, Jefferson attended the University of Central Florida where he starred as a wide receiver and return specialist. Jefferson completed his collegiate career with 1,087 yards and 11 touchdowns on 67 receptions. As a return specialist, Jefferson returned 39 kickoffs for 782 yards.

Jefferson and his wife, Marla, have two daughters, Paige and Faith, and a son, Shawn Jr.

Clayton Lopez
Defensive Backs Coach
Detroit Lions

Wilbert Montgomery
Running Backs Coach
Detroit Lions

Clayton Lopez begins his first year with Detroit as the Lions' defensive backs coach. He worked the past two seasons as the Oakland Raiders defensive backs coach after spending the previous five seasons with the Seattle Seahawks.

Lopez began his coaching career as a graduate assistant at the University of Nevada from 1995 to 1996. He was promoted to running backs coach and recruiting coordinator where he worked from 1997 to 1998.

In 1999 Lopez entered the NFL coaching ranks with the Seahawks as their defensive assistant and quality control coach. He also assisted with the linebackers and secondary. After three seasons, he was promoted to assistant secondary coach.

Lopez received a master's degree in counseling and education and a bachelor's in psychology from the University of Nevada. As a defensive back at Nevada, Lopez helped the team to three conference titles, finishing his career with 150 career tackles and three interceptions.

Lopez grew up in Los Angeles, where he was a three-sport letterman in football, basketball and track at Serra High School in Gardena.

Wilbert Montgomery joins the Lions this year after spending his entire nine-year NFL coaching career with the St. Louis Rams. He spent six seasons (1997-99, 2003-2005) coaching running backs and three seasons (2000-2002) coaching tight ends. He helped the Rams win their first championship in Super Bowl XXXIV.

Drafted in 1977 by Philadelphia, Montgomery was an NFL running back for nine seasons. He played eight seasons (1977-84) with the Eagles, and holds seven franchise records. Montgomery led the NFL in yards-from-scrimmage in 1979 and was selected to his second Pro Bowl. He played his last year with the Lions in 1985. In 1987 Montgomery was voted to the Philadelphia Eagles Honor Roll.

At Abilene Christian University, Montgomery played running back and set the NAIA record for touchdowns. He also helped lead the Wildcats to the NAIA Division I national championship in 1973.

Montgomery is one of four brothers who played in the NFL. He and his wife Patti have three children, twins Briana and Brendan, and a son, Tavian. Montgomery also has a daughter, Sherrita, and a son, Derron.

Fred Reed
Defensive Assistant Coach
Detroit Lions

Cedric Saunders
Assistant to the Head Coach
Football Operations
Detroit Lions

Fred Reed joined the Lions this year after coaching cornerbacks for Ohio University last year. He also coached five seasons at the University of Nebraska-Omaha (UNO), two as defensive coordinator and three coaching linebackers and safeties. In his five seasons at UNO, the Mavericks won the 2000 and 2004 North Central Conference Championships.

Reed originally joined Nebraska-Omaha's coaching staff as a graduate assistant in 1995 coaching wide receivers. He rejoined UNO in 2000 as the secondary coach and coached special teams in 2001.

Reed began coaching at South Dakota in 1994. He also coached at Minnesota Morris in 1996 and was the recruiting coordinator and linebackers coach at Michigan Tech from 1997 to 1999. In 1999 he helped lead the Huskies to their first winning season in five years.

Reed earned a bachelor's degree in recreation management from Mesa State College where he played free safety from 1991 to 1992. He earned a master's degree in sports management from the United States Sports Academy.

Reed and his wife, LaShannon, have twins, Amare and Khamara.

Cedric Saunders joined the Lions this year after five seasons with Tampa Bay. Saunders works directly with the head coach, Rod Marinelli, overseeing player development, strength and conditioning, athletic training and football support. He also serves as a liaison between the head coach, players and staff.

Previously at Tampa Bay, Saunders directed player development. He assisted players with continuing education programs, off-season internships and their post-NFL careers. He was also the main contact between the players and the community relations department where he encouraged player involvement in charities and community activities. Saunders also spent two seasons as a college scout for the Kansas City Chiefs.

A native of Sarasota, Florida, Saunders played for Tampa Bay from 1994 to 1996 as a tight end and on special teams. He also played with the Scottish Claymores of NFL Europe in 1997. Saunders played college ball at The Ohio State University, earning second-team All-Big Ten honors as a senior in 1993.

Saunders and his wife, Bashi, have a daughter Reegan, and sons, Cayden and Kai.

Sheldon White
Director of Pro Personnel
Detroit Lions

Charlie Sanders
Assistant Director
Pro Personnel
Detroit Lions

Sheldon White has been with the Lions for ten seasons. He evaluates and scouts current Lions, NFL and NFL Europe players. He also assists with free agency, the draft, and negotiating contracts for the team's choices. White was also the area scout with the BLESTO scouting organization where he worked in college scouting.

Drafted by the New York Giants, White made the All-NFL Rookie team in 1988. In 1990 he signed with the Lions. He was a member of the 1991 team that won the NFC Central and advanced to the NFC Championship game. He also played with the Cincinnati Bengals in 1993. Following a six-year NFL playing career, White coached receivers at his alma mater, Miami University in Oxford, Ohio.

White played at Miami from 1984 to 1987 and was a key contributor to the Redskins' MAC title in '86. Graduating with a bachelor's degree in business administration and finance, he also completed the NFL's career development program at Stanford's Graduate School of Business.

Sheldon and his wife, Amy, have four children, Sheldon II, Jordan, Cody and Lacy.

Long-time Lions' player and coach, Charlie Sanders rejoined the club in a scouting capacity in February of 1998. Sanders compiles reports and evaluations on opponents and players and aids with the NFL Draft.

After eight years coaching the Lions' tight ends and wide receivers, Sanders spent the 1997 season as a radio broadcaster on the team's flagship station. He was also the club's color commentator from 1983 to 1988.

Drafted by the Lions in the third round, Sanders was the only rookie that season to play in the Pro Bowl. He went on to appear in six additional Pro Bowls, was named All-Pro twice, and missed only 12 games during his nine-year career. Sanders was inducted into the Michigan Sports Hall of Fame in 1990, the North Carolina Sports Hall of Fame in 1997, and the Guilford County Sports Hall of Fame in 2005. He was elected as a finalist for the Pro Football Hall of Fame's Class of 2007.

Sanders and his wife, Georgianna, have nine children, Mia, Charese, Mary Jo, Georgianna, Charlie Jr., Nathalie, Tallisa, Wayne and Jordan.

Dennis Gentry
Personnel Scout
Detroit Lions

Dennis Gentry scouts for the player personnel department and is in his sixth season with the Detroit Lions. Previously, Gentry worked for the XFL's Chicago Enforcers in scouting and coaching capacities. In his role, he concentrated heavily on offensive quality control and was responsible for analyzing the computerized breakdown of all games for the team's offense.

Prior to his stint in the XFL, he worked the 1998-99 season as a high school coach in Texas.

Gentry's first job in the NFL, after his own playing career, came in 1997. At that time he was hired, as part of the NFL's Minority Coaching Internship program, as an intern wide receivers coach during training camp for the Arizona Cardinals.

Gentry played 11 seasons as a running back, wide receiver and kick returner for the Chicago Bears, and was a member of their Super Bowl XX championship team. Gentry was drafted by Chicago in the fourth round of the 1982 NFL Draft after graduating from Baylor University with a bachelor's degree in health and mathematics.

Gentry and his wife, Jaye, reside in McGregor, Texas.

Silas McKinnie
Personnel Scout
Detroit Lions

Silas McKinnie is entering his fourth season as personnel scout with the Detroit Lions. Prior to joining the club in 2003, McKinnie spent five NFL seasons, from 1997 to 2002, as a regional scout with the Minnesota Vikings.

Before joining the Vikings, McKinnie enjoyed a 20-year career as a college basketball coach, including a three-year stint as assistant coach, for the University of Miami.

McKinnie played football at the University of Iowa from 1965 to 1967, where he earned All-Big Ten honors as a running back. He graduated in 1968 with a bachelor's degree in speech and dramatic arts. Following graduation, McKinnie played five seasons of professional football with the Saskatchewan Rough Riders of the Canadian Football League, from 1968 to 1971 and 1973. He signed with the St. Louis Cardinals in 1972, but played the season with the Atlanta Falcons and the Kansas City Chiefs.

Born in Detroit, McKinnie attended Robichaud High School in Dearborn, where he earned all-state honors in both football and basketball. He has a daughter, Ixchel, and a son, Lance.

Al Bellamy
Head Athletic Trainer
Detroit Lions

Al Bellamy enters his sixth season as the Lions' head athletic trainer. Chief among Bellamy's responsibilities is overseeing the Lions' medical staff.

Bellamy, 44, arrived in Detroit following 13 years as assistant trainer with the Washington Redskins. Bellamy was a member of the team's medical staff when Washington won Super Bowl XXVI. Prior to joining the Redskins, he spent a year as an assistant athletic trainer with the University of Miami football team in Florida. There, he worked with the Hurricanes' 1987 National Championship team that included former Lions' safety, Bennie Blades, and wide receiver, Brett Perriman. That assignment was his first full-time job after grad school.

Graduating from Archbishop Caroll High School in Washington, D.C., Bellamy received a bachelor's degree in health education from Michigan State University (MSU). While at MSU, he worked NFL training camp internships with the St. Louis Cardinals and San Francisco 49ers. He earned a master's degree in physical education from Syracuse University.

Bellamy and his wife, Sharon, reside in Northville, Michigan with their children, Chase and Ashley.

Courtney Alexander
Director of Guest Services

Earle Fisher
Senior Director of Corporate
Sales & Marketing

Phyllis Anding
Director of Housekeeping
& Conversion

Toya Hankins
Events Manager

Risa Balayem
Director of Communication

Allen "Jocko" Hughes
Executive Direcctor of
Team Relations

Al Brooks
Director of Security

Rhoda Jones
Director of Human Resources

Shawn Crockett
Retail Manager

Michael Richardson
Assistant Video Director

C O M M U N I T Y

Northwestern Dodge, established in 1967, is an integral part of the Northwest Detroit and Southern Oakland County community. We are active in the growth and vitality of our surrounding neighborhoods. Your involvement with Northwestern Dodge is an affirmation of our contribution to the community.

C O M M I T M E N T

Commitment is best expressed by loyalty. We, the Northwestern Dodge family, are loyal to our community. We are loyal to our customers. We are committed to positive community contributions, quality service to our customers, and providing a happy, qualified workforce.

C O N V E N I E N C E

Northwestern Dodge is ideally located for easy access from any point in Southeast Michigan. We are located on a major thoroughfare, West Eight Mile Road, only minutes from the Southfield and Lodge freeways, I-696 and I-75 freeways. All of Northwest Detroit and Southern Oakland County can reach us in minutes.

NORTHWESTERN DODGE

10500 West 8 Mile Road • Ferndale, Michigan 48220 (810) 399-6700

"Dawn helps mentor Metro Detroit area students and helps prepare them for entrance into the "corporate" world."

"La'Trise has helped develop the East Michigan region diversity council and is committed to Huntington's associates and business partners alike."

"Jennel has become a regular face within the community...she provides financial education for kids."

"Maxine receives great joy and satisfaction from helping others to the best of her ability."

"Gwendolyn is an active member of the community. She works with...the United Way, Leadership Macomb and Chamber Detroit."

"Navia works to promote diversity awareness at Huntington and enjoys participating in community events...."

WE COULDN'T HAVE
SAID IT BETTER OURSELVES

The words of your colleagues and friends say it best. You invest your talent, time and passion helping others which pays dividends for us all.

huntington.com

Huntington

A bank invested in people®

Dawn K. Lucas
Banking Office Manager
Oakman Office
Huntington National Bank

D awn Lucas is the banking office manager of the Oakman Office of Huntington National Bank in Dearborn, Michigan. In this position, Dawn manages the day-to-day operations of an office with more than $30 million in assets. Her responsibilities include implementing sales and business plans, coaching and developing a staff of 15 and the acquisition of new business.

Dawn has had many accomplishments during her tenure at Huntington, including acquiring more than $3.5M in business loans within two years. As a result, Dawn was named "Member of the Year" in the 2005 Million Dollar Club for business sales. She also was one of a select group of bankers named to Huntington's 2005 Summit Club, a recognition program that rewards bankers for outstanding performance.

Throughout her 16-year career in banking, Dawn has remained active in the community. She serves on various volunteer committees and was named one of the 2006 YMCA Minority Achievers.

A native of Detroit, Dawn received a bachelor of business administration degree from the University of Michigan in Ann Arbor.

She is the proud mother of one daughter, Jayla.

Navia McCloud
Vice President
Commercial Real Estate
Huntington National Bank

N avia McCloud is a vice president and senior relationship banker at Huntington National Bank. In this position, she manages a commercial real estate portfolio in excess of $100 million and acts as an essential partner to local real estate developers.

Navia is the chair of the bank's East Michigan Diversity Council. She has been working to promote diversity awareness at Huntington by participating in and promoting community events such as the Lawrence Tech Diversity Series and other bank-sponsored awareness activities.

Navia earned a bachelor of science degree in business administration and finance from Saint Louis University in 1998.

She is the wife of Terrence McCloud and the proud mother of two young daughters, Morgan and Mackenzie.

Gwendolyn Norman is vice president of the north retail market in the East Michigan region of the Huntington Bank. In this position, she manages the development of market share for her district and is responsible for staff development of her associates. She has been in the financial industry for over 19 years.

Gwendolyn is an active member within the community. She works and currently sits on the local community committee for the United Way of Macomb. Gwendolyn is an alumni of Leadership Macomb. She is also an active member of the Urban Financial Coalition Services and the Detroit Regional Chamber.

Gwendolyn is the wife of Jeffrey Norman, who she has been married to for 20 years. She is the proud mother of three teenage sons, Justin, Marcus and Corey.

Gwendolyn Norman
Vice President
Retail Market Manager
Huntington National Bank

Jennel Proctor is Huntington Bank's East Michigan community development specialist. With 26 years of dedicated service with Huntington, Jennel has worked in numerous departments and in various capacities. These include customer service, human resources, and as a retail teller trainer and a banking office manager.

As a community development specialist, Jennel coordinates and manages the Community Reinvestment Act (CRA) program for Macomb, Oakland and Wayne Counties. This includes working with various departments within the bank to ensure the delivery of financial products and services. She works in the community to determine their needs and, through active business development efforts, markets bank products and services to meet those needs.

Jennel has become a regular face within the community and maintains an open dialogue with government officials, community development corporations, and community and civic leaders. Jennel is also an active board member of numerous community organizations. Her greatest fulfillment is training youth on financial education.

Jennel and her husband of 38 years, Tyrone, are the proud parents of three adult children, six grandchildren and one great-grandchild.

Jennel Proctor
Vice President
Community Development
Huntington National Bank

La'Trise Smith
Assistant Vice President
Human Resources
Huntington National Bank

La'Trise Smith is an assistant vice president of human resources for Huntington National Bank in Troy, Michigan. In this position, La'Trise hires, retains and develops associates to deliver the best customer service when delivering the banks products and services. In addition to her daily business objectives, La'Trise has helped develop Huntington's East Michigan region diversity council. She is committed to providing awareness to all company associates and business partners.

La'Trise has a bachelor's degree in human resources from Ferris State University and a master's degree in educational leadership from Western Michigan University. She is also the owner of DeMerial Smith Events, an event planning and decorating company, and holds bridal and decorating certifications.

She is also very active with her sorority, Zeta Phi Beta, where she volunteers countless hours mentoring young women and working within the community.

A native of Detroit, La'Trise is the wife of Edward Smith and mom to her adorable shiatsu Zyon.

Maxine Thomas-Grimes
Customer Service Representative
Huntington National Bank

Maxine Thomas-Grimes is a customer service representative at Huntington National Bank where she has served for nine years. Her positive and competitive attitude has helped her maintain the spirit needed to contribute to the Huntington's winning team.

Maxine has been an assertive and goal-oriented person since grade school, where she was the blue-ribbon winner in track, high jumping, and varsity volleyball. Last year she coached the Butzel Recreation Center Yankees to an undefeatable 11-game championship. Maxine receives great joy and satisfaction helping others achieve to the best of their ability.

After raising three children of their own, the youngest being 32, she and her husband adopted four foster children ranging in ages from 12 to 17 years old. The children keep her busy with weekly baseball, basketball, football, skating and swimming. At any given time, there are as many as 13 children spending the night in her home. Neighborhood children affectionately know Maxine as "Grandma."

She is a choir director and vice president of the church choir. Maxine is devoted to her job and enjoys working with the public.

Marriott
DETROIT
AT THE RENAISSANCE CENTER

CORPORATE SPOTLIGHT

Raynard Lawler
Resident Manager
Detroit Marriott at the Renaissance Center

David L. Simmons, PHR
Multiple Property Director, Human Resources
Detroit Marriott at the Renaissance Center

Raynard Lawler is the resident manager of the Detroit Marriott at the Renaissance Center. In this position, he is responsible for the operations of the 1,328-room hotel, which also holds 1,000 square feet of banquet and meeting space.

Raynard joined Marriott Hotels & Resorts in October of 2004. He is involved in organizations such as the National Coalition of Black Meeting Planners, the Black United Fund Detroit, Marriott's central region diversity committee and Marriott's ROARS advisory council. Prior to joining Marriott Hotels & Resorts, Raynard spent 18 years with Hyatt Hotels & Resorts holding various positions from assistant general manager to regional executive based in New York City. He was also general manager, assistant general manager and hotel manager of Adam's Mark Hotels and Loews Hotels & Resorts.

Raynard is a native of Flint. He attended the University of Michigan-Flint and has been in the hospitality industry for more than 25 years. Raynard and Beverly are the proud parents of three sons, Donté, Brandon and Derek, all attending their colleges of choice.

David L. Simmons joined Marriott International in November of 1987. Since that time, he has transitioned through multiple food and beverage leadership positions. Simmons has completed meaningful work assignments across the Midwest as director and market lead of human resources and as a certified professional of human resources (PHR).

He has acquired years of experiential knowledge and skills in organizational development, while continuing his education in business administration. Recently, Simmons had the pleasure of leading the New Orleans Employment Center recovery effort after Hurricane Katrina, wherein he helped locate and successfully place 3,000 Marriott associates.

Marriott
DETROIT
AT THE RENAISSANCE CENTER

Lisa Williams
Senior Account Executive
Multicultural Segment
Marriott Detroit at the Renaissance Center

Kendron L. Winslow
Assistant Front Office Manager
Detroit Marriott at the Renaissance Center

A native Detroiter, Lisa Williams is a 13-year Marriott associate. She has held various leadership positions within Marriott. Prior to her current role, she was director of sales at the Southfield Marriott. Her earlier positions with Marriott were at Dearborn Inn, A Marriott Hotel, where she held a variety of management positions. Williams currently holds the position of senior account executive, multicultural segment. This allows her to pursue gay/lesbian/bisexual/transgender (GLBT), ethnic and other diversity segments.

Williams is a graduate of the Northern Michigan University School of Business. There, she made a significant impact for students through her leadership in various organizations and as a resident advisor.

Williams is an active member of the National Coalition of Black Meeting Planners, the Michigan Hispanic Chamber, the Asian Chamber of Commerce, and the NAACP.

Kendron L. Winslow currently holds the position of assistant front office manager at the Detroit Marriott at the Renaissance Center. In this position, he manages approximately 100 associates including four managers, doormen, bell staff, the front desk, the concierge, rooms control and valet. Likewise, he is "at your service" while overseeing the check-in and checkout process of the hotel's 1,300 guest rooms. He has been in the hotel industry for seven years with various leadership positions in the operations department.

Kendron has coached little league football for the past seven years with the Northwest Detroit Cougars football organization.

Gertha Inez Dodson
Assistant Director of Services
Detroit Marriott at the Renaissance Center

James Ward
Director of Restaurants
Detroit Marriott at the Renaissance Center

Gertha Inez Dodson is a seven-year veteran of Marriott and currently holds the position of assistant director of services at the Detroit Marriott at the Renaissance Center. In this position, she manages approximately 200 associates, 1,300 guest rooms, 110,000 square feet of public space, as well as an on-site laundry/valet facility. She is also a facilitator for Marriott's National Training Cadre, delivering key management and customer service courses.

Gertha received a bachelor of science degree from Detroit College of Business in Dearborn, Michigan and has studied elementary education at the University of Detroit Mercy.

Born in Columbus, Ohio and raised in Detroit, Michigan, Gertha Inez has two adult children, Lauren and Ernest Dodson, and resides in metropolitan Detroit.

On August 26, 2006, James Ward joined the Detroit Marriott at the Renaissance Center where he currently serves as director of restaurants. He has been a member of Marriott International since 1991. Ward has held the position of restaurant manager at Atlanta Perimeter Center and the Cleveland Marriott at Key Center. In addition, Ward has held the positions of chef manager, banquet chef, and sous chef in various North American hotels.

Ward is a three-time Manager of the Quarter in various hotels. He is a graduate of St. Louis Community College at Forest Park in hotel and restaurant management and a member of the Society for Hospitality Management.

Ward is married with one son.

Marriott.
DETROIT
AT THE RENAISSANCE CENTER

Jerome Scott
Room Service Manager
Detroit Marriott at the Renaissance Center

Wangombe (Dobie) Keeling
Senior Sous Chef
Detroit Marriott at the Renaissance Center

Jerome Scott joined the Detroit Marriott at the Renaissance Center in 1992. He attended the University of Michigan-Dearborn. Scott joined the Marriot management team in 1996 as assistant restaurant manager at the Marriott Southfield. In 1998 he was promoted to restaurant manager.

Scott joined the Detroit Marriott at the Renaissance Center in 2002 as assistant restaurant manager. His current position is room service manager.

Scott is married and has two children.

Wangombe (Dobie) Keeling has been with the Marriott team since 1993. Keeling started with at the Southfield Marriott and worked there for eight years, his last position as sous chef.

Keeling is a New Orleans native and is currently the senior sous chef at the Detroit Marriott at the Renaissance Center. Some of his responsibilities at this property have included overseeing operations of the Rivercafe Restaurant as the specialty restaurant chef. He routinely travels to other Marriott locations to support the opening of other hotels or implementation of new processes.

Lisa Moore Rozier
Manager, Starbucks &
Beverage Manager
Detroit Marriott at the Renaissance Center

Carlton S. Ross, CWP
Event Manager
Detroit Marriott at the Renaissance Center

Lisa Moore Rozier is part of the Marriott management team. She has an associate degree from William Rainey Harper College in Palatine, Illinois and is currently a junior at Eastern Michigan University working on her bachelor of arts degree in hotel and restaurant management.

Rozier is currently the manager of the Starbucks and beverage manager located at the Detroit Marriott at the Renaissance Center. Prior to that time, she was part of the restaurant management team for RiverCafé and RiverBar starting in October of 2002.

Rozier previously worked at the Courtyard Marriott in Wooddale, Illinois, and the Schaumburg Marriott in Schaumburg, Illinois. She has seven years of experience with the restaurant division of Nordstrom.

Rozier is a member of Triumph Church in Detroit and has two children.

Carlton Ross joined the Detroit Marriott at the Renaissance Center in 2004 working in various capacities before his current position as event manager. He handles the religious market, corporate meetings, and various social events, including weddings and family reunions. Carlton has 30-plus years of management/supervisory experience with an extensive background in customer service and sales. He is a self-motivated professional with excellent interpersonal skills. Carlton enjoys providing his clients with everything they need to have a successful, enjoyable experience at their meetings and events held at the Detroit Marriott. He is frequently requested by clients for future meetings and events.

Carlton has demonstrated his leadership abilities in his professional life as well as in his involvement in many organizations in the community, including the Mayor's Steering Committee, the Presidential Electoral Committee, the NAACP, the Detroit I-Care Team, the National Religious Ministerial Alliance, and as a member of the Association for Convention Operations Management.

He completed his studies at Wayne State University in the field of business administration. Carlton looks forward to a bright and promising future in the hospitality industry.

National City®

CORPORATE SPOTLIGHT

Charles Banks Jr.
Vice President
Small Business Area Manager
National City Bank

Charles Banks is vice president and small business area manager for National City Bank. In this position, he manages small business lending activities for the Northern Michigan region, which consists of 21,000 square miles. Charles was previously a relationship manager in the corporate banking division. He has 25 years of banking experience and is a two-time National City Excel Award winner, an award that annually recognizes sales achievements throughout the corporation.

Charles' civic and personal affiliations include the Genesee Regional Chamber of Commerce, where he serves on the strategic planning committee, Genesee County Metropolitan Planning Commission, and the Youth Leadership Institute. Charles attends Macedonia Missionary Baptist Church in Flint, Michigan and is chairman of the board of trustees.

Charles received a bachelor of arts degree from Spring Arbor College. In 2005 he was awarded a diploma for completion of the National City Business of Banking School.

Charles' hobbies include basketball, bowling, jogging and traveling. Charles and his wife Gloria reside in Flint.

Joyce Conley
Vice President
Corporate & Community Development
Public Sector
National City Bank

Joyce Conley is vice president with the public sector group for National City Bank in Troy, Michigan. In this position, she specializes in providing an array of financial services to municipalities, public school districts, institutions of higher education, nonprofit organizations and labor unions. Joyce started her career in banking in 1981 and has a wide variety of experience and expertise in the field of treasury management.

Joyce is active in various organizations. She is a member of the Detroit Treasury Management Association and an executive board member of the Urban Financial Services Coalition. Her professional memberships include the Treasurer Associations of Wayne County, Oakland County, Macomb County and Michigan Municipal. Additionally, she holds membership with Michigan Government Finance Officers, and the Detroit Economic Club and Inforum.

Joyce received a bachelor of arts degree from Loyola University in Chicago. She is a Certified Treasury Professional (CTP).

A native of Chicago, Illinois, Joyce is the proud mother of two children, Kenya and Trevor.

A s community president of National City Bank in Jackson, Michigan, Bruce Davis is responsible for managing and developing National City's corporate banking portfolio and market development for all other lines of business. These include investor real estate, retail banking, private client group, leasing, small business banking, insurance services and capital markets. Bruce received the Excel Award for revenue growth, National City's highest award.

Bruce has served on several community boards, including the YMCA of Jackson, Greater Jackson Chamber of Commerce and Jackson Nonprofit Support Center. He was selected as the 2006 chairman of the United Way of Jackson County's annual fundraising campaign.

Graduating from Clark College in Atlanta, Georgia, with a bachelor's degree in accounting, Bruce received a master of business administration degree from Atlanta University. He also passed the Uniform Certified Public Accounting Examination.

Bruce and his wife, Shawn, were selected as the 1995 Minority Business People of the Year by the Lansing Regional Chamber of Commerce and The National Negro Business and Professional Women's Club of East Lansing, Michigan. They have three children, Bruce II, Br'Shawn and Brawn.

Bruce R. Davis
Community President
National City Bank

C arlton Faison is a senior vice president and group manager in National City's corporate banking group. He oversees several relationship managers who are responsible for maintaining and growing National City's business with corporations in the Detroit area. Prior to assuming his current position, Carlton worked in National City's Cleveland, Ohio headquarters in a variety of positions. These include member of the structured finance division, manager of the international division sales team, and manager of National City's branch in Toronto, Canada.

In addition to his professional activities, Carlton is actively involved in his community. He is a former member of the board of trustees of the Coleman A. Young Foundation and a volunteer for the Detroit Executive Service Corps.

Carlton received a bachelor of science degree from Georgetown University in Washington, D.C. and a master of business administration degree from Columbia University in New York.

A native of New York City, Carlton currently resides in Troy, Michigan with his wife, Wendy, and children, Maya and Aaron.

Carlton M. Faison
Senior Vice President
National City Bank

Cynthia D. Ford
Assistant Vice President &
Branch Manager
National City Bank

Cynthia Ford is assistant vice president and branch manager for National City Bank's Buhl Building branch located in downtown Detroit. Cynthia is responsible for managing $50 million in branch assets. She manages a staff of five employees and is responsible for providing financial services to customers located primarily in the business district.

Cynthia is a 2005 Excel Award winner, National City's highest honor of recognition. She is also a 2004 and 2005 Branch Sales Champion.

Cynthia received a bachelor of science degree, in finance, from the University of Detroit Mercy and is currently pursuing a master of business administration degree from Walsh College.

She enjoys spending quiet time and weekend activities with her husband Steven and two children, Austin and McKenzie.

Marshalynn D. Johnson
Vice President
Branch Market Grower
National City Bank

Marshalynn is a branch manager at the National City Baldwin/Waldon Road office located in Orion, Michigan. She manages a branch with $50 million in deposit base and $12 million in assets. In her position, Marshalynn's expertise drives sustainable deposit and revenue growth in an aggressive, team-oriented and goal-driven environment. She demonstrates a thorough understanding of competitive landscape and a deep knowledge of each competitor's product offerings.

Having joined National City Bank in 1989, Marshalynn is extremely involved in outside small business activities that benefit both the bank and the community. She coaches, guides and directs her branch team, including licensed employees, on sales activities related to consumer and small business deposits, investments and lending.

Marshalynn received a bachelor of business administration from the University of Phoenix. She obtained her NASD Series 6 and 63 licenses in 2002.

A resident of Bloomfield Hills, Michigan, Marshalynn is the proud mother of Whitney, 11 and Myles, 7.

M ary Mays is human resources officer and senior recruiter for National City's corporate employment division in Michigan. Her responsibilities include developing sourcing relationships with outside agencies, recruiting on local college campuses, conducting interviews and negotiating offers for open positions, and facilitating new-employee orientation. With 28 years in banking, Mary has worked in the operations division, in various branches and extensively in human resources.

Mary has been nominated for the Excel Award, National City's highest honor, for two consecutive years. In 2004 a district manager nominated her for "Living the Customer Champion Brand Promise" and in 2005 she was nominated, by a different district manager, for "Being Best in Class - a National City Hero." Mary truly cares about *doing what's right,* National City's brand promise. These recognitions exemplify Mary's work ethic, commitment and excellent service. They are also a testament to the relationships she has built over the years.

A native of Ann Arbor, Michigan, Mary is the wife of Roy Mays and the proud mother of three children, Jason, Justin and Monica.

Mary A. Mays
Human Resources Officer &
Senior Recruiter
National City Bank Corporation

J o Obasuyi is a branch network district sales executive for National City Bank in the Detroit /Toledo market. She joined National City in 1994. In this position, Jo manages branches in the North Oakland district with a deposit base of $600 million and an asset base of $150 million.

Jo drives the growth and profitability of her district and builds sales and expertise within the branch management team. With knowledge of credit, risk management and loan structuring, she inspires service excellence within the branch team.

Jo obtained her NASD Series 6 and 63 in 2002 and will graduate from the Consumer Bankers Association's Graduate School of Retail Bank Management in 2007. This program is a fast-paced, quality-focused educational opportunity for bankers that are destined for greater management opportunities in all areas of retail banking.

Married to Solomon Obasuyi, Jo is the proud mother of son, Owen, 1 and stepdaughter, Irese, 9. They reside in Bloomfield Hills, Michigan.

Josephine Obasuyi
Vice President
District Sales Executive
National City Bank

Jason Paulateer
Vice President & Executive Director
National City Community
Development Corporation
National City Bank Corporation

J ason Paulateer is vice president and executive director of the Michigan branch of National City Community Development Corporation. He is responsible for managing the tax credit and equity investing activities for National City throughout Michigan, excluding the southeast portion of the state.

Jason's community involvement was recognized by the Grand Rapids Area Chamber of Commerce, which named him Minority Financial Services Advocate of the Year. He also received the "Up and Coming Alumnus of the Year" Award from Grand Valley State University's Seidman College of Business. In addition, National City Corporation recognized Jason's team, including the Greater Detroit branch, with the Local Corporate Excel award, one of the highest honors bestowed by the organization.

Jason holds a bachelor's and master's degree from Grand Valley State University. He resides in Grand Rapids, Michigan with his wife, Chapri, and their three daughters, Micha, Michaila and Michaya. A member of Tabernacle Community Church, he serves on the stewardship ministry. Jason is also a life member of Omega Psi Phi Fraternity, Inc.

Cynthia T. Pearson
Assistant Vice President
Michigan Regional Human Resources

C ynthia Pearson is the regional human resource consultant for the southeastern area of Michigan. In this position, she provides and supports the delivery of human resource services for National City's various regional business units. She contributes to each unit's decision-making regarding human resource initiatives and supports strategic objectives. Cynthia delivers advisory services and makes recommendations to senior and mid-level managers regarding significant employee relations and key human resource issues.

Cynthia was nominated for National City's highest honor, the Excel Award. She was part of the human resources team that was nominated for operating effectively and efficiently. Additionally, she received two awards for exemplifying Customer Champion management principles. These awards recognize her outstanding contributions to the company.

Cynthia received a bachelor of arts degree from Washington University in St. Louis, Missouri. She is a member of the National Association of African Americans in Human Resources and the Urban Financial Services Coalition. A native of Brooklyn, New York, Cynthia loves to travel, enjoys the arts, plays the piano and is a fan of the NBA.

Detroit's

SKILLMAN SCHOLARS

SPONSORED BY
THE SKILLMAN FOUNDATION

The **YES** Foundation®

Youth Employment Services · Youth Education Services · Youth Enrichment Services

Dominic Babb
Class of 2009
Cranbrook Kingswood Upper School
Skillman Scholar

Ashley N. Bibbs
Youth Initiatives Project
Neighborhood Service Organization

Dominic Babb is a sophomore at Cranbrook Kingswood Upper School, where he participates in advanced acting, basketball, football, track and field, the winter play, and the Youth Enrichment Program. He is also a member of the African American Awareness Association (4A).

Dominic is active in the community by serving as a youth council member for Wayne County Parks and Recreation. Still uncertain about a definite career path, he is considering the fields of architecture, engineering, acting, writing, and professional football.

His mottos for life are: "Live for the moment because tomorrow may never come" and "Seeing is believing."

Ashley N. Bibbs is a senior at University Preparatory High School in Detroit. She is an aspiring journalist who hopes to make a difference in her community.

Ashley is a community activist and peer mediator. She is currently an intern and peer educator with Youth Initiatives Project (YIP), a youth-driven program of the Neighborhood Service Organization (NSO). YIP provides youth leadership and advocacy training focused on violence prevention and substance abuse prevention. Through the guidance of YIP, she has received training in public speaking, writing news releases, planning town hall meetings and other essential skills for an activist and communicator. YIP has proven to be a conduit through which she has developed and displayed her skills, including the ability to speak positively in reacting to the tragic death of her father due to gun violence. Through her inspirational story, Ashley has persuaded teens and adults to become positive role models.

In addition to being the 2005 United Way Torchlighter, she has received numerous awards, including the Peacemakers Award, the Spirit of Detroit Award and the Do the Right Thing Award.

Raymond Brown III
Class of 2009
University Liggett School
Skillman Scholar

Raymond Brown III is a sophomore at University Liggett School in Grosse Pointe Woods. A Skillman Scholarship recipient, Raymond currently participates in the theatre program, tennis and student government.

In the community, he volunteers at St. James Nursing Home and is active in his church's youth group ministry, S.T.O.N.E.D. (Searching Toward Our Never Ending Destination).

Raymond hopes to pursue a career in comparative world religious studies and/or cultural anthropology. He names Mahatma Gandhi, Musashi and Ozzy Osbourne as his heroes.

His motto for life is: "It is good to have an end to journey toward; but it is the journey that matters, in the end" (Ursula K. Le Guin).

Johnathan Craig
Class of 2007
University Liggett School
Skillman Scholar

Johnathan Craig is a senior at University Liggett School in Grosse Pointe Woods. He is a Skillman Scholarship recipient and plays baseball and football at University Liggett School.

Johnathan has narrowed his career options to the field of medicine. He would like to become a biomedical engineer, cardiologist or pediatrician. Johnathan names his mother as his sole hero.

His motto for life is: "It's not where you came from, but where you are going."

SKILLMAN SCHOLARS®

Gabriel Wynton Doss
Freshman
Brown University
Skillman Scholar

Derek E. Dunlap Jr.
Class of 2010
The Roeper School
Skillman Scholar

Gabriel Wynton Doss has a four-year full scholarship to Brown University, where he is currently enrolled as a freshman. He graduated from Cranbrook Kingswood Upper School with a 3.7 grade point average.

While at Cranbrook, Doss was a writer/editor of the student newspaper and literary magazine all four years. He received several awards including the Madday Summer Artistic Award from the Interlochen Center for the Arts in 2004, and was named Most Outstanding Speaker on the forensics team. Doss was senior class president, vice president of the African American Awareness Association, president of the Resident Council, captain of varsity track and field, president of the Gold Key Club, and a member of the varsity football team. He also volunteered as a film editor at Brookside School.

Doss plans to study public policy at Brown, which may lead to a career in government and law. He also wants to concentrate on modern culture and media studies in order to examine culture and language in film.

His hero is Malcolm X and his motto for life is: "Persistence alone is omnipotent."

Derek E. Dunlap Jr. is a freshman at The Roeper School in Bloomfield Hills. Previously, he attended Hally Magnet Middle School in Detroit. At Hally, he was class president and was elected to student council, and participated in the Science Bowl, the Academic Games, track and field, eCYBERMISSION, and Albion College's basketball camp.

Derek has served as an usher and participated in the youth summer camp at his church. Additionally, he has volunteered at the Capuchin Soup Kitchen and worked as a volunteer at Roeper Summer Camp.

Derek's career objectives involve owning an entertainment business in the National Basketball Association or becoming the first black President of the United States. His heroes are his parents.

His motto for life is: "Preparation + Opportunity = Success."

Dominique L. Evans
Youth Initiatives Project
Neighborhood Service Organization

Raven Fisher
Class of 2010
University Liggett School
Skillman Scholar

Dominique L. Evans is a senior at Denby Technical & Preparatory High School. She is an aspiring singer and community activist.

Dominique is currently serving as a peer educator with Youth Initiatives Project (YIP), a youth-driven program of the Neighborhood Service Organization (NSO). As a YIP youth leader, she works with her peers to promote gun violence prevention and substance abuse prevention and to improve neighborhood and community organizations through the coordination of town hall meetings, peer mentoring and youth advocacy. Dominique has dedicated her life to working with young people to raise awareness of the consequences of gun violence.

Her avid love of singing and poetry continues to provide an avenue for her to artistically express her mission to end gun violence in Detroit.

Dominique has been a member of the Denby High School JROTC, a section leader of the school choir and a member of the National Honor Society. "It doesn't matter where you start, it only matters where you finish," is her motto.

Raven Fisher is currently a freshman at University Liggett School. A first-year Skillman Scholarship recipient, Raven previously attended the YMCA Learning Academy for her middle school education.

While at YMCA Service Learning Academy, she was a cheerleader and played on the girls' soccer team. She also completed a competitive 14-month academic preparation in YES for the PREP program that ran concurrent with her middle school attendance.

Raven's community involvement includes volunteering her time with Meals on Wheels. Her current career objectives include earning a degree in childhood education and to one day own or administrate a child daycare and education center. Her hero in life is her father.

Raven's motto for life is: "Keep your head up."

Britany Hamilton
Class of 2010
The Roeper School
Skillman Scholar

Umar Henry
Freshman
University of Pennsylvania
Skillman Scholar

Britany Hamilton is a freshman at The Roeper School. She is a Skillman Scholar, a cheerleader, and a member of the dance committee and the Michigan School Vocal Music Association choir. She also volunteers her time at the Capuchin Soup Kitchen.

For her career, Britany would like to pursue either the field of education and become a teacher, or the field of medicine, and become a pediatrician.

Britany's hero is her mother, Tonya Hamilton, and her motto for life is: "Move forward not backward."

Umar Henry is currently a freshman at the University of Pennsylvania. He graduated from Cranbrook Kingswood Upper School in 2006. At Cranbrook, Umar was a Skillman Scholar, president of the African American Awareness Association, president of student council, president of Passage of Leadership, and vice president of residence hall council.

He has contributed 20 hours of community service through his church and has invested 200 hours working with a youth leadership program to serve the community at large.

Umar lists four things he would like to accomplish during his career. He would like to be a lawyer, the chief executive officer of a company, an entrepreneur, and a bond salesman. His hero is Malcolm X.

His motto for life is: "I am the captain of my fate...I am the master of my soul."

Brandon Hill
Class of 2009
Detroit Country Day School
Skillman Scholar

Candise Hill
Class of 2007
Detroit Country Day School
Skillman Scholar

Brandon Hill is a sophomore at Detroit Country Day School in Beverly Hills. He participates in soccer, track and field, and strength and conditioning training at the school.

At church, Brandon attends Bible class and prayer, and he helps manage/operate the candy store. Elsewhere in the community, he helped with the Sharon McPhail campaign and has served as a ball boy for soccer games at school.

He would like to pursue a career in mechanical engineering, receive his master's degree and work for General Motors Corporation.

Brandon's hero is his dad, and his motto for life is: "Take life one step at a time."

Candise Hill is a senior at Detroit Country Day School where she maintains summa cum laude status. A Skillman Scholarship recipient since 2003, she has served as junior class president and received recognition for her work as class board treasurer and her team leadership. Candise has participated in school recruitment and prepared new candidates for interviews, served as class representative to the Pumpkin Festival, and played varsity basketball.

Her community involvement includes volunteering her time at Logan Elementary School to help students with class projects and holiday events. Candise would like to pursue a career in medicine, law or engineering. She does not name one particular hero or role model but looks up to her many friends and family members and considers them all significant in her life.

Her motto in life is, "I am more than a conqueror."

Blendia K. Hubbard
Class of 2009
The Roeper School
Skillman Scholar

Blendia Hubbard is a sophomore at The Roeper School in Bloomfield Hills. She is a Skillman Scholar, a member of the school's pep squad, Hype Squad, and a representative for Umoja.

In the community, Blendia is a volunteer at Marygrove College, and she serves on a Roeper board committee. Her career objectives involve writing, becoming an animator, novelist, or poet; and biology, perhaps as a high school teacher.

Blendia's hero is her father, Dan R. Hubbard (deceased). Her motto for life is: "Live life to the fullest type of crazy."

Daniel Jackson
Class of 2009
Detroit Country Day School
Skillman Scholar

Daniel Jackson is a sophomore at Detroit Country Day School. He is a Skillman Scholar and participates in the Academic Games, the school band, basketball and track and field.

In addition to his school involvement, Daniel helps younger children during Sunday school at church. He also donates his time and energy to The Salvation Army.

His career objective is to become chief executive officer of his own company. He names Nelson Mandela as his hero because he never gave up. Likewise, Daniel's motto for life is: "Never give up on your dreams."

Charles McDonald II
Class of 2008
University Liggett School
Skillman Scholar

Brandon McNeal
Class of 2008
Detroit Country Day School
Skillman Scholar

Charles McDonald II is a junior at University Liggett School. He is a Skillman Scholar, a student senator, a delegate for the Student Diversity Leadership Conference and a member of the African American Awareness Association (4A) executive council. He is also a member of his church's youth choir, PYC.

For his career goals, Charles would like to become both a successful chemical engineer and a successful entrepreneur. His hero in this world is his mother.

Charles' motto for life is: "Live your life for God, and He will give you anything you desire."

Brandon McNeal is a junior at Detroit Country Day School in Beverly Hills. He is a Skillman Scholarship recipient and a member of the Contemporary Issues Club, the Academic Games Club, and the basketball and track teams.

An active member of his community, Brandon volunteers with the United Way and spends time reading to elementary students.

With respect to a potential career, he currently has his sights set on attending a four-year university followed by law school. Of all the people who have influenced Brandon, his grandfather is his hero.

Brandon's motto for life is: "Life is like a game of chess. Every move has consequences."

SKILLMAN SCHOLARS

Jihad A. Mims
Class of 2009
Detroit Country Day School
Skillman Scholar

Larry Sanders II
Class of 2010
Cranbrook Kingswood Upper School
Skillman Scholar

Jihad A. Mims is a sophomore at Detroit Country Day School. His school activities include being a Skillman Scholar and parlor games. He is also a wide receiver and cornerback on the football team, a point guard/shooting guard on the basketball team, and a sprinter on the track team.

Jihad has participated in several community activities including Chris Webber's Hurricane Katrina Relief Efforts, the Bates Academy Athletics Pancake Breakfast, and Bates Academy's L.S.C.O. beautification committee cleanup efforts. He also served as a chaperone for summer youth activities held in Rosedale Park and Southfield.

Looking towards a career, Jihad would like to become an engineer in the areas of architecture and biochemistry. In addition, he is passionate about pursuing a future in urban planning and real estate investing.

Jihad's parents are his heroes, and his motto for life is: "Just Do It!"

Larry Sanders II is a Skillman Scholar completing his freshman year at Cranbrook Kingswood Upper School. Immediately prior to enrolling at Cranbrook, he attended Bates Academy, where served on the leadership team and participated in the Academic Games, chorus, and varsity basketball. Active in his church, Northwest Unity Baptist Church, Larry is an audio/visual technician, a member of the youth choir, and a junior trustee.

His potential career objectives include becoming a journalist, a politician, and a musician. The person he looks up to more than anyone else is pastor Oscar W. King III.

He gets his motto for life from Philippians 4:13: "I can do all things through Christ who strengthens me."

Kalin Sellers
Class of 2009
The Roeper School
Skillman Scholar

Imani Sims
Class of 2009
Cranbrook Kingswood Upper School
Skillman Scholar

Kalin Sellers is a sophomore at The Roeper School. A Skillman Scholar, he plays on the Roeper baseball and basketball teams. In the community, Kalin has helped coach little league baseball and basketball teams.

With respect to his future vocation, he would like to pursue a career in banking or become a real estate agent. He considers his parents his heroes.

Kalin's motto for life is: "Live life to its fullest."

Imani Sims is a Skillman Scholar and a sophomore at Cranbrook Kingswood Upper School. She is currently involved with the Golden Key International Honour Society, the African American Awareness Association, Listen Up the Poetry Club, the pep squad and softball.

In her church Imani is a youth usher, a junior Big Sister and participates in Gospel Hands. She is also active in her community with YES for PREP and People to People. Her career ambitions include a future in business law with a focus on being an agent. Imani's heroes are the character Flor from *Spanglish* and Jesus.

Her motto in life is: "Learn something from everyone you meet."

Danielle Smith
Class of 2009
Detroit Country Day School
Skillman Scholar

Danielle Smith is a sophomore at Detroit Country Day School. She is a Skillman Scholar and is currently involved with the *Spectrum Literary Magazine,* the Day Times (school paper), the orchestra, theatre tech and the stage crew. Danielle also plays volleyball and lacrosse.

She also participated in the Summer in Service program at the Plymouth YMCA. Danielle's career objectives are to become either a doctor or a teacher. Her mother is her hero and source of inspiration.

Danielle's motto for life is: "Knowledge is power."

Katricia Smith
Freshman
Duke University
Skillman Scholar

A four-year Skillman Scholar, Katricia Smith is currently enrolled as a freshman at Duke University, where she is majoring in biology and cultural anthropology. She graduated from The Roeper School in Bloomfield Hills with a 3.8 grade point average, and received a four-year scholarship to pursue her higher education at Duke.

While at Roeper, Katricia participated in Skillman Scholar activities, dance, choreography, writing and poetry clubs. She is a member of Umoja and Amnesty International.

Although somewhat undecided on her career objectives, Katricia is currently leaning toward a vocation in the fields of biology or anthropology.

Damiana Sorrell
Class of 2010
University Liggett School
Skillman Scholar

Christian Starling
Freshman
Harvard College, Harvard University
Skillman Scholar

Damiana Sorrell is a Skillman Scholar currently completing her freshman year at University Liggett School. Previously, she attended Hally Magnet Middle School in Detroit, where she was an office aide and served on the student council. In addition, she participates in the youth ministry at her church, and her short story, "The Golden Jewel," was recently published.

Potential career paths for Damiana include becoming an actress, an ice skater or a writer. She names her mother as her hero.

Her motto for life is: "Succeed always."

Christian Starling graduated from University Liggett School in 2006. He is currently a freshman at Harvard College, Harvard University.

At University Liggett, Christian was a four-year Skillman Scholar, president of student council as a senior, yearbook editor for his junior and senior years, and he played three varsity sports. In addition, he headed the community outreach Mission Minded Kids for five years and planned and coordinated prayer walks and bicycle trips for his church. His current community activities include the Freshman Urban Outreach Program at Harvard College.

Christian's career objectives include starting a college counseling program for inner-city youths and becoming a writer/journalist and photojournalist for a major news publication. His hero is his godfather, Ron Patterson.

His motto for life is: "The biggest problem in the world is misunderstanding; take the time to understand people, not tolerate them."

Gabriela Sullen
Class of 2010
Cranbrook Kingswood Upper School
Skillman Scholar

Cherry Tolbert
Class of 2010
Cranbrook Kingswood Upper School
Skillman Scholar

Gabriela Sullen is a freshman at Cranbrook Kingswood Upper School. A Skillman Scholar, she has participated in the after-school gifted and talented art program, career club, dance team and has played basketball and served as president of student council.

She is an acolyte, an usher, and a member of the choir and high school youth group at her church. In the community, Gabriela is a volunteer at the recreation center, on teen council, and has helped feed the homeless.

Currently, her career objectives are set. She wants to maintain a 3.5 or higher grade point average, earn a scholarship to attend college and become a doctor. Her hero is her mother.

Gabriela's mottos for life are: "Do it right the first time, or not at all" and "Always keep a smile on your face."

Cherry Tolbert is a freshman at Cranbrook Kingswood Upper School where she is a Skillman Scholar and involved in art and choir. Her current church activities include participating in choir and dance. In the community, Cherry is active with the Big Brothers Big Sisters organization, is a member of the Block Club and is a student at the College of Creative Studies (CCS).

For career objectives, she wants to be involved in politics or fields related to math, science, and art. Her heroes in this world are Oprah, Stevie Wonder and her own mother.

Cherry's motto for life is: "Anything is possible if you apply yourself."

Detra Danielle D'Shawn Ward
Class of 2009
University Liggett School
Skillman Scholar

D etra Danielle D'Shawn Ward is a sophomore at University Liggett School. She was a student council representative during the 2005-2006 school year. A Skillman Scholar and a class officer, Detra is involved in a variety of clubs and activities including Casa Maria, the African American Awareness Association, French Club, musicals, seasonal plays, and tennis.

At her church, she serves on the youth praise team and is a member of the dance troop and hospitality staff. Detra loves mentoring children, volunteering at colleges, singing and writing music, swimming, writing poetry and short stories and preparing for college. Her largest activity is reading and expanding her outlook on life.

Detra plans to complete high school at University Liggett and study performing arts and journalism at an East Coast college or university. She hopes to act, sing, and dance; however, if that does not pan out, she would like to make a difference in the world with her motivational speeches and/or literature.

Detra's heroes are Patti LaBelle and Lena Horn. Her motto for life is: "With great power comes great responsibility."

Terrence Way
Class of 2009
The Roeper School
Skillman Scholar

T errence Way is a sophomore at The Roeper School in Bloomfield Hills. A Skillman Scholarship recipient, Terrence participates in the concert band and competes on the school's junior varsity basketball and varsity track and field squads. He also serves as a sound technician at his church and volunteers at an arts camp for kids between the ages of six and ten.

Still somewhat unsure of a definite career path, Terrence would like to pursue a vocation in the fields of advanced math or programming. His heroes in life are his parents.

Ebony LeShanda Williams
Freshman
Mount Holyoke College
Skillman Scholar

E bony LeShanda Williams is enrolled as a freshman at Mount Holyoke College in South Hadley, Massachusetts. A Skillman Scholar, she graduated from University Liggett School in 2006.

As a University Liggett School student, Ebony was a class officers class representative for two years, a member of student government for two years, and president of the African American Awareness Association. Active in her church, she is a youth representative in the vicariate, youth group president, and a planner of outreach activities. Ebony has also served as a tutor for students in math and Spanish.

Her career objective is to eventually become a pediatrician. Ebony plans to achieve her goal by excelling at Mount Holyoke and maintaining a good grade point average, and then graduating from medical school with a good foundation laid for her future. Her mother, Caroline Williams, is her hero.

Ebony's motto for life is: "Even though things may not be great now, the future holds the key to your dreams."

Detroit's

JUDGES

"Democracies die behind closed doors."

JUDGE DAMON KEITH

JUDGES

**The Honorable
Deborah Ross Adams**
Judge, Family Division
Third Judicial Circuit Court

The Honorable Deborah Ross Adams is a judge in the Third Judicial Circuit Court (Family Division), Wayne County, Detroit, Michigan. She was elevated to this position by appointment of Governor Jennifer Granholm on April 10, 2006. Adams previously served nine years as an outstanding judge in the 36th District Court, Detroit, Michigan, where she was the top vote getter in two citywide judicial races. She also served three years as a respected magistrate in that court as well, following a distinguished career as a trial attorney in the law department of the City of Detroit.

Adams received her undergraduate degree from the University of Michigan and her law degree from Georgetown University Law Center.

Adams is active in numerous civic and community organizations, serving on boards that promote child advocacy, women's rights and mental health issues. A frequent lecturer at schools across metropolitan Detroit, she has mentored many children throughout her career.

She has been married to Detroit Deputy Mayor Anthony Adams, Esq. for 27 years. They have three lovely children: Ashley (25), an attorney, Arin (21), and Aric (16).

**The Honorable
Alex J. Allen Jr.**
Visiting Judge
36th District Court

Judge Alex J. Allen Jr. served on the 36th District Court for 17 years, during which he served as chief judge for six years. Specializing in alternative dispute resolution, he currently sits as a visiting judge. He is also the president of The Allen Legal Group.

Allen earned a bachelor of arts degree from Wayne State University and a juris doctor degree from the Detroit College of Law. He currently attends the Ashland Theological Seminary.

Allen is a member of many professional, civic and community organizations, including the State Bar of Michigan, the National Bar Association and the Association of Black Judges of Michigan. He is a founder of the Wolverine Law Student Association, and a member of Omega Psi Phi Fraternity, Inc., and the Prince Hall Grand Lodge of Michigan. Allen is active in senior issues and rescue mission activities.

He is married to Nancy Green Allen. They have three sons, Alex III, Michael and Derek.

Eric L. Clay is a judge on the United States Court of Appeals for the Sixth Circuit where he has served since his appointment to the federal bench by President Clinton in 1997. Clay previously practiced with the Detroit law firm of Lewis, White & Clay, P.C., where he chaired the litigation department. He began his career as a law clerk for U.S. District Court Judge Damon J. Keith, and currently serves with Keith on the United States Court of Appeals.

Clay has served as a member of the executive committee of the Yale Law School Association and on the board of visitors for the University of North Carolina. He has received numerous awards for his community involvement, including the 2004 Trailblazer Award from the D. Augustus Straker Bar Association in recognition of his pioneering efforts to promote diversity, equality and justice.

A native of Durham, North Carolina, Clay graduated Phi Beta Kappa from the University of North Carolina at Chapel Hill, and received his juris doctor degree from Yale Law School.

The Honorable Eric L. Clay
Judge
U.S. Court of Appeals, Sixth Circuit

The Honorable Julian Cook Jr. was appointed to the U.S. District Court on September 25, 1978 by President Jimmy Carter. He served as chief judge of the Eastern District of Michigan from 1989 to 1996.

He currently serves as chairman of the Fellows of the Michigan Bar Foundation. Since 1986 he has served as chairman of the Sixth Circuit committee of standard criminal jury instructions. He has served as an instructor at the Harvard University trial advocacy workshop, the Trial Advocacy Institute at the University of Virginia School of Law, and the Criminal Trial Advocacy Program for the Department of Justice. Cook has received numerous accolades and awards for his professional and civic contributions.

A graduate of The Pennsylvania State University and Georgetown University Law School, he holds a master's degree in law from the University of Virginia. He also holds honorary doctorate of laws degrees from Georgetown University, the University of Detroit Mercy, Wayne State University, and Michigan State University.

Cook and his wife, Carol, are proud parents of three children.

© PINDERHUGHES

The Honorable
Julian Abele Cook Jr.
U.S. District Court Judge
Eastern District of Michigan

**The Honorable
Edward Ewell Jr.**
Judge
Third Circuit Court, Criminal Division
State of Michigan

E dward Ewell Jr. was born and raised in Detroit. After graduating from Cass Technical High School, he attended the University of Michigan Ann Arbor. Ewell pursued a master of science program through Atlanta University and graduated from Wayne State University Law School. After his admission to the Bar, he clerked for the Honorable Damon J. Keith for two years.

Governor Jennifer Granholm appointed Ewell to the Third Circuit Court of Michigan, criminal division, on which he sits as the presiding judge.

Ewell was an associate at the law firm of Pepper, Hamilton & Scheetz before working as a criminal prosecutor in the United States Attorney's Office. There, he was responsible for all criminal civil rights violations.

In 1997 Ewell became general counsel for Wayne County. He managed a municipal corporate law office, employing more than 70 people. He also oversaw a team of lawyers who handled an array of lawsuits and claims against various Wayne County departments.

Ewell lives in Detroit with his wife of 17 years, Florise Neville Ewell, and their two children, Edward, 15, and Simone Alyse, 11.

**The Honorable
Sheila Ann Gibson**
Judge, Family Division
Third Judicial Circuit Court

T he Honorable Sheila Gibson is a Wayne County Third Judicial Circuit Court judge of the family division, where she handles domestic, neglect and juvenile cases. She has served as presiding judge of the family division's domestic and juvenile sections. She was previously assistant corporation counsel for the City of Detroit and assistant general counsel for Blue Cross Blue Shield of Michigan.

Gibson obtained a bachelor of arts degree from the University of Michigan in 1980 and a law degree from the University of Pittsburgh School of Law in 1983.

She has legal affiliations with the Michigan Judges Association, the Association of Black Judges, the Wolverine Bar Association and the Women Lawyers Association. She is also chair of the Michigan Judges Association family law committee.

Gibson developed and serves as director for the Wayne County Juvenile Drug Court Program. She also handles the school truancy docket.

She has served as chair/co-chair of the Detroit Association of University of Michigan Women, the American Corporate Council, Alpha Kappa Alpha Sorority, Inc., Oak Grove A.M.E. Church scholarship committees and several other private scholarship committees.

J udge Judy A. Hartsfield was appointed by Governor Jennifer M. Granholm to the Wayne County Probate Court, where she hears child abuse and delinquency cases.

Before joining the bench, Hartsfield worked for more than 15 years for the State of Michigan Office of the Attorney General. In 1997 she became the first African-American female to head a division in the history of the attorney general's office when she became head of the child abuse and neglect division in Detroit.

Hartsfield is frequently a guest lecturer in child welfare law at Wayne State University and Marygrove College. She is currently on the board of directors for the Children's Aid Society, the Children's Charter of the Courts of Michigan, and the Association of Black Judges of Michigan. She also serves on the Governor's Task Force for Children's Justice.

Hartsfield graduated with honors from Detroit Central High School and the University of Michigan, and earned her law degree from the University of San Diego. She is a member of the State Bars of California and Michigan. She is married with one daughter.

**The Honorable
Judy A. Hartsfield**
Judge
Wayne County Probate Court

J udge Beverly Hayes-Sipes was elected to the 36th District Court in November of 2002, and is dedicated to the principle that justice is where law and compassion meet.

Hayes-Sipes serves in many community and professional organizations. She is president of the Association of Black Judges of Michigan, which was the host organization for the Judicial Council of the National Bar Association (NBA) for its 81st Annual Conference in Detroit, Michigan. During the convention, she was elected to the board of directors for the Judicial Council.

In addition to other acknowledgements of her judicial excellence and commitment, Judge Hayes-Sipes was awarded the NBA President's Award for 2006. Additionally, she was given the 2006 Judicial Council Chair's Award.

Hayes-Sipes received a bachelor of science degree from Wayne State University and her juris doctorate from Michigan State University College of Law.

A Detroiter, Judge Hayes-Sipes is married to Victor L. Sipes, an educator, and has three children, Martin (Karen), David (Michele) and Valencia, seven grandchildren and a great extended family. She is a member of Hartford Memorial Baptist Church.

**The Honorable
Beverly J. Hayes-Sipes**
Judge
36th District Court

JUDGES

**The Honorable
Denise Page Hood**
U.S. District Court Judge
Eastern District of Michigan

The Honorable Denise Page Hood, a graduate of Yale University and Columbia School of Law, is a United States District Court judge for the Eastern District of Michigan. She was appointed to the bench by President Bill Clinton in 1994.

Hood has worked as assistant corporation counsel in the City of Detroit Law Department and has served on the benches of the 36th District Court, Recorder's Court, and Wayne County Circuit Court. She was the first black female president of the Detroit Bar Association.

Hood is an active member of the State Bar of Michigan, the Detroit Metropolitan Bar Association, and the Association of Black Judges of Michigan, to name a few. She also volunteers in various community groups including, but not limited to, the Olivet College board of trustees, the Lula Belle Stewart Center, Cyprian Center and the Inside/Out Literary Arts Project. Hood has been honored with many honors and awards.

She is married to Reverend Nicholas Hood III, senior minister of Plymouth United Church of Christ and former Detroit city councilman. They have two sons, Nathan and Noah.

**The Honorable
Karen Fort Hood**
Judge
Michigan Court of Appeals
Detroit, Michigan

In November of 2002, the Honorable Karen Fort Hood made history as the first African-American woman elected to the Michigan Court of Appeals. A former Detroit Public School teacher and probation officer, Hood was elected to the Recorder's Court bench in 1992. In 1999 she became presiding judge of the Wayne County Circuit Court, Criminal Division.

Previously, Hood was a special assistant prosecutor in the Wayne County Juvenile Court, where she prosecuted juvenile offender and abuse and neglect cases. She transferred to the appellate division of the Prosecutor's Office, and was appointed assistant prosecuting attorney, serving until 1992, when she took the bench.

An active member of the community, Hood is past president of the Association of Black Judges of Michigan, and a member of the Wolverine Bar Association. She is on the executive board of the Detroit NAACP and a member of the Western Wayne County NAACP. Hood is active in the National Council on Alcoholism, and is currently on the board of B.A.B.E.S. (Beginners Alcohol Addiction Basic Education Studies). She is a member of Word of Faith International Christian Center.

P ast Judicial Council chair of the National Bar Association (NBA), Sylvia James was the first female judge and first African-American woman elected citywide in the history of Inkster. A University of Michigan graduate, James obtained her law degree from the University of Wisconsin School of Law.

During her tenure, James has instituted three highly successful programs: Save African American Boys, the Community Service Program, and the Annual Law Day Program and Essay Contest.

James served as president of the Wolverine Bar Association, regional director of the NBA, and on the Public Safety and Justice Committee of New Detroit. A gubernatorial appointee to the State Board of Ethics, she served on the board of directors of SCLC (Detroit). James is a life member of Delta Sigma Theta Sorority, Inc.

James has received numerous awards including The Raymond Pace Alexander Distinguished Jurist and Humanitarian Award from the Judicial Council of the National Bar Association. In 2000 she penned the foreword in the inaugural edition of *Black Judges in America*®.

James' most significant accomplishment is her daughter, Alexxiss S. Jackson, a National Merit Scholar.

**The Honorable
Sylvia A. James**
Chief Judge
22nd District Court
Inkster, Michigan

A native Detroiter, Judge Patricia L. Jefferson is a graduate of the Wayne State University School of Law. Jefferson practiced as a civil trial attorney, specializing in automobile insurance law, medical malpractice and construction site accidents. She later entered into private practice with her husband, Melvin D. Jefferson Jr., specializing in criminal defense.

Elected to the 36th District Court in 1996, Jefferson was instrumental in implementing Detroit's first Drug Treatment Court, becoming the court's first judge. She is currently serving her second term on the bench.

Jefferson served as vice president and board member of the Michigan Association of Drug Court Professionals, and as past president of the Association of Black Judges of Michigan. Appointed by the mayor, she currently serves on the City of Detroit Health Department's substance abuse advisory council.

Jefferson has received numerous awards for her work on the bench and in the community, including special Congressional recognition, the Governor's Certificate of Tribute, the Spirit of Detroit Award, and the National Coalition of 100 Black Women Achievement Award.

**The Honorable
Patricia L. Jefferson**
Judge
36th District Court

JUDGES

**The Honorable
Shelia R. Johnson**
Chief Judge Pro Tempore
46th District Court

The Honorable Shelia R. Johnson is chief judge pro tempore of the 46th District Court, which serves the Detroit suburban communities of Southfield, Lathrup Village, Beverly Hills, Bingham Farms, Franklin and Southfield Township, Michigan. She is the first African American to serve as judge in the 46th District Court and the first African-American female district judge in Oakland County. Johnson spearheaded the establishment of the community Court in Schools Program, where court is held offsite at various schools, with the goal of deterring youth from criminal behavior and inspiring future career choices.

Johnson is a graduate of Dartmouth College and The University of Michigan Law School, where she served as the first African-American president of the Law School Student Senate and delivered the commencement address to her class. She served in the prestigious position of law clerk to a federal judge and thereafter, as an attorney in private practice.

Johnson has received numerous awards, and she actively serves in civic, judicial and legal associations. She is single and enjoys weight lifting, waterskiing and the arts.

© Glenn Triest Photographic

**The Honorable
Damon J. Keith**
Judge
United States Court of Appeals
for the Sixth Circuit

Born and raised in Detroit, Damon J. Keith graduated from West Virginia State College. He earned a juris doctor degree from Howard Law School, where he was elected chief justice of the Court of Peers. He received his master of laws degree from Wayne State University Law School. From 1950 to 1967, Keith was a partner in one of Detroit's first all-black law firms, Keith, Conyers, Anderson, Brown & Wahls.

In 1967 President Johnson appointed Keith to the United States District Court for the Eastern District of Michigan. After ten years on the District Court, including two years as chief judge, he was elevated by President Carter to the United States Court of Appeals for the Sixth Circuit.

Keith is the recipient of numerous awards and honors, the latest being an endowment to build the Damon J. Keith Center for Civil Rights at Wayne State University Law School.

Keith is married to Rachel Boone Keith, M.D. They have three daughters, Gilda, Debbie, and Cecile. Cecile and her husband, Daryle Brown, are the parents of Keith's granddaughters, Nia and Camara.

Born in Detroit, the Honorable Leonia J. Lloyd taught at Cass Technical High School in 1971. She received a bachelor of science degree in education and juris doctor degree from Wayne State University. She was elected to the 36th District Court in 1992, and became a Drug Treatment Court judge in 2002.

Lloyd was a partner in the law firm of Lloyd and Lloyd with her late sister, the Honorable Leona L. Lloyd. The country's first twin judges to sit on the same bench at the same time, they were affectionately dubbed, "twins for justice." In memory of her sister, Lloyd has endowed two scholarship funds that assist undergraduate students in the field of education and law.

Currently, Lloyd is the presiding Drug Treatment Court judge, which includes Project Fresh Start, a program designed to help women in the sex trade to remain drug free, restore self respect, acquire housing and employment, and become productive citizens. This program was the second place winner in the National Association of Drug Court Professionals for 2006-2007.

Llyod is married to DeMarcus Holland.

**The Honorable
Leonia J. Lloyd**
Judge
36th District Court

The Honorable Miriam B. Martin-Clark is a judge of the 36th District Court in Detroit, where she has served since 1997. As a judge on the second-busiest court in the nation, Martin-Clark has general jurisdiction of criminal and civil cases ranging from felony preliminary exams to civil matters, including landlord tenant summary proceedings.

Martin-Clark is a graduate of both Howard University, where she earned her bachelor of arts degree in English literature, and Wayne State University, where she earned a post degree in education and a juris doctorate.

Martin-Clark is the former assistant general counsel of Wayne State University. A native of Detroit, she lives there with her husband, Dr. Frank M. Clark, a physician. She is an active member of several community organizations and a recipient of numerous awards and citations. She is also the proud mother of two adult children, Frank II, a lawyer, and Christina, a physician.

**The Honorable
Miriam B. Martin-Clark**
Judge
36th District Court

JUDGES

**The Honorable
B. Pennie Millender**
Judge
36th District Court

Governor Jennifer Granholm appointed Judge B. Pennie Millender to the 36th District Court in December of 2003. She was elected to serve a full term on the Court in November of 2004.

Prior to her appointment, Millender served as a magistrate in the 36th District Court for five years. She earned a bachelor's degree in psychology from Southern University in Baton Rouge, Louisiana; a master of arts in vocational rehabilitation counseling from Wayne State University; and a juris doctorate from Detroit College of Law.

While studying law, Millender received several awards including the American Jurisprudence Book Award. She held internships with the Honorable Claudia House Morcom (Wayne County Circuit Court) and the Honorable Dennis W. Archer (Michigan Supreme Court).

The former president of the Association of Black Judges of Michigan, Millender is a member of the Wolverine Bar Association and a life member of the NAACP. She has received numerous awards and honors.

Millender credits her parents, the late Robert and Louise Millender, with influencing her commitment to public service and the pursuit of justice and equality for all Americans.

**The Honorable
Cylenthia LaToye Miller**
Judge
36th Judicial District Court

The Honorable Cylenthia LaToye Miller serves on the third-busiest district court in the nation. She presides over cases from all of the court's dockets, including real estate, traffic and ordinance, general civil, and criminal cases.

Cylenthia is first vice president of the National Bar Association (NBA) Women Lawyers Division and a trustee of the Charles H. Wright Museum of African American History. She is also a past president of the Wolverine Bar Association (WBA) and the Women Lawyers Association of Michigan.

Her awards include the NBA President's Award (2000 and 2006); the WBA Shining Star (2005) and Member of the Year (2001); State Bar of Michigan's Citizen Lawyer (2005); Wolverine Student Bar Association Distinguished Alumni (2003); and *Michigan Lawyers Weekly*'s Top 5 Up & Coming Lawyers (2001).

Cylenthia earned a bachelor of arts degree from Wayne State University and a juris doctor degree, cum laude, from Michigan State University-Detroit College of Law, becoming the first African-American woman class president in its history.

Cylenthia enjoys all music, swimming, movies, and reading. She believes, "What you make of yourself is your gift to God."

Denise Langford Morris is Oakland County's first African-American judge. She has served on the Circuit Court since 1992. Morris received a master's degree, cum laude, in guidance and counseling from Wayne State University and a juris doctorate degree from the University of Detroit Mercy School of Law. Previously, Morris was an assistant Oakland County prosecutor and assistant United States attorney.

Morris is active in many law-related organizations including the National and American Bar Associations. She is a board member of the Michigan Supreme Court Historical Society, president of the Association of Black Judges of Michigan, and a founding member of the D. Augustus Straker Bar Association. She is also very active in youth mentoring, church events, and community organizations.

Morris has received numerous awards, including the ABA Judicial Certificate of Recognition, the Southeastern Michigan Association of Chiefs of Police Certificate of Appreciation, the Wonder Woman Award from the Woman's Survival Center, the Pontiac Urban League - Break the Glass Ceiling Award and the NAACP Judicial Award.

Morris has handled numerous high-profile cases, including Dr. Jack Kevorkian, Eminem, and Selena Jones.

**The Honorable
Denise Langford Morris**
Judge
Oakland County Circuit Court
Detroit, Michigan

John A. Murphy was first elected to the Court of Common Pleas on November 7, 1978. He also served with distinction on the 36th District Court until his election to the Third Judicial Circuit in 1986.

A graduate of Southeastern High School, Murphy received an undergraduate degree from the University of Michigan. He received his law degree from the Wayne State University Law School.

Murphy is a member of numerous professional and civic organizations. These include the American Trial Lawyers Association, the American Judges Association, the Wolverine Bar Association, the Association of Black Judges of Michigan, and Optimist International.

Murphy is married to the former Patricia Ann Van Dyke and is the father of one son, John Brandon. His family resides in a happy home in Plymouth Township.

**The Honorable
John A. Murphy**
Circuit Court Judge
Third Judicial Circuit of Michigan
Detroit, Michigan

JUDGES

**The Honorable
Jeanette O'Banner-Owens**
Judge
State of Michigan
36th District Court

The Honorable Jeanette O'Banner-Owens serves as a judge of limited jurisdiction for Michigan's 36th District Court. She presides over the court, determining controversies between parties in preliminary examinations, civil trials, small claims and landlord-tenant disputes.

Owens is a member of the Phi Alpha Delta Law Fraternity, International, and is a lifetime member of the National and International Associations of Women Judges. She is a former president of the Michigan District Judges Association and she is the Judicial Council treasurer.

A candidate for a master's degree in judicial studies, Owens has traveled the world studying the law of different countries with the National Judicial College. She is a board member of the New Judicial College and the Trial Lawyers School in Dubois, Wyoming.

At 21, Owens came in first in sales in the U.S. for Avon Products, Inc. and was featured in *Who's Who in America*. She has also been included in *Who's Who in Law Enforcement* and the *International Who's Who of Professionals*.

A native Detroiter, Owens is a member of Straight Gate International Church.

**The Honorable
Mark A. Randon**
Judge
36th District Court
City of Detroit

Mark Randon serves as a judge of the 36th District Court in Detroit, one of the largest and busiest district courts in the nation. In this position, he presides over a wide variety of civil and criminal cases that occur in Detroit.

Appointed by the governor in 2001 at age 32, Randon holds the distinction of being the youngest judge appointed to the bench in Michigan since the constitutional requirements were changed. In 2002 the citizens of Detroit elected him to a six-year term, which he is currently serving.

Randon has authored several articles that have appeared in newspapers and legal journals. He has received many awards for his community service, including *Crain's Detroit Business* 40 under 40. In 2005 he established an educational program for young offenders through Wayne County Community College.

Randon is a graduate of Cass Technical High School and Michigan State University. He received a law degree from the University of Michigan in 1992. He has been married for ten years to Dr. Lisa Marie Randon, and together they have two children.

Judge Deborah A. Thomas is the middle child of three daughters born into a working-class family. At the age of three, she contracted polio. She recalls the loving attention and encouragement from her father during the challenges of her early years. Following her father's death, when she was ten years old, it was her mother, extended family and the church that guided her to become the person she is today.

Thomas is a lifetime resident of Detroit and was educated in the Detroit Public Schools. A graduate of Cass Technical High School, she attended Western Michigan University where she earned a bachelor's degree in education and sociology. She also has a master's degree in criminal justice and a law degree.

Thomas' favorite pastime is community volunteer service. She is a member of the Order of the Elks, the Mary McLeod Bethune Association, the A. Phillip Randolph Institute and many other organizations. She believes that working with youth is an especially important use of time.

**The Honorable
Deborah A. Thomas**
Judge
The Third Judicial Circuit of Michigan

Youth Employment Services · Youth Education Services · Youth Enrichment Services

YES for PREP: Future Leaders Wanted

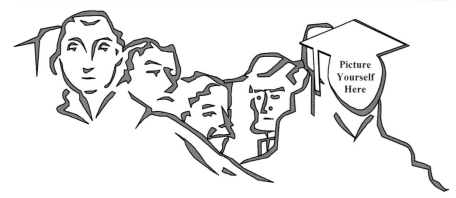

Prepare to compete successfully for college preparatory high school admission!

Rigorous Academic Preparation with Social and Cultural Experiences
Scholarship Opportunities

The Talent Search begins in October; the 14-month program begins in the summer before 8th grade.

Eligible Students Must:

- reside in Detroit, Hamtramck, Highland Park, or Pontiac.
- be currently enrolled in 7th grade.
- be currently enrolled in a public, charter or home school.

- be from a low-income minority group background.
- exhibit high performance capacity in school, with at least a 'B' average.
- achieve a score in the 90th percentile or above on a qualifying examination administered by The YES Foundation®.

For more information, call (248) 646-2203 today!

Sponsored by The YES Foundation® and Marygrove College;
Funded by The Skillman Foundation and The Knight Foundation

Explorers' Learning Community
Presents
Summer Academic Camp

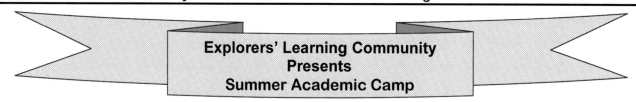

Goal: Six week intensive study aimed at preparing participants to have a sound footing in select courses upon entering 7th grade.

Eligibility: Students who reside in Detroit, Hamtramck, Highland Park, or Pontiac.

When: Begins the last week in June and runs six weeks.
Monday through Thursday, 8 am – 12 pm; Field trips every Friday.

Call (248) 646-5696 for more information.

Sponsored by The YES Foundation®; Funded by The Knight Foundation

Detroit's

COUNSELORS AT LAW

"The test of character is the amount of strain it can bear."

CHARLES HAMILTON HOUSTON (1895-1950)

LAWYER AND CIVIL RIGHTS ACTIVIST

Vernon Baker
Senior Vice President
General Counsel
ArvinMeritor, Inc.

Jerome P. Barney
Attorney at Law
Jerome Barney & Associates, PLC

Vernon Baker is senior vice president and general counsel of ArvinMeritor, Inc. There, he is responsible for the legal aspects of all ArvinMeritor's global operations and its subsidiaries. In addition, Baker directs all legal activities in the corporation, including corporate governance, acquisitions and divestitures, litigation, business standards compliance, regulatory compliance and intellectual property. He also has functional oversight responsibility for the environmental and health and safety areas.

Before the July 2000 merger with Arvin Industries Inc., Baker was senior vice president, general counsel and secretary of Meritor Automotive Inc., a global supplier of components and systems for commercial, specialty and light vehicle OEMs and the aftermarket.

Baker holds a bachelor's degree from Dartmouth College in Hanover, New Hampshire, and a juris doctorate from American University Washington College of Law in Washington, D.C. He was recently honored with the Minority Corporate Counsel Association's Trailblazer Award, which recognizes the outstanding achievements of minority in-house counsels who also act as role models in the legal profession.

Jerome P. Barney has practiced law in the Detroit area for 29 years. While he still manages a successful criminal and entertainment law practice, Jerome Barney & Associates, PLC, Jerome is shifting his focus to strategizing innovative means to bring economic revitalization to metropolitan Detroit.

First on his agenda is bringing a new franchise to Michigan by opening several Fatburger restaurants. Additionally, Jerome is planning Movie Town in Highland Park. He is assembling a coalition of Hollywood experts and accredited investors to be part of this exciting new industry. Movie Town will locally produce and market movies worldwide, blending Detroit-area and Hollywood talent to create a wide variety of employment and business opportunities.

Jerome has written and published a collection of poetic monologues, *The Other Side of the Rainbow*, which he is adapting into a stage play, *From the Other Side: Live!* Most importantly, he is the proud father of four wonderful children and happily married to Karen.

Linda D. Bernard, J.D., LL.M.
Principal, Attorney at Law
Linda D. Bernard and Associates

Niccole J. Blocker
Managing Partner
Blocker & Associates

Linda D. Bernard, principal in the law firm, Linda D. Bernard and Associates, specializes in business, labor, contract and entertainment law. An excellent business strategist, she excels in problem solving and litigation/business strategy.

Linda argued and won three precedent-setting cases in the Michigan Supreme Court, and has broad public and private sector experience as an attorney, business leader, general counsel, and president and chief executive officer. She is a licensed attorney in Michigan, Massachusetts, Pennsylvania, Washington, D.C., and the U.S. Supreme Court, Court of Claims, and Court of International Trade. She has received numerous local and national awards and serves on various boards.

She received her bachelor of arts and juris doctor degrees from Wayne State University, and a master of laws degree from the University of Pennsylvania Law School. She hosted her own radio and television shows, and is an editorial columnist, arbitrator, mediator and administrative hearings officer.

Niccole J. Blocker is the managing partner of Blocker & Associates. The firm's core competency includes total media/public relations, campaign management services and executive positioning for its clients. Blocker & Associates continues the legacy of Jerry Blocker, Michigan's first African-American anchorman at WDIV-TV in Detroit.

Niccole inherited her father's strong work ethic and through her many resources has cultivated positive relationships with the community, corporate America and local government. She has a natural zest for life and enjoys the challenges associated with building bridges among diverse cultures. She is also the vice president of corporate affairs for GE Distribution Services.

Niccole is the proud mother of two sons, Jordan and Noah.

COUNSELORS AT LAW

Erika Butler-Akinyemi
Partner
Jaffe, Raitt, Heuer & Weiss P.C.

Alan L. Canady
Member, Attorney At Law
Clark Hill PLC

Erika Butler-Akinyemi is a partner with Jaffe, Raitt, Heuer & Weiss P.C. She was admitted to practice law in 1999 and is a member of the firm's litigation group. Erika's areas of practice include commercial litigation, employment defense, negligence and products liability defense, probate and trust administration, education law and real estate litigation. Within these areas, she provides litigation services to business clientele, including managing case files; maintaining client relationships; drafting motions and briefs; and representing clients in state and federal courts.

In 2003 Erika received the State Bar of Michigan's Regeana Myrick Outstanding Young Lawyer Award and the Wolverine Bar Association's Margrette A. Taylor Distinguished Young Lawyer Award. She is also the 2005 recipient of the National Bar Association's Outstanding Region Award, and the 2006 National Bar Association's Presidential Award.

Erika received her bachelor of arts degree, magna cum laude, from Amherst College in 1995, and her juris doctor degree from The University of Michigan Law School in 1998.

Alan L. Canady is a member of Clark Hill's government policy and practice group and specializes in government relations and legislative affairs. Prior to Clark Hill, Canady served as chief of staff to several Michigan leaders, including Michigan House Democratic leader Dianne Byrum, former Michigan House Democratic leader Kwame Kilpatrick, and former Democratic leader Buzz Thomas.

Canady joined government in 1987 as an attorney and policy analyst for the Michigan State Senate in the areas of local government and taxation. He was appointed Senate Democratic counsel in 1989, where he served as chief legal counsel and parliamentarian for the Senate Democratic Caucus. He advised the caucus on all legal matters as well as Senate rules, parliamentary procedure, campaign finance and election law. In 1998 Canady was given the title of deputy chief of staff by then Senate Democratic leader John Cherry.

Prior to working in the government, Canady was in private practice in Lansing, specializing in litigation within state and federal courts.

Canady earned a bachelor's degree from the University of Michigan, and his juris doctorate from George Washington University.

COUNSELORS AT LAW

Michelle A. Carter
Associate, Attorney at Law
Bodman LLP

George A. Chatman
Principal Attorney
George A. Chatman and Associates
Attorneys at Law

Michelle A. Carter, an associate at Bodman LLP, represents clients in complex commercial litigation. Carter also has experience with labor and employment law, counseling employers regarding claims of sexual harassment, discrimination and wrongful termination.

Carter received her juris doctorate from Rutgers State University-Camden. In law school, she interned as a clerk for the Honorable Joel B. Rosen of the U.S. District Court of New Jersey. She also served as vice president of the Black Law Students Association. She began her practice in New Jersey and Pennsylvania, and clerked for the Honorable Theodore Z. Davis of the Superior Court of New Jersey.

Carter serves on the board of directors for the Wolverine Bar Association, the Detroit Metropolitan Bar Association, the Rutgers-Camden School of Law Alumni Association, and Volunteers of America, Michigan. She is a member of Delta Sigma Theta Sorority, Inc., the American Bar Association, the National Bar Association, the Pennsylvania Bar Association and the New Jersey Bar Association.

A native of Detroit, Carter received her bachelor of arts degree from the University of Michigan.

George A. Chatman is principal attorney at George A. Chatman and Associates. His law practice includes criminal, personal injury, family law and appeals. He has more than 24 years of trial experience. In 2004 he was a candidate for judge of the 36th District Court and was rated Outstanding by the Detroit Metropolitan Bar Association.

George has received many awards during his legal career, including Lawyer of the Year, 1989-1990, by the Wolverine Bar Association; WCNLS Private Attorney Involvement Program Award for 1986-1987; Certificate of Appreciation from the Southern Poverty Law Center in 2004; and Certificate-Volunteer from the Legal Aid and Defender Association, Inc. in 2005.

George graduated from Cass Technical High School and received his bachelor of science degree from Wayne State University. He received his master's and juris doctor degrees from the University of Detroit. He has consulted on two high school textbooks: *Law in American History* and *American Government – Principles and Practices.*

George is married to Marian Williams-Chatman and has one daughter, Sharyl, a graduate of Spelman College.

COUNSELORS AT LAW

Reginald G. Dozier
Shareholder & Corporate Secretary
Lewis & Munday, PC

Arthur Dudley II
Shareholder, Attorney at Law
Butzel Long

Reginald G. Dozier is a shareholder and the corporate secretary of Lewis & Munday, PC. A 1985 graduate of the Detroit College of Law, he is the former president of Dozier, Turner & Braceful, PC, and the commanding officer of the Detroit Police Department's legal advisor section.

Reginald represents Fortune 500 corporations, municipal corporations and small businesses in premises and personal injury matters, as well as commercial, contract and condemnation matters.

Reginald is licensed to practice in Michigan state and federal courts, and the United States Supreme Court. He is the past chair of the State Bar of Michigan's law practice management section council, and a former member of the board of directors of the Wolverine Bar Association. He was featured in *Crain's Detroit Business* 40 Under 40 in 1997. Reginald attended Howard University, and received a bachelor of arts degree from the University of Michigan-Dearborn in 1980. He is involved in numerous professional and community activities.

A native Detroiter, Reginald is the husband of Dr. Karen Gunn, and the father of MaToya, Reginald II and Karla.

Arthur "Art" Dudley II is a shareholder in Butzel Long's Detroit office. He has practiced law for more than 25 years, specializing in securities law, mergers and acquisitions, executive compensation, emerging growth companies, and general corporate representation.

Art received a juris doctor degree from Yale Law School and a master of arts degree in economics from Yale University. He attended Harvard College as a National Merit Scholar, graduating cum laude with a bachelor of arts degree in economics.

Art is involved in numerous civic and charitable organizations. He is a graduate of Leadership Detroit; a member of the Michigan Minority Business Development Council (MMBDC); current chair of the CIC Professional Services Sector; and recipient of the MMBDC's 7 GEMS Award. He is a director of the Legal Aid and Defender Association; past vice chair of the Detroit Urban League; and past chair of the Black United Fund of Michigan and a recipient of its Hampton Award. Art's passion is to increase minority wealth through economic development.

Art and his wife, Doreen, are the proud parents of two sons, Alexander and Frederick.

Stephen C. Glymph, Esq.
Chief Financial Officer & General Counsel
The Basketball Warehouse, LLC

Marcia B. Marsh Goffney
Vice President, Secretary & General Counsel
Yazaki North America, Inc.

Stephen Glymph is a member, chief financial officer and general counsel of The Basketball Warehouse, LLC. The Basketball Warehouse is an indoor sports and entertainment company, with the mission of providing clean, safe, affordable and accessible recreation and entertainment facilities in urban communities. It employs a business model that focuses on building partnerships with local government, community-based nonprofit organizations, schools and churches.

The Basketball Warehouse opened its first location, a 33,000-square-foot facility on Detroit's east side in February of 2006. Children of all ages can enjoy activities such as pick-up basketball, leagues, tournaments, instructional camps, boxing, volleyball, weight training and batting practice. The facility includes a family entertainment center, snack shop, barbershop, and retail sports apparel shop, making The Basketball Warehouse the first of its kind in Detroit.

A native of Detroit, Stephen received his bachelor of science degree in mechanical engineering from Michigan State University, and his juris doctorate from William and Mary School of Law in Virginia.

Stephen manages The Basketball Warehouse with fellow members and native Detroiters Jermaine Woods, CEO and Terrence Willis, COO.

Marcia B. Marsh Goffney is vice president, secretary and general counsel of Yazaki North America, Inc., a multi-billion-dollar supplier of wire harnesses, data solutions and electronic and electrical components to the global automotive industry. YNA is part of the Japan-based Yazaki Group.

Goffney manages all legal services for YNA and Yazaki entities throughout North America, South America, Canada and Mexico. She also oversees governance activities. Previously, she was managing counsel at Dow Corning Corporation.

Goffney co-founded the Charting Your Own Course Foundation for the career advancement of minority lawyers. She is a member of the Executive Leadership Council and has served on the Michigan Open Justice Commission and the American Bar Association ethics and professional responsibility committee. She is an alumna of Leadership America and serves as a director on the boards of the 20,000-member Association of Corporate Counsel and the Straker Bar Association.

Goffney's awards include the Dow Chemical/Dow Corning Amory Houghton Community Service award, the Mitten Bay Girl Scout Region's Outstanding Woman of the Year, and the Association of Corporate Counsel National Diversity Award.

COUNSELORS AT LAW

Elliott Hall
Of Counsel, Attorney at Law
Dykema Gossett PLLC

David Baker Lewis
Chairman & Chief Executive Officer
Lewis & Munday, PC

Elliott Hall's practice focuses on government policy and practice matters, with an emphasis on legislative issues pertaining to the automotive industry, as well as matters relating to municipalities. Active in the business community, Hall serves on many corporate boards in Detroit and Washington, D.C.

Prior to joining Dykema, Hall was the first African-American vice president and former vice president of Washington affairs and dealer development for Ford Motor Company. There, he was responsible for the development and growth of new Ford dealers, with an emphasis on recruiting qualified minorities and women.

Hall was the first African-American chief assistant prosecutor for Wayne County, Michigan and the first African-American corporation counsel for the City of Detroit.

He is a past president of the Detroit Metropolitan Bar Association and the Wolverine Bar Association. Hall is board chairman of both the Joint Center for Political and Economic Studies in Washington, D.C., and the Music Hall Center for Performing Arts in Detroit. He is also a board member of Georgetown University, Clark Atlanta University and the Congressional Black Caucus Foundation, Inc.

David Baker Lewis serves as chairman and chief executive officer of Lewis & Munday. He has specialized in municipal finance since 1974. Lewis is a former member of the board of directors of the National Association of Bond Lawyers and is former chairman of the National Association of Securities Professionals.

Lewis was educated in the Detroit Public Schools. He received his bachelor of arts degree from Oakland University. He earned his master of business administration degree from the University of Chicago Graduate School of Business and was awarded his juris doctor degree from the University of Michigan Law School.

Currently, Lewis serves as a member of the Kroger Company board of directors and is chairman of the Kroger audit committee. He is also a member of the H&R Block board of directors. Lewis is a former director of Comerica Inc., TRW Inc., LG&E Energy Corp., M.A. Hanna Company and Consolidated Rail Corporation.

Denise J. Lewis
Partner, Attorney at Law
Real Estate Department
Honigman Miller Schwartz and Cohn LLP

Kathleen McCree Lewis
Member, Attorney at Law
Dykema Gossett PLLC

Denise J. Lewis is a partner in the real estate department of Honigman Miller Schwartz and Cohn LLP's Detroit office. She represents and counsels real estate developers, owners, and investors with projects including retail, office, multi-family, industrial, single-family and mixed-use hotel/office development. She represents corporate clients engaged in real estate transactions, such as the downtown headquarters projects for General Motors Corporation and Compuware Corporation. Lewis focuses on projects in urban centers involving public/private partnerships and issues of redevelopment and restoration, environmental planning, land use planning, brownfield financing, tax abatement and tax increment financing.

Lewis is the first woman and the first African American from Michigan elected to the prestigious American College of Real Estate Lawyers. She has been recognized in the 2006 Super Lawyers for Michigan listing, *Chambers USA: America's Leading Lawyers for Business*, and *Crain's Detroit Business*.

Lewis graduated cum laude from the University of Michigan Law School in 1983. She earned a master of arts degree from Wayne State University in 1969 and graduated cum laude with a bachelor of arts degree from Columbia University in 1966.

Kathleen McCree Lewis is Dykema Gossett PLLC's appellate litigation specialist. She handles appeals involving all substantive areas of civil law, including antitrust, banking, bankruptcy, environmental, general commercial, insurance, intellectual property, land use, municipal finance, professional malpractice and product liability. She is admitted to practice in the state and federal courts in Michigan and in the U.S. Court of Appeals for the Sixth, Seventh, Eighth, Ninth, Tenth, Eleventh and Federal Circuits, and the United States Supreme Court.

Lewis served as president of the American Academy of Appellate Lawyers in 2005-2006. She is a past co-chairperson of the American Bar Association section of litigation appellate practice committee, and is a founding member of the State Bar of Michigan appellate practice section. In 1999 and 2001, she was nominated by President Clinton to serve on the U.S. Court of Appeals for the Sixth Circuit.

Lewis and her husband received the 1995 Learned Hand Award from the Detroit chapter of the American Jewish Committee's Jacob Blaustein Institute for the Advancement of Human Rights. In 1977 she was named one of Detroit's Most Influential Women.

COUNSELORS AT LAW

Angelique Strong Marks
Vice President, Corporate Legal Counsel
Handleman Company

Bonnie Mayfield
Member, Attorney at Law
Dykema Gossett PLLC

Angelique Strong Marks serves as the vice president of corporate legal counsel of Handleman Company. Handleman is a Troy-based music distribution company with operations throughout the United States, Canada and the United Kingdom and revenues of $1.2 billion. She is the only African-American woman in Michigan to head the legal department of a publicly traded company. She is also the company's first in-house counsel in its more than 70-year history.

Marks earned her bachelor of science degree in finance from the University of Akron, her master in business administration degree in finance and management from Miami University, and her juris doctor degree from The Ohio State University College of Law.

Marks is also active in several civic and community organizations. In 1995 *Michigan Lawyers Weekly* honored her as an Up & Coming Lawyer. In 1996 she was acknowledged as one of *Crain's Detroit Business* 40 under 40.

Bonnie Mayfield, a member of Dykema Gossett's employment law and litigation practice groups, specializes in employment discrimination, product liability (pharmaceutical, medical device, chemical and toxic tort), the Petroleum Manufacturing Practices Act, and commercial litigation.

Mayfield has been selected by several major clients to defend their employment, products, and commercial matters and to be Dykema's responsible partner managing the client/law firm relationships. As a responsible partner, she enhances the client/law firm relationships, facilitates constructive feedback, and provides a common focal point and conduit for both lawyers and client contacts, in addition to substantively defending the clients' legal matters.

A frequent lecturer, Mayfield has spoken to the International Association of Defense Counsel and the State Bars of Michigan and Wisconsin. She was a panelist at the American Bar Association's 1996 and 2002 mid-year products liability meetings. Prior to joining Dykema, she clerked at the United States Court of Appeals for the Sixth Circuit (for the Honorable Nathaniel R. Jones) and at the United States District Court for the Eastern District of Michigan (for the Honorable Julian Abel Cook Jr.).

Dolores Preston Merritt
Attorney and Counselor at Law
Dolores Preston-Cooper, P.C.

Reuben A. Munday
Senior Partner
Lewis & Munday, PC

Dolores Preston Merritt graduated from Wayne State University in 1955 with a bachelor of science degree in elementary education and social studies combined, and a master of education degree in 1970. She worked as a teacher and administrator until retiring in 1988. While employed with the Detroit Public Schools, she received a Fulbright-Hayes Grant which provided her the opportunity to teach in Zimbabwe.

In 1975 Dolores received a doctorate of educational sociology and in 1982, a juris doctor degree. She currently practices family law.

Dolores is a member of Greater New Mt. Moriah Baptist Church, the NAACP, the State Bar of Michigan, the Wolverine Bar and the Detroit Bridge Unit.

She has traveled extensively to locations including Hong Kong, Buenos Aires, Rio de Janeiro, Zimbabwe, Kenya, Egypt, Ethiopia, the Caribbean, Canada, England, Spain, China, Argentina, Italy, and France.

Dolores married James D. Merritt in February of 1996. They have four children: Deborah Lovepeel, designer; Lynnette A. Love, 1998 and 1996 Olympian in taekwando; Esther R. Cooper, Detroit school police officer; and Stephen B. Cooper, chiropractor.

Reuben A. Munday is a senior partner at the Detroit law firm of Lewis & Munday, PC, where he has practiced law since 1977. Munday served as president and chief executive officer of the firm from 1994 to 2003.

His primary areas of practice include real estate acquisition and sale, commercial leases, mortgage financing, commercial and industrial real estate development and construction law. Munday served on the council of the real property section of the State Bar of Michigan for six years.

Munday holds bachelor of arts and master of professional studies degrees from Cornell University, and received his juris doctor degree from the University of Michigan Law School in 1976.

Munday is an active or past member of the boards of the St. John Riverview Hospital, the City of Detroit board of ethics, the National Conference of Community Justice, Mosaic Youth Theater, City Year Detroit, Leadership Detroit and Big Brothers Big Sisters of America. He also serves on the finance committee of St. John Health System.

COUNSELORS AT LAW

Medina D. Abdun Noor, Esq.
Executive Director
Department of Administrative Hearings
City of Detroit

Alex L. Parrish
Partner, Attorney at Law
Corporate and Securities
Honigman Miller Schwartz and Cohn LLP

Medina Abdun Noor is executive director of the Department of Administrative Hearings for the City of Detroit. In this position, she successfully implemented the first municipal quasi-judicial administrative hearings tribunal in the state of Michigan and created a comprehensive administrative hearings process that ranges from proper ticket issuance to appeals to the Third Judicial Circuit Court. The Department of Administrative Hearings has become the standard for the best practices in municipal code enforcement and has been featured in local and national publications.

In addition to managing the department, Medina serves as chief hearings officer, adjudicating motions and violations of the zoning, property maintenance, and solid waste and illegal dumping ordinances.

Medina received a bachelor of arts degree from Oakland University, and Michigan State University School of Law awarded her a juris doctor degree, cum laude.

Alex L. Parrish is a partner and serves on the board of directors at Honigman Miller Schwartz and Cohn LLP. He is a key legal adviser to numerous minority and women-owned companies. He also represents a number of Fortune 500 manufacturing and services companies and major financial institutions. Parrish concentrates his practice in transactional matters including capital formation, mergers and acquisitions, joint ventures, securities regulations and general corporate matters. He also has significant experience with business reorganizations, workouts and bankruptcies.

Parrish is active in a number of civic and charitable institutions. He is currently chairman of the board for Detroit's Music Hall Center for the Performing Arts.

Parrish was named in *The Best Lawyers in America*, 2006, and as one of Michigan's outstanding business leaders in *Crain's Detroit Business*.

Parrish earned his juris doctor degree from Harvard University Law School in 1980. He graduated summa cum laude with a bachelor of arts degree from Howard University in 1977.

Harold D. Pope III
Member, Attorney at Law
Jaffe, Raitt, Heuer & Weiss, PC

Gregory J. Reed
Attorney at Law
Gregory J. Reed & Associates, P.L.C.

Harold D. Pope III has been a member in the Detroit firm of Jaffe, Raitt, Heuer & Weiss, PC since August of 1999. A graduate of Concordia College and Duke University School of Law, Pope began his legal career in a New Jersey firm.

Pope is a former president of the National Bar Association and was chair of the National Bar Institute from 2002 to 2006. He is an active leader in the State Bar of Michigan. Pope is chair of the American Bar Association's Council on Racial and Ethnic Justice and a member of their Center for Racial and Ethnic Diversity.

Pope received the State Bar of Michigan's Champion of Justice Award in 2000 and the NBA's C. Francis Stradford Award. He has worked with the Garden State Bar Association; the Michigan chapter of the American Diabetes Association; and the Detroit Public Schools Student Motivational Program. Pope is a member of Tabernacle Missionary Baptist Church and Alpha Phi Alpha Fraternity, Inc.

Pope was born in Newton, New Jersey. He is married to Renay, and has two children, Daman and Ebony.

Gregory J. Reed, one of the most dynamic attorneys in the area of sports and entertainment law, has gained national and international attention.

The author of twelve award-winning books, Reed has produced Broadway plays, *Ain't Misbehavin'* and *The Wiz*, and the nationally toured productions of *We Are the Dream* and *A Soldier's Play*.

Reed's passion for education materialized into an online course specializing in entertainment and media. He has served as a taxation professor at a major university, lectured at universities across the U.S., and appeared on major cable and radio talk shows.

Reed is a renowned artifact preservationist. He negotiated the acquisition of the Malcolm X biography and unpublished chapters. He is the founder of the first music exhibit, "100 Plus One, Celebrating America's Music...Before Motown and Beyond," which premiered at Chicago's DuSable Museum with a record-breaking attendance of 200,000 visitors.

Reed represented Rosa Parks, with the late Johnnie Cochran Jr., against media giant BMG. His achievements in arts, entertainment and sports law have been recognized by the Michigan Bar Association with the highest honor, The John Hensel Award.

COUNSELORS AT LAW

Jacqueline H. Sellers
Member, Attorney at Law
Clark Hill PLC

Lionel Sims Jr.
Assistant General Counsel
Detroit Board of Education

Jacqueline H. Sellers is a member in Clark Hill's Detroit office where she focuses her practice in the areas of warranty, product liability, commercial litigation and premises liability.

Sellers serves as the national alternative dispute resolution counsel for a major automobile manufacturer where she manages all warranty, fire and accident claims. Previously, she served for 15 years as the corporation's national supervising counsel for its warranty litigation group and 12 years as national product liability discovery counsel for its product liability import matters. Additionally, Sellers is a mediator for the Wayne County Mediation Tribunal and a panelist for the Michigan Attorney Discipline Board.

Sellers serves on the board of directors for the CYOC Foundation and Forgotten Harvest, the nation's third largest "food rescue organization." She is also a member of the Defense Research Institute.

Presenting on topics such as profitable attorney-client relationships, rainmaking and diversity, Seller has served as a panelist for the National Bar Association, the CYOC In-House Counsel Career Conference, the Women Lawyers Association of Michigan, and the Augustus Straker Bar.

Lionel Sims, assistant general counsel to the Detroit Board of Education, concentrates his practice in the areas of commercial litigation, labor and employment and contractual litigation. He is lead counsel on many litigation matters including a million-dollar lawsuit filed on behalf of the Detroit Board of Education. Sims has also co-authored a chapter on public employers' drug testing policy.

A recipient of the Wolverine Bar Foundation Scholarship, Sims earned his law degree from the University of Detroit Law School in 2000. He holds a bachelor of science degree in corporate finance from Wayne State University. He is a member of the State Bar of Michigan and the National Bar Association. Sims also serves as president of the Wolverine Bar Association and general counsel for the International Detroit Black Expo.

Recently, Sims formed GGE Management, a sports management company tailored to provide legal service, real estate purchasing, and financial guidance to professional athletes. He is certified by the National Football League as an agent and contract advisor and has successfully negotiated contracts for basketball players in South America and Europe.

Stephanie M. M. Smith
Attorney at Law
Clark Hill PLC

Joseph E. Turner
Member, Attorney at Law
Business Practice Group
Clark Hill PLC

Stephanie M. M. Smith is an attorney at Clark Hill PLC, and concentrates her practice in the areas of real estate, affordable housing and corporate matters. She earned a juris doctor degree from Rutgers University School of Law, a bachelor of arts degree in analytical philosophy with an emphasis in mathematics from Howard University, and a certification for the studies of French civilization at the University of Paris - Sorbonne in Paris, France.

An expert on affordable housing law, Stephanie is an avid speaker and published writer on affordable housing issues related to community economic development in urban communities.

Stephanie is co-chair on the affordable housing committee for the real property section of the American Bar Association. She also serves on the board of directors for the Detroit Urban League, the board of trustees for Friends School in Detroit, and is chair of the housing committee for the Northeast Village Community Development Corporation.

Born in Chicago, Illinois, Stephanie lives in Detroit with her husband Tony and their daughter, Skylar. She enjoys playing classical piano, downhill skiing and golf.

Joseph E. Turner is a member of Clark Hill's Business Practice Group, specializing in real estate, municipal finance, school law and business finance matters. His clients include the City of Detroit, the County of Wayne, the Policemen and Firemen Retirement System of the City of Detroit (PFRS), and the General Retirement System of the City of Detroit (GRS). As a former commercial bank manager, he offers invaluable institutional lending experience with respect to various complex finance-related transactions.

Turner is experienced in creative commercial transactions. He has served as special counsel to the PFRS and GRS in credit enhancement arrangements, pension fund investments, real estate leasing and real estate finance matters, including major development projects. He has also served as co-bond counsel on County of Wayne and Oakland County Road Commission public financings. He has served as local counsel to national companies involved in multi-state financings and real estate-related acquisitions.

Turner is a member of the board of directors of the Development Corporation of Wayne County, and is a former member of the board of directors of the Metropolitan Coalition.

COUNSELORS AT LAW

Reginald M. Turner
Member, Attorney At Law
Clark Hill PLC

Allen Wade Venable
Associate, Attorney at Law
Bodman LLP

Reginald M. Turner is a member of Clark Hill PLC. He is a member of the firm's executive committee, labor and employment practice group, and the government policy and practice group. A noted national leader in legal and civic circles, Turner is a past president of the National Bar Association and the State Bar of Michigan. Turner is named in The Best Lawyers in America. He is also a fellow of the American Bar Foundation, a designation reserved for less than one percent of the profession.

Turner regularly counsels clients in negotiation, drafting and administration of labor and employment contracts in both the private and public sectors. With governmental experience at the federal, state and local levels, Turner also counsels and advocates clients on important matters of public policy. He has handled a wide variety of litigation in state and federal civil courts, state and federal administrative tribunals, and grievance and interest arbitrations.

Turner remains active in numerous public service, civic and charitable organizations.

Allen Wade Venable is a native Detroiter and an attorney with Bodman LLP. He focuses his legal practice on complex commercial litigation and intellectual property law. He has represented commercial businesses, religious institutions, government entities, school districts and individuals in matters involving contract, copyright/trademark, trade secret, construction, real estate and shareholder/member disputes.

Allen serves on the boards of directors for the Detroit Urban League and Kabaz Cultural Center, Inc., and on the executive committee of the Detroit Urban League Young Professionals.

Allen also provides pro bono legal services to indigent clients through several nonprofit organizations, including Volunteer Lawyers for the Arts, and Community Legal Resources.

He received a bachelor of arts degree in interdisciplinary studies and pre-law, a certificate of specialization in Africa studies, and a master of labor relations and human resources degree from Michigan State University. He received his law degree from Howard University.

Allen lives in Detroit and he enjoys professional sports, music, film and politics.

Kenneth T. Watkins
Attorney at Law
Sommers, Schwartz P.C.

Marcus A. Williams, Esq.
Attorney at Law
Butzel Long

Kenneth T. Watkins is a medical malpractice and personal injury attorney at Sommers, Schwartz P.C. Beyond earning multimillion dollar verdicts and settlements within the Michigan court system and representing the seriously injured and families who are subject to the wrongful death of a loved one, Watkins is quite the altruist.

He has maintained a strong dedication to reciprocating community outreach efforts that once supported him as a youth. He is a volunteer coach for the Southfield Lathrup Falcons and a frequent speaker at Metro Detroit's schools.

A sustaining member of the Michigan Trial Lawyers Association executive board, Watkins is also a past president of the Wolverine Bar Association, a charter member of the Motor-City Optimist Club, an executive board member of Black Family Development, Inc., and vice president of Urban Solutions, Inc., an organization that provides scholarships for inner-city students.

A graduate of Northwestern University, Watkins earned his legal degree from Detroit College of Law. His proudest contribution to society has been nurturing the growth of his daughter, KenNath Marie, and son, Kenneth II, with his lovely wife, Nina Maria.

Marcus A. Williams practices in the Detroit office of Butzel Long, where his primary areas of practice are corporate transactions, corporate finance, securities and business law. He is involved in negotiating, drafting and closing complex corporate transactions. He deals with domestic and international transactions for public and privately held companies, including mergers and acquisitions, venture investments in growth companies, joint ventures and strategic alliances.

Marcus graduated with a juris doctor degree from the University of Michigan Law School in 1996. He earned his bachelor of business administration degree from the University of Michigan Business School, specializing in corporate finance.

Marcus is director and chair of the audit committee of Think Detroit Police Athletic League, a nonprofit corporation which is widely recognized for its management excellence. He is also a director of the Boll Family YMCA in downtown Detroit, where he serves on the leadership development committee. He is on the executive board of the National Association of Black Accountants, Detroit chapter, co-chairperson of the student affairs committee, and a member of the University of Michigan Business School Club of Detroit.

COUNSELORS AT LAW

Jermaine A. Wyrick
Attorney at Law
Law Offices of
Jermaine A. Wyrick P.L.L.C.

A successful trial attorney, Jermaine A. Wyrick began the Law Offices of Jermaine A. Wyrick P.L.L.C. His areas of practice are civil rights law, criminal defense, juvenile law, personal injury and probate law.

Wyrick has numerous professional affiliations, including the Detroit Metropolitan Bar Association, the State Bar of Michigan, the Michigan Trial Lawyers Association, the National Bar Association and the Wolverine Bar Association.

The recipient of many honors, Wyrick was awarded the Civil Rights and Education award from the United States Attorney's Office, the Black History Month Award, the Outstanding Leadership in Affirmative Action award from the Detroit Chapter NAACP, and many others.

Among his civic activities are the Coleman A. Young Foundation, the Rainbow/PUSH Coalitions's 2nd Tuesday Network, the NAACP legal redress committee, the State Bar of Michigan Imprint Mentoring Program, and the U.S. Department of Justice program, Project Safe Neighborhoods, Project Sentry-Youth Gun Violence Prevention Program.

Born in Detroit, Wyrick graduated from the University of Michigan with a bachelor's degree in political science. He received his juris doctorate from the Wayne State University Law School.

Detroit's

PHYSICIANS

"Do your best and let God do the rest."

DR. BEN CARSON

PEDIATRIC NEUROSURGEON

PHYSICIANS

William Gilchrist Anderson, D.O.
Director of Medical Education
St. John Detroit Riverview Hospital

William G. Anderson, D.O. is a respected director of medical education at St. John Detroit Riverview Hospital. Additionally, he serves as associate dean of the Michigan Region Kirksville College of Osteopathic Medicine, and associate clinical professor at Michigan State University College of Osteopathic Medicine.

A civil rights activist, Anderson lectures throughout the country about his experience during the civil rights movement in the 1960s and walking alongside Dr. Martin Luther King Jr. This living legend has received numerous outstanding distinguished resolutions, awards, and honorary degrees from nine colleges of osteopathic medicine, and a doctorate of humane letters from Michigan State University.

Anderson is the former president of the American Osteopathic Association, former director of the Southern Christian Leadership Conference, founder and first president of the Albany Movement for Civil Rights, and a member of the NAACP and YMCA.

In his spare time, Anderson enjoys golf, traveling and reading. He and his wife, Norma, authored the book *Autobiographies of a Black Couple of the Greatest Generation*. They have five children, three in osteopathic medicine, and ten grandchildren, two in osteopathic medicine.

Alfred E. Baylor III, M.D.
Assistant Professor of Surgery
Wayne State University

Alfred Eugene Baylor III, M.D. is an assistant professor in the department of surgery at Wayne State University. He is also a general surgeon and attending staff physician for the Detroit Medical Center, with special interest in trauma and critical care. Alfred has been actively involved as captain of the U.S. Army National Guard/ Reserve since 1988, in addition to holding the position of assistant chief medical officer of the Military Entrance Processing Station in Troy.

Alfred earned his baccalaureate from Hampton University in 1991. He received his medical degree from Georgetown University in 1998. There, he was the first African-American male class president in its more than 150-year history. He successfully completed his internship and residency at Wayne State University, where he is currently a doctoral candidate with an emphasis in immunology and microbiology. A member of several local and national medical associations and societies, Alfred has authored and co-authored several peer-reviewed publications in medical journals.

A native of Oxon Hill, Maryland, Alfred is the husband of Michelle, and the proud father of three daughters, Amber, Ashley and Alexis.

Stanley M. Berry, M.D., is chairman of the department of obstetrics and gynecology at William Beaumont Hospitals in Royal Oak and Troy, Michigan. He is responsible for overseeing all of the medical care provided to obstetrical and gynecological patients. His educational responsibilities include teaching medical students, residents, nurses, and attending physicians. He is also a professor at Wayne State University.

Berry practices the subspecialty of maternal-fetal medicine, which encompasses the care of high-risk obstetrical patients. These patients include women who have medical illnesses such as diabetes, hypertension, or disorders unique to pregnancy. Within this subspecialty, Berry's expertise includes fetal diagnosis and fetal therapy.

Berry attended Macalester College in St. Paul, Minnesota. In 1984 he earned his medical doctor degree from Mayo Medical School in Rochester, Minnesota. He completed his residency at Saint Louis University in 1988 and finished a fellowship in maternal-fetal medicine at Wayne State University in 1990.

A native of Minneapolis, Berry is the proud father of one son, Akin, and two daughters, Niambi and Ayanna.

Stanley M. Berry, M.D.
Chairman, Department of
Obstetrics & Gynecology
William Beaumont Hospital

Arthur I. Bouier, D.O. is an internal medicine physician of osteopathic medicine and surgery. He graduated in 1977 from Michigan State University College of Osteopathic Medicine. In 1981 Bouier established his own private practice, and in 1982 he received board certification for internal medicine. He is a member and program director of the American College of Osteopathic Internists.

Bouier is the medical director for the department of internal medicine at Wayne State University. He provides patient-centered medicine of the highest standards, using critical medical evaluations to aid in the prevention, diagnosis, treatment and management of disease.

Bouier specializes in internal medicine, geriatrics, home visits, obesity and EECP cardiac treatment. He adheres to the highest ethical standards, displays integrity, and communicates with compassion to patients and their families in order to sustain effective medical care.

Arthur I. Bouier, D.O.
Medical Director
Department of Internal Medicine
Wayne State University

PHYSICIANS

Robert A. Chapman, M.D.
Director of Josephine Ford Cancer Center
Henry Ford Hospital

D r. Robert A. Chapman is the director of the Josephine Ford Cancer Center (JFCC) at Henry Ford Health System. The JFCC has thrived under his leadership. Chapman secured a competitive Medicare grant to study disparities in cancer care in the African-American population.

He is an expert physician and clinician-researcher in medical oncology. Chapman is well known for his lung cancer research and involvement and his leadership as head of Henry Ford's hematology/oncology division. He was listed as a Top Doc in *Hour Detroit* magazine the last three years and was listed in America's Top Doctors for Cancer in 2005.

Chapman obtained his medical degree from Cornell Medical School. He completed his internal medicine residency at Henry Ford Hospital and his medical oncology fellowship at the Memorial Sloan Kettering Cancer Center in New York City.

The JFCC is the focus of all cancer-related services. It is ranked among the top cancer programs in the country and provides a variety of services in six treatment facilities throughout the metro area, including radiation therapy, chemotherapy, surgical oncology and support services.

Paul A. Edwards, M.D.
Chairman, Department of
Ophthalmology & Eye Care Services
Henry Ford Hospital

D r. Paul Edwards believes in giving his patients the highest possible quality care and providing them with information about their disorders so they can make better-informed decisions. In partnership, together, they take better care of the problem.

Edwards is the distinguished Cornelius E. McCole chair of ophthalmology and eye care services at Henry Ford Hospital. He is responsible for one of the largest eye care departments in the United States. In partnership with Henry Ford OptimEyes, Henry Ford has 375,000 patient visits per year for eye care.

He graduated from the University of the West Indies, completed his residency in ophthalmology at Henry Ford Hospital and completed a research fellowship at the National Eye Institute. Edwards is named as one of America's Top Ophthalmologists by the Consumer Research Council of America and by *Hour Detroit* magazine as a Detroit Top Doctor.

In addition to his medical career, he co-founded two charitable nonprofit organizations and currently serves as president of Student Mentor Partners.

He resides with his wife, Jennifer, daughters, Nikeisha and Tiffany, and son, Paul II, in West Bloomfield.

O tis B. Ferguson III, M.D., ophthalmologist at St. John Detroit Riverview Hospital, believes good vision is not negotiable. Ferguson specializes in the treatment of cataracts, glaucoma and diabetic eye disease. He also performs laser surgery.

Ferguson is certified by the American Board of Ophthalmology. He received his bachelor of science degree from Howard University, and his medical degree from Wayne State University School of Medicine. He completed his residency at the Kresge Eye Institute as well as a National Eye Institute Fellowship at Washington University in St. Louis, Missouri. Ferguson is a member of the American Academy of Ophthalmology and the Michigan State Medical Society.

When the native Detroiter completed his ophthalmology rotation, he knew it was the field for him. Ferguson is very active in the community that the hospital serves. He often speaks on radio shows about comprehensive eye care.

Ferguson is married with four children. When he is not treating patients, he enjoys basketball, golf, movies, family outings and playing the guitar.

Otis B. Ferguson III, M.D.
Ophthalmologist
St. John Detroit Riverview Hospital

D r. Janice Fields is a practicing gastroenterologist in metropolitan Detroit, and a partner in Digestive Health Associates, PLC, a private practice specialty group. She is a fellow of the American College of Gastroenterology, and holds staff privileges at several Detroit area hospitals. She regularly speaks on colon cancer and other important health issues to her colleagues and the community.

Fields is an executive board member of the James Tatum Foundation for the Arts, a nonprofit organization that awards college scholarships to study the visual and performing arts and raises community awareness of jazz music and other arts. She is also very active in her church, Tabernacle Missionary Baptist Church, co-chairing the health and human services ministry.

Fields was awarded her bachelor of arts and medical degrees in a dual degree six-year program at the University of Missouri-Kansas City.

A Missouri native, Fields is married and has three stepdaughters.

Dr. Janice Fields
Gastroenterologist
Digestive Health Associates, PLC

PHYSICIANS

Nicole T. Fields, D.D.S.
Owner & Dentist
Feels Best Dentistry, P.C.

Dr. Nicole T. Fields is a general dentist in private practice where she especially enjoys treating young children and senior citizens. Her office philosophy is "We put our hearts into improving your smile." Fields has been an adjunct professor at the University of Detroit Mercy School of Dentistry for the past ten years, supervising students as they treat low-income citizens of Detroit. In 2004 she was presented with the Faculty Community Service Award.

Fields is a native Detroiter and a graduate of Renaissance High School. She received a bachelor of science degree in chemistry from Spelman College and earned a doctor of dental surgery degree at the University of Michigan in 1993.

Fields is currently serving as president of the Wolverine Dental Society, which represents African-American dentists in the Detroit area. She is a frequent career day speaker and is a faithful member of Tabernacle Missionary Baptist Church, the NAACP and Delta Sigma Theta Sorority, Inc.

Nicole's greatest achievement and joy is being a mother to her ten-month-old daughter, Morgan Janae.

John M. Flack, M.D.
Professor and Interim Chair
Department of Internal Medicine
Wayne State University

John M. Flack, M.D. is a specialist in clinical hypertension and currently serves as the interim chairman and chief quality officer in the department of internal medicine at Wayne State University. He is director of translational research and clinical epidemiology, and principal investigator for the Wayne State University Center for Urban and African American Health.

Flack received a bachelor of science degree in chemistry from Langston University in 1978, and spent the next ten years at the University of Oklahoma Health Sciences Center in Oklahoma City, Oklahoma.

Flack's research interests are clinical trial design, implementation, hypertension in African-Americans, and utilization of software-based approaches to support optimal clinical decision-making.

Flack is the author of more than 125 peer-reviewed manuscripts and book chapters. He was selected as one of the Best Doctors in America for several years, and was awarded the Pillar of Excellence by the Michigan Peer Review Organization. He was selected as a Health Care Hero by *Crain's Detroit Business*, for leading multidisciplinary and cutting-edge research into root causes of obesity and lifestyle-related diseases in African Americans.

C heryl Gibson Fountain, M.D., is chief of staff and attending physician in obstetrics and gynecology at St. John Detroit Riverview Hospital. She is also a clinical preceptor at Wayne State University College of Pharmacy and Health Sciences.

Gibson Fountain's primary interests are adolescent medicine, teenage pregnancy and menopause. Extending her genuine regard for the community, she partnered with her late husband, Pastor Renzo L. Fountain Sr., to provide free annual health screenings, immunizations and clothing drives for local residents, and obstetric and gynecologic care to women in Nigeria during a medical mission.

Gibson Fountain is board certified in obstetrics and gynecology. She completed her undergraduate studies at the University of Michigan, received her medical degree from Wayne State University, and completed her ob-gyn residency at Hutzel Hospital in Detroit.

A native Detroiter, she is a member of the American College of Physician Executives, the National Medical Association, the American Medical Association, the Michigan State Medical Society, the Wayne County Medical Society, the Detroit Medical Society, and a lifetime member of the NAACP.

Gibson Fountain resides with her daughter, Anne Marie.

Cheryl Gibson Fountain, M.D.
Chief of Staff & Ob-Gyn
St. John Detroit Riverview Hospital

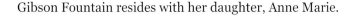

C rystal R. Gardner-Martin, M.D., was recently elected a member-at-large of the medical executive team for St. John Detroit Riverview Hospital. In addition, she is the newly appointed chairman of the medical care and evaluation quality committee at the hospital.

Gardner-Martin specializes in nephrology. She performs hemodialysis and peritoneal dialysis for patients suffering from kidney disorders, and she treats patients afflicted with acute and chronic renal failure.

A graduate of the University of Michigan in Ann Arbor, Gardner-Martin completed her internship and residency at the University of Illinois in Chicago.

Gardner-Martin is board certified in nephrology and internal medicine. She has received numerous awards and co-authored articles that have been published in multiple journals and research magazines. In addition, she has presented at several national conferences. She is a member of the American College of Physicians and the Alpha Kappa Alpha Sorority, Inc., Beta Eta Chapter.

Gardner-Martin is married to David and they attend City Temple Seventh Day Adventist Church with their two children, Daisha, ten, and Devin, five.

Crystal R. Gardner-Martin, M.D.
Nephrology
St. John Detroit Riverview Hospital

PHYSICIANS

Dr. Herman Glass II, D.C.
Owner and Director
Glass Chiropractic

D r. Herman J. Glass II owns and operates Glass Chiropractic, accommodating more than 10,000 patients annually. He currently serves as an independent medical examiner consultant with the American Medical Evaluation and Phoenix Evaluation Companies.

Glass has served the chiropractic community in many positions throughout his 22-year career. He was the president of the American Black Chiropractic Association from 1989 to 1992, and was the 1992 American Black Chiropractic Association Chiropractor of the Year. He was the first black chiropractor appointed to the State Board of Chiropractic Examiners by Governor James Blanchard, from 1988 to 1992, and was re-appointed by Governor John Engler, from 1992 to 1996.

In 1985 Glass served as an adjunct professor at Texas Chiropractic College in Houston, and is a past consultant for Blue Cross/Blue Shield of Michigan's utilization review department.

A native Detroiter, Glass is a member of the Jim Dandy Ski Club and the National Association of Black Scuba Divers.

Herman B. Gray Jr., M.D., MBA
President
Children's Hospital of Michigan

H erman Gray, M.D., is president of Children's Hospital of Michigan, the only freestanding children's hospital in Michigan. He is the first African American in the history of the hospital to serve as president. At Children's, Gray established innovative programs, such as the hospital's first sleep apnea program to monitor babies for sudden infant death syndrome; family-centered care to engage families in the decision-making process of their child's medical care; and a school-based health clinic in Detroit.

Gray has previously held leadership roles with Michigan SIDS Center, Project Uptown, and the Pediatric AIDS Prevention and Control Program. He also served as the first medical director of children's special health care services at the Michigan Department of Public Health. Gray has served on numerous national and international committees to improve health care services and access for children. He has been repeatedly recognized for his humanitarian efforts related to pediatric health care.

Gray earned his medical degree from the University of Michigan and his physician executive MBA from the University of Tennessee.

He and his wife, Shirley Mann Gray, have two daughters.

W. Anthony Greer, M.D. is the chief medical officer at St. John Detroit Riverview Hospital. He provides clinical and administrative leadership for the 285-bed hospital with multiple outpatient sites. He enjoys translating mission and vision statements into achievable action plans.

Greer is board certified in ophthalmology. He received his medical degree from Loyola University in Chicago, and his graduate degree in technology management from the University of Phoenix. Greer completed his internship in general surgery at Rush Presbyterian – St. Luke's Medical Center, and his residency in ophthalmology at Howard University Hospital.

Greer is a member of the American Medical Association, the American Academy of Ophthalmology, the American College of Healthcare Executives, the American College of Physician Executives, the State of New York Medical Society, the Michigan State Medical Society, the National Medical Association, the Healthcare Information and Management Systems Society, and the Project Management Institute. He has received several awards and recognitions, and received an honorable discharge from the U.S. Military.

In his spare time, Greer has interests in tai chi, complementary medicine, boating, motorcycling, computer graphics and animation.

W. Anthony Greer, M.D.
Chief Medical Officer
St. John Detroit Riverview Hospital

Dr. Barbara Hannah is the owner and president of Women's Center/HealthCare Physicians, PLLC, located in the Detroit suburb of Lincoln Park. There, she has practiced obstetrics and gynecology for eight years. Hannah works to treat the complete patient by addressing their physical, emotional, spiritual and mental needs.

Hannah is committed to giving back to the community and the world. She is the founder of Imhotep Development, which introduces high school and college students to careers in medicine. She travels to Africa and Jamaica to provide medical care, helping to fulfill her desire to empower African people.

A native of Indianapolis, Barbara is a graduate of Wayne State University School of Medicine. She received her master of science degree in biomedical science from Western Michigan University and her bachelor of science degree from Kentucky State University.

Barbara is active in local and national medical societies. A member of Alpha Kappa Alpha Sorority, Inc., she enjoys tennis and liturgical dancing.

Barbara, a single woman, enjoys acting and creative writing. She is writing her first poetry and short story book.

Barbara A. Hannah, M.D.
Owner & President
Women's Center/HealthCare
Physicians, PLLC

PHYSICIANS

Melvin L. Hollowell, M.D.
Urologist
Sinai-Grace Hospital

Melvin L. Hollowell, M.D, a urologist at Sinai-Grace Hospital, has been a servant to Detroit and the United States for almost 50 years. His medical career includes many prominent positions at the Detroit Medical Center serving as a chairman at almost every Detroit Medical Center hospital. At Sinai-Grace Hospital, Hollowell's positions have included vice president of medical affairs, senior medical director and member of the board of trustees. Additionally, he served on the board of directors for both the Wayne County Medical Society and the Michigan State Medical Society.

Outside of the medical community, Hollowell is an associate professor of urology at Wayne State University School of Medicine. He also mentors schoolchildren in Detroit and assists with a variety of fundraising and charity efforts.

Hollowell received his undergraduate degree in chemistry and biology from Wayne State University and his medical degree from Meharry Medical College. He served as a captain and a surgeon in the U.S. Army and as the police surgeon for the City of Detroit.

He is married to Sylvia Hollowell and they have seven children.

Theodore B. Jones, M.D.
Medical Director
Perinatal Infectious Disease

Theodore B. Jones, M.D., received his degree from Temple University School of Medicine in Philadelphia, and completed a residency in obstetrics and gynecology at Baylor University Medical Center in Dallas, Texas. He completed his fellowship in maternal fetal medicine at Wayne State University/Hutzel Hospital. Following the completion of his fellowship, he has been a faculty member at Wayne State and is currently an associate professor.

Jones is medical director of the Perinatal Infectious Disease Clinic. He is also the obstetric principle investigator for perinatal trials sponsored by the Perinatal AIDS Clinical Trials Group. His department administrative posts have included: residency program director, associate director for education and vice president for medical affairs for Hutzel Women's Hospital. Jones also serves as a board examiner for the maternal fetal medicine subspecialty examination by the American Board of Obstetrics and Gynecology.

C onrad Cuthbert Maitland is a board-certified urologist specializing in the study and treatment of adult and pediatric urology. His special areas of interest include prostrate diseases, infertility, incontinence, impotency and bed wetting.

A graduate of Wayne State University School of Medicine (WSUSOM), Maitland completed his general surgery residency at Sinai Hospital in 1978 and completed his urology residency at WSUSOM in 1983.

Maitland's professional affiliations include Wayne State Medical Society, Michigan State Medical Society, Black Medical Alumni Association and Alpha Epsilon Delta Honor Fraternity.

Maitland has participated in many advanced-training classes. His participation occurred most recently at the Cleveland Clinic, Kimmel Cancer Center in Dearborn, and the Postgraduate Institute for Medicine in Detroit to learn new techniques and treatments of urological diseases.

His staff privileges are with Detroit Medical Center affiliates, Sinai-Grace Hospital, Huron Valley-Sinai Hospital and Harper University Hospital.

Conrad Cuthbert Maitland, M.D.
Urologist
Detroit Medical Center Affiliates

M ildred C. Matlock, Ph.D. is chief operating officer of Detroit Medical Center's Rehabilitation Institute of Michigan, one of the country's largest freestanding, academic rehabilitation hospitals. She is responsible for the hospital's overall operating effectiveness and outpatient satellites.

Matlock completed a doctorate in speech-language pathology at Wayne State University (WSU), and a master of science degree in administration at Central Michigan University. She is a clinical assistant professor in the WSU department of physical medicine and rehabilitation.

Recognized as the Minority Achiever of the Year from the YMCA of Metropolitan Detroit, Matlock also received Ameritech's Living the Dream award for achievements in health administration. In addition, Matlock has earned numerous competitive speaking awards as a member of Toastmaster International.

Active in other leadership roles, Matlock is a graduate of Leadership Detroit – Class XV, and is a member of several professional and civic organizations, including the American College of Healthcare Executives, the Neighborhood Services Organization, and WSU's Alumni Association.

Matlock resides in Farmington Hills and is an avid tennis player.

Mildred C. Matlock, Ph.D.
Chief Operating Officer
Rehabilitation Institute of Michigan
Detroit Medical Center

PHYSICIANS

Sharon D. Minott, M.D.
Anesthesiologist
Huron Valley-Sinai Hospital

D r. Sharon Minott is a graduate of the University of Michigan Medical School. She is a board-certified anesthesiologist, with an additional certification in pain medicine. She enjoys her work as an anesthesiologist at Huron Valley-Sinai Hospital, where she has worked with the Detroit Medical Center since 1999.

Minott also serves as the medical director of the Michigan Interventional Pain Associates. There, she is committed to improving patients' quality of life. She and her partners have established a state-of-the-art practice with a noted reputation of excellent care and compassionate support. Her areas of interest include interventional and conservative management of acute and chronic pain. She also has an evolving interest in the management of pelvic pain conditions.

Minott is a native of Detroit and enjoys cooking, shopping, traveling and dancing.

Gerard M. Mosby, M.D.
Chair of Pediatrics
St. John Detroit Riverview Hospital

G erard M. Mosby, M.D., pediatrician and chair of pediatrics at St. John Detroit Riverview Hospital, was one of four local physicians recognized for their efforts to improve immunization levels in the city of Detroit. He serves on several committees at St. John Detroit Riverview Hospital including medical executive and medical care and evaluation-quality. He has served as president of the Physician Hospital Organization.

Mosby received his undergraduate and master's degrees from Prairie View A&M University. He earned his medical degree from the University of Texas at Galveston. Mosby furthered his training by completing his internship and residency at Children's Hospital of Michigan, and he received a master of business administration degree in health care management from Oakland University.

Mosby has served as medical director for three school-based clinics in Detroit and was a member of the Detroit Asthma Coalition. He has received numerous awards and recognition for his efforts to improve pediatric care, including the Southeastern Michigan Childhood Immunization Registry Award.

A native of Austin, Texas, he is married to Dr. Lynetta Mosby.

G ail Parker is a psychologist and president of Parker Counseling and Consulting Services, P.C., specializing in counseling adults, adolescents, families and couples.

An adjunct professor at the University of Michigan Ross School of Business - Executive Education since 1995, Parker teaches managerial coaching and counseling. She also serves as a consultant to various businesses, organizations and school districts.

Parker is well known for her work on local and national newscasts. She has appeared as an expert on a variety of nationally syndicated talk shows, including several appearances on *The Oprah Winfrey Show*. Likewise, she has served as a script consultant and expert on local and nationally featured documentaries for the Public Broadcast System. She has also hosted her own talk show, *Ask the Psychologist*, on WXYT radio in Detroit.

Parker completed her bachelor of arts degree at Duquesne University in Pittsburgh, Pennsylvania and her master's and doctoral degrees at Wayne State University in Detroit, Michigan.

A native of Detroit, Parker is married and the mother of one son.

Gail Parker, Ph.D.
Psychologist & President
Parker Counseling and
Consulting Services, P.C.

I saac J. Powell, M.D. is professor of urology at the Wayne State University School of Medicine, Harper University Hospital, Karmanos Cancer Institute. He is chief of urology at the John D. Dingell Veterans Administration Medical Center. Powell is board certified with the American Board of Urology and is a fellow of the American College of Surgeons.

Powell has been involved in prostate cancer research for more than 16 years. His work on prostate cancer in African-American men is nationally known, and he completed a community-based education and early detection study in men who are at high-risk. It was the first successful early detection program among African-American men.

Powell's research explores ethnic differences in the biology of prostate cancer. He is principal investigator of a nationwide consortium of recruitment centers to examine hereditary prostate cancer among African Americans. He is co-investigator on a grant comparing genetic alterations and clinical findings in men who have undergone radical prostatectomy. In collaboration with institutions across the United States, this research examines the androgen gene variation and diet in correlation to clinical outcomes.

Isaac J. Powell, M.D.
Professor, Department of Urology
Wayne State University
Harper University Hospital

PHYSICIANS

Michael H. Rainer, M.D.
Senior Associate Physician
Rehabilitation Medical Specialists, LLC

D r. Michael Rainer is the senior associate at Rehabilitation Medical Specialists, LLC. He recently left the academic department of physical medicine and rehabilitation at the Detroit Medical Center (DMC) for private practice, but maintains affiliation with the DMC. Rainer evaluates and treats patients with musculoskeletal, neurologic, trauma-related conditions and provides pain management.

He graduated from Wayne State University School of Medicine in 1988. He completed two-and-a-half years of core general surgery residency at the DMC. He subsequently worked at the Detroit Mercy emergency room for five years. Rainer finished a residency in physical medicine and rehabilitation at the University of Pittsburgh and is board certified. In addition, he was associate professor at The University of Texas Southwestern, where he was medical director of a 14-bed inpatient unit, multidisciplinary spine/injection clinic and amputee clinic.

Rainer's clinical interests and expertise include the evaluation and treatment of musculoskeletal conditions, neck and back pain, arthritis, headache management, sports medicine, EMG evaluation and interpretation and treatment of spasticity.

Michael W. Roberts, D.O.
Orthopedic Surgeon
St. John Detroit Riverview Hospital

M ichael W. Roberts, D.O., a board-certified orthopedic surgeon at St. John Detroit Riverview Hospital, has been in private practice for eight years.

Roberts received his bachelor of science degree from Wayne State University and his medical degree from Michigan State University. Additionally, he interned and completed his residency at Bi-County Osteopathic Hospital in orthopedic surgery.

Roberts is a member of the American Osteopathic Academy of Orthopedics, the American Osteopathic Association, and the Michigan Osteopathic Association. He is an associate clinical professor at Kirksville College of Osteopathic Medicine. Two years ago, his students honored him with a plaque for his commitment to clinical excellence.

A native Detroiter, Roberts has been married to his beautiful wife, Linda, for 15 years. They have three children, Michael II, 14, Lauren, 12, and Maya, 9.

In his spare time, Roberts enjoys golf and basketball. He and his family are members of Hope United Methodist Church in Southfield, Michigan.

A board-certified ob-gyn, George H. Shade Jr., M.D. is the vice president of medical affairs and department chief of obstetrics and gynecology at Sinai-Grace Hospital. In this capacity, he leads the affairs of the Sinai-Grace medical staff. With a passion for teaching, Shade is an associate professor of gynecology at Wayne State University School of Medicine and Michigan State University College of Medicine. He is a published author and lecturer.

Active in his profession, Shade serves on numerous boards, including the advisory council of the American College of Obstetrics and Gynecologists, Michigan section, and the board of medicine for the State of Michigan. He is also a member of Kappa Alpha Psi Fraternity, Inc., and Sigma Pi Phi Fraternity, Iota Boulé.

A native of Detroit, Shade attended Detroit Public Schools, earned a bachelor's and medical degree from WSU, graduating with honors every time.

He has been married for 30 years to Carlotta A. Johnson-Shade and is the father of two children, Carla and Ryan. He is a parishioner of Hartford Memorial Baptist Church.

George H. Shade Jr., M.D.
Vice President of Medical Affairs &
Chief of Obstetrics and Gynecology
Sinai-Grace Hospital

A native Detroiter, Richard E. Smith, M.D., completed his undergraduate education at the University of Michigan in Ann Arbor, his medical degree with honors from Howard University College of Medicine in Washington, D.C., and his residency in obstetrics and gynecology at Wayne State University. He is a senior staff physician at Henry Ford Hospital. During his 27-year tenure, Smith has delivered more than 7,000 babies and has served as medical director of obstetrics.

He played a leading role in advocating for both state and federal legislation that improved prenatal care for women and teens across the country. Smith has also been honored by *Hour Detroit* magazine as one of Metro Detroit's Top Docs, and by the Detroit Board of Education for his work as chairman of the health education advisory committee. As chair, he helped to establish the middle school health curriculum.

Smith is a member of many professional societies. He is a past president of the Wayne County Medical Society of Southeast Michigan and serves on the board of directors of the Michigan State Medical Society.

Richard E. Smith, M.D.
Chairman, Board of Governors
Henry Ford Medical Group

PHYSICIANS

Natalia M. Tanner, M.D.
Pediatrician
Children's Hospital of Michigan

Natalia Tanner is a pediatrician affiliated with the Children's Hospital of Michigan and serves as clinical professor of pediatrics at the Wayne State University School of Medicine. During her 50 years of private practice in adolescent medicine, Tanner has received many distinguished service awards and honors for her outstanding contribution to pediatrics and the recruitment of minorities.

Recognized as Detroit's first board-certified African-American pediatrician in 1951, Tanner is well known as an activist in the community. She is also the first female and African-American fellow of the American Academy of Pediatrics, later becoming the Michigan Chapter president in 1983.

Tanner has served on many national committees and boards, including the Society for Adolescent Medicine and the National Medical Association. She earned her medical degree from Meharry Medical College. She and her husband, Waldo Cain, M.D., a surgeon, have two daughters.

Thomas J. Trueheart, M.D.
Pediatrician & Allergist-Immunologist
TrueCare Asthma and Allergy Center

Dr. Thomas J. Trueheart is certified in both pediatrics and allergy-immunology. His goal is to provide personal, quality and effective care for all persons, of all ages, in the treatment of asthma and allergies. His office motto is "Not only do we treat, but we teach."

To his credit, he has a published writing, "The Improvement of Intractable Asthma with Treatment of Gastroesophageal Reflux." He presently serves as a Pfizer-physician consultant, a fellow in the American College of Asthma Allergy and Immunology, and a member in the American Academy of Asthma Allergy and Immunology. He is active in Hope United Methodist Church, the Prince Hall Masonic Fraternity, and the NAACP.

Trueheart holds a bachelor's degree from Canisius College, a master's degree from Roswell Park Memorial Cancer Institute, and a medical degree from the State University of New York Upstate Medical University. His medical training was conducted entirely at Detroit Medical Center.

He and his wife, Kimberly, are the proud parents of Janelle, Marcus and Nia.

Director of breast radiation oncology for the Henry Ford Health System (HFHS), Dr. Eleanor M. Walker is board-certified in radiation oncology and active in integrative medical research. She received a grant from the Susan B. Komen Breast Cancer Foundation examining acupuncture in the treatment of hot flashes in women with breast cancer. Walker is active in many medical organizations including the National Medical Association; the Radiation Therapy Oncology Group; the Southwest Oncology Group; the American Society for Therapeutic Radiology and Oncology; the American Medical Association; and the Wayne County and Michigan Medical Societies.

A graduate of the University of Notre Dame, Walker is active in the alumni association, and serves on the College of Science advisory board for the university. Walker received her medical degree from Washington University. She completed her internship at Vanderbilt University and her residency at the University of Maryland.

Walker is active in the community through her church and through HFHS, educating African Americans about cancer.

Her hobbies include traveling, scrapbooking, reading and jazz. She is a native of Brooklyn, New York.

Eleanor M. Walker, M.D.
Director, Breast Radiation Oncology
Henry Ford Health System

Dr. Felicia D. Wilson is a board-certified prosthodontist practicing in Detroit, Michigan. Prosthodontists are referred to as the quarterbacks of the dental profession. They often lead teams of dentists, oral surgeons, periodontists and other health professionals in the pioneering and development of advanced dental solutions. Prosthodontists developed the techniques used on the television series, *Extreme Makeover*.

Less than one percent of dentists in the country are board-certified prosthodontists. Wilson is the only African-American female in Michigan to hold that distinction. She is also the only dentist in metropolitan Detroit certified in the breakthrough technology of completing full-mouth permanent dental implants in one office visit, a process that normally takes six months to a year.

Wilson earned her degrees at the University of Detroit Mercy and the University of Michigan, Ann Arbor. She is a diplomat of the American Board of Prosthodontists, and a member of the American College of Prosthodontists, the American Dental Association and the American Academy of Fixed Prosthodontics.

Felicia D. Wilson, D.D.S.
Prosthodontist

PHYSICIANS

Stephen Wilson, M.D.
Chief Executive Officer
Advanced Physical Medicine, P.C.

D r. Stephen Wilson is the chief executive officer of Advanced Physical Medicine, P.C. He is board certified in physical medicine and rehabilitation and pain management. He is also certified in medical acupuncture. Wilson incorporates the use of traditional and complementary medicine to improve the quality of life for his patients.

Wilson was honored in the 2004-2005 edition of *Guide to America's Top Physicians* and also in the October 2005 *Hour Detroit* magazine's Top Docs, as voted by doctors and nurses. He received a proclamation from the City of St. Clair Shores to publicly recognize his dedication and concern for others.

Wilson received a bachelor of science degree from the University of Detroit in 1989 and his doctor of medicine degree from Wayne State University in 1993. He completed his medical internship at Grace Hospital and his residency at Schwab Rehabilitation Hospital in Chicago.

A native of Detroit, Wilson is the husband of Maria, and the proud father of two children, Stephen and Isabella.

Dr. Michael Wood
Surgeon
Wayne State University

D r. Michael H. Wood is a clinical professional of surgery at Wayne State University in Detroit. He is board certified and a fellow of the American College of Surgeons. He serves as the medical director of the CORI Centers and of the Bariatric Surgical Services at Harper University.

Wood is also an active member of the American Society for Bariatric Surgery (ASBS). He has more than 25 years of experience and an extensive background in weight loss surgery. Throughout his career, he has performed several thousand bariatric surgeries and is the co-inventor of the patented Sapala-Wood Micropouch procedure.

Detroit's

SPIRITUAL LEADERS

"Faith is taking the first step even when you don't see the whole staircase."

REV. DR. MARTIN LUTHER KING JR.

MINISTER AND CIVIL RIGHTS ACTIVIST

SPIRITUAL LEADERS

Dr. Allyson D. Nelson Abrams
Pastor & Founder
Speak The Truth Baptist Church

E. L. Branch
Pastor
Third New Hope Baptist Church

The Reverend Dr. Allyson D. Nelson Abrams is a pastor, preacher, teacher and lecturer. She preaches in many pulpits across the United States. Abrams founded Speak The Truth Economic Empowerment Corporation. Additionally, she authored two books, serves on the faculty of two local schools and as assistant editor of the national magazine, *Baptist Progress*.

Two of her sermons have been nationally published in *The African American Pulpit* and she was featured in *Baptist Times*, a Detroit-based magazine. Abrams received the Spirit of Detroit Award in 2004. Additionally, she is a certified board member for the Detroit Public Schools Board.

Abrams is the second female to serve on the executive board of the Council of Baptist Pastors. She is a member of Council of Clergywomen of Greater Detroit, the Progressive National Baptist Convention, Alpha Kappa Alpha Sorority, Inc., the Order of the Eastern Star and the Black Caucus of Michigan.

A graduate of Howard University, Abrams received a master of divinity degree and a doctor of ministry degree from United Theological Seminary.

She has three children, Chevonne, Adam and Allyson.

Pastor E. L. Branch is God's visionary for Third New Hope Baptist Church located in Detroit, Michigan. Serving as pastor since 1977, his obedience to God has taken the Third New Hope church family from glory to glory. Pastor Branch's uncompromising and bold teaching and preaching of God's Word is changing the lives of people both at Third New Hope and around the world. Pastor Branch is a community advocate, humanitarian, scholar, lecturer, and musician.

Educationally, Pastor Branch has earned a master of arts degree in biblical studies and a master of divinity degree in religious studies from the Ashland Theological Seminary, where he presently continues his studies toward a doctor of ministries degree.

Pastor Branch profoundly lives by and proclaims the words of Luke, "The Spirit of the Lord is upon me, for he hath anointed me to preach the gospel..." (St. Luke 4:18). This prophet-preacher is "...committed to making the wounded whole!"

Pastor Branch and his wife, Lanell, have one daughter, Nikkiya, who is a graduate of Clark-Atlanta University and Touro Law School in Huntington, New York.

Faithe Brooks
Founder and President
Faithe Brooks Ministries International Inc.

Bishop P. A. Brooks
National General Board
Church of God in Christ, Inc.

Faithe Brooks is the founder and president of Faithe Brooks Ministries International Inc., a multicultural, interdenominational evangelistic ministry. Faithe ministers from a rich background of more than 20 years in the ministry. She is a noted television and radio personality hosting a weekly television broadcast entitled *Faithe to Faith,* which currently airs on the Christian Television Network. She also conducts a weekly Bible study in the city of Southfield, Michigan. Faithe is a conference host, seminar speaker, author, educator and worship leader.

She is a graduate of Kenneth E. Hagin's Rhema Bible Training Center and holds degrees in education and theology from Oral Robert's University in Tulsa, Oklahoma.

Faithe has traveled to South Africa conducting evangelistic meetings in Cape Town, Durban and Johannesburg motivating the masses to "rise up and go forward in faith."

Faithe is the daughter of Bishop and Mrs. P. A. Brooks, prelate of the Northeast Michigan Jurisdiction. Her father is also a member of the national presidium of the Church of God in Christ, Inc.

Bishop P. A. Brooks is one of the twelve members of the presidium of the Church of God in Christ, Inc. headquartered in Memphis, Tennessee. In this position he helps to direct 6 million members worldwide, with churches in the United States and more than 57 foreign countries. Bishop Brooks is co-author of *Understanding Bible Doctrine as Taught in the Church of God in Christ*, a widely-used training manual for ministry leaders and new converts.

Bishop Brooks is the recipient of an honorary doctorate degree from Lewis College of Business. He also serves as president of the New St. Paul Tabernacle Non-Profit Housing Corporation and as chief executive officer of Faith Community Mortgage, which is licensed to operate in 50 states.

A native of Chicago, Illinois, Bishop Brooks and his wife, Doris, are celebrating more than 55 years of marriage. They are the parents of Evangelist Faithe Brooks, hostess of the *Faithe to Faith* television broadcast, and Minister Phillip Brooks III, a musician and recording artist.

SPIRITUAL LEADERS

Samuel H. Bullock Jr.
Pastor
Bethany Baptist Church

Bishop Keith A. Butler
Founder & Senior Pastor
Word of Faith International Christian Center

Dr. Samuel H. Bullock became pastor of Bethany Baptist Church of Detroit, Michigan in 1982. He was called and ordained to the gospel ministry while a member of the New Mount Vernon Baptist Church of Ferndale, Michigan.

Bullock received an associate of arts degree from Highland Park Community College and a bachelor of science degree from Wayne State University. He continued his education at Andover Newton Theological School in Massachusetts and Drew University in New Jersey where he received his master and doctor of ministry degrees.

Bullock is highly involved in the church and community, serving as president of the Joan Ann Bullock Academy, the Spear Community Development Corporation, and the Council of Baptist Pastors of Detroit and Vicinity, Inc. He also sits on the board of directors for the Red Cross of Southeastern Michigan, New Detroit, Inc., and the Detroit Medical Center. He is a past president of the Michigan Progressive Baptist Convention, the Southeast Area American Baptist Churches Ministers Council, and the West Detroit Interfaith Community Organization.

Bullock is married with four sons and two grandchildren.

Bishop Keith A. Butler is the founder and senior pastor of Word of Faith International Christian Center. Founded January 14, 1979, Word of Faith is a congregation of over 21,000 members and 300 employees. The church is located on a beautiful 110-acre campus in Southfield, Michigan, where multiple services are held in the 5,000-seat auditorium.

Along with Word of Faith Christian Center in Southfield, Bishop Butler pastors satellite churches in San Francisco, California and Toronto, Canada. He also oversees international operations in England, Bulgaria, Africa and Brazil.

With the support of his lovely wife, Pastor Deborah L. Butler, and their children, Pastor MiChelle A. Butler, Minister Kristina M. Butler and Pastor Keith A. Butler II and his wife Minister Tiffany Butler, who are the proud parents of Alexis Nichole and Angela, Bishop Butler continues to plant churches worldwide.

He ministers extensively in churches, conferences and seminars throughout the U.S. and abroad, with an emphasis on instruction, line-upon-line teaching and a no-nonsense practical application of God's Word. Bishop Butler is the author of several books.

Rev. Reginald A. Caldwell Sr.
Senior Pastor
Greater Emmanuel Missionary
Baptist Church

Bishop Charles H. Ellis III
Senior Pastor
Greater Grace Temple

Reginald A. Caldwell Sr. is the senior pastor at Greater Emmanuel Missionary Baptist Church where he teaches God's word to approximately 300 members. With a congregation that is growing rapidly, Caldwell currently has four associate ministers and one youth minister.

A member of the Council of Baptist Pastors of Detroit and Vicinity, Caldwell is the past chairman of the political and social action committee. He also served as council liaison to the Detroit Public Schools Board and as a chaplain for the Detroit Police Department. He is currently a chaplain for the Wayne County Sheriff's Department and the third vice moderator of the Fellowship District.

Caldwell attended Oakland and Wayne State Universities in pursuit of life enrichment. He has taken a variety of classes concentrating in social and personal development. These classes have enhanced his ability to impart his biblical principles through personal life experiences.

A Detroit native, Caldwell is the husband to First Lady Sharon Diane and the proud father of five children, Renita, Reginald Jr., Raquel, Ryan and Shavon. He is the grandfather of Shantique and Benjamin.

Bishop Charles H. Ellis III is the senior pastor of the 6,500-member Greater Grace Temple, one of Detroit's largest churches. Under his leadership, the church touches its congregation and community with more than 250 ministries and outreach programs. Most of these are headquartered at their 20-acre complex known as the "City of David."

In 2004 Bishop Ellis was elected assistant presiding bishop of the 1.3 million-member Pentecostal Assemblies of the World. He ministers daily on nationwide television via *The Word Network*.

Bishop Ellis is also a highly respected civic leader sitting on several boards, including the YMCA, the Detroit Zoo and Sinai-Grace Hospital. His honors include being named Michigan Pastor of the Year by the state chapter of the Southern Christian Leadership Conference and receiving a Distinguished Leader of the Year award.

A graduate of Wayne State University, Bishop Ellis received a degree in business administration. He also holds an honorary doctorate from Aenon Bible College. He is married to Crisette Michelle, and is the proud father of two children, Kiera, and Charles IV.

SPIRITUAL LEADERS

Reverend Julius Caesar Hope
National Director
Department of Religious Affairs
NAACP

Rev. Julius Caesar Hope has served as national director of the NAACP's department of religious affairs for 28 years. He is also pastor of New Grace Missionary Baptist Church in Highland Park, Michigan.

An NAACP branch president for 15 years, he has run for city council in Brunswick, Georgia. Hope was president of the Georgia State Conference of NAACP Branches for 18 years while hosting a radio program. Former Georgia Governor Jimmy Carter appointed him to the Human Relations Council of Georgia.

Hope is in the Civil Rights Hall of Fame at Clark University Center in Atlanta. He has received the NAACP's Medgar Evers Award, and had an award established in his honor, The Reverend Julius C. Hope Hall of Fame Award.

A graduate of Alabama State University, he received ASU Distinguished Alumni status in 2005. Hope earned a master of sacred theology degree from Interdenominational Theological Seminary. He is a member of Alpha Phi Alpha Fraternity, Inc.

He is married to Louise Hope and is the father of Rev. Julius E. and Tonya Hope-Davis.

Bishop Wayne T. Jackson
Senior Pastor
Great Faith Ministries International

Bishop Wayne T. Jackson is the senior pastor of Great Faith Ministries International in Detroit, Michigan. Bishop Jackson holds an honorary doctorate of divinity degree from St. Thomas Christian College in Jacksonville, Florida.

As a pastor, Bishop Jackson's primary responsibilities are teaching the Word of God and developing disciples of Jesus Christ. He also oversees the ministry's day-to-day administrative activities.

A vital portion of Bishop Jackson's ministry is to help those that cannot help themselves. Under his administration, he has developed and implemented several programs to help the underprivileged. He has ministered to the homeless and fed them both spiritually and naturally.

The founder of Wayne T. Jackson Ministries, he has been called to bring the demonstration of the power of God to the world. His miracle crusades have changed the lives of thousands of individuals. Many have been healed of cancer, diabetes, AIDS, high blood pressure and many other diseases.

Bishop Jackson has been married to his wife, Pastor Beverly Y. Jackson, for 26 years. They have seven children and a number of grandchildren.

James A. Jennings Jr.
Pastor
Shield of Faith Ministries

Dr. Wilma Robena Johnson
Senior Pastor
New Prospect Missionary Baptist Church

James A. Jennings Jr. is the pastor of Shield of Faith Ministries in Detroit. There, he preaches and teaches the word of God, counsels, mentors and nurtures the congregation. Shield of Faith is an empowerment ministry teaching principles of faith and successful living.

Jennings received an honorary doctor of divinity degree. He was the recipient of the highest civilian award by the late Mayor Coleman A. Young and the Detroit City Council. He also received the 1994 Reverend C.L. Franklin Preaching Award for his inspirational style of preaching.

Jennings completed his undergraduate studies at Macomb County Community College and Wayne State University. He received his bachelor of arts degree from the American Baptist Theological Seminary, in Nashville, Tennessee. He pursued his master of divinity degree at Southern Baptist Theological Seminary in Louisville, Kentucky. Jennings earned master of arts degrees at Wayne State University, and the University of Louisville.

A native of Forkland, Alabama, Jennings grew up in Detroit. He is a husband, father and grandfather. He is married to Helen Watkins-Jennings.

The Reverend Dr. Wilma Robena Johnson is an ordained Baptist minister and woman of God. On March 1, 1999, she became the senior pastor of New Prospect Missionary Baptist Church in Detroit, Michigan. For 32 years Dr. Johnson has continued to teach, conduct workshops and preach the Gospel of Jesus Christ.

Johnson enjoys loving and meeting the needs of her growing congregation. They affectionately call her "Pastor J." Johnson and her husband, Deacon David L. Johnson, have two sons, David Lawrence, 21 and Brian Langston, 17.

Johnson holds a bachelor of arts degree in business administration, a master of arts degree in pastoral ministry, and a doctor of ministry degree from the Ecumenical Theological Seminary in Detroit, Michigan. She is the accomplished author of *Giving Away My Joy*.

Johnson is the third vice president of the Detroit branch of the NAACP. She is a member of the board of trustees of American Baptist College in Nashville, Tennessee and Ecumenical Theological Seminary.

Her motto is "Jesus is the best thing that ever happened to me."

SPIRITUAL LEADERS

Larry T. Jordan
Founder & Senior Pastor
Family Victory Fellowship Church

Larry T. Jordan is the founder and senior pastor of Family Victory Fellowship Church in Southfield Michigan, a family-orientated ministry with the vision of building, strengthening and restoring families.

Jordan is the chief executive officer and founder of Generation 2 Generation, Inc., a youth development organization focusing on maximization of individual potential. He is also founder of Children Technological Academy, a Christian school committed to training children to be leaders in society. He also serves as a chaplain with the City of Southfield Police Department.

Jordan is a graduate of Lawrence Technological University in Southfield Michigan. Prior to his pastorate, he utilized his architectural degree as a senior staff architect with Albert Kahn Associates, a major architectural firm located in Detroit, Michigan.

Jordan is a member of the board of trustees for the International Third World Leadership Association where Dr. Myles Munroe is founder and president. Jordan is also the founder of Covenant Pastor's Association, a network of senior pastors in the metropolitan Detroit area.

He is married to Southfield Councilwoman Sylvia Jordan and the father of two children.

Reginald M. Lane
Founder & Senior Pastor
Dunamis Outreach Ministries
Worldwide, Inc.

Reginald M. Lane is the founder and senior pastor of Dunamis Outreach Ministries Worldwide, Inc. This growing, Detroit-based, 1,000-member church is known for its non-traditional services, dynamic praise and worship, and Lane's unique and powerful ministerial style. His lecture topics, which focus on Christ's way of life as the solution to the issues we face, have been presented in Europe, South America and across the United States.

Described as "a breath of fresh air to the church today," by Professional Sports Planning's president and CEO, Kevin Poston, Lane is reaching and positively affecting today's generation. An accomplished songwriter and producer, Lane has achieved this level of impact through various media outlets including television, radio and music albums.

In addition to his flourishing ministry in Detroit, Lane has established churches in Atlanta, Georgia, Madras, India and New Delhi, India. Dedicated to a life that serves Christ, Lane continues in his pursuit to make the work of Christ a reality in people's lives.

He is married to Kelly Lane, and the father of four children.

Prince A. Miles
Pastor
International Gospel Deliverance Center

Reverend Dr. James C. Perkins
Pastor
Greater Christ Baptist Church

The third son to Dr. Luvenia Miles and the late Apostle Charles O. Miles, Prince A. Miles was born in Detroit, Michigan on July 8, 1956. He is married to Lady Monica Miles and father to three sons, Matthew, Joseph and the late Prince A. Miles II.

A graduate of Southfield High School, Miles attended Detroit Business Institute. In 1975 he was called into the ministry and in 1977 he was ordained to preach. Miles attended William Tyndale College and received his doctor of divinity degree in 1990 from the United Bible College and Theological Seminary. In 1999 he received the Spirit of Detroit Award and a certificate of recognition from the mayor.

The pastor of International Gospel Deliverance Center in Southfield, Michigan, Miles was consecrated an apostle on July 8, 2006. He serves on the executive council of the National Clergy Council and as chaplain for MADD of Wayne and Oakland Counties. A leader and shining light in the community, Miles is a witness for Jesus Christ, with a desire to see lives changed by His saving grace.

The Reverend Dr. James C. Perkins was ordained to gospel ministry in 1974. He has served as pastor of Greater Christ Baptist Church in Detroit for 25 years. He received his doctor of ministry degree from United Theological Seminary and is a nationally-recognized minister.

Perkins is the author of *Building Up Zion's Walls: Ministry for Empowering the African American Family*. His other writings, as well as profiles of his ministry and details of his community activism, have been included in publications such as *Black Enterprise*, *USA Today*, *Ebony*, *American Baptist*, several edited works published by Judson Press, and the best-selling *Success Runs in Our Race: The Complete Guide to Effective Networking in the African-American Community*.

Perkins has established numerous enterprises that support his vision. In 1992 he founded the Fellowship Nonprofit Housing Corporation as a vehicle for community economic development. In 1993 he instituted the Benjamin E. Mays Male Academy, a Christian school for boys in grades kindergarten through seven.

A native of West Virginia, Perkins is married to Linda Adkins Perkins and has two daughters and one grandson.

SPIRITUAL LEADERS

Glenn R. Plummer
Chairman & Chief Executive Officer
Christian Television Network

J. Drew Sheard
Senior Pastor
Greater Emmanuel Institutional
Church of God in Christ

Glenn R. Plummer founded the Christian Television Network (CTN) in 1982 and has gone on to own and operate three local, independent stations. He is well known as the host of a daily, live one-hour television program, *CTN Live!* Passionate and confrontational, Plummer is admired for his courage and leadership in dealing with controversial issues from a foundation of biblical principles. Recently ending his three-and-a-half-year term, Plummer was the first African American to serve as chairman and chief executive officer of the National Religious Broadcasters in their 63-year history.

Several years ago, Plummer had a vision for Israel and black America, but 2004 proved to be pivotal in unfolding his new role of leadership in this area. Thus, the Fellowship of Israel and Black America (FIBA) was launched in February of 2006 as a partnership with the International Fellowship of Christians and Jews.

Plummer is the senior pastor of Ambassadors for Christ Church. He sits on the board of directors of the NRB and the board of advisors of El Al Israel Airlines.

Intelligent, confident, and diligent are three of the many words used to describe J. Drew Sheard, senior pastor of Greater Emmanuel Institutional Church of God in Christ in Detroit, Michigan. His awesome leadership abilities have established his position as one of the most influential leaders in the Church of God in Christ (COGIC).

The current president of COGIC's International Youth Department, Sheard is an advocate for youth and wayward souls and has implemented several programs during his tenure. He also serves as chairman of the Auxiliaries in Ministries (AIM) Convention, superintendent of the Emmanuel District, and administrative assistant of the North Central Ecclesiastical Jurisdiction of Michigan.

Sheard has held several other positions on national, jurisdiction and local levels within COGIC, including national adjutant overseer, executive secretary of the International Youth Department, and vice president of the AIM Convention.

Graduating from Wayne State University. Sheard received a bachelor's degree in education and a master of education degree in Mathematics. He is the dedicated husband of Evangelist Karen Clark-Sheard and father to Kierra Sheard and J. Drew Sheard II.

The Reverend Horace L. Sheffield III
Pastor
New Galilee Missionary Baptist Church

André L. Spivey
Pastor
St. Paul AME Church

The Reverend Horace L. Sheffield III was born in Detroit to Horace L. Jr. and Mary Sheffield. He was called to preach at 11 years of age and was ordained by Howard Fauntroy Jr. Presently, he is the pastor of New Galilee Missionary Baptist Church.

Sheffield is a published writer having co-authored two plays with Yolanda Denise King. He has published articles in *The Michigan Chronicle*, the *Detroit News*, *The Michigan Front Page*, and *African American Parent Magazine*.

In concert with the local church community, Sheffield organized The Safe Center, Inc., a faith-based nonprofit human service agency, which is housed inside New Galilee. Previously, Sheffield worked on the staff of Mayor Dennis W. Archer. He has served as president of Michigan Chapter of the National Action Network, board member of St. John Northeast Community Hospital, chairperson of the Ecumenical Ministers Alliance, and a life member of the NAACP. Additionally, he is the executive director of the Detroit Association of Black Organizations.

Sheffield has two children, Horace Lindsey IV and Mary Christine.

André L. Spivey is the pastor of St. Paul African Methodist Episcopal Church in Detroit, Michigan. Prior to this charge, he served as pastor of Pleasant Valley AME Church in Belleville, Michigan and Saunders Memorial AME Church in Detroit, Michigan.

Spivey received a bachelor of arts degree from Morehouse College, a master of divinity degree from Colgate Rochester Divinity School, and is currently working toward a master of arts degree in administration at Central Michigan University.

Spivey served on the Detroit School Board transition team and is currently serving on the Wayne County Economic Development Corporation and the Brownfield Redevelopment Authority. He also serves on the boards of the International Detroit Black Expo and the Detroit Omega Foundation. He is a member of the Detroit chapter of the Morehouse College Alumni Association, Phi Mu Alpha Sinfonia, a professional music fraternity, and Omega Psi Phi Fraternity, Inc.

A native of Detroit, Spivey is married to Shema Spivey and they have two children, a son André II and a daughter, Kendall.

SPIRITUAL LEADERS

Dr. Edgar L. Vann
Senior Pastor
Second Ebenezer Church

Bishop Corletta J. Vaughn
President & Chief Executive Officer
Go Tell It Ministry Worldwide, Inc.

Since 1976, Dr. Edgar L. Vann has served as the senior pastor of Second Ebenezer Church in Detroit, Michigan. He is also the founder and chair of Vanguard Community Development Corporation.

Vann has traveled and preached extensively throughout the world, using every spiritual gift given to him to spread the gospel. The mission of Second Ebenezer is to make an impact in the world and bring persons into a saving and redemptive relationship with Jesus Christ. During his tenure, the church's membership has grown from 66 to more than 5,000 committed Christians with more than 50 active church ministries.

He is the visionary behind over $60 million of real estate development in Detroit, including a new 15-acre worship center, affordable housing and commercial developments.

The recipient of numerous awards and acolades, Vann received The Skillman Foundation's 2006 President Award. He was also inducted into the Board of Preachers at Morehouse College, alongside notables such as Dr. Martin Luther King, Jr. and Benjamin Hooks.

Pastor Vann is married to Minister Sheila R. Vann and they have two children, Edgar III and Ericka.

A Michigan native, Bishop Corletta J. Vaughn is the first female in Detroit to be consecrated to the office of bishop. For 20 years she has been the senior leader of The Holy Spirit Cathedral of Faith, formerly Holy Ghost Cathedral. She is president and chief executive officer of Go Tell It Ministry Worldwide, Inc. and the Corletta J. Vaughn Foundation, a nonprofit organization with a passion for youth.

Founder of Two Sisters Publishing, she served as the executive producer of her CD *There's A Flow*. Bishop Vaughn's spectrum is endless as she travels the nation for the primary purpose of "knowing God to make Him known." She is sound politically and spiritually as she encourages all to stay focused, believing in the power of the Holy Spirit. A chameleon with unlimited abilities, she is an entrepreneur, designer, musician, vocalist, writer, registered nurse, teacher and minister, showing no signs of slowing down in the race to save souls.

Corletta is the wife of Gilbert, mother of Shannon, Stephen, Apprille and Nadia, grandmother to several and spiritual mother to thousands.

Pastor Marvin L. Winans has focused his life on bringing joy and good works to his community, people and country. Growing up in a musical and religious family, Winans is the youngest twin, and the fourth of ten children. The Winans are well-known as the First Family of contemporary gospel and have gained international acclaim. Three generations have earned numerous Dove, Stellar and more than 20 Grammy Awards.

Winans acknowledged his ministry call in the l970s, delivering his first sermon on December 18, 1976. On May 27, 1989, Winans founded Perfecting Church in Detroit. The Lord has blessed Perfecting to grow into a ministry campus of over 165,000 square feet with 3,500 members.

In 1992 Winans created Perfecting Community Development Corporation to ignite economic growth, offer transitional housing, and provide recreational activities for youth. In 1997 he established the Marvin L. Winans Academy of Performing Arts for students in grades K-12.

Although amassing numerous awards and accolades, Pastor Winans' greatest joy is to see people come into the full knowledge of Jesus Christ and live victoriously forever.

Marvin L. Winans
Pastor
Perfecting Church

T.J. Adams & Associates

SPECIALIZING CONFIDENTIALLY SINCE 1985 IN

EXECUTIVE SEARCH

MANAGEMENT CONSULTING

CORPORATE SUPPORT TRAINING

TEMPORARY STAFFING

500 Griswold Street, 10th Floor, Suite 1050, Detroit, Michigan 48226-3501
Tel: 313.965.7772 Fax: 313.965.9294
www.tj-adams.com

Detroit's

COMMUNITY LEADERS

"We need to dream big dreams, propose grandoise means if we are to recapture the excitement, the vibrancy, and pride we once had."

MAYOR COLEMAN A. YOUNG (1918-1997)

COMMUNITY LEADERS

Tonya Allen
Program Director
The Skillman Foundation

Tonya Allen is program director of the Skillman Foundation, a private nonprofit organization that makes annual grants of $23 million to improve the lives of children through their homes, schools and neighborhoods. Allen is responsible for implementing the Foundation's newest strategy to invest deeply and more strategically into key neighborhoods where there are many children and limited resources.

Allen attended the University of Michigan, where she completed her bachelor's degree in sociology and African American studies. In 1996 she received a master's degree in public health and a master's degree in social work.

Allen is an active member of her community. She is co-chair of the CDC-sponsored CENTERED Project, aimed at eliminating ethnic and racial health disparities, and co-chair of the Tavis Smiley Foundation Detroit advisory committee. She also serves as a trustee of the Southfield Community Foundation, the Child Care Coordinating Council of Detroit/Wayne County and the Detroit Parent Network.

She lives in Southfield with her husband, Louis, and daughters, Phylicia, Brianna and Alana. She worships at Hope United Methodist Church.

Elizabeth W. Brooks
Philanthropist &
Community Leader

Elizabeth "Betty" W. Brooks is a patron of the arts and a tireless community leader. She writes inspirational poetry and is a columnist for a local newspaper.

Elizabeth is a member of the board of directors of the Michigan Opera Theatre; the Lewis College of Business; the Music Hall for Performing Arts; the Charles H. Wright African American Museum; the Michigan Humanity Council; and The Greening of Detroit. She is also chair of the board of directors for the Sphinx Organization and the After School All-Stars. She is co-chair of the Capital Campaign for Communities in Schools. Elizabeth serves on the Belle Isle Women's Committee and the advisory board for the Metro Parent Publishing Group. She is chair of the council for African American dance at the Detroit Opera House.

Elizabeth was appointed by Governor John Engler to three terms as a member of the Michigan Council for the Arts and Cultural Affairs.

Elizabeth is the recipient of many service awards including the Shirley Chisholm Award of recognition as the 1997 Woman of the Year.

A native Detroiter, Akua Budu-Watkins is dedicated to the advocacy of human rights and women's empowerment. Her journey as an activist began in 1963 when she participated in the Detroit march with Rev. Martin Luther King Jr.

Akua was director of field operations for former Detroit Mayor Dennis Archer and was appointed director of Neighborhood City Halls. She coordinated the community outreach plan for U.S. Senator Debbie Stabenow's campaign and was appointed director of the Southeast Michigan office. She has been called the "field general" of community organizing.

Akua has a broad range of expertise in political strategy and organizational development. She is well known and respected for building and maintaining key alliances and partnerships in both the public and private sectors.

Akua has traveled to Europe, South America, the Caribbean and Africa to address important issues. She is the founder of Sisternomics' Health and Finance seminars for women. Akua is deeply committed to the struggle for economic equality and equity.

Akua Budu-Watkins
Chief Administrative Officer
Interstate Traveler Company, LLC

A nnie Carter is a board member of the Detroit Board of Education. In this position, she was elected to represent District 3 for the Detroit Public Schools. She is the chairperson of the committee on parent and community involvement, Title I (Parent Involvement Fund).

Annie served as chairperson at three Detroit Public Schools and was a Chapter 1 parent delegate for the State of Michigan. She also served as a member of the district parent advisory council, the citywide parent organization, the juvenile accountability advisory and many other committees within the Detroit Board of Education.

Annie is involved in many organizations including the NAACP, the National Coalition of Title I, 14th Congressional Democratic Party, the Detroit Federation of Teachers, the United Dairy Workers, the Barton McFarlane Neighbor Association and Hope United Methodist Church.

Annie has received several certificates in leadership (MASB), business industry and computer skills, basic computer skills, understanding the law, and general education.

Annie Carter
Board Member, District 3
Detroit Board of Education

COMMUNITY LEADERS

Sheilah P. Clay
President & Chief Executive Officer
Neighborhood Service Organization

Sheilah P. Clay is the president and chief executive officer of Neighborhood Service Organization (NSO), a Detroit-based $23 million nonprofit human services organization that provides mental health, substance abuse and problem gambling treatment. The organization supports financial literacy, crisis intervention, youth violence prevention, home-based Head Start, and assistance for the homeless, developmentally disabled, and kinship care providers.

Clay holds a master of arts degree in guidance and counseling from Wayne State University and a bachelor of arts degree in psychology from Spelman College.

Clay's affiliations include the Association of Behavioral Healthcare Management, the Michigan Association of Community Mental Health Boards, the Detroit Regional Chamber, Alpha Kappa Alpha Sorority, Inc., Women Executives, the United Way for Southeastern Michigan, and Karmanos Cancer Institute Community Network Partnership.

Appointed by Governor Jennifer Granholm to the State Commission on Community Action and Economic Opportunity, Clay also serves on several boards, including the Michigan Non-Profit Association, CareLink Network, ConsumerLink Network, and Behavioral Health Professionals, Inc. She was recently appointed to the Farmington Board of Education.

Clay resides in Farmington Hills with her husband and two children.

Rochelle E. Danquah
Director of Education and
Public Programs
Charles H. Wright Museum
of African American History

Rochelle E. Danquah is director of education and public programs for the Charles H. Wright Museum of Natural History. She also owns and operates Sankofa Tutoring & Educational Services in Southfield. Rochelle is a historian, lecturer, genealogist, researcher and educator.

A former college instructor, Rochelle also taught middle and high school. She holds a State of Michigan secondary education teaching certificate, and has taught in Ghana, West Africa. Recognized as an Outstanding Young Woman in America, Rochelle is highly sought after as a speaker on black history and education.

Rochelle conducts major research related to the African-American experience and the Underground Railroad in Michigan. She is a member of the Association of African-American Museums, the Association of American Museums, the Fred Hart Williams Genealogy Society, the Great Lakes African American Quilters Network and the Association of University Women.

Rochelle earned a bachelor's degree from Western Michigan University and a master's degree from Central Michigan University.

A native of Port Huron, Rochelle is married to Eugene O. Danquah, and has two children, Jaimi and Asante.

Bamidele Agbasegbe Demerson is director of exhibitions and research at the Charles H. Wright Museum of African American History. Prior to this, he served as the museum's curator of education.

A graduate of the University of Michigan, Demerson has conducted anthropological fieldwork in Nigeria, Brazil and the United States. His research interests include African-American culture and history, comparative social organization in Africa and the African diaspora, and political consciousness in visual art created by African Americans. Presented at domestic and international conferences, his research also appears in anthologies and periodicals.

Demerson has curated numerous exhibitions, including "New Eyes for Ancient Gods: Yoruba Orisa in Contemporary Art," and "Unmasked: Stereotypes in American Material Culture." He also collaborated in the development of the 22,000-square-foot, longterm exhibition, "And Still We Rise: Our Journey Through African American History and Culture" at the Wright Museum.

Demerson participates in the Paradise Valley Commemorative Park Working Group, serves on the board of directors of the National Conference of Artists, Inc., and provides consultative services to the Edo Arts and Cultural Heritage Institute, USA.

Bamidele Agbasegbe Demerson
Director of Exhibitions and Research
Charles H. Wright Museum of
African American History

Aaron P. Dworkin is founder and president of the Sphinx Organization. An accomplished electric and acoustic violinist, he received his bachelor's degree and master's of music in violin performance from the University of Michigan School of Music, graduating with high honors. He previously attended the Peabody Institute, the Philadelphia New School and the Interlochen Arts Academy. He has studied with Vladimir Graffman, Berl Senofsky, Jascha Brodsky, John Eaken, Renata Knific, Donald Hopkins and Stephen Shipps. Additionally, Dworkin studied piano with Robert Alexander Böhnke in Tübingen, Germany.

In 2005 Dworkin was awarded a MacArthur Fellowship. He is the recipient of *Newsweek*'s Giving Back Award, a National Governors Award, and SBC Ameritech's Excellence Award. In 2003 the *Detroit News* named him a Michiganian of the Year. He serves on the board of directors for the University Musical Society in Ann Arbor, ArtServe Michigan, Walnut Hill School, and WRCJ.

Dworkin is a frequent panelist, lecturer and speaker on the topic of diversity in the arts, and he recently gave commencement addresses at the University of Michigan, Bowling Green State University, and the Longy Conservatory.

Aaron P. Dworkin
Founder & President
The Sphinx Organization

Louversey Green
Founder & Director
Mediation Outreach to the Blind

L ouversey Green in a weekend board operator, engineer and hostess of her own radio program on WMUZ and WEXL in Detroit. She is the producer and engineer of "Gospel Melodies."

Louversey is the founder and executive director of Meditation Outreach to the Blind and the organizer of a program called the Music Enrichment Project, which teaches visually impaired students how to play musical instruments and sing in an orchestra setting. They present concerts at nursing homes, prisons, senior buildings and churches.

Loversey, an evangelist, is an associate minister of her church, Greater Grace Temple. She is also the mother of eight children. Recently, her children and grandchildren gave her an eightieth birthday celebration. She has received numerous awards for her community and religious work.

Her favorite quote is "Let not your heart be troubled, ye believe in God believe also in me. In my father's house are many mansions."

Minetta Hare
Director of Annual Giving
Museum of African American History

M inetta Hare is the director of annual giving for the Museum of African American History in Detroit, Michigan. In this position, she manages individual donors and fund development campaigns for the museum.

Minetta is a global humanitarian and the founder of ARISE & BUILD International, an organization that addresses issues of health care, education, economic and spiritual development. Minetta has had a great impact on lives in Jamaica, South Africa, Kenya, Haiti, Venezuela and the city of Detroit. She was featured in the *Michigan Chronicle* as a Woman of Purpose, one of the women who can lead and empower people for the new millennium.

Minetta received a bachelor of business administration degree from Western Michigan University. She has several business and training certifications and is a licensed minister. She is the owner of a Christian entertainment, event planning and travel consultation company.

A native of Montgomery, Alabama, Minetta is single and the proud sponsor of several children's educational needs around the world. She enjoys golf, the Detroit Pistons, reading and traveling.

D r. Alison J. Harmon is a 30-year veteran educator. She has a doctor of education degree in educational administration, a master of education degree, and a bachelor of science degree in education. Currently, she is a program director and education specialist for the Skillman Foundation, a private grant-making foundation that applies its resources to improve the lives of children in metropolitan Detroit.

Harmon is committed to participating in community activities. She is the president of the Delta Research and Educational Foundation and a national executive board member of Delta Sigma Theta Sorority, Inc. She is also a member of the board of directors of the Detroit Area Pre-College Engineering Program and the Coleman Young Foundation, and an active member of Trinity Missionary Baptist Church in Pontiac.

She is married to Robert F. Harmon Sr. They have two sons, Aaron, 20, an honors student at Bowling Green State University, and B.J., 24, a third-year law student at the University of Michigan.

Alison J. Harmon
Program Director
The Skillman Foundation

M argaret Harris steps in to help Detroit Public School students when no one else does. She started by helping a high school student get a new outfit for an awards program. Margaret saw a need and stepped in, and she keeps doing that for the students at Hutchins Middle and Loving Elementary Schools. Margaret's son, Brandon, now a junior in college, went to both schools, and the single mother made sure that she made time to help Brandon's teachers, while running her own home cleaning business, My Margaret.

Margaret helps students rise to a level of excellence and accomplish greatness. Brandon traveled to Africa twice to visit students. His success is a testament to Margaret's fortitude as a single mother. Now, she fights for other students to be successful by volunteering her services to the Academic Games Team, the All-City Dance Competition, and the Henry Ford Teen Health Center.

She has received awards from the governor, mayor and city council for her dedicated community leadership in Detroit's North End as an elected precinct delegate for more than 25 years.

Margaret Harris
Community Volunteer

COMMUNITY LEADERS

Teola P. Hunter
Partner
Sloan/Hunter Group

Teola P. Hunter is a native Detroiter, mother, grandmother, entrepreneur, teacher and political leader. She taught in the Detroit Public Schools for 14 years. In 1971 she founded the Buttons and Bows Nursery and Kindergarten. In 1974 she developed an additional nursery and a preparatory school.

Hunter was elected to the Michigan House of Representatives in 1980. There, she was chairperson of the House Social Service and Youth Committee, chairperson of an ad hoc committee on children and families, and subcommittee chair of the committee on AIDS. Testimony on AIDS led Hunter to establish Resource Endowment Aiding Children Together, a nonprofit organization dedicated to helping children and families affected by AIDS.

In 1989 Hunter was the first female elected to the leadership position of speaker pro tempore. In 1992 she was appointed deputy director for Health and Community Services and became the first female elected to the office of Wayne County Clerk.

Hunter resigned from the office in 2000. She became the founding partner of the Sloan/Hunter Group, a lobbying and consultant business specializing in public affairs services and fund development.

Arthur L. Johnson
Retired Vice President
University Relations
Wayne State University

In 1995 Arthur L. Johnson retired as vice president for university relations and professor of educational sociology from Wayne State University after 23 years of service. During his tenure, Johnson established a number of new programs including the Detroit Festival of the Arts.

Johnson served as president of the Detroit NAACP from 1987 to 1993, following years of service to the branch, beginning as executive secretary in 1950. He also served as deputy director of the Michigan Civil Rights Commission.

Johnson has received honorary degrees from Morehouse College, Wayne State University and the University of Detroit Mercy. He is the recipient of the Detroit Bar Association's Liberty Bell Award, the Afro-Asian Institute's Histadrut Humanitarian Award, the National Bar Association's Gertrude E. Rush Award and many others.

Johnson serves on the board of the Detroit Symphony Orchestra, the Detroit Science Center, the Detroit Institute of Arts, and the governance committee of the Detroit Riverfront Conservancy.

A student of sociology, Johnson earned his bachelor's degree from Morehouse College and master's degree from Atlanta University. He completed a research fellowship at Fisk University.

Cheryl Johnson joined the Coalition on Temporary Shelter in 1990 as shelter director. She managed a staff and oversaw emergency shelter and program services for thousands of homeless people. In 1994 she was named deputy director of COTS, and helped shape a long-range strategic plan. She became chief executive officer in March of 1998. Since then, she has pushed the agency in several innovative directions and secured the move into the permanent supportive housing arena. In her role as CEO, Johnson has increased the permanent supportive housing units from 23 single room occupancy units to 154 multi-family units.

Johnson has received numerous awards and recognitions, including *Crain's Detroit Business* 40 Under 40, the Women's Information Network's Most Influential Black Women for Metro Detroit, a Eureka Detroit Fellowship, and Woman of the Year by Zeta Phi Beta Sorority, Inc.

Johnson received a bachelor's degree in psychology from Kalamazoo College and worked as a licensed social worker before her employment at COTS.

She is married to Gerald Johnson Jr. and is the mother of four children.

Cheryl P. Johnson
Chief Executive Officer
Coalition on Temporary Shelter

Attorney Paula Johnson is a member of the Detroit Board of Education where she is chair of the committee on contracting and procurement, one of the most vital committees on the board. In this position, she is responsible for overseeing the award and administration of all contracts for goods and services totaling more than $50,000, with an annual school budget of approximately $1.3 billion.

Admitted to the Michigan State Bar in November of 2002, Johnson is a solo practitioner focusing on child custody, divorce, guardianship and employment matters. She has been honored by the Legal Aid and Defender Association for her pro bono work with victims of domestic violence.

Johnson is an alumna of Cass Technical High School, the University of Detroit Mercy, and the Wayne State University School of Law, where she was a recipient of the Krell Scholarship.

A lifelong Detroiter, Paula Johnson is married and the proud mother of three children. Her motto is, "A greater passion leads to a greater promise."

Paula Johnson, Esq.
Member
Detroit Board of Education

COMMUNITY LEADERS

Stephanie L. Jones
Director, Marketing and
Public Relations
Cass Technical High School
Alumni Association

Stephanie L. Jones is director of marketing and public relations for the Cass Technical High School Alumni Association, which represents the 100,000 graduates of Cass Technical High School in Detroit. In this position, she coordinates events, creates marketing campaigns and assists in the areas of strategic planning and fund development.

Stephanie, who is also a freelance publicist, works with several best-selling book authors in the areas of marketing and media relations. She has successfully worked on marketing campaigns to help catapult the careers of many authors. Before retiring from corporate business, she served as an award-winning team member for Charter One Bank and SBC.

Stephanie earned her associates degree in business administration from Wayne County Community College and is a candidate for a dual bachelor's degree in management and marketing from the University of Michigan - Dearborn. She has been awarded and recognized for her community service work with teen girls, and as a mentor in the Detroit Public Schools.

Stephanie, a Detroit native, is the wife of Robert A. Jones Jr.

Patricia Anne McCann
Director of Volunteer Services
United Way for Southeastern Michigan

Patricia McCann is director of volunteer services for United Way for Southeastern Michigan. There, Patricia is responsible for developing and maintaining relationships with a variety of community partners and internal and external volunteers. To this end, she oversees a Web-based volunteer matching system, which receives approximately 350,000 hits annually, plans and executes one of the largest volunteer recognition luncheons in the country, and provides training and resources to other community groups related to volunteerism. She has positioned the volunteer center to be a community resource and an integral tool in making positive community change.

As director of volunteer services, Patricia served on the volunteer advisory committee for the Super Bowl XL host committee and had significant supervisory responsibilities over many volunteers during that time.

Patricia holds a bachelor of science degree in psychology from Michigan State University. Dale Carnegie certified, she has received extensive professional training at the National Academy of Voluntarism in Alexandria, Virginia, and at Michigan State University.

Patricia resides in Detroit with her husband and two sons.

A s the executive director of Mothers Against Drunk Driving, Wayne County Chapter, Ne'chole Drake McClendon has more than fifteen years of nonprofit experience. She is an advocate of MADD's mission to stop drunk driving, support victims of this violent crime and prevent underage drinking. She is dedicated to educating the public on MADD's core programs and servicing victims.

A native of Grand Rapids, Michigan, Drake McClendon is a product of the Grand Rapids Public School system. She holds undergraduate degrees from Grand Rapids Community College and Eastern Michigan University. She also earned a master's degree in industrial relations from Wayne State University. A proud Wayne State University Multicultural Experience in Leadership Development (MELD) alumna, she is committed to cultivating an understanding between leaders of diverse communities through cross-cultural collaboration, cultural immersion, personal assessments and relationship building.

Drake McClendon is a member of the Black Alumni Association at Eastern Michigan University and the Organization of Black Alumni at Wayne State University. She enjoys reading, traveling and attending sporting events with her son. She and her family live in Detroit.

Ne'chole Drake McClendon
Executive Director
Mothers Against Drunk Driving
Wayne County Chapter

T racey Theodoria Miree-Marks assumes many responsibilities in her commitment to achieve full accessibility by connecting the global hearing majority to the deaf, hard of hearing, and deaf/blind minority cultures.

Tracey is actively implementing services in the Detroit Public Schools to provide visual language education interpreting, while setting precedents in the Wayne County Judicial System for legal interpreting services. Tracey plays a vital role in the Homeland Security CEPIN Project, protecting the safety of the communities. Successfully petitioning to the Detroit City Council, her "campaigning for full accessibility" has made a tremendous impact.

Tracey has received numerous awards and honors for her professional community affiliations and involvement, now making her mark on Capitol Hill by lobbying and advocating for the rights of the people she serves. She is a member of the Disability Task Force, a board member of DDOT's paratransit appeals board and a member of the citizens review committee.

Tracey is inspirited by the enormous support from both the hearing and non-hearing communities to be the best at creating value in our society.

Tracey T. Miree-Marks
Founder & President
Connections for Deaf Citizens, Inc.

COMMUNITY LEADERS

Carmen A. N'Namdi
Founder & Principal
Nataki Talibah Schoolhouse of Detroit

Carmen A. N'Namdi founded the Nataki Talibah Schoolhouse of Detroit as a private school in 1978 to immortalize her daughter, Nataki, who died in 1974. N'Namdi served as headmistress and classroom teacher to her original 18 students. The school now serves 450 students as a public school chartered by Central Michigan University.

In 1979 the *Detroit News* spotlighted N'Namdi as an "unconventional educator" in People to Watch. She was awarded the National Professional Best Award by Oldsmobile, Michigan State University and *Learning Magazine*. N'Namdi was appointed to the McPherson Commission to study charter schools and served as chair of the National Charter School Institute board for three years. She sits on the board of the Michigan Association of Public School Academies, as well as ArtServe Michigan, where she advocates for the arts in education.

A native of Cincinnati, Ohio, N'Namdi holds bachelor's and master's degrees in education from The Ohio State University and Wayne State University, respectively. She is married to George N'Namdi of G.R. N'Namdi Galleries, and has three adult children, who are alumni of the Nataki Talibah Schoolhouse.

Dr. Delila Owens
Assistant Professor
Theoretical and Behavioral Foundations
Wayne State University

Delila Owens is assistant professor of the theoretical and behavioral foundations division at Wayne State University. A graduate of Ferris State University and Central Michigan University, Owens received her doctorate degree in counselor education from Michigan State University in East Lansing, Michigan.

As an assistant professor at Wayne State University, Owens' research focuses on school counseling practices in urban settings, closing the achievement gap, parental attachment, and later, adult adjustment. A former school counselor, Owens serves on both the *Journal of School Counseling* and *Professional School Counseling* editorial boards.

Governor Granholm appointed Owens to the Michigan Board of Counseling. This licensure board oversees the practices of counselors in Michigan. She also serves on the public advocacy and support committee for the American Counseling Association (ACA), the Rosa Parks Foundation board of directors, and formerly served as an Americorps*VISTA.

In 2005 she was awarded the OHANA Award by the Counselors for Social Justice Association, a division of ACA, for her contributions to the field of counseling and her fight for social justice.

V. Lonnie Peek Jr. is an instructor, professor and ordained minister. A previous department chair of the Black Studies Department, he is currently district director of religious studies at Wayne County Community College District. Peek founded and served as the first president of Wayne State University's Association of Black Students in 1967, serving as a springboard into Detroit's political and civic arena. He later founded the Concerned Citizens Council, a citywide advocate organization.

Peek serves on the board of New Detroit, the Detroit Economic Growth Corporation, and the Detroit Riverfront Conservancy. He has worked with mayors Coleman Young, Dennis Archer and Kwame Kilpatrick; served as executive assistant to Governor James Blanchard; and is chief executive officer of eBusiness Strategies and Diversified Temporaries. He serves on the executive committee of the Council of Baptist Pastors and is the assistant pastor at Greater Christ Baptist Church.

Peek is a radio talk show host and columnist with the *Michigan Chronicle*, appearing on local and national television.

He is married to Eunice and has four children, Monique, Lonnie III, Ricky and Ki.

The Reverend V. Lonnie Peek Jr.
District Director of Comparative
Religious and Cultural Studies
Wayne County Community College District

Orena "OP" Perry is a Christian mother of five children, D'Lila, Dezaré, Anthony, Elijah and Joyce.

A graduate of Redford High School, Perry was known as the Strong Songs Teen Reporter for four years on WJLB 98 FM. She earned a bachelor's degree in general marketing from Davenport University.

In 2004 Perry organized a nonprofit organization, now called the Girlfriend Network, which led her to start the *Girl Talk* radio show on WDRJ 1440 AM. She hopes to inspire females, one city at a time, while healing their pain through inspirational thought and conversation. "We can all make a difference and it will begin with me," Perry says.

During 2005 Perry helped to organize "Jazz on the Blvd." Her company, The Acquisitionist, handled all bookings and promotion for the event.

In fall of 2005, Perry became the president of the Wayne County Mothers Against Drunk Driving, where she currently serves.

Orena Perry
President
Wayne County Mothers
Against Drunk Driving

COMMUNITY LEADERS

Oliver Ragsdale Jr.
President
The Arts League of Michigan, Inc.

O liver Ragsdale Jr. is president of The Arts League of Michigan, Inc., one of the largest minority arts organizations in Michigan. Through its core programs of presenting visual and performing arts and community arts and education, The Arts League serves as a center in the development, presentation, preservation and promotion of the African and African-American cultural arts. President since 1991, Ragsdale serves as the organization's chief executive and program director.

Ragsdale is the immediate past president of the Michigan Association of Community Arts Agencies, having served on the board since 1996. He is a member of the board of the University Cultural Center Association (Detroit) and the Michigan Festivals & Events Association.

An accomplished percussionist, Ragsdale has an extensive professional background. He has performed with such organizations as the Pittsburgh Opera and Ballet Orchestras, the West Shore Symphony Orchestra, the Virginia and Michigan Opera Theatre Orchestras and numerous bands, musicals, touring companies and road shows including Dionne Warwick, Earl "Fatha" Hines, Steve Alien and others.

Arlene M. Robinson
Chief Executive Officer
Girl Scouts of Metro Detroit Council

A rlene M. Robinson, the first black Girl Scout executive in Michigan, has served as chief executive officer of the Girl Scouts of Metro Detroit Council since 2001. Of 312 councils nationwide, GSMD is the seventh largest, providing opportunities to more than 30,000 girls in the metro area. Girls, ages 5 to 17, take advantage of programs including computer safety, diversity awareness, human sexuality, substance abuse prevention, conflict resolution and myriad age appropriate services.

Previously, Robinson served as a City of Detroit mayoral appointee, building the youth department from the ground up. Her past positions include administration vice president of the Detroit Economic Growth Corporation; president of Efficacy Detroit; and president of the Community Training & Development Corporation.

A licensed counselor, Robinson holds a master of arts degree from the University of Detroit, and a Wharton School executive leadership development certificate. She has advanced education in business administration from Wayne State University.

Robinson served as the first black working president of the Junior League of Birmingham. She works on numerous boards, commissions and committees and has received recognition for her community service.

A da Smith is the director of chapter development and community relations for the Detroit chapter of the Black Alliance for Educational Options. There, she is responsible for coordinating membership activities and community events for the chapter. She facilitates workshops, meetings and conferences for the local and national organization, and advises local affiliate organizations.

Ada is quickly becoming a local advisor on issues concerning educational choice and youth. She spearheaded a new summer festival for the city of Highland Park, Market on Manchester. In 2006 *Crain's Detroit Business* honored her as one of Detroit's Top 30 Under 30.

Ada received a bachelor's degree and a master's degree in counseling from Xavier University of Louisiana. In 2005 she was one of the youngest graduates of the Detroit Regional Chamber of Commerce Leadership Detroit program.

A native of Detroit, Ada is a graduate of Cass Technical High School, where she serves as vice president of the alumni association. She is a partner is JAS Events, a local full-service event planning company.

Ada Smith
Director, Chapter Development &
Community Relations
Black Alliance for Educational Options

P reviously serving as grants manager, Christopher Smith became chief operating officer for the Southeast Michigan Community Alliance (SEMCA) in March of 2002. Since then, he has made his mark as a leader and continues to bring his knowledge and expertise to the forefront. His role as chief operating officer includes overseeing the daily operations of the Substance Abuse Services program and the Workforce Development program.

Before working at SEMCA, Smith was a relation's consultant for United Way Community Services, and assistant regional director and director of grants and government affairs for New Passages, a mental health treatment agency.

Active in numerous organizations, Smith is a member of the National Association of Social Workers, the American Society for Public Administration, the Detroit-Wayne County Mental Healthy Agency advisory council, the Michigan Association of Substance Abuse Coordinating Agencies and Alpha Phi Alpha Fraternity, Inc.

Smith received his bachelor's degree from Michigan State University and two graduate degrees from Wayne State University.

Smith is an avid runner and enjoys spending quality time with his wife and two children.

Christopher B. Smith
Chief Operating Officer
Southeast Michigan
Community Alliance

COMMUNITY LEADERS

Claudette Y. Smith, Ph.D.
Executive Director
Coleman A. Young Foundation

Dr. Claudette Y. Smith is executive director of the Coleman A. Young Foundation. In this role she oversees an organization that provides college scholarships and other programs for personal and academic growth to Detroit's youth.

Before joining the Coleman A. Young Foundation, Smith was program officer at the Skillman Foundation. She came to Skillman after ten years in various positions with New Jersey's Department of Higher Education. She previously worked as a statistician/demographer for the United Nations in New York City.

Smith earned her doctorate in sociology and demography from Princeton University, a master's degree in demography from the London School of Economics and Political Science, and a bachelor's degree from the University of the West Indies. She is an adjunct professor of Wayne State University's sociology department. She sits on several boards and is a graduate of Leadership Detroit Class XXV.

She is married to Locksley A. Smith and is the proud mother of a daughter, Najwa Smith Schmookler, married to Benjamin, and a son, Dia Smith.

William W. Tandy
Director, Upward Bound
Wayne State University

William Tandy is the director of Wayne State University's Upward Bound Program. As the director of Upward Bound, William prepares young students from the city of Detroit for success in a program of post secondary education. He is also the owner and operator of Evolution Lounge, and vice president of Times Square 200, which owns Detroit hot spot, Club Icon. William's nightclubs and lounges are Detroit's best.

Known throughout the Midwest as Detroit's most aggressive and outspoken developer of youth, William has consistently demonstrated a great talent for motivation and leadership. He has the most wins of any coach in Detroit's little league history and he holds the PAL record for most consecutive victories and championships.

William received a bachelor of arts degree from Tennessee State University and was awarded his master's degree in clinical social work from Wayne State University.

A native of Detroit, William is married and belongs to Kappa Alpha Psi Fraternity, Inc.

Alison Vaughn is the founder and chief executive officer of Jackets for Jobs, Inc., a nonprofit organization that provides employment etiquette, career skills training and professional clothes to low-income individuals. Since opening the doors in 2000, the organization has assisted more than 5,000 individuals with employment. This high-profile organization has been supported and applauded by Donald Trump, ABC's *The View*, NBC's *The Today Show*, and Oprah's *O* magazine. A highlight of Alison's career was the distinct honor of ringing the closing bell on NASDAQ.

Alison received a bachelor of science degree from Michigan State University and graduated from the Women's Campaign School at Yale University, sponsored by Yale Law School. She is active with the NAACP and was a candidate for the 2006 Michigan State Senate.

A former model, Alison was a Miss America Petite Pageant contestant, *Jet* Beauty, auto show model and high school homecoming queen.

In her spare time, she enjoys traveling, reading and attending sporting events. She is a loyal Detroit Lions season ticket holder.

Alison Vaughn
Founder & Chief Executive Officer
Jackets for Jobs, Inc.

E'lon-Eloni Wilks is president and founder of the Hospice of Metropolitan Detroit and director/producer of Detroit's longest running radio/television youth and senior citizen program. For more than 30 years, this refreshing, award-winning community affairs program has provided young broadcasters with the opportunity for training in the media.

Wilks works with youth and seniors who have experienced trauma in their lives. She provides counseling and training in the trades of media, construction, plumbing, and electrical skills to help young people find their place in life. She communicates with more than 200,000 students weekly through TV 33, WHPR 88.1, Comcast 20 and Legacy News.

Wilks earned a doctorate from the University of Michigan. She has received numerous awards from organizations including the Black Educators Association, Detroit Public Schools, the Michigan Supreme Court, the Gospel Music Hall of Fame and Museum, BMI Publishers, AIDS Consortium, the Boys & Girls Club of America, Girl Scouts of Metro Detroit, and Easter Seals. She is most proud of her work with emotionally disturbed children, media and the hospice.

E'lon-Eloni Wilks
President & Founder
Hospice of Metropolitan Detroit

COMMUNITY LEADERS

Michael E. Williams
President & Chief Executive Officer
Orchards Children's Services, Inc.

As president and chief executive officer of Orchards Children's Services, Inc., Michigan's premier foster care and adoption agency, Michael Williams has dedicated his life and career in support of all children and their families.

Williams' involvement as a community leader includes active participation in the National Black Child Development Institute. He is president of the Association of Accredited Child and Family Agencies (AACFA). He is a board member for Deaf Options, a corporation providing support services for the hearing-impaired, and MINDS, whose mission is to educate young people about mental illness.

Before becoming president and CEO of Orchards in 2003, he was president of StarrVista care management organization. He is a former executive director of the Hannah Neil Center, a program of Starr Commonwealth. Williams has held a variety of positions, including family services worker and director of several community-based programs. In 1994 he was elected mayor of the City of Albion. He is married and has one daughter.

Cherrie Woods
President
National Black Public
Relations Society
Detroit Chapter

Cherrie Woods is a communications consultant with Eclectic Communications, a company she founded in 1997. She recently held the position of internal communications specialist at the Detroit Institute of Arts and served as chair of the African American subcommittee of the community outreach committee. She has more than eight years of experience in public relations, marketing and community relations.

Woods serves as president of the National Black Public Relations Society – Detroit chapter, and is also a member of the Public Relations Society of America.

Woods has completed a bachelor of arts degree and graduate certificates in corporate communications and human resources management. A native of Canada, she has held high-profile communications positions with Toronto Social Services, Toronto Public Health, and Harbourfront Center, Canada's premier arts and entertainment center. She was featured in *Toronto World Art Scene* and *Sister to Sister* magazine.

Detroit's

MEDIA PROFESSIONALS

"Ability may get you to the top, but it takes character to keep you there."

STEVIE WONDER

SINGER AND COMPOSER

MEDIA PROFESSIONALS

Chuck Bennett
Society Columnist
Detroit News

Sheri Clark Brooks
Chief Executive Officer &
Television Host
WHPR-TV 33/Dynasty Publications

Chuck Bennett gained notoriety at the *Detroit News* for his innovative fashion presentations with multicultural models, and as the first reporter regularly covering R&B. He went on to become interior design editor, men's fashion editor and a weekly columnist. Winner of several local and national awards, including the prestigious Lulu Award for excellence in men's fashion reporting, Bennett left the paper in 1984.

Bennett worked as senior editor at *Detroit Monthly Magazine*; men's fashion editor at *The Jewish News*; fashion director at Broadway Clothing; and editor-in-chief at *Recovery Magazine, Chicago* and *Metro Exposure Magazine*.

Today, back at the *Detroit News*, Bennett continues to be a trailblazer and a rarity among major metropolitan dailies as one of the few African-American males working as a society columnist. Co-founder of *The Real Scoop*, Detroit's online magazine, he also contributes to *Ambassador Magazine, Hour Detroit, African American Family Magazine* and the *Michigan Chronicle*.

Currently, Bennett is a fundraising consultant for Detroit Holiday Meals on Wheels, an organization committed to delivering every homebound senior a nutritious meal every day of the year.

Sheri Brooks is host and executive producer of the literary talk show *Wordz in Motion* on WHPR-TV 33. She is responsible for developing and overseeing production of literary and entertainment projects that have a positive impact on the community. Sheri is chief executive officer of Dynasty Publications, an independent press that publishes books and a literary magazine.

Sheri sits on the National Association of Black Writers' board of directors, is executive chair for Women in Film and Television, Michigan chapter, and is a member of NABFEME. She was featured as one of the top ten Powerhouses in Publishing in the July issue of *WIM* magazine.

In an effort to promote self-publishers and increase literacy rates, Sheri hosts Metro Detroit Literary Collective's Annual Writers Conference and Awards Banquet. She co-sponsors the Beyond the Bars Prison Writing Contest. An active member of Linwood Church of Christ, Sheri is co-founder of Michigan's Leading Ladies of Business.

A native of Detroit, Sheri is a speaker, songstress and spoken word artist. She enjoys teaching a writer's workshop for teens and ministering to young women.

Gary Chandler
Music Director & Mix Show Coordinator
WHTD-FM HOT 102.7
Radio One Detroit

Donafay Collins
On-Air Personality
WMXD MIX 92.3
Clear Channel Radio

DJ Gary Chandler, Detroit's bad boy, has been in and around the music business for 22 years. Best known for his versatility, Gary can rock a party whether the attendees are eight or 80.

Gary's got his start in an unconventional way. His best friend, a local DJ at the time, left town and happened to leave his turntables with Gary. Upon his return, he was astonished to see that Gary was an even better DJ than he was.

Capitalizing on his newfound skill, Gary soon hit the streets, clubs and any party that would have him. After becoming the house DJ for the well-known Club UBQ, his reputation began to precede him. In 1991 a local urban radio station contacted Gary and asked him to come on board.

Gary has been with Radio One Detroit for three years. In his spare time, he enjoys collecting eclectic music, DVDs, hanging out with family and friends, and shopping.

Donafay Collins is an on-air personality for WMXD MIX 92.3 Clear Channel Radio. He is the host of *Black Jam*, a live broadcast in the Greektown Casino in downtown Detroit. It is held every Friday night from 7 p.m. to 12 a.m. The broadcast was originally scheduled for only two weeks, but has now been running for nearly two years.

Donafay is also a police lieutenant in the Wayne County Sheriff's Department. He has been an officer for 17 years and is currently assigned to the Andrew C. Baird Detention Facility, one of the largest jails in America. Donafay has been assigned to several units but has found great satisfaction in his assignment as a school resource officer in the COPS in Schools program.

Donafay attended the University of Detroit and the Specs Howard School of Broadcast Arts.

A native of Kansas City, Kansas, Donafay is the husband of Ranae Collins, and the proud father of two sons, Viticus and Carlos. He also has two daughters, Kristal and Rakya.

MEDIA PROFESSIONALS

Denise Crittendon
Editor
African American Family Magazine

Frankie Darcell
Radio Personality
WMXD Mix 92.3 FM

Denise Crittendon is editor of *African American Family Magazine*, an award-winning lifestyle magazine for black families in metropolitan Detroit. A former editor for the NAACP's *Crisis Magazine*, Crittendon worked for 15 years as a reporter and features writer for the *Detroit News*. She is also a motivational speaker and author of the self-help book, *Girl In The Mirror: A Teen's Guide To Self Awareness*. The book, which focuses on the character development and empowerment of pre-teen and teenage girls, was inspired by her volunteer work at Vista Marie Girls' Home in Dearborn.

Crittendon's awards include the Life Directions' Mary Ball Children's Advocacy Award 2004, the Aisha Shule W.E.B. Dubois Academy's Legacy Award and the Detroit City Council's Spirit of Detroit Award. She was honored by the Women's Informal Network as one of the Most Influential Black Women in Metropolitan Detroit, 2000. Crittendon spent ten months in Harare, Zimbabwe as a 1987 Rotary Foundation ambassador of goodwill. She has received writing awards from the National Association of Black Journalists, Best of Gannett, and Parenting Publications of America.

Before moving to Detroit in 1993, Frankie Darcell started her career at Morgan State University's WEAA FM in Baltimore as an engineer. Since then, she has worked in Raleigh-Durham and Charlotte, North Carolina as a music director and assistant program director.

Frankie is the host of the award-winning shows, *The Mid-day Mix* and *Sunday Morning Talk of the Town*. An author, lecturer and businesswoman, Frankie has appeared on four magazine covers and has been featured in more than 65 newspaper articles and publications. She appears frequently on local and national television and radio programs, discussing topics that matter to the community, specifically, issues relating to the quality of life for women and children. Frankie has a unique way to inspire and empower her listeners and readers, often with great humor.

A graduate of Morgan State University, Frankie has a bachelor of arts degree in telecommunications. She is a member of Alpha Kappa Alpha Sorority, Inc., and the recipient of several major industry awards and recognitions. Her greatest achievement is being a mom. Her daughter, Phallon, gives her the greatest joy.

Kyra Dillard
On-Air Personality
WKQI Channel 955

DJ DDT
Local Music Coordinator
WJLB-FM

K yra Dillard is an on-air personality at WKQI Channel 95.5 on Mojo in the Morning. As a member of the team, she brings her dynamic energy and raw talent to the quirky cast. Since Kyra's addition to the station, the morning show has experienced a rise in ratings.

Kyra has been featured as a hot new addition to Detroit radio in *Michigan Frontpage*, *The Oakland Press* and the *Detroit News*. She compels audiences with her innovative humor and girl-next-door personality. Kyra keeps Detroit on its toes, mingling with stars like socialite Paris Hilton and R&B diva Mary J. Blige. She has matched wits with the best that Hollywood and the music industry have to offer. She has interviewed such artists as Busta Rhymes, P. Diddy, 50 Cent and Detroit's own Eminem.

Kyra earned her bachelor of arts degree in mass communications from Bennett College in Greensboro, North Carolina. She was a founding member of the campus chapter of the Association of Women in Communications.

A native of Columbus, Ohio, Kyra is the youngest daughter of Clarence and Sheila Dillard.

D DT, a DJ of 23 years, began his career at age five. His love of music began with a huge record collection that his father, a former drummer, started for him at age two. In high school, DDT, born Desmond Travis, took a radio class at Golightly Career & Technical Center.

While at Golightly, DDT earned an internship in FM 98 WJLB's promotions department. Showing impressive editing skills, DDT worked as an evening show producer. He succeeded greatly, working as producer of the evening show and afternoon show, mix-show DJ, production assistant, making commercials, and as an on-air personality.

By 1999 he became the DJ for monster group D12 (Shady/Interscope Records). He later became a producer for the morning show, where he had a segment every Wednesday and Thursday called *DDT's New Music Report*. He is now host of *What's Next on the Menu* every Saturday, bringing unsigned Detroit artist to the airwaves. DDT is now producing hit records at Mr. Porter Productions for major artists like D12 and Pharoahe Monch (Universal Records).

MEDIA PROFESSIONALS

DJ Zap
On-Air Personality & Mixer
WHTD-FM HOT 102.7
Radio One Detroit

D J Zap is a connoisseur of music. His broad musical knowledge led him to be dubbed "The Junglist." Zap says he got the name by being the first DJ to make jungle music, a form of music found and played widely in Europe, acceptable for clubs and radio in the U.S.

The HOT 102.7 on-air personality and mixer has been with the station for eight years. Many listeners love him for his immensely popular segment, *Sexin' Next to the Radio* where Zap dons his "slow jams" hat.

Zap, a native Detroiter, got his start in the industry by disc jockeying everywhere he could. A talented turntablist and on-air personality, he has been a presence during some high-profile industry events including the Detroit Electronic Music Festival. He has also been featured in a number of national and local publications. His name was forever imprinted on wax when he, along with Disco D, laid down the 2000 club bangers, "Club Talk" and "I Can Make U." His distinctive style can be heard in the hottest club scenes in the area.

Karen Dumas
Columnist
The Michigan Chronicle

K aren Dumas is a columnist for *The Michigan Chronicle*, a respected local media personality, and president of her own public relations firm. She formerly served as director of culture, art and tourism for the City of Detroit, and as director of community relations for Mayor Kwame M. Kilpatrick.

Dumas joined the Kilpatrick administration after more than 14 years as president of her own PR firm, where she served an impressive list of corporate, entertainment and community clients. She returned to private practice after her tenure with the Kilpatrick administration and hosting her talk-radio show, *Up Front with Karen Dumas*.

Dumas serves on the Michigan Film Commission, the Arts League of Michigan, Sphinx, the Tourism Economic Development Council, and the communication committee for the Riverfront Conservancy. Her achievements have been recognized by The Black Women's Contracting Association, the City of Detroit, and the State of Michigan.

Dumas graduated from East Catholic High School and received a bachelor of science degree in merchandising from Michigan State University. She and her husband, Timothy Cook, reside in Detroit with their two children.

Kenneth H. Frierson Jr.
National Sales Manager
WMYD-TV20 Detroit
My Tv20 Detroit

Mildred Gaddis
Host, *Inside Detroit*
WCHB AM News Talk 1200
Radio One Detroit

In January of 2004, Granite Broadcasting Corporation announced Ken Frierson as the national sales manager for Detroit's WDWB-TV20, now WMYD-TV20. With 16 years of experience, he has solidified the station's market position and made a greater presence in national sales.

Prior to joining TV20, Frierson served as general sales manager/national sales manager at another Granite station, WTVH-TV in Syracuse, New York, and as national sales manager of Granite-owned WEEK-TV in Peoria, Illinois. Frierson began his sales career in the Flint, Michigan market. His background at WEYI and WNEM-TV in Flint included positions as national sales manager, regional sales manager and account executive. There, he distinguished himself as Sales Person of the Year, and received several New Business Awards and the Human Relations Award. He was named the Distinguished Sales Achiever by sales and marketing executives in 1997 and 1998.

A native of Saginaw, Michigan, Frierson received a bachelor of science degree in speech communications from the University of Wisconsin-Superior. He later joined the staff of Flint's WSMH-TV as an account executive before moving to WNEM-TV.

Mildred Gaddis, a 28-year radio veteran, has been described by the *Detroit Free Press* as one of ten African Americans to watch in Detroit.

In the car, at home or in the office, listeners tune in to her sometimes no-nonsense, warm and inspiring style as the host of *Inside Detroit* on WCHB AM News Talk 1200 weekday mornings from 6 a.m. to 10 a.m. According to Arbitron Ratings Services, Gaddis continues to rank as the top morning show host with listeners who spend the longest time listening.

A native of Hattiesburg, Mississippi, Gaddis arrived in Detroit 17 years ago and has built an immensely successful career in Detroit radio. Her skills enabled her to travel to China with former Detroit Mayor Dennis Archer and former Michigan State Governor John Engler.

Gaddis was recently named Professional Woman of the Year by the National Association of Negro Business Women. She is also a member of the Detroit Urban League board.

A graduate of Texas Southern University, she is the mother of a 16-year-old daughter, Khia.

MEDIA PROFESSIONALS

Angelo B. Henderson
Host, *Your Voice with Angelo Henderson*
WCHB-AM 1200
Radio One Detroit

Pam Jackson
Anchor, Reporter & Producer
WWJ Newsradio 950

Your Voice with Angelo Henderson airs weeknights on WCHB-AM 1200 from 7 to 9 p.m.

A Pulitzer Prize-winning host, Angelo B. Henderson has a wealth of journalism experience with *The Wall Street Journal*, the *Detroit News*, the *St. Petersburg Times* in Florida and *The Courier-Journal* in Louisville, Kentucky. He was named one of 39 African-American Achievers to Watch in the Next Millennium by *Success Guide* magazine. Angelo has also been honored by Columbia University as one of the nation's best reporters on race and ethnicity in America.

Angelo was an ordained deacon at Hartford Memorial Baptist Church in 1999 and was ordained and licensed as a member of the clergy under Pastor Charles G. Adams in December of 2003. He is currently the associate pastor of worship, vision and emerging ministries at Hope United Methodist Church in Southfield.

A member of Phi Beta Sigma Fraternity, Inc., Angelo earned a bachelor of arts degree in journalism in 1985 from the University of Kentucky.

He is married to Felecia Dixon Henderson. They reside with their son in Pontiac, Michigan.

Pam Jackson has been an anchor, reporter and producer for WWJ Newsradio 950 since November of 2003. She recently became producer, in addition to her responsibilities of anchoring and serving as an in-house and field reporter.

Pam's love for writing has taken her down many avenues in life. Writing for *The Lima Voice*, she had a column, "It's a Spiritual Thang". The column allowed her to voice her opinion on how spirituality drives everything. It also sparked her passion to write her first book.

Pam received a bachelor of arts degree in journalism from Wayne State University, and a diploma from the Specs Howard School of Broadcast Arts in 1995.

A native of Detroit, Pam loves reading, writing and dancing. She is currently working on her first short film.

Kim James
Mix Show Coordinator
FM98 WJLB & WMXD-FM

Keith Jones
On-Air Personality
WHTD-FM HOT 102.7
Radio One Detroit

A Detroit native, Kim "The Spin Doctor" James, has been on air for 15 years at a station that has been ranked in the top ten for nearly thirty years. He is the mix show coordinator for both FM98 WJLB and WMXD-FM. Kim is the man behind *High Noon Hot Mix* and *Lunch Music Café*. He was recently named assistant programming director for the new sister station to WJLB, WJLB HD. Kim is the official DJ for *Old School Sundays*, which has been going strong for more than ten years. He is also one of six nationally recognized DJs with the New Pepsi DJ Division.

In 2000 this driven mixer launched The Seven Deadly Techniques, a group comprised of Kim and six additional mixers, to set the tone of what a radio mixer and a party/club jock should be.

In addition to his many accomplishments, Kim is now venturing into other business affairs. He recently unleashed his own company, Millennium Marketing, which is quickly becoming one of the city's premiere companies in the entertainment world.

K eith Jones began his career at the age of 11 years, singing in the youth choir. Shortly thereafter, he was introduced to hip-hop. He immediately took a liking to disc jockeying, making mix tapes for his buddies in junior high school and spinning at school dances.

Keith continued disc jockeying and working as an MC until his true calling presented itself in the form of on-air Cleveland personality, Lynn Tolliver. Keith listened to Lynn faithfully and soon decided that he wanted to be an on-air talent like his idol. Upon graduation from high school, he enrolled at Columbus State, where he majored in business management, aspiring to own his own radio station. In the fall of his sophomore year, Keith began an internship with a local Ohio radio station.

Keith is a member of Alpha Phi Alpha Fraternity, Inc. His community service includes speaking to students, as well as working with less-privileged families.

Keith is a devoted father, and a recently married man. He can be heard on HOT 102.7, weeknights from 6 p.m. to 10 p.m.

MEDIA PROFESSIONALS

Kapri
Morning Show News Producer
Producer, *That's What Up*
FM98 WJLB

Emery C. King
Director of Communications
Detroit Medical Center

Born and raised in Detroit, Kapri has always been in love with radio. As a child, she was given a boom box and a microphone. Instead of singing or rapping along to songs, Kapri pretended to be an MC.

While studying radio and television at the Specs Howard School of Broadcast Arts, she earned an internship at Detroit's heritage station, WJLB. In 2003 Kapri's hard work, dedication and passion paid off. WJLB hired her as the afternoon show producer, and she landed her first on-air shift at WQHH in Lansing. Kapri is currently holding down two positions, WJLB morning show/news producer, and producer of WJLB's Sunday talk show, *That's What's Up.*

Kapri believes that in order to succeed in this industry, you have to have a positive attitude and the right mentality. She has two jobs, but she is also a 4.0 full-time student.

Kapri strongly believes in giving back to the community. She speaks at local schools, volunteers for the Boys & Girls Club and donates to positive community causes.

For 19 years, Emery King served as a key member of WDIV-TV's number one rated news team. He was a White House correspondent for NBC-TV's national news. Currently, King serves as director of communications for the Detroit Medical Center, which operates nine hospitals and institutions.

King and his wife, Jacqueline Casselberry King, started Kingberry Productions in 1993 and produced a series of documentaries exploring the history of African Americans.

NBC's white paper documentary, *America: Black and White*, earned King a first place award in the Monte Carlo International Film Festival. He received an Emmy award for Best News Anchor in Detroit, and won awards for Best Hard News Reporting and Best Documentary (*The Rouge*). Kingberry Productions won local and national awards for its documentaries, most of which are currently part of university and library collections.

Governor Jennifer Granholm appointed King as chairman of the Michigan Film Advisory Commission. He also sits on the board of the Michigan Multiple Sclerosis Society and the board of visitors for Wayne State University's School of Communication and Performing Arts.

MEDIA PROFESSIONALS

Lady BG
On-Air Personality
WDMK 105.9 Kiss-FM
Radio One Detroit

Ed Love
Host, *Destination Jazz: The Ed Love Program*
WDET 101.9 FM
Detroit Public Radio

Lady BG joined the Radio One family at the inception of Kiss in August of 1999 as an on-air personality and assistant program director. She has lived in Detroit and worked in the radio industry for more than 12 years.

Born and raised in Institute, West Virginia, a small college community that surrounds West Virginia State University, Lady BG has always felt a passion for music and was bitten by the radio bug long ago. After graduating from West Virginia State University with a bachelor's degree in mass communications, she pursued a career in radio.

Her 20-year radio career has taken her to numerous cities across the country. In addition to her radio career, Lady BG has done an incredible amount of voice-over work. Her voice can be heard on commercials throughout the country on radio and television. She is also a member of the Screen Actors Guild.

Listeners love the vibe of her *Kisses After Dark* show on weeknights from 6 p.m. to 11 p.m. Lady BG is also a newlywed.

For nearly 25 years, Ed Love has delighted listeners with *Destination Jazz: The Ed Love Program* on weekday evenings on WDET 101.9 FM. Ed's passion for jazz and radio dates back to his youth in Parsons, Kansas. He began broadcasting in Detroit in 1960 and joined WDET in 1983. Ed also hosted *The Evolution of Jazz*, a nationally syndicated program, which was carried on 125 stations.

Ed was honored with the Distinguished Achievement Award from the Motor City Music Foundation. He has received two Spirit of Detroit Awards, and recognition by two Wayne County executives, the Michigan House of Representatives, the Michigan Senate, the Congressional Black Caucus and the National Broadcast Awards.

The Southeast Michigan Jazz Association recognized Ed for his outstanding contribution to jazz and the arts. In 2005 he received the Detroit Jazz Guardian Award from the Music Hall Center for the Performing Arts and the Detroit International Jazz Festival. He was also recognized by the Oakland County Chapter of The Links, Inc. Ed has served as senior program consultant for the Detroit International Jazz Festival since 2000.

MEDIA PROFESSIONALS

Sharon McClendon
Director of Community Affairs/Producer
WMYD-TV20 Detroit
My TV20 Detroit

Sharon McClendon serves as WMYD-TV20's primary community liaison. She firmly believes that creating stronger ties and partnerships will benefit the community and she continually works to expand and strengthen those ties on behalf of the station.

McClendon has 17 years of experience in broadcasting, both in front of and behind the camera. She worked in news at WKBD-TV and WMXD 92.3, as well as for several independent production companies. She has received honors for her work on documentaries. *A Woman's Town* is catalogued in the Library of Congress and *A Basilica for Africa* was accepted as an official chronicle for Africa's Ivory Coast.

McClendon developed, produced and co-hosted her own show, *Studio Detroit* (1996-97). She is a governor and education coordinator of the Michigan Chapter of the National Academy of Television Arts and Sciences. She serves on several community advisory boards, and is the recipient of a variety of community service awards.

McClendon is the co-creator and producer of TV20's long-running community affairs campaign, Positively Detroit. She is a two-time Emmy Award recipient.

Montez Miller
President & Chief Executive Officer
The Montez Group

Montez Miller is president and chief executive officer of The Montez Group, a national television production company that offers production services, video promotions and celebrity bookings. In this position, she has worked with such media giants as Bishop T.D. Jakes, Bow Wow, Will Smith, Diddy and Janet Jackson.

With a career in entertainment spanning more than 20 years, Miller has worked for Fortune 500 companies including Black Entertainment Television and PolyGram's Island Black Music.

Following God's inspiration, Miller returned to Detroit and joined GlobalHue as executive talent director. There, she continued to build and maintain relationships, which led her to form her own company, The Montez Group, in July of 2004.

Miller's work can be seen on BET. She is the producer of Comcast Detroit's *City Highlights* with host Kathy Young-Welch. She is the executive producer of the Telly Award-winning reality show, *A Dose of Reality* on Comcast Detroit and the Black Family Channel.

A graduate of the Specs Howard School of Broadcast Arts, Miller is a member of Second Ebenezer Church.

Monica Morgan
Photographer

Jamillah A. Muhammad
Program Director
WMXD/Clear Channel Radio

Monica Morgan is more than just a photographer - she lives her life through the lens. One of Detroit's most widely acclaimed photojournalists, Monica has been honored as the recipient of a 2003 SBC African American Excellence Award, and was voted one of Detroit's Most Influential Women, and a Leader of the 21st Century. She is featured in a national 30-minute documentary.

Monica's work has appeared internationally via the Associated Press Worldwide, Wireimage.com and *Newsweek Japan.* Her credits include *Ebony, Jet, O* magazine, AOL, ESPN.com, *In Touch Weekly, Entertainment Weekly, US Weekly* magazine, the *New York Daily News, Black Enterprise Magazine, Essence* and *TV Guide.* It has appeared in the *Detroit News,* the *Detroit Free Press,* the *Michigan Chronicle,* MTV, VH-1 and more.

Currently, Monica has many Fortune 500 clients, including General Motors, DaimlerChrysler, Coca-Cola, HBO, Comcast Cable, Marriott, PepsiCo, Kentucky Fried Chicken, Wyndham, Absolut, Anheuser-Busch, and Pizza Hut.

The late Mayor Coleman Young said that Monica was Detroit's best photographer, or as he so aptly put it, "the sure shot." Rosa Parks selected her as her personal photographer.

Jamillah A. Muhammad, affectionately called "Jam," is the program director for WMXD-FM. She is also the president of Image First Productions Inc., an up and coming production company.

Jamillah started her radio career 15 years ago at WGCI-AM in Chicago. She later moved to Milwaukee where she was music director, then assistant program director for WVAZ-FM. She went on to program for WKKV-FM, taking the station's Arbitron ranking from No. 8 to No. 1.

During her early years in radio, Jamillah also worked as an assistant for the Mayor's Office of Special Events helping to coordinate the Chicago Gospel Festival and other special projects.

She is a member of the Chicago Chapter of The Recording Academy, the National Association of Black Female Executives, and the National Association of Black Journalists.

Jamillah has won various community and industry awards, including Urban Adult Contemporary Program Director of the Year Awards from Radio & Records and the Urban Network. She was nominated to be featured in *Crain's Detroit Business'* 40 under 40.

Jamillah resides in Southfield. She is single with no children.

MEDIA PROFESSIONALS

Sarah Norat-Phillips
President & General Manager
WMYD-TV 20

I n May of 1998, Sarah Norat-Phillips was named president and general manager of WDWB-TV, better known as WB20, and currently WMYD-TV. In doing so, she became the first black female to head a major television station in Detroit. Since her appointment, she has committed herself to improving the station's market share, delivering quality programming, and building stronger ties with the Detroit community.

Under her leadership, WB20 became one of the nation's strongest performing WB network affiliates, experiencing both ratings and revenue growth while building a solid foundation and track record of service. Norat-Phillips was successful in acquiring the broadcast rights to the Detroit Pistons after nearly 30 years on WKBD.

Throughout her career, Norat-Phillips has been honored with numerous awards, including the 40 Under 40 Award from *Business First Magazine* and several New York State Associated Press Awards. She is an Emmy Award-winning television writer and producer. She is also a graduate of Leadership Buffalo VI and Leadership Detroit XXII. Involved in various community organizations, she serves as vice chairman of the Arts League of Michigan.

A.J. Parker
On-Air Personality
WDMK 105.9 Kiss-FM
Radio One Detroit

K nown to listeners as "The Diva," A.J. Parker is a 26-year radio veteran. Check her out on WDMK 105.9 Kiss-FM as A.J. delivers today's hottest R&B and yesterday's old school hits during the midday shift, weekdays from 10 a.m. to 2 p.m.

A dynamic public speaker, A.J. calls her start in radio a "fluke." She landed an on-air spot while a student at Michigan State University. A.J. cites her father, Al Benson ("The Ol' Swingmaster"), as her inspiration. He was on the air from 1950-1975.

A.J. is also the voice of the WNBA champions, the Detroit Shock. Gaining experience in various markets before landing in Detroit, A.J. co-hosted the nationally syndicated talk show *Jerry Springer*, and facilitated the nightly Illinois State Lottery drawing on the Superstation WGN before the Chi-town wind blew her to WDMK 105.9 Kiss-FM. From co-hosting the morning show to now hosting her own slot during middays, 105.9 Kiss-FM would be incomplete without "The Diva."

Deborah Smith Pollard, Ph.D.
Associate Professor
University of Michigan Dearborn

Ramona Prater
Traffic & News Director
MIX 92.3

D r. Deborah Smith Pollard is an associate professor of English and humanities at the University of Michigan Dearborn. From 2002 to 2006, she served as director of the African and African American studies program.

Pollard, who has lectured internationally on gospel music, has published articles in academic and popular journals. Her latest research will be featured in her upcoming book, *When the Church Becomes Your Party: Essays on Gospel Music at the Turn of the Twenty-First Century*, and in two anthologies, *More Than the Blues* and *Contemplating Black Music*.

Pollard, host/producer of *Strong Inspirations*, can be heard Sundays from 6 a.m. to 10 a.m. on FM98 WJLB. She was named Gospel Announcer of the Year during the 2005 Stellar Awards. An Emmy Award-winning producer for *GodSounds*, which aired on WDIV-TV Channel 4, Pollard has also produced events since the 1980s, including the McDonald's GospelFest and the Motor City Praisefest.

Pollard earned her bachelor's degree and doctorate from Michigan State University. She holds a master of arts degree in teaching from Wayne State University.

She has been married to Basil since 1997.

R amona Prater was raised on the northwest side of Detroit with her 13 brothers and sisters. They lived on Archdale Street near the Grand River/Fenkell/Southfield intersection. Ramona went to Cooke Elementary School in Rosedale Park, learned how to skip at Cervany Middle School on Puritan and Hubbell Streets, and won "Class Hair" and "Class Clown" superlatives at Redford High School.

Growing up she shopped on Grand River Avenue and Greenfield Road. Ramona later permed and cut hair at her own salon on Burt Road near 6 Mile. She is a 7 Mile-cruising, Belle Isle-picnicking, gator-having, weave-wearing Lions fan and Pistons fanatic!

Ramona spends her mornings broadcasting live news, weather and traffic reports on MIX 92.3-FM to Detroit commuters driving along the Lodge, Jeffries, Reuther and Southfield freeways. Many of whom are driving Ford-modeled cars, which her daddy assembled for 37 years!

Ramona lives, drinks, dances and dines in downtown Detroit. She is a self-professed Detroitaholic, to which there is no cure!

MEDIA PROFESSIONALS

Charles Pugh
Newscaster
FOX 2

Reverend Mother
Host
WMUZ Gospel Station

Born and raised in Detroit, Charles Pugh is a newscaster, talk show host, commentator, public speaker, college instructor and business owner. He started Charles Pugh Productions in 2006.

Born on August 3, 1971, Pugh grew up on the west side near Dexter and Davison, and in a community called Research Park. His parents were George and Marcia Pugh. He was raised primarily by his grandmother, Margaret Pough, after the deaths of his parents.

Pugh attended Balch Elementary, Edmonson Elementary, Pelham Middle School and Murray-Wright High School. He graduated from the University of Missouri-Columbia with a degree in broadcast journalism in 1993.

One of very few openly gay African-American journalists in America, Pugh has reported and anchored at KOMU-TV in Columbia, Missouri; WIBW-TV in Topeka, Kansas; WKJG-TV in Fort Wayne, Indiana; and WAVY-TV in Norfolk, Virginia. In Detroit, he has worked for WJBK-TV; WCHB-AM; and WJLB-FM.

Pugh has guest lectured at several universities including the University of Michigan and Hampton University. He also taught class at Wayne County Community College.

Pugh has one brother, one sister, two wonderful nieces, and one marvelous nephew.

Known as "Reverend Mother" to her many listeners, Norma Jean Pender hosts *In the Spirit with Rev. Mother* on 1340-AM, the WMUZ gospel station. Her radio show has been rated the No. 1 gospel music show in the state of Michigan. Pender is also an ordained minister and has served as the assistant pastor at New Jerusalem Baptist Church in Detroit, Michigan for two years.

Pender has distinguished herself with more than 50 years of participation in the realm of gospel music. Her extensive knowledge of gospel music history, artists and music personalities has given rise to her acclaim and prominence. A native of Pittsburgh, Pennsylvania, Pender began her formative piano training, singing and directing in the gospel choir at Central Baptist Church under the pastorate of the late Dr. Cornell E. Talley.

At the inception of the Gospel Music Workshop of America in 1967, the founder and president, Reverend James Cleveland, appointed Pender as the national public relations director, a position she has held for 39 years.

Rochelle Riley
Columnist
Detroit Free Press

Smiley
On-Air Personality
WHTD-FM HOT 102.7
Radio One Detroit

Rochelle Riley writes an op-ed column for the *Detroit Free Press*. She co-hosts a weekly talk show on Detroit Public Television, *Am I Right?* She also offers commentary on National Public Radio and MSNBC.

Rochelle has been nominated four times for the Pulitzer Prize, and the Michigan Press Association has twice named her the state's Best Local Columnist. She has won writing awards from the Charles E. Scripps Award Foundation, the Society of Professional Journalists, the Detroit Press Club Foundation, the National Association of Black Journalists, Michigan Associated Press, and the American Association of Sunday and Feature Editors. In 1996 her debut column for *The Courier-Journal* in Louisville, Kentucky helped spur an $80 million campaign to build a museum honoring boxer and humanitarian Muhammad Ali. It opened last November in Louisville, Ali's hometown.

Rochelle earned her journalism degree from the University of North Carolina at Chapel Hill. She is a member of Delta Sigma Theta Sorority, Inc., and is completing her first novel. She is the proud mother of a 17-year-old actress and future pre-school teacher.

Detroit's own Smiley has been an on-air personality at HOT 102.7 for three years, but she has 15 years of experience in the entertainment industry under her belt.

Those who listened to Detroit hip-hop in the late 1980s probably remember the line, "Smiley... but I'm not friendly, for the simple fact that it's just not in me..." That was from this industry vet's first rap single, *Smiley, But I'm Not Friendly*, released in 1989 and certified gold.

In addition to hearing her funny wit and charm over the airwaves, Smiley can also be seen in action on television every Saturday at noon on Comcast Channel 6. She is the executive producer/editor and host of Detroit's number one music video show, *The Smiley Show*. Every local and national artist or group passing through town stops by *The Smiley Show*. She is always out and about, covering every hot event in the city.

Smiley can be heard every Monday through Thursday, and again on Sundays, from 10 p.m. to 2 a.m. on HOT 102.7.

MEDIA PROFESSIONALS

Spudd
Program Director & On-Air Personality
WHTD-FM HOT 102.7
Radio One Detroit

Suga Rae
On-Air Personality
WHTD-FM HOT 102.7
Radio One Detroit

Socially conscious, fiercely dedicated and undeniably gifted, Spudd is the program director and afternoon drive personality at WHTD-FM HOT 102.7. He is a major influence on what is hot in Detroit's music scene.

Spudd listens when the streets are talking, translating records and urban lifestyle into ratings. Consistently number one in his time slot, listeners turn to him for everything ranging from politics to entertainment. He is informative and entertaining, often raising thought-provoking topics. As program director, Spudd leads a creative team of on-air personalities and mixers. "Every program director wants to be number one in the market, and I'm no exception, but my ultimate goal in this position is to make radio legends; personalities that go on to do great things for the community and the music industry," he says.

Hailing from Junction City, Kansas, Spudd has been with Radio One since 1998. His radio career spans 15 years and various cities.

Spudd has one son. He credits his mother and grandmother, who played major roles in shaping his life, with the old school lessons he has learned.

Starting her career with Radio One Detroit as a high school reporter, Suga Rae's talent, strong personality, will, drive and determination soon led her to an on-air position with the company's urban mainstream station. After advancing from a nighttime gig to a morning show, Suga Rae is showing the city how the ladies do it, holding down her own timeslot during the day with the famed *Suga's House*.

Suga Rae's hobbies include traveling, reading and listening to her favorite artist, Common. A self-proclaimed shopaholic, Suga loves perusing through vintage stores for pieces that complete her unique style. She is truly a trendsetter. A powerhouse in the clubs, Suga is frequently requested as host and MC for various events throughout the city.

With show staples that keep her listeners laughing and informed at the same time, Suga Rae gets them through the day with Suga's Celeb News, Gimmie 5 and Suga's Music Trivia.

Suga can be heard on HOT 102.7, weekdays from 10 a.m. to 2 p.m.

Vickie Thomas
City Beat Reporter
WWJ Newsradio 950
CBS Radio

Melissa Thrasher
Public Relations Practitioner
Southeast Michigan Community Alliance

Vickie Thomas is the city beat reporter for WWJ Newsradio 950. In addition to covering Detroit politics, Thomas covers breaking news, as well as an array of stories as the morning drive reporter. She also hosts *Ask The Mayor*, a live call-in show with Detroit's mayor.

Thomas is the recipient of awards from the Detroit Press Foundation, the Michigan Association of Broadcasters, the Michigan Associated Press and the National Association of Black Journalists. She received the national Gabriel Award from UNDA-USA for the WWJ Black History Month series, *The African-American Church: The Heart and Soul of Metro Detroit's Black Community*.

Thomas attended Michigan State University and graduated cum laude from Wayne State University with an honors degree in broadcast journalism. The highlight of her academic career was serving as an intern for Congressman Louis Stokes' office on Capitol Hill. She was instrumental in getting legislation passed honoring Olympic gold medalist Jesse Owens.

Thomas loves to travel. Among her favorite trips are the South of France, Italy, England, Greece and Spain.

Melissa Thrasher is creative, unique, and a strong communicator. She works as a public relations practitioner for the Southeast Michigan Community Alliance (SEMCA), where she organizes events and writes and pitches stories to the media. Previously, she worked at Campbell and Company in Dearborn, Michigan, where she conducted public relations for Ford Motor Company's special events.

Thrasher graduated from Michigan State University with a degree in journalism and an emphasis in broadcasting. Her knowledge of the media stems from her print and broadcast internships at WLNS Channel 6, Meridian Government Access Channel, Capitol News Service and the CNN Student News Bureau.

Thrasher's accomplishments include implementing a media training seminar for SEMCA and receiving three awards for her work on the Healthy You Tour. She was recently featured in the *Nonprofit Communications Report* regarding two special events she organized for SEMCA. She credits her success to her ability to build and maintain relationships with the media, as well as with colleagues.

Thrasher is a member of PRSA and enjoys spending quality time with her family and friends.

MEDIA PROFESSIONALS

Tune Up
On-Air Personality
WHTD-FM HOT 102.7
Radio One Detroit

Wax Tax-n Dre
Mixer
WHTD-FM HOT 102.7
Radio One Detroit

Tune Up embodies the dynamic power and energy that is radio. The HOT 102.7 on-air personality has been with Radio One Detroit since 1998.

A native of Detroit, his professional radio career began as an unpaid college intern. Tune Up graduated from Northern Michigan University with a degree in language arts and journalism. While working nights for a pop station, he worked another full-time job from 8 a.m. to 5 p.m. His break came when a local urban radio station offered him the traffic reporter/producer position for a popular morning show. From there, the personality "Tune Up Man" was born.

Tune Up is in constant demand from retailers, businesses and clubs. Loyal listeners "tune in" to HOT 102.7 as Tune Up's energy, passion and laughter radiate over the airwaves. Those who happen to meet him while out and about, either at a live broadcast, appearance or club, are quickly pulled in by his intense and infectious enthusiasm.

Tune Up's inspiration for reaching new heights comes from his wife and two sons.

With experience from disc jockeying to promotions, Wax Tax-n Dre began his career thinking that disc jockeying was only a hobby. Soon, people insisted that he DJ parties for them and from there it was on.

After nervously auditioning for a local radio station while spinning live on the air at a club, he waited for a callback, only to learn that the station had already created a commercial announcing Wax Tax-n Dre as their newest DJ. The world famous Wax Tax-n Dre has been with Radio One Detroit for ten years.

Wax is multitalented. As a prominent cast member of the sketch/comedy show, *Switch Play TV*, he has found another love, acting.

A self-proclaimed "tech freak," Wax also loves video games. A native of Ecorse, Michigan, he graduated from Ecorse High School and the Detroit Business Institute.

Throughout his years of spinning, Wax has won numerous awards and clawed in major DJ battles. He is looking forward to his next phase of life, when he plans to make his own video game.

Carolyn K. Worford
Operations & Program Manager
WMYD-TV20 Detroit
My TV20 Detroit

Ya Girl Cheron
Radio Personality
FM98 WJLB

Carolyn Worford's career began as an executive secretary at KMBC-TV in Kansas City, Missouri. After three years, she knew she wanted to stay in television, so she made the move to another station in order to advance. Worford walked in the door as a receptionist and left seven years later as program director.

In 1984 Worford moved to Detroit to work at WJBK-TV as program director. There, she was promoted five times, with her last position being station manager/vice president of program development. In 1998 WDWB-TV/WB20, now WMYD, opened their doors to her as program director. Her duties include managing the programming, community affairs, Internet and news departments, and station operations.

A lifetime member of the National Association of Television Program Executives, Worford served on their board and was board chair in 1995. She is a member and award recipient of the American Women in Radio and Television, a lifetime member of the NAACP, a former board member of the Michigan Chapter of NATAS, a Silver Circle honoree and an alumna of Leadership Detroit IX.

Cheron is the host of *The Quiet Storm* for FM98 WJLB, a Clear Channel station. Her program airs weeknights from 10 p.m to 2 a.m., as she slows it down with a mix of current hits and R&B. Every night, she features a poem from a listener in "Cheron's Spoken Word." At 11 p.m., she opens the Apology Line for listeners' calls. Cheron recently kicked off *Quiet Storm LIVE*, a series of live concerts on the radio, broadcast from a secret location in the city.

Cheron places great importance on giving back to the community. She has been involved in numerous community organizations including Jack & Jill of America, Girl Scouts of America and the American Red Cross. A former debutante, she was honored to host the 2003 Debutante et Les Mere Cotillion Ball.

A member of Bethel AME Church, Cheron lives everyday by the golden rule, "Do unto others as you would have them do unto you."

Detroit's

ENTREPRENEURS

"Any river that forgets its source will dry up."

FRANK YUGO

FROM *AFRICAN QUOTES & PROVERBS*

ENTREPRENEURS

Ty Adams
Founder & President
Heaven Enterprises

A life coach, author and entertainment mogul, Ty Adams is the founder and president of Heaven Enterprises. Her mission and gift is unlocking the hidden potential in both men and women.

Ty is celebrated as the voice of faith and purpose, as well as the pen behind *Single, Saved, and Having Sex.* This bestselling book has everyone talking, including Warner Books, who republished the book after it landed on *Essence* magazine's bestseller list. She has appeared on numerous television and radio programs, including TBN's *Praise the Lord* and *The 700 Club.* Her book landed at number seven on Amazon.com's Top 100.

Often called by her peers, "the Juanita Bynum" of her time, Ty's unique ministry illuminates, yet extends outside the four walls of the church with exploits on the big screen, books, stage plays and lifestyle summits. Her bold approach makes her one of the most sought after speakers in the country. Her motto is, "Helping life, live!"

Brian Alexander
President
Alexander Productions

Brian Alexander is the president of Alexander Productions, a marketing and communications company located in Oak Park, Michigan. He has been in the music media industry as a music/video producer and event coordinator for more than 20 years. In 2003 his company was one of the lead media sources for Jennifer Granholm's gubernatorial campaign, composing the campaign theme song and radio ads. In January of 2005, he directed and produced the entertainment for the Michigan delegation's Inaugural Ball festivities for President George W. Bush at the Smithsonian Museum in Washington, D.C.

Brian recently returned from West Africa as a guest of His Excellency Yahya Jemmah, president of the Republic of The Gambia, where he produced a tourism documentary on the African nation.

Alexander Productions' clients include Mr. Roof, Avis Ford, Merollis Chevrolet, *The Frank Beckman Show,* Hanson's Windows and Siding, Metro Foodland, and the National Multiple Sclerosis Society.

He is a highly sought after motivational speaker, and co-founder of Alexander Briggs & Associates, a multimedia multicultural consulting firm.

Karen Anderson became the first woman president and chief executive officer of City Cab Company since it began more than 70 years ago. Her commitment to inclusion, bringing the owners/operators and staff together, has cultivated a strong since of pride. Karen believes that no one person is bigger than the company.

After receiving numerous awards and accolades for leadership, Karen is reluctant to take credit for doing what she feels is her purpose, serving the community. Her love for people is apparent in all areas of her life. Under her leadership, the City Cab Scholarship Fund was instituted. This scholarship was created for special needs children, and is awarded annually to qualified applicants.

Karen has a degree in business administration and with that she has been able to patent City Cab's logo and market the company in new and innovative ways. City Cab t-shirts and hats have been seen all over the world.

Karen Anderson
Owner & Chief Executive Officer
City Cab Co.

Sarah Bates is the president and chief executive officer of New Technology Steel, LLC. In this position, she is responsible for the profitability of the entire organization. NTS currently has three facilities located in Detroit, Michigan; Erie, Michigan; and Toledo, Ohio. Sarah's objective has always been to build a world-class, minority-owned steel service center by using her developmental, organizational, communication and leadership skills to form a strong and educated workforce.

Sarah is a member of the National Minority Supplier Development Council; Corporate Plus One; the National Association of Women Business Owners; the National Association of Black Automotive Suppliers; the Michigan Minority Business Development Council and many more organizations. She has been featured in *Corp!* as one of the Top 10 Michigan Business Women in 2006; *Fortune;* and is featured in the August 2006 issue of *American Executive*.

A native of Toledo, Ohio, Sarah is happily married to John C. Bates.

Sarah Bates
President & Chief Executive Officer
New Technology Steel, LLC

ENTREPRENEURS

Kimberly A. Black
President & Chief Executive Officer
Black Diamond Entertainment Group
Diamond Acres Urban Network Fund

Kimberly A. Black is the president and chief executive officer of Black Diamond Entertainment Group. With more than two decades of communications experience, Black specializes in advertising, marketing, promotions, media production and special events. Black and Black Diamond Entertainment are committed to maintaining a standard of promotional excellence by leading the market in creativity and originality.

Black Diamond Entertainment has always been on the cutting edge of national special events, advertising, marketing and public relations. Black has worked and produced many promotional events in local, regional and national markets. Among her past clients are Dr. Bobby Jones, Dr. Creflo Dollar, T.D. Jakes Productions, Sound of Gospel record label, The O'Jays, Puff Daddy, Lil' Kim, Slum Village, Eve, Ruff Riders, The Pjazz jazz series, *The Contender* television series, and Emanuel Steward and the Kronk boxing team.

Black also serves as president and chief executive officer of Diamond Acres Urban Network Fund, a nonprofit youth outreach organization, which provides youth with life skills, promotes literacy, and offers boxing and other recreational activities.

Jillian Blackwell
Chief Executive Officer
4LIFE Productions, LLC

Jillian Blackwell is the founder of Urban Gospel Promo the premier advertising and marketing company. Urban Gospel Promo promotes Christian events, artist, businesses, entertainers, etc. In addition, they partner with companies seeking to increase sales and profits through corporate sponsorships. The urban Christian community looks to Jillian's company to provide them with "what's happening" in their community. She is also the founder of First Sundays Detroit. First Sundays Detroit, "A place for the Praise Professional," is the official monthly networking social of Urban Gospel Promo and is designed exclusively for young, professional Christians (21 and older).

Jillian has a passion for young people, which she demonstrates through launching *Urban Gospel News*, an online magazine dedicated to youth written by youth; and by volunteering at Word of Faith International Christian Center's youth department and children's ministry, and the Reggie McKenzie Foundation.

Jillian attends Central Michigan University. She graduated from Domata International Training Bible School in Tallinn, Estonia and Word of Faith Bible Training Center in Southfield.

Happily married to Robert Glynn Blackwell, she has two handsome sons, Mackenzy and Johnathan.

Willie E. Brake is president and chief executive officer of All About Technology, Inc., a company that provides high-quality computer sales, service, training and upgrades for residential and business customers. Willie is also the executive director for the Center for Creative Arts, Inc. and a faculty member at the University of Phoenix. Additionally he serves as a speaker for various organizations.

Prior to the creation of All About Technology, Willie spent more than 12 years in positions of increased responsibility in the automobile, consulting, education and manufacturing industries in locations around the world.

An award-winning hometown hero and international freedom fighter, Willie is a member of various civic, community and philanthropic organizations. These include Alpha Phi Alpha Fraternity Inc., the United Way and Service Corps of Retired Executives (SCORE).

Willie earned a bachelor's degree from Wayne State University and a master of business administration degree specializing in technology management from the University of Phoenix.

A native of Detroit, Michigan, Willie is the proud father of one daughter, Olivia Madison.

Willie E. Brake
President & Chief Executive Officer
All About Technology, Inc.

Wade L. Briggs is an inspiration for African Americans interested in broadcast journalism, business and music production. Known as Butterball Jr., Briggs became a hit DJ at radio station WCHB. In 14 years, he served as program director and operations manager. His talk show, *Rap with Butter*, earned numerous awards for his handling of local and national issues. He coined the phrase "Take your souls to the polls and vote," encouraging listeners to elect Detroit's first black mayor, Coleman A. Young.

In 1982 Briggs became vice president of Barden Communications, Inc., and helped co-found Barden Cablevision of Detroit. Following 14 years as vice president of programming and advertising with Barden, he founded Voice Net Communications and Wade L. Briggs Enterprises, Inc.

Briggs continues to serve his community as an investor in major economic development projects. He is a partner of Alpha Restaurant Group, and Alexander Briggs & Associates. He holds a patent for a home security device, and as a producer, Briggs secured first recording contracts for The Floaters, with *Float On*, and Grammy Award-winning recording artist Anita Baker.

Wade L. Briggs
Founder
Voice Net Communications
Wade L. Briggs Enterprises, Inc.

ENTREPRENEURS

Anthony G. Brogdon
President
Strong Fragrances and Apparel

A consummate entrepreneur, Anthony Brogdon is the president of Strong Fragrances and Apparel. The company produces fragrances for men and women as well a line of signature casual apparel.

Prior to getting into the clothing and fragrance business, Anthony spent ten years in the marketing merchandise business. He has also authored several books on being an entrepreneur in particular states and produced motivational African-American history calendars.

Anthony received a bachelor of science degree in accounting and management information systems from Oakland University in Rochester Hills, Michigan. He has been featured in numerous local and national publications including *Jet* magazine. He has also conducted seminars on the subject of entrepreneurship at the University of Michigan and the University of Cincinnati. He is a member of Oak Grove A.M.E. Church and Alpha Phi Alpha Fraternity, Inc. Anthony also serves as a mentor for V.I.P. Mentoring.

A native of Detroit, Anthony travels extensively throughout the United States and abroad promoting his business. He is married to Marsha Brogdon and has two children, Danielle and Wesley.

Rev. Dr. Velva D. Burley
President
anSpire, LLC

The Reverend Dr. Velva D. Burley was educated in the Detroit Public School system from elementary through high school. After graduating from Detroit Central High School she matriculated to college where she received a bachelor of arts degree in business administration from Michigan State University and a master of science degree in health administration from the University of Detroit Mercy. In May of 2003 she received a master of divinity degree from Ashland Theological Seminary, and in June of 2006 she received a doctor of ministry degree in black church studies from Ashland Seminary in Cleveland, Ohio.

Burley is currently president of anSpire, LLC, a women-owned training and development business. She is one of the co-founders of anSpire Ministries, an outreach ministry based in Detroit.

Burley is an ordained minister and currently serves as an associate minister at Third New Hope Baptist Church in Detroit. She is the proud mother of James Ronald, affectionately known as "big boy James." Her favorite scripture is Philippians 4:13, "I can do all things through Christ who strengthens me."

Annivory Calvert represents winning accomplishments. Recently, she ran successful political campaigns for City Councilwoman Barbara-Rose Collins and for State Representative Elect Coleman A. Young II, her son. This single mom's greatest passion is helping others to accomplish their goals in the spotlight of the stage of life.

She describes herself as both an entrepreneur and intrapreneur. She is a businesswoman who can bring the entrepreneurial mindset to any environment, whether she's running the business or helping employees to be intrapreneurs.

Her work experience spans government, grant funding for AIDS public health services, major housing construction, public and private education, defense engineering administration, a weekly news column, television production/writing and being a non-denominational pastor.

Calvert holds both undergraduate and graduate degrees from Oakland University, where she graduated as the top female student of her class. She also completed graduate studies in educational administration and law at Wayne State University and California Southern Law School. She has certificates in public administration and radio, television and film production, and scriptwriting. She believes life is a journey to help others succeed.

Annivory Calvert
Proprietor
Calvert & Associates

Through the power of radio, television and public speaking, Monique S. Carter has created an unparalleled connection with people around the nation. As a broker and owner of Remerica MSC Realty, she has enlightened and uplifted countless people as she helps them persevere and overcome the trials of today's real estate market.

Monique's accomplishments as a real estate pioneer, educator and businesswoman have established her as a respected and admired public figure, which has granted her the ability to become the finest luxury homes consultant. She was featured in *Unique Homes Magazine*, and is known by her peers and clients as the 30-day specialist, as featured on WMUZ-1340AM.

A Detroit native and devout Christian, Monique attends Second Ebenezer Church under the leadership of Dr. Edgar L. Vann. She strives for excellence and integrity in serving people and promises to give everyone a professional, honest and ethical real estate transaction.

Monique S. Carter
Broker & Owner
Remerica MSC Realty

ENTREPRENEURS

Gwendolyn Esco Davis
President & Chief Executive Officer
The Hascom Group, LLC

Gwendolyn is president and chief executive officer of The Hascom Group, LLC. With more than two decades of operational and management experience, she has developed a keen eye for how businesses get bloated with inefficiencies, cross-purposes, and clouded missions, and how they can retool for a sleeker, smoother, strategically focused organization. As an entrepreneur who is building her own successful consulting practice, Gwendolyn also helps business owners make priorities to create balance.

Gwendolyn is a leader in her community, serving as board vice chair of the Matrix Theatre Company; volunteer for the Detroit Executive Service Core; member of the Detroit Regional Chamber's small business advisory council; and past board president of Preservation Wayne. She was featured in *Who's Who in Professional and Executive Women* in 1987.

Gwendolyn received a bachelor of science degree in math from Shaw College. In 2006 she was awarded a certificate of achievement from Leadership Detroit. She has received numerous commendations from social and civic organizations.

A native of Detroit, Gwendolyn is married to Alex Davis. She is the proud mother of three daughters.

Claudette de la Haye
Event Planner & Photographer

Claudette de la Haye is a self-employed event planner, photographer and reporter in metro Detroit. A former corporate executive administrator and accountant, Claudette now caters a wide range of special events. Her creativity is unlimited, as failure-to-launch projects are not an option. Gumption, commitment and integrity are key to accomplishing tasks on time with exceptional value and service that exceed expectations.

Born and raised in Great Britain, this Afro-Caribbean European native resides in Oak Park, Michigan. Claudette earned a degree in accounting and computer science, as well as a business studies diploma in Nottingham, England. She has also studied French, economics, sociology, English and literature.

While Michigan's recent economic climate has presented challenges, Claudette has managed to network her way to success.

Angela F. Dodd
Regional Director
Decor & You

Angela F. Dodd began her career as a regional director with Decor & You® in 2002. Since launching her interior decorating franchise, Angela has compiled a long list of commercial and residential clients, and her designs have been featured in several local publications, including *Detroit Home Magazine*. As a regional director, she educates her community about unique possibilities for decorating their homes and offices.

Angela came to Decor & You as a marketing and planning professional with a broad base of experience in managing large projects and budgets. Her extensive background in the automotive industry, where she worked in marketing and communications, has provided her the opportunity to combine her analytical skills with her natural creativity.

Angela holds degrees from the University of Chicago Graduate School of Business and the Purdue University College of Engineering. She is a graduate of the Decor & You decorating program, conducted by the company's principals and other industry experts. Of particular significance was her study of advanced design concepts with internationally acclaimed author and designer Mary Gilliatt.

Tanisha Dukes-Parnell
Owner & Operator
A Nu U Mobile Luxury Day Spa

Tanisha Dukes-Parnell is the owner and operator of A Nu U Mobile Luxury Day Spa, servicing the metro Detroit area. The spa offers a variety of services including massage and bodywork techniques for special events such as bridal showers, baby showers, health fairs and pamper parties.

A Nu U was an exclusive participant in the VIP pre-Super Bowl bash for Super Bowl XL, which was hosted on February 5, 2006 in Detroit.

Tanisha is a member of the Associated Bodywork & Massage Professionals. She graduated at the top of her class from the National Institute of Technology Massage Therapy program.

Tanisha is a native of Detroit. She shares her success with her husband, David Parnell Jr., and her three lovely children, Dejah, David and Donovan.

ENTREPRENEURS

Greg Dunmore
President
Jazz Jewels International, Inc.

G reg Dunmore is co-partner of Jazz Jewels International/Pulsebeat International, Inc., an entertainment and special markets promotional agency. He is co-publisher and executive editor of *Venhue Magazine*, an art, entertainment, culture and lifestyle publication. *Venhue* is considered to be one of the finest new magazines produced out of Detroit. Additionally, he is the co-chair of the arts and entertainment task force for the National Association of Black Journalists.

Ivy-league educated and multitalented, Greg has an impressive background. Graduating from Cornell University and the National University of Mexico, he is the former "Hot Happenings" columnist for *Detroit News*. Many Detroiters also remember him as being the "About Town" columnist for the *Michigan Chronicle*. Greg is also the producer and writer of the Emmy-nominated *Detroit Jazz Jewels* television special.

An award-winning fashion designer, he and his mother, Jo Thompson, design elegant women's eveningwear under their label Carlos Nina Couture. Greg is the former vice chair of the Detroit Cable Commission and a former correspondent for Black Entertainment Television.

Victoria B. Edwards
Chief Executive Officer & Founder
vbEdwards Consulting

V ictoria B. Edwards is the chief executive officer and founder of vbEdwards Consulting, a process improvement firm specializing in administration, communications, event planning, time management and leadership training for community, faith-based and nonprofit organizations.

Edwards graduated from Renaissance High School and received her undergraduate degree in business from Marygrove College in Detroit. Her active memberships include the Detroit Association of Women's Clubs, The Mission, Pilgrim Village Association and Westside Mothers. In addition to serving on various committees of the Charles H. Wright Museum of African American History and the Adopt-A-Child Christmas program, Edwards is an independent beauty consultant for Mary Kay cosmetics.

In 2004 Edwards was appointed to the Third Circuit Court of Michigan to provide judicial support, control access to, and coordinate the speaking, public service and committee obligations of a Circuit Court judge.

In all that she does, Edwards' strength comes from the Lord. She attends Northwest Church of God where she serves on the pastor's anniversary committee and is president of the Sisterhood. Her greatest achievement is her daughter Kelly, a senior at Central Michigan University.

Mark England is vastly becoming a household name. As a designer, his close attention to detail is paramount in his designs. His women's collection has received rave reviews and some might say that Mark has the unique ability to bridge the gap between couture in America and ready-to-wear.

Mark has dressed some of the most influential women in Detroit and around the world. From several artists at Bad Boy Entertainment to Omarosa from the famed reality show, *The Apprentice.* These days, Mark is consistently being asked to serve as style expert for celebrities and recording artists such as The Temptations and The Four Tops.

From his humble beginnings in the 1980s as a costume designer to the present, Mark has remained true to his belief that there are no rules in the game of design. If there were, he would break them. Currently Mark is very busy with his successful flagship store located on the hot, trendy block known as "Merchants Row" in downtown Detroit. The focus for this new location is to support Detroit-based designers by carrying their collections.

Mark England
Designer
Mark England De Mode

ViLinda Everett is the founder of Intimate Touch Collections LLC in Westland, Michigan. ITC specializes in sales and professional installation of an array of custom window treatments, special event planning and decorating. Their hallmark is the ability to combine critical aspects of design from conception to completion.

ViLinda's leadership skills are exemplified in a high level of ethical business practices, extensive product knowledge and a strict code of ethics. A member of several trade organizations, she has been recognized as one of the top 100 America's Master Tradesmen in 2005, the 2000 Entrepreneur of the Year, and the 2000 Spirit of Detroit. Her achievements have also been featured in *Window Fashions* magazine and she has received certificates for volunteer services.

ITC is in the development stages of a nonprofit apprenticeship, Windows of Opportunity, teaching the trade of professional installation of custom window treatments. Through classroom instruction, students will learn professionalism, industry terminology, measuring techniques, use of tools and self-sufficiency on a budget.

ViLinda R. Everett
Founder & President
Intimate Touch Collections LLC

ENTREPRENEURS

Grace Gentry
Owner
MissGG Silkscreening

Grace Gentry is the sole proprietor of MissGG Silkscreening in Detroit, Michigan. Her company is certified as a Wayne County Minority and Women Business Enterprise (MBE/WBE). She also participated in the Super Bowl XL Emerging Business program and is listed in the Emerging Business Directory.

Her company screen prints custom and pre-designed graphics for wearable and nonwearable products. Her specialty is decorating T-shirts, tote bags and umbrellas with inspirational messages.

Grace is currently an honor student at Davenport University majoring in health information technology. She will receive her degree in 2007. She has also studied vocal music and piano at Marygrove College and the College for Creative Studies. Grace is a member of Greater Ecclesia Temple and has participated in the Detroit Public Schools as a consultant for the Junior Achievement program.

A native of Trenton, New Jersey, Grace is the daughter of Flora M. Gentry and the late Grady Gentry Sr. Her favorite quote is "Life is a grindstone. But weather it grinds or polishes you is determined by the stuff you are made of."

David Gough
Founder
The International Gospel Music
Hall of Fame and Museum

An entrepreneur, artist, songwriter and producer, David Gough is one of the defining voices in the world of gospel music and entertainment. To many, he is known as the Mayor of Gospel because of his commitment to introducing gospel music and entertainment to mainstream audiences. He started his own gospel label, founded the International Gospel Music Hall of Fame and Museum, and was the first gospel artist to perform at The Festival of the Arts in Kunming, China.

In the early 1970s after completing active duty, Gough moved back to Detroit to pursue his music career. He married his wife, Carolyn, who inspired him to focus his talent on creating gospel music.

To further demonstrate his commitment, in 1995 Gough founded the International Gospel Music Hall of Fame and Museum, dedicated to the preservation and education of gospel music and entertainment.

Today, Gough continues to oversee the growth and direction of the hall of fame, as well as DoRohn Entertainment.

Tyree Guyton is an internationally renowned artist. Primarily a painter and sculptor, he has been described as an urban environmental artist. Tyree has waged a personal war on urban blight on Detroit's east side, transforming his neighborhood into a living indoor and outdoor art gallery. Through his art, he has drawn attention to the plight of Detroit's forgotten neighborhoods and spurred discussion and action.

Tyree studied at the College for Creative Studies in Detroit. His work is featured in the Detroit Institute of Arts, the Studio Museum of Harlem and many others. His work has earned him over eight awards.

Tyree has been featured extensively in major publications, books, magazines, documentaries, and on television, including *The Oprah Winfrey Show*. He was the subject of an Emmy award-winning documentary entitled, *Come Unto Me, the Faces of Tyree Guyton*.

Tyree continues to live and work in the city. He and his wife Jenenne Whitfield, director of the Heidelberg Project, travel and lecture throughout the country and the world.

Tyree Guyton
Founder
Heidelberg Project

Frederick E. Hall is founder and president of Novatech Computer Services and Training Center. This multifunctional operation focuses on computer networking and Web site design, as well as providing training in courseware development. Boasting more than 24 years of experience in the computer service industry, Frederick attributes the company's longevity to the committed efforts of many qualified and dedicated individuals, and their combined vision of superior customer service.

Frederick received a bachelor of science degree from Austin Peay State University in Clarksville, Tennessee. In 1989 he received a master of business administration degree from Wayne State University.

Frederick recently acquired H&P Protective Services, Inc., a security company specializing in providing guard services for corporate events and trade shows.

A member of Alpha Phi Alpha Fraternity, Inc., Frederick serves as a trustee at Tabernacle Missionary Baptist Church, and is actively involved in other community-based organizations.

Frederick E. Hall
Founder & President
Novatech Computer Services and
Training Center

ENTREPRENEURS

Marc W. Hardy
Founder & Chief Executive Officer
SMART Management Group, LLC

Marc W. Hardy is a licensed certified public accountant (CPA) in Michigan and has an extensive background in corporate, financial and business management. He is the founder and chief executive officer of SMART Management Group, LLC, which supplies its clients with professional accounting, fiscal and operational management, general business and administrative related consultation, resources and support services. SMART helps businesses meet and exceed organizational goals to achieve financial accountability, productivity, growth and succession.

A graduate of Morehouse College, Marc is a member of the American Institute of certified Public Accountants, the Michigan Association of Certified Public Accountants, and the National Association of Black Accountants.

Marc is active in his community and has served many organizations including Greater Grace Temple, Omega Psi Phi Fraternity, Inc., 100 Black Men of Greater Detroit, Big Brothers Big Sisters of Metropolitan Detroit, Detroit Regional Chamber's Leadership Detroit, the Booker T. Washington business Association, and the YMCA of Metropolitan Detroit. He has also been appointed to various boards and commissions for the City of Southfield, Michigan by its mayor and city council.

Jeanetta Hill
Chief Executive Officer
Personal Touches by Jeanetta

Jeanetta Hill, president and chief executive officer of Personal Touches by Jeanetta, has managed her company for more than 18 years. Personal Touches is a multifaceted special events production company that provides décor for corporate and social events, grand openings, new product launches, press conferences and marketing promotions.

Hill transforms venues and open spaces by creating image, ambience and excitement. After working in sales for ten years, and education for six, Hill began designing. She discovered a knack for designing and a long list of clients. Using her sales experience and business savvy, she turned her desire into a successful company.

Hill operates her business from an office in St. Louis, and recently opened a new office in Detroit. She has produced a half million-dollar event at the America's Center in St. Louis, dropped 6,000 balloons for President George W. Bush in Arkansas, and provided décor for numerous corporations and organizations.

A native Detroiter, Hill strongly believes that it is our responsibility to give back, so she uses her business as a platform to share with other young entrepreneurs.

Carolyn J. Hopkins
President
De'Spa Elite, Inc.

Carolyn J. Hopkins is president of De'Spa Elite, Inc., and De'Elegance Floral Designs in Detroit. She has been in business for more than 15 years. As the president of two businesses, she oversees day-to-day operations, interacts with customers to ensure good customer relations, and secures major accounts and events for business.

Carolyn is also the owner of Lifestyle Solutions, a company that focuses on educating African Americans on the importance of changing their lifestyles to live longer, healthier lives. She has been featured in *Women's Health Style Magazine* as an outstanding female entrepreneur in the Detroit area.

Carolyn is affiliated with numerous organizations, including the Small Business Administration, the Michigan Minority Business Council board, the Chamber of Commerce, the Booker T. Washington Business Association, the National Association of Women Business Owners, and the Women's Economic Club.

Carolyn's hobbies include decorating, floral designing, walking, working out and cooking. A native of Tennessee, she is married to Larry Hopkins, and is the mother of Frenchie LaMont Hopkins in Brentwood, Tennessee. She is the grandmother of Layla Simone, age two.

Jacob B. Keli
President & Chief Executive Officer
Kaskel Construction Company, Inc.

Jacob Keli is president and chief executive officer of Kaskel Construction Company, Inc. He has more than 20 years of experience in finance and accounting, banking, economic development, public relations, international trade and corporate management. Previously, he was assistant vice president of civic and community affairs for NBD Bank, now JP Morgan Chase, a leading national and international financial service institute in the U.S. In his role as president and CEO of Kaskel, a successful and reputable construction company, Jacob has successfully secured construction and rehabilitation projects in both the private and public sectors.

Jacob graduated from Wayne State University with bachelor's degrees in economics and international relations. He earned master's degrees in international economics and political science from the University of Detroit-Mercy.

Jacob is a member of Phi Sigma Alpha, a political science honor society. He is a recipient of the President's Commission on the White House Fellowship Regional Award. An active member of the Detroit Lions Club and the International Rotary Club of Metropolitan Detroit, Jacob recently received the Paul Harris Rotarian Award for his humanitarian achievements.

ENTREPRENEURS

Lyn Lewis
President
LL & Associates Inc.

D r. Lyn Lewis is the former chair of the sociology department and currently professor of sociology at the University of Detroit Mercy. She is also a prominent consultant, educator, evaluator, researcher and motivational speaker. President of LL & Associates Inc., Lewis has appeared on CNN, BET and FOX national news. In addition, she has established a solid reputation in the media in metropolitan Detroit. She has appeared on numerous shows and newscasts on all television stations in the Detroit area.

At the age of 20, Lewis entered the graduate program at the University of Tennessee, becoming the first African American to earn a master of arts degree in sociology. She became an instructor of sociology at Spelman College at 21 years old, remaining there for three years.

Motivated by her thirst for knowledge, Lewis completed her doctor of philosophy degree at Wayne State University in 1978, with a major in sociology. Her specialties were industrial sociology and ethnic and race relations. Lewis was one of the first three African Americans to earn this degree in the history of the institution.

Sharon Mann
Chief Executive Officer
GE Distribution Services L.L.C.

S haron Mann is the chief executive officer of GE Distribution Services, a full-service promotional products agency. She has more than 20 years of experience helping customers achieve their marketing and advertising objectives by providing them with corporate awards, image apparel and advertising specialties.

Sharon has a passion for the business and always strives to exceed her customer's expectations. She builds strategic relationships with her clientele to ensure repeat business and referrals. The company's motto is "to provide excellent service at exceptional prices with on-time delivery."

Sharon has received awards for outstanding member in the National Coalition of 100 Black Women, outstanding member in the Southern Oakland County branch of the NAACP, and the Spirit of Detroit proclamation. She was also published in *Who's Who of Women Executives* and *Who's Who of American Women*.

Most recently, Sharon's company secured and executed a contract to manage and operate four stores selling official licensed 2006 Superbowl merchandise at the NFL Detroit headquarters in the GM Renaissance Center.

Sharon received a bachelor of arts degree from the University of Iowa.

D arci E. McConnell, president and founder of McConnell Communications, Inc., is an established communicator whose company has experienced great growth and success since its inception in 2004. Her clients include Governor Jennifer M. Granholm, casino mogul Don H. Barden, Think Detroit PAL, Siebert Brandford Shank & Co., the Wayne State University School of Social Work and Laborers Local 1191. Located in the heart of downtown Detroit, her company provides media relations, crisis management and media training services. The company is a member of the Detroit Regional Chamber and is MMBDC certified.

Before launching her company, Darci spent 14 years as an award-winning journalist, working in Washington, D.C., Detroit, Grand Rapids and Lansing, Michigan newspapers, including *USA Today*. She regularly provides political analysis to area mediums, including WDIV-TV, WWJ Newsradio 950 and WXYZ-TV.

Darci attended the University of Michigan and holds a bachelor's degree in English and communication. She is also an adjunct professor of communication and fine arts at Wayne State University.

Currently, Darci sits on the board of the Detroit Community Initiative.

Darci E. McConnell
President & Founder
McConnell Communications, Inc.

S haron L. McWhorter, president of American Resource Training System, Inc., is an alumna of Cass Technical High School. She is a highly intensive individual with a talent for identifying problems and developing effective solutions.

McWhorter has more than 25 years of experience in the areas of business management, innovation, credit awareness, customer care and strategic planning. She is highly respected as a course developer, strategist, relationship specialist, violence/conflict and change management facilitator and lecturer.

Active in community affairs, McWhorter serves as chair on the Detroit Empowerment Zone Development Corporation, and is a gubernatorial appointee to the Collections Practices board. She sits on the board of directors for Matrix Human Services, ZIAD Health Services, and the Inventors Council of Michigan. An NANBPW member, she has also been involved with the Museum of African American History, the Detroit Public School transition team, and the Wayne County chapter of MADD. McWhorter is a contributing writer for *OurPC Magazine*.

A graduate of Wayne State University, McWhorton has two patents and certifications in sound board engineering and international training.

Sharon McWhorter
President
American Resource Training
System, Inc.

ENTREPRENEURS

Terri Moon
Owner
Terri Moon and Associates

Terri Moon is a dynamic business executive with more than 20 years of operations, global purchasing, and strategic planning experience. She is a visionary who creates opportunities, builds strong teams and delivers results. Moon is an outstanding communicator with finely-honed negotiation skills and a reputation for leadership.

Moon has excelled in nontraditional roles in one of the world's most traditional business sectors, the automotive industry. She held executive positions at General Motors and The Bing Group. Her accomplishments in the auto industry are widely-recognized and she often mentors young business professionals with executive aspirations.

In 2005 Moon launched her consulting firm, Terri Moon and Associates and has developed a reputation among her clients as a dedicated, creative and results-focused consultant with a talent for resolving complex organizational issues. Moon helps transform businesses and nonprofit organizations so that they can deliver great products and services.

Today, Moon continues to welcome challenges, taking them on with impressive confidence and enthusiasm. She is an accomplished motivational speaker and serves the community through several civic and local board affiliations.

Danielle M. Morgan
Chief Executive Officer
**The Insurance Agency
with Grace, LLC**

Danielle Morgan is the chief executive officer of The Insurance Agency with Grace, LLC. As a representative for this new and upcoming agency, her position involves providing competitive insurance rates, building business relationships and providing excellent service to her clients.

Danielle has been in the insurance business for ten years, winning multiple awards for high sales, group coordinating, and new group opening. She has won National Leaders Conference trips and performed as the number two new agent in the nation for one of the companies she currently represents.

Danielle received a bachelor of arts degree in finance from Michigan State University and a master of arts degree in business administration from the University of Phoenix. She has received her life, health, Series 63, property and casualty licenses from the State of Michigan.

A Detroit native, Danielle is the proud mother of two sons. She devotes her time to her sorority, Eta Phi Beta Sorority, Inc. (Delta Chi chapter), the International Detroit Black Expo, Inc., the Michigan Business Professional Association, and her church, Greater Grace Temple.

Rochelle Morton is an emerald manager with Warm Spirit. Warm Spirit markets a comprehensive collection of nature-based beauty and healthcare products created specifically for person-to-person distribution. Founded in 1999, the company is based in Exeter, New Hampshire, and markets its products throughout the U.S. Morton started with the company in May of 2003 and today leads a national team of over 85 consultants.

Morton was second in sponsoring and awarded the Shining Star. She also received the President's Club Award for March and August of 2006. Morton received this honor for her hard work to promote and build growth for Warm Spirit. Morton surpassed sales and recruiting goals for March of 2006, further demonstrating her dedication to the company and her community.

A native of Detroit, Rochelle is the wife of Anthony C. Morton and proud mother of three children, Lauryn, Aaron and Evan. She enjoys the occasional domestic travel that her Warm Spirit business affords.

Rochelle Morton
Emerald Manager
Warm Spirit

Georgella Bascom Muirhead is the president of Berg Muirhead and Associates (BMA), one of Southeast Michigan's premier public relations firms. She has more than 30 years of expertise in community affairs, event planning and media relations.

Muirhead served as director of the Department of Public Information for the City of Detroit, under both Mayor Coleman A. Young and Mayor Dennis Archer. Muirhead received the Public Relations Society of America's coveted Silver Anvil Award for excellence in government communications for the 1992 City of Detroit's Devil's Night campaign.

Muirhead's specialty is coordinating special events of national and local significance. Her most memorable public relations campaigns are the 2003 Detroit Democratic Presidential Candidates Debate, the grand opening of YouthVille Detroit, a $15.8 million youth development center, and orchestrating 26 events for the 2002 inaugural celebrations of Mayor Kwame M. Kilpatrick.

Muirhead serves on the board of trustees of The Parade Company and the Booker T. Washington Association. She is a former board member and trustee of the Museum of African American History and Detroit Public Television.

Georgella Bascom Muirhead
President
Berg Muirhead and Associates

ENTREPRENEURS

Duvale Murchison
Owner
Laughalujah Comedy Tours &
DME Entertainment

A native of Lansing, Michigan, Duvale Murchison has been active in the gospel entertainment industry for more than 20 years. His experience includes promoting concerts, multiple years in radio and working in promotions at GospoCentric Records.

Duvale Murchison Entertainment (DME) birthed the *Laughalujah Comedy Jam*, a national tour featuring some of America's best Christian standup comedians, including Marcus Wiley, Rod Z, Vyck Cooley and Darian Perkins. The tour showcased in churches and venues throughout the United States in cities such as Lansing, Flint, Philadelphia, Peoria, Memphis, Raleigh, Cleveland, Columbus, Phoenix, Orlando, Jacksonville and Kansas City.

In 2006 DME introduced another pioneering comedy tour called *Gurlfrienz* featuring talented female comediennes, Meshelle, Debra Terry and Mrs. V.

The Laughalujah brand has become so popular and the demand so great that DME has taken initiatives to bring its family of comedians to the forefront of gospel entertainment by offering their comedy through platforms such as theater, home video, television broadcast and other new media configurations.

Duvale resides in Lansing with his wife of 18 years, Roxanne. They have two children, Kelvin and Destini.

Regina Ragland
Owner
Essence Upscale Promotions

As the owner of Essence Upscale Promotions, Regina Ragland manages a small staff that produces large-scale results with the attentiveness of a small business. She oversees the daily operations of her company.

Regina is a member of the Michigan Minority Business Development Council, the Promotional Products Association International, and is a team leader in the Making Strides Against Breast Cancer walk. She is an active member of Hartford Memorial Baptist Church.

Regina entered the promotional business after leaving the spirit industry in 2003. Her venture into the promotional industry was a smooth transition because of her orientated position in the spirit industry. Her attentiveness to customer loyalty has allowed her to locate and offer upscale products that are essential to any business.

Regina studied at Wayne State University with a concentration in marketing. A native of Detroit, she is the wife of Nathaniel Ragland and the mother of Rekira.

Lawrence R. Roberson is president of Wealth Management Group, Inc. (WMG). WMG provides a myriad of financial planning and money management services. Roberson has more than 30 years of experience in finance. He served in several managerial positions at Ford Motor Company. After 13 years, he started his own firm in 1985. His transition from Ford to an entrepreneur was featured on the front page of the *Wall Street Journal*.

Roberson graduated from Alabama A&M University with a bachelor of science degree in mathematics. He received his master of business administration degree from Indiana University. He was one of the first African Americans to obtain the CFP (Certified Financial Planner) designation in Michigan. He is also a past president of the Detroit chapter of the National Black MBA Association.

Roberson was born in Birmingham, Alabama. In the 1960s, he participated in the civil rights struggle of the South. Most notable was a bombing that took place on December 24th. Although no one was killed, Roberson's home, Bethel Baptist Church, and many other homes were damaged.

Lawrence R. Roberson
President
Wealth Management Group, Inc.

Ralph Robinson is a freelance photojournalist for *Today's Photographer* magazine. Robinson's career has been an arduous journey. He has photographed numerous events. Well known in the music and entertainment world, Robinson was the photographer of the award-winning jazz musician, the late Dr. Teddy Harris Jr. He has also photographed government dignitaries such as the United States president, mayors, congressmen, and governors.

Robinson is a lover of people. He overcame a bout with cancer, which he believes made him better at his skilled craft. Robinson has earned several applicable degrees in photography. He has studied under world-class teachers including Bill Tolbert, Russell Keen and Elijah Bowie.

After viewing Robinson's work, some viewers have classed him as one of the world's top photojournalists.

Ralph Robinson
Photojournalist
Today's Photographer

Mona Ross
Owner & Operator
234 Winder Street Inn

Mona Ross is the owner and operator of 234 Winder Street Inn, an elegant bed and breakfast located in the Brush Park district of Detroit.

Ross was born in New Orleans, and moved to Detroit at an early age. As an adult, she raised a family and explored her interests in cooking, antique collection and home restoration. For 15 years, Ross was a real estate investor and owner of the Southern Cuisine Restaurant.

As the former president of the Brush Park Development Corporation, Ross has been instrumental in securing landmark status for Brush Park, and soliciting other development projects as well.

Her pioneer spirit and vocational interest culminated in restoring a 134-year-old dilapidated mansion to its original prominence, and creating an upscale bed and breakfast. 234 Winder Street Inn is located in the heart of downtown Detroit, directly across from Detroit's Ford Field and Comerica Park Stadiums.

234 Winder Street Inn opened for business during the summer of 2005, and has already hosted an impressive mix of VIP clientele.

René Thomas
Chief Executive Officer &
Creative Director
Cambrey Noelle Designs, L.L.C.

René Thomas is the chief executive officer and creative director of Cambrey Noelle Designs, an elegant line of custom knitwear and fashion consultation service.

René began her career in fashion as a runway model in her teens. She later branched out into film and print modeling. To expand her knowledge and gain more experience, René pursued and received licenses in cosmetology and barbering. With both licenses, she has won numerous awards in hair shows and worked as an independent contractor for Chanel, Clinique and Clarins.

René incorporated her first company, Just Bands & Fragments, in 1987 and flourished making unique headpieces. Cambrey Noelle Designs, named for her daughter, was started after she recognized a gap in stylish and custom-made clothing for women of all sizes. Believing that women should always feel beautiful and fashionable, her designs fit sizes 0-32.

When she is not modeling or designing, René is an active member of Word of Faith Christian Center and enjoys volunteering for the UNCF and the Detroit Opera House.

René is the mother of Cambrey Noelle, a student at Northwestern University.

Sherry Washington is founder of Sherry Washington Gallery and co-founder of BWW Group, Inc. and Associates for Learning, Inc. Sherry Washington Gallery (SWG) opened in 1989 in Detroit, providing museum quality art, art appraisal and curating services to corporations, museums and private collectors. SWG represents artists among the world's finest, including Benny Andrews, David Driskell, David Fludd, Richard Lewis, Richard Mayhew, Gilda Snowden and Shirley Woodson. The consulting firm BWW provides expert diversity contracting solutions. Associates for Learning markets and implements corporate wellness products and services.

Washington is a member of several boards and organizations, including Detroit Public Schools' Detroit School of the Arts; the Downtown Development Authority; the Detroit Public Library Commission; the Black Women Contracting Association, Inc.; Detroit Institute of Arts, Friends of African and African American Art; Music Hall Center for the Performing Arts; the Detroit International Jazz Festival; Delta Sigma Theta Sorority, Inc.; and Detroit Athletic Club.

Born in Detroit, Washington is a 1977 graduate of the University of Michigan. Her family includes son Khalid R. W. Haywood, also a graduate of the University of Michigan.

Sherry Washington
Founder
Sherry Washington Gallery

A graphic design teacher and owner of LT Graphics, God has blessed Lititia White by making her a multitalented individual. This is reflected in every aspect of her life and work. Lititia is also a lead case manager, marketing resource specialist and MIS specialist for the Michigan Reentry Initiative "Walk With Me" program.

With a master of fine arts degree from Michigan State University, Lititia designs for various organizations, from major corporations to local mom-and-pop operations. Some of her clients include Daimler Chrysler, Comerica Bank, Inter Court Music Group and numerous churches in the Detroit area. Lititia is an international artist whose work has reached Europe, Africa and the Caribbean.

Lititia is a member of The Lydia Circle of Christian Business and Professional Women and Delta Sigma Theta Sorority, Inc. Her vision and goal is to develop a community technology and communications center and provide services and training to the community in the areas of graphic design, printing and business development.

Born and raised in Detroit, Michigan, her interests include painting and selling large oil paintings, singing and African dance.

Lititia White
Owner & Art Director
LT Graphics, Inc.

ENTREPRENEURS

Margo E. Williams
President
Margo E. Williams & Associates, Inc.

Margo E. Williams is president of Margo E. Williams & Associates, Inc. (MEWA), an award-winning public relations and advertising firm in Detroit and Las Vegas. The agency opened in 1990 and specializes in media relations, event planning, video production, graphic design and crisis management.

With successful careers as a talk show host and reporter, Margo worked alongside Regis Philbin and opposite Oprah Winfrey in St. Louis and Baltimore. Margo has also written for *The Detroit News*, *Crain's Detroit Business*, *Black Enterprise* and *The Crisis*.

Margo served as president of the Detroit chapter of the National Association of Black Journalists and Women in Communications. She also served on the board of directors for the Detroit Urban League, Leadership Detroit, the National Kidney Foundation and the National Association of Women Business Owners.

MEWA clients include Molina Healthcare, White Castle, Honeywell, IBM, The Chisholm-Mingo Group, Detroit Medical Center, Cobo Hall, Detroit Public Schools, Wayne State University, W.K. Kellogg Foundation, Museum of African American History and the Detroit Institute of Arts.

Williams graduated from Harris Teacher's College and Southern Illinois and St. Louis Universities.

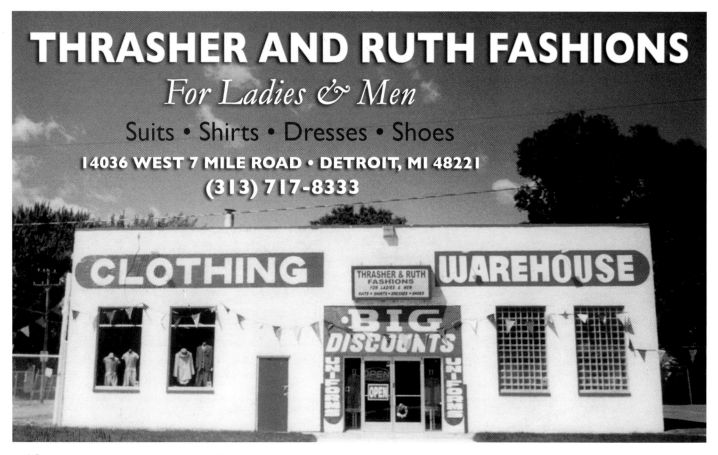

Detroit's

PROFESSIONALS

"Great artists suffer for the people."

MARVIN GAYE (1939-1984)

SINGER AND SONGWRITER

PROFESSIONALS

Linda Jaye Arogundade
Internal Communications
Specialist
St. John Detroit
Riverview Hospital

Linda Jaye Arogundade is an internal communications specialist for St. John Health. She provides communication support to St. John Detroit Riverview and North Shores Hospitals.

A proud graduate of Martin Luther King Jr. Senior High School, Linda Jaye received her bachelor of arts degree in journalism from the University of Detroit Mercy. She will continue pursuing her master's degree in public relations and organizational effectiveness at Wayne State University.

Some of her honors include the Spirit of Detroit, City of Detroit Youth Initiative, and a Detroit 300 choir performance. Linda Jaye has volunteered in many community activities and health fairs, entertaining children as Giggles the Clown.

A born again Christian, Linda Jaye is a member of Mt. Vernon Missionary Baptist Church in Detroit. Additionally, she is a member of the National Association of Black Journalists (Detroit chapter), the National Black Public Relations Society-Detroit, Sisters Cycling Bicycle Club, Full & Fabulous, Inc. and a former member of the Mack Alive board of directors.

A native Detroiter, Linda Jaye resides with her husband, Aros. She enjoys singing, acting, traveling and reading.

Ronald Neil Bennett
Principal Analyst/Supervisor
Computer Operations
DTE Energy

Ronald Neil Bennett is a principal analyst/supervisor for computer operations for DTE Energy. He has attended Detroit Institute of Technology and has more than 37 years of professional training and experience, mostly in information technology. He has won the Sarah Sheridan Award in 2001 and 2002, an award honoring DTE employees for exceptional customer satisfaction achievements that exemplify the company's core values and principles.

A business manager for Paradise Travels and Wedding Center, Bennett has more than ten years of experience in the travel business. He also heads the graphic arts department and gives seminars and group presentations on travel details and destinations.

Bennett is an activist in community improvements, specifically in relationships between neighborhood residents and businesses. He is a member of the Russell Woods Association and the Russell Woods Radio Patrol. Additionally, he is CERT trained and qualified (Community Emergency Response Team, Homeland Security) and is treasurer of the Russell Woods Quadrangle Block Club.

A native Detroiter, Bennett is the husband of Brenda Bennett and is the proud father of two sons, Kwayana and Jarron.

Lanar "Kern" Brantley
Music Director, Producer

Kern Brantley is a talented music director, producer, songwriter and arranger. Most recently, he toured with Beyonce and Destiny's Child as music director and bassist. Other artists Kern has worked with include Sean "P Diddy" Combs, R. Kelly, Teddy Riley, Bobby Brown, Keith Sweat, Lil Wayne, Nelly, the legendary Aretha Franklin and the late Grover Washington Jr.

Kern has served as musical director for many artists on numerous network television shows such as *The Tonight Show* with Jay Leno, *Late Night* with David Letterman, *Saturday Night Live* and *The Oprah Winfrey Show*. Kern has also recorded with several top artists, including Will Smith, L.L. Cool J., Jay-Z, Aretha Franklin, and 98 Degrees, to name a few.

He has produced records for the likes of Mary J. Blige, and worked as director and music arranger to Chris Brown , KeKe Wyatt, Salt 'n Peppa, and Carl Thomas.

Additionally, Kern is a member of the American Federation of Musicians, the American Federation of Television and Radio Artists, Broadcast Music, Inc. and the National Academy of Recording Arts and Sciences.

Marsha A. Brogdon is a realtor associate with Robinson Realty Group, located in Bingham Farms, Michigan, Detroit and Atlanta. Her 25-year marketing, communications and public relations experience, as well as her proficiency in developing strategic partnerships, has provided the backdrop for her customer-centric approach to real estate.

Prior to Robinson Realty, Marsha spent more than 15 years as a marketing communications executive at St. John Health. One of her many accomplishments during her tenure was designing the infrastructure and operational blueprint for the organization's customer relationship management center. Marsha received a bachelor of arts degree from Michigan State University, where she majored in telecommunication and journalism. She also received her master's degree in public relations and organizational communication from Wayne State University.

A member of Oak Grove AME Church, Marsha is involved with Alpha Kappa Alpha Sorority, Inc., the Neighborhood Service Organization, the Michigan Association of Realtors and the National Association of Realtors.

A native Detroiter, Marsha enjoys gardening and interior decorating. She is married to fragrance designer Anthony B. and has two children, Danielle and Wesley.

Marsha A. Brogdon
Realtor Associate
Robinson Realty Group

Myrna Burroughs is a commercial real estate broker in the Detroit office of CB Richard Ellis. She works with landlords, tenants, buyers and sellers of all types of commercial properties, including office, retail, industrial and vacant land. She is a member of the CB Richard Ellis African-American Network Group, which consists of brokers from major markets around the country working together to provide real estate services to companies that have established diversity practices. Myrna is also a member of the CB Richard Ellis Women's Network, and Commercial Real Estate Women (CREW).

Myrna received a bachelor's degree in Japanese language and literature, and a master's degree in international business from San Francisco State University.

A native of Chicago, Myrna lives in Detroit with her husband, Ed. She has two sons, Jordan and Alexander.

Myrna Burroughs
Real Estate Broker
CB Richard Ellis

Xenia Castillo-Hunter is an account executive in conference and events services for the Detroit Metro Convention & Visitors Bureau (DMCVB). In this role, Castillo-Hunter is responsible for providing meeting management professionals with assistance in arrangements necessary for holding an event in metropolitan Detroit, and offering services to maximize the fulfillment of the DMCVB mission. She is responsible for assisting with planning, implementing and managing assigned special projects, events, and programs including attendance promotions, hospitality and other programs.

Castillo-Hunter joined the DMCVB in 1998. She brings a solid history of sales success and creative marketing ideas to the DMCVB as well as a proven ability to develop sales potential in new market areas.

Castillo-Hunter is currently pursuing a bachelor of science degree in marketing from the University of Phoenix.

Xenia Castillo-Hunter
Account Executive
Detroit Metro Convention &
Visitors Bureau

PROFESSIONALS

Roy Christmon
Global Service
Delivery Manager
Electronic Data Systems

As global service delivery manager at Electronic Data Systems (EDS), Roy Christmon is responsible for data center services provided to one of EDS' largest clients of automotive aftermarket supplies. He led the activity to transition this new client's services into the EDS delivery model, and he has responsibility and oversight of day-to-day operations.

Roy has 22 years of operational and leadership experience in the information technology industry. He drives efficiency by taking advantage of "best in class" practices, consistency in process and tools, while continuing to deliver quality service and driving down expenses.

Roy sits on a regional diversity council focused on providing leaders and employees with continuous learning through awareness, education and training on diversity. He is a regional ambassador for EDS Employee Network Group Unity In Action (UIA) and is the EDS program director for INROADS.

Roy attended Oakland University in Rochester, Michigan, where he majored in business management and computer science. An accomplished musician, he loves listening to and playing music. Roy enjoys a variety of sports including basketball, football and golf.

Pearl Cotton
Catering Sales Manager
Hotel St. Regis

Pearl Cotton is the catering sales manager for the Hotel St. Regis where she specializes in meeting planning for corporate, sports, social and religious markets. In her current role, she endeavors to assist with community programs such as Wayne State University, the Chamber of Commerce of Greater Detroit, the NAACP and Henry Ford Health Systems, which are just a sampling of her scope and range. Pearl has a wealth of collaborative dexterity in her hospitality career and exudes the personable warmth and spirit of Detroit.

Her attention to detail and the professionalism of her services have earned her numerous letters of recognition. Pearl is the devoted spouse of David Cotton. They have three daughters and are the proud grandparents of eight wonderful grandchildren.

She is a proactive member of the Nurses Guild and a member of the Greater Faith Baptist Church Choir, where Frank Robinson Jr. is pastor. Pearl still finds the time to counsel and promote healthy skincare products.

John W. Cromer Jr.
Corporate Developer
America Works

John W. Cromer Jr. is corporate developer for America Works, and chairman of the employee committee at Hartford Memorial Baptist Church. In this position, he has formed relationships with employers, resulting in hundreds of jobs for people with barriers to employment and self-sufficiency.

John is an incredible advocate for re-entry efforts on behalf of the prison population. He establishes the support mechanisms that will keep ex-offenders in the community, in jobs and contributing to society.

John speaks to churches, schools and community centers, and conducts employability workshops for Wayne County Community College District and Michigan Works affiliates. When Detroit got involved with helping Hurricane Katrina survivors, John organized one of the most successful jobs fairs that resulted in on-the-spot-hiring of many.

John received the Rosa Parks Tolerance Award, the State of the African American Male Recognition and various honors for his efforts to change people's lives by helping them to be productive and gain employment.

A native of Detroit, John is a proud single father of one daughter, Josalyn.

Cheryl Davis has 25-plus years of sales and management experience in a corporate and self-employed environment with a proven track record. She holds a bachelor's degree in business administration from Wayne State University.

Davis and her family have resided in North Rosedale Park for 20 years and have been active with various neighborhood committees. The most recent activity was the Rosedale-Grandmont Community Open House, an event that educated realtors and prospective homeowners of the advantages of living in this community.

As a Realtor, her objective is to provide the highest possible level of professionalism and unsurpassed customer service. Her role is to educate and inform clients on all aspects of their real estate transaction.

Davis is a member of the Western Wayne and Oakland County Board of Realtors, the Association of Women Realtors, the Michigan Association of Realtors, the Better Business Bureau and the National Association of Realtors.

Cheryl Davis
Realtor Associate
Robinson Realty Group

A native of Lansing, Michigan, J. Otis Davis is court administrator for the 36th District Court in the City of Detroit. He is responsible for the day-to-day operations of all court functions, which includes the supervision of over 400 employees, and an annual budget of approximately $50 million.

Prior to his current position, Otis was director of the Bureau of Juvenile Justice for the State of Michigan, a position he held for ten years.

Otis received a bachelor's degree in social science from Western Michigan University and a master's degree in social work and criminal justice from Michigan State University, where he also served as an adjunct professor in the School of Criminal Justice. He is a member of Omega Psi Phi Fraternity, Inc.

Otis has conducted youth basketball camps in Lansing, Detroit, Indiana and Los Angeles. He has worked for Magic Johnson, Isaiah Thomas and other professional basketball players through his affiliation with Dr. Tucker's Basketball Camp of Champions.

J. Otis Davis
Court Administrator
36th District Court

U olanda Davis-Campbell is an event coordinator for Cobo Conference Center. In this position, she manages the planning and arrangements relating to the use of 80 meeting rooms, eight ballrooms with river views and 700,000 square feet of exhibit space. Her responsibilities include coordinating facility arrangements for local, national and international meetings, conventions, dinners, trade shows and major public events.

Uolanda is also the chief executive officer of Creative Concepts in Planning, a full-service planning and referral service that she established in 1989. She is the facility coordinator for the Rho Sigma chapter of Sigma Gamma Rho Sorority, Inc. Uolanda's expertise is shared as a board member for the International Detroit Black Expo, Inc.

She majored in organizational communications while attending Eastern Michigan University. Uolanda is a registered meeting planner (RMP) and a certified event planner (CEP) through the International Society of Meeting Planners. Her other affiliations include memberships with the International Association of Exhibit Management and the National Coalition of Black Meeting Planners.

Uolanda is a native Detroiter and is the proud mother of one son, Timothy Campbell Jr.

Uolanda Davis-Campbell,
RMP, CEP
Event Coordinator
Cobo Conference
Exhibition Center

PROFESSIONALS

Cathy Dockery
Administrative Director of
Nursing
Sinai-Grace Hospital

Cathy Dockery, administrative director of nursing at Sinai-Grace Hospital, is highly skilled in managing key patient-care service areas. She has worked on numerous hospital and ambulatory operation initiatives, including the emergency department 29-minute guarantee to improve hospital throughput. Cathy co-presented this topic at the Society of Health Service Engineers Annual Forum.

In 2005 Sinai-Grace Hospital was awarded a grant to address disparities in healthcare for Latino and African Americans. As nursing executive, Cathy was actively involved in establishing the Healthy Heart Project.

With a career that spans 25 years, Cathy has served the healthcare industry in other capacities. These include, respiratory therapist, registered nurse, director of emergency services, and interim vice president of patient care services. A member of several healthcare professional organizations, Cathy earned a bachelor of science degree in nursing and a master of business administration degree in health care management from the University of Phoenix.

Cathy is married to James Dockery, mother to Kendall, Kelly and Katrina, and grandmother to Kamani. She is a member of Hartford Memorial Baptist Church in Detroit.

Gail A. Echols
Global Deskside
Services Integration
Software & Hardware Manager
Ford Motor Company

Gail is an information technology (IT) senior manager with 15 years of experience in IT infrastructure, networking, manufacturing systems and security and controls. She is the global deskside integration software and hardware manager for Ford Motor Company. Gail's organization has ultimate responsibility for the PC/Unix hardware standards, operating system images, image/fax and printer strategy, integration lab certification, and mobile wireless technology. Her team is currently responsible for launching Vista/Longhorn clients, Windows Mobile 5.0 utilizing ActivSync and smart phone technologies.

She has managed multi-million dollar capital and expense budgets. Gail has also been responsible for all IT applications and infrastructure at the largest manufacturing plant facility in North America. She excels in organization, communication, leadership, team building and project delivery.

Gail holds a bachelor's degree in computer science from Wayne State University. She has been instrumental in Ford IT recruiting and Ford college graduate mentoring efforts. Gail is an active member of the Michigan Council of Women in Technology and The Ford African American Network (FAAN). She is also an active member of her church, Original New Grace Missionary Baptist Church.

Michael Griggs
Real Estate Developer

A lifelong Detroit resident, Michael Griggs is deeply committed to the revitalization of Detroit by expanding well-established neighborhoods and creating contemporary suburban housing options to the city.

After graduating from Chadsey High School, Griggs attended the University of Detroit Mercy and earned a bachelor of arts degree in history with a specialization in Egyptology. During his undergraduate education, he studied in Egypt under the world renowned Egyptologist Dr. Yosef Ben Jochannon. Following his graduation, he immediately entered the liberal arts program and earned a master of arts degree in a record six months.

Griggs has lectured on Egyptology and history at colleges and universities across the state of Michigan and served as executive director of development at SOSAD (Save Our Sons and Daughters). At 27, he opened what was at the time the second-largest black-owned bookstore in Michigan, Black World Books.

His commitment to community development is highlighted by his effort in developing beautiful three-story brownstones and single-family homes on Detroit's west side. Griggs' resume differs from most developers because he is deeply rooted and heavily involved in community affairs.

Janice Hale is a professor of early childhood education at Wayne State University. She has spoken and consulted at numerous colleges, professional organizations and early childhood education programs across the United States and Jamaica. She served as a consultant for *Sesame Street* and *Mister Rogers' Neighborhood*.

Hale has written numerous articles and three books in her field. Her second and third books, *Unbank the Fire: Visions For the Education of African American Children* and *Learning While Black: Creating Excellence for African American Children*, were both nominated for the Pulitzer Prize.

Hale received a bachelor of arts degree from Spelman College, a master of religious education degree from the Interdenominational Theological Center, and a doctoral degree in education from Georgia State University. She completed post-doctoral work at Rockefeller University, the University of California San Diego and Yale University. In 1981 she was named a Distinguished Alumna of the College of Education at Georgia State University.

Hale attended public schools in Columbus, Ohio. She is the daughter of Rev. and Mrs. Phale D. Hale and the mother of Keith A. Benson Jr.

Janice E. Hale
Professor,
Early Childhood Education
Wayne State University

Julia Hunter is a marketing education teacher at Martin Luther King, Jr. Senior High School in Detroit. She is responsible for teaching international marketing and marketing education coop. She developed the international marketing curriculum (the only one in Detroit and one of a few in Michigan) in 1995.

In addition to teaching three preps, serving as the advisor for DECA (vocational student organization), and serving as coop coordinator, Hunter is a senior class advisor. In this capacity, she is responsible for coordinating all activities, meetings and events for more than 400 seniors.

Hunter has been awarded numerous awards for her performance and dedication, including WDIV/ Newsweek Teacher of the Year, Michigan Marketing Educator of the Year, Michigan Consumer Educator of the Year and The Jim Boyce Foundation Outstanding Service Award, to name a few.

She holds a bachelor of science degree from Alabama State University and an MBE degree from Eastern Michigan University.

Hunter operates a small book publishing company in her spare time. In the past year, her client base has grown from one to forty-plus clients.

Julia Hunter
Educator
Martin Luther King, Jr.
Senior High School

LaToya Johnson-Fowlkes is a realtor associate and brokers' assistant with Robinson Realty Group. She embraces the beauty of individuality and recognizes the need to tailor life's tools to fit each unique personality when pursuing results. Her clients find comfort in knowing that as their advocate, Johnson-Fowlkes represents them with an optimum balance of passion, humility, knowledge and commitment.

Prior to her career in real estate, she specialized in the rehabilitation of people with traumatic brain injuries for nearly ten years. She embraced the opportunity to teach, to advocate, and to empower people on different levels.

Johnson-Fowlkes received her associate degree in arts from Henry Ford Community College and then majored in communications at Wayne State University. She enjoys writing, public speaking and the art of dance. She devotes time to the youth of today working as a youth sponsor at her church, Church of the Living God, CWFF Temple#69.

Johnson-Fowlkes is a member of the Michigan and National Associations of Realtors.

She has been happily married to her soul mate for the past eight years.

LaToya Johnson-Fowlkes
Realtor Associate
Robinson Realty Group

PROFESSIONALS

Dichondra Johnson-Geiger
Community Relations Specialist
St. John Detroit Riverview
Hospital

Dichondra Johnson-Geiger heads the community relations division for St. John Detroit Riverview Hospital. As the liaison between the Detroit community and the hospital, she is responsible for promoting the understanding of the hospital, its services, the St. John Health System and a variety of health-awareness programs. She does this by developing relationships and maintaining communication with external stakeholder groups and the community at large.

In addition, Dichondra is co-owner of Verondee Consulting Co., an event management and logistical services company. Additionally, she is a joint partner with Verondee/Domaine Detroit Productions, which focuses on wine and spirit education via private and public tasting events throughout Metro Detroit. In 2002 the Association of Performing Arts Presenters named Dichondra "Emerging Leader" for her groundbreaking work in the performing arts.

Dichondra received her master of business administration degree in marketing and global business from Davenport University. She holds a bachelor of science degree in arts administration and marketing from Eastern Michigan University.

A native of Detroit and Lansing, Michigan, Dichondra is the wife of Michael Leo Geiger Jr.

Rita L. Jordan
Membership Development
Officer
Charles H. Wright Museum
of African American History

Rita Jordan is the membership development officer for the Charles H. Wright Museum of African American History. She is responsible for the acquisition and retention of museum members.

Before joining the Museum, Rita spent 14 years at Detroit newspapers in eleven different positions. Her experience ranges from circulation accounting, circulation marketing, telemarketing, business development, advertising and distribution center management to sales crews. Rita is driven by excellence and was recognized by the Detroit Regional Chamber as One of Southeast Michigan's Future Leaders.

She received a bachelor's degree in business administration with a minor in marketing from Tennessee State University. She is a certified trainer and enjoys training others on sales and marketing. Rita has an entrepreneurial spirit and is passionate about making a difference. Additionally, she is president and chief executive officer of Rita Jordan & Associates, L.L.C., a marketing and public relations agency, and an image consultant.

Born in Huntsville, Alabama and raised in Detroit, Rita is single and is a member of Corinthian Missionary Baptist Church. She enjoys reading, traveling, dancing and shopping.

Anthony E. O. King
Associate Professor
Wayne State University

Anthony E. O. King is an associate professor at Wayne State University, where he teaches social work research. He is an expert on social work practice with criminal justice populations, and has served as a program development and evaluation consultant to federal, state and county corrections departments in several states.

King's practice with African-American male inmates, and his research on black male/female relationships and violence among African-American males are published in scholarly journals, edited books and newspapers.

King graduated cum laude from Cleveland State University with a bachelor of arts degree in sociology and social services. He earned his master's degree and doctor of philosophy degree in social work from Washington University in St. Louis, Missouri.

King served six years in the United States Marine Corps and 20 years as a psychological operations and social work officer in the Army National Guard and Army Reserves. During his military career, he earned the Marine Corps Good Conduct Medal and Meritorious Unit Commendation, the National Defense Service Ribbon with Bronze Star, the Armed Forces Reserve Medal, and the Army Service Ribbon.

Valerie Lott
Realtor
Robinson Realty Group

Valerie Lott prides herself in making sure that her clients are stress free and that they understand all phases of home buying and selling. She is a million dollar seller and enjoys working with first-time homebuyers.

A native Detroiter and a licensed realtor for more than 20 years, Valerie retired from the City of Detroit. She completed her career on the human resources department's administrative team, where she helped administer a $32 million budget. She has also worked with charitable organizations and city employees, raising more than $2 million for the March of Dimes, the United Negro College Fund, the Black United Fund of Michigan, Goodfellows Fund of Michigan, the Coleman A. Young Foundation and the Charles H. Wright African American Museum.

Valerie is a member of the NAACP, the National Association of Realtors, and Oak Grove AME Church, where she serves on the Richard and Sarah Allen Usher Board and the liturgical dance ministry team. She is the proud mother of one son, Ronnie.

Krystal L. Love
Branch Sales Manager
Flagstar Bank

Krystal Love is sales manager of an in-store banking center for Flagstar Bank. In this position, she is responsible for developing activities to help her branch reach its sales goals, ensuring branch compliance with regulatory policies and procedures, and coaching staff in skill development and personal growth.

Since joining Flagstar in 2003, Krystal has received a number of recognitions, including a Shining Star Award for outstanding performance and being named "CRA Star of the Month" for her community activities.

Krystal frequently participates in homebuyer seminars and works with a local nonprofit organization to help participants save money to buy their first home. She also opened the first in-school bank in Detroit for Flagstar. Additionally, she is a Junior Achievement volunteer and a partner for a student at Cornerstone School.

Krystal majored in business administration at Central Michigan University and holds licenses to sell life, health, accident, and property and casualty insurances.

The wife of Walter Love Jr. and the proud mother of Marquel and Walter III, Krystal enjoys spending time with her family.

Tania M. McGee
Director of Education &
Community Affairs
Sphinx Organization

Tania M. McGee graduated from De Montfort University in Leicester, United Kingdom, with a bachelor's degree in arts management. She joined the Sphinx Organization in 2003 as an artistic coordinator. Currently she is the director of education and community affairs, handling the coordination and implementation of all programs for the organization. Additionally, she is the director of the Sphinx Competition for young African-American and Latino string musicians. McGee frequently speaks on behalf of the organization at various national and local events.

Having worked for "Music In The Sun," in Sheffield, U.K. and as festival coordinator for the Charles H. Wright Museum in Detroit, McGee has national and international festival experience. She also worked at Best Efforts, Inc., where she was involved in planning and producing educational and cultural community programs.

A volunteer with The United College Negro Fund's women's group, McGee is closely involved with the Ebony Fashion Fair in Detroit. She helps to coordinate all aspects of the event, including advertising, merchandising and venue coordination. She also serves on the board of directors for the Ann Arbor Film Festival.

PROFESSIONALS

Brandi Mitchell
Makeup Artist &
Image Consultant

Brandi Mitchell has been key in developing the images of actors, models, singers and corporate executives throughout the United States and Europe for more than 12 years. Known for making people look polished and naturally beautiful, her work can be seen in magazines, television, film and on some of your favorite celebrities, political figures and radio personalities.

Recently, Mitchell made history by becoming the first African-American department head of makeup in Michigan with her work on the Columbia/Tristar film, *Crossover*.

Mitchell's experience and trained eye for both makeup and hair allows her the opportunity to work on a number of projects and give her clients the visual "total package." She divides her time between film, television, print and live performance jobs. She works in the Los Angeles, New York and Atlanta areas, in addition to serving clients at her private studio.

Mitchell is also an author, educator, and platform artist, traveling across the country to teach makeup techniques and service clients nationwide.

Sgt. Elton Moore
Administrative Sergeant
Tactical Operations
Detroit Police Department

Sergeant Elton Moore is a 29-year veteran of the Detroit Police Department. He is the proud husband of Lydia Nolan and is the father of twelve-year-old Karyn Moore.

Promoted to the rank of sergeant in 1999, Moore is currently the administrative sergeant at tactical operations. The tactical operations section is responsible for planning many high-level events that are held in the city of Detroit, such as the North American International Auto Show, the Thanksgiving Day Parade and numerous dignitary visits and annual city events.

Moore has attended the Center for Creative Studies (photography and advertising design) and Wayne County Community College (law enforcement and political science). He attends First Baptist Church in southwest Detroit where he serves as a deacon.

Moore's philosophy is simple: "When you visit anyone's home, they want you to be comfortable. You never enter into someone's home and turn on the lights and set the temperature yourself. So when native Detroiters and visitors attend special events in the city, it is the job of tactical operations to 'Turn On the Lights So Detroit Can Shine.'"

Joseph B. Moton
Physician Relations Specialist
St. John Detroit
Riverview Hospital

Joseph B. Moton, a 14-year veteran in the healthcare industry, is the physician relations specialist for St. John Detroit Riverview Hospital. In this position, Joseph is responsible for managing the local day-to-day infrastructure and reporting activities that support physician relations and business operations.

Having worked both in hospital systems and with health insurance plans, Joseph has a successful track record for establishing and maintaining medical service networks to ensure access to medical care for patients in the state of Michigan.

Joseph received his bachelor of arts degree in business management from Siena Heights University in Adrian, Michigan. Additionally, he is a certified physical ability test administrator by Advanced Ergonomics, Inc. Because of his genuine commitment to excellence, Joseph serves as a service excellence ambassador and super coach for St. John Health's customer service initiative. He is a member of the National Association of Occupational Health Professionals.

A native Detroiter, Joseph is married to the beautiful Tracy L. Moton. They attend Second Ebenezer Baptist Church in Detroit. In his leisure time, Joseph enjoys golf, music and theatre.

Shirley Y. Myrick
Global Program Manager
Electronic Data Systems

Shirley Myrick supports the General Motors Acceptance Corporation Financial Services account as global program manager for Electronic Data Systems (EDS). She is responsible for all activities to transition to the GM third generation information technology operating model. Shirley's GM/EDS career spans 30 years. Her career achievements were recognized with an Outstanding Technology Leader Award in 1998.

Shirley is national president of the American Business Women's Association (ABWA), and is chair of the ABWA Metropolitan Detroit Area Council. Additionally, she serves as president of Sisters with a Vision Investment Club and is a member of Toastmasters International and Alpha Sigma Nu Honor Society. In March of 2006, Shirley was honored as one of the Top Ten Most Influential African Americans of Metropolitan Detroit.

Her volunteer efforts include mentoring pregnant teens at The Salvation Army Denby Center. She is a trustee and president of the women's ministry at Hartford Memorial Baptist in Detroit.

A graduate of the University of Detroit Mercy, Shirley holds a bachelor of science degree in business. She and her husband, Cornelius, reside in North Rosedale Park, Detroit.

Sheila R. Neal
Account Executive
Detroit Metro Convention &
Visitors Bureau

Sheila R. Neal, account executive with the Detroit Metro Convention & Visitors Bureau (DMCVB), handles the religious and multicultural markets. Neal has worked for the Bureau for more than 16 years, and she has held her current post as a sales account executive for the past five years.

Neal was recently named one of Detroit's History Makers Under 40 by the *Michigan Chronicle*, the state's leading African-American newspaper. Her passion for providing outstanding sales and client service has helped her secure a number of high-profile conventions in Detroit. Among conventions that have been or will be held in Detroit are the National Alliance of Black School Educators; the National Association for the Advancement of Colored People; Progressive National Baptist; the National Urban League; Alpha Phi Alpha Fraternity, Inc.; the National Head Start Association; Black Data Processing Associates; the National Dental Association; and the National Bar Association.

Neal is a member of several professional associations and recently obtained her association sales executives certification for the Professional Conference Managers Association.

Samuel Pittman
Application Engineer
Industrial Automation
Dynetics, Inc.

Samuel Pittman serves as an application engineer within the industrial automation group for Dynetics Inc., a full-service engineering company. With demanding customers domestically and internationally, Samuel is responsible for supporting custom engineering solutions involving computer hardware and software, wireless networks, electrical analysis, marketing and business development. His work helps ensure product quality and process efficiency within automakers' assembly facilities throughout the United States, Canada, Mexico, Europe and Australia.

Samuel has been recognized for leadership and accomplishment within numerous organizations such as INROADS, Inc. and the National Society of Black Engineers, Inc. He is an entrepreneur, public speaker and founder of "Minority Speak," a new and forthcoming minority-focused magazine.

Samuel received his bachelor of science degree in computer engineering from the University of Missouri-Rolla, and was the first African-American male to do so at the university. He also holds associate of arts degrees in engineering science and mathematics.

Samuel is a native of St. Louis, Missouri, currently single and proud to be a Detroit resident.

PROFESSIONALS

Pamela Powell
Benefit Representative
United Auto Workers

Pamela Powell currently serves as a benefit representative for the United Auto Workers at the Ypsilanti Plant. She represents Ford employees, both active and retired. Her duties encompass the addition of new employees to the various healthcare plans, plan management and retirement preparation. Pam also serves as a financial advisor and liaison between the active and retired workers and the International Executive Board, National Retirement Board, Fidelity Investments, National Programs Center and the National Employee Service Center.

She holds a degree in library science from Oakland University and is currently enrolled in classes in education and labor at the University of Michigan.

Pam is a member of the UAW Regional Advisory Council on Civil and Human Rights, Detroit chapter; the A. Phillip Randolph Institute; the Detroit chapter of the NAACP; the Trade Union Leadership Council; the Michigan Reading Association and the Platinum Stars LLC Co.

She loves people and recognizes that her purpose is to touch and be touched by others. Her hobbies include music, art, travel and cooking. Pam is the mother of a ten-year-old daughter.

Tracye Robinson-Blount
Principal Broker
Robinson Realty Group

By emphasizing reliability, integrity and commitment, Tracye Robinson-Blount has built a successful career as an associate broker and now owns her own company.

Tracye knows that combining knowledge and service, she can ensure the best interests of her clients. With her lengthy background in marketing, strong negotiating skills and expertise in analyzing market trends, she can quickly match clients with the perfect property at the right price.

Tracye's ability to meet her clients' needs is seen in a 97% rate of repeat and referral business, a true sign of success. A metropolitan Detroit native, Tracye has a unique knowledge of the area and communities. She has a high regard for the area and thrives on introducing clients to all that the metro area has to offer.

An excellent listener, Tracye is devoted to educating herself, her agents and her clients on a market that is fueled by change. She is the recipient of numerous awards including the President's Circle and the Council of Excellence.

Tracye is very active in the community and is a member of several local organizations.

Nicholas Schrock
Sales Representative
Cintas Corporation

At age 23, Nicholas Schrock has been affiliated with Cintas Corporation for six years. Nicholas began working with Cintas as an intern through INROADS, a national organization that places talented minority youth with corporations during their senior year in high school.

After graduating from Southfield High School, Nicholas attended the University of Michigan. He spent each summer with Cintas learning different operational aspects of the corporation. He graduated from the University of Michigan with a bachelor of arts in organizational studies at age 21 and accepted full-time employment as a management trainee with Cintas. He graduated from the management trainee program in May of 2005, and is currently responsible for maintaining and acquiring new business in Detroit, Dearborn, and Dearborn Heights.

Nicholas is the youngest of three brothers and values time with his family and friends. He is a member of Renaissance Baptist Church. His love of sports can be traced to lifelong participation in team sports, beginning with soccer at age four. He attributes his ability to work successfully with different people and cultures to those team experiences.

Gerald L. Scruggs Sr. is a territory manager for Colonial Supplemental Insurance. In this position, he specializes in custom designing employee benefit programs that are tailored to the specific needs of businesses, for the purpose of reducing overhead costs. Gerald also orchestrates benefits communications systems for employers, which help attract and retain top-quality employees. He completes this service with little or no direct cost to the employer.

Gerald has been Agent of the Year for two consecutive years. He also received the Eagle Award, honoring the top agent in the Midwest region (17 states), as well as recognition as the Top Agent in Michigan. In addition, Colonial awarded him a seven-day Caribbean cruise one year and a seven-day trip to Hawaii another year.

Gerald earned a bachelor's degree in business management from Eastern Michigan University. He is a member of Word of Faith International Christian Center in Southfield.

Gerald is the husband of Marta A. Scruggs and is the proud father of Gerald II, Rasheed, Quinton, Crystal, Bahati, and Quinte.

Gerald L. Scruggs Sr.
Territory Manager
Colonial Supplemental
Insurance

Alison Streaty has prided herself on being able to professionally and efficiently provide the best service to all of her clients. With a seven-year combined background in the title and mortgage industries, Alison knows what it takes to make any real estate transaction a smooth success. Having the best resources available for marketing, and a drive for negotiating, she tries her best to meet each and every one of her clients' real estate needs.

Alison is aware that the needs of her clients are more than just finding or selling the perfect home for them; it entails being able to listen and comprehend what is required of her services and educate not only her clients, but herself as well. She attends seminars, training classes, and continuing education classes in order to enhance her real estate career.

Alison Streaty
Real Estate Associate
Robinson Realty Group

Born in Detroit, jazzy cabaret pianist and singer Jo Thompson has appeared on television and in swank nightclubs all over the world. She was the very first to sing, "For Once in My Life."

Jo, along with jazz singer Harvey Thompson, starred in Comcast Cable's nationally televised special, *Detroit Jazz Jewels*. This award-winning show received an Emmy nomination and won both the prestigious Beacon and Telly Awards. She often works with the JC Heard Orchestra directed by Walt Szymanski. Jo and the big band received rave reviews in July of 2006 at the world-renowned Lincoln Center as well as at engagements at two of New York's most noted jazz clubs, The Iridium and the Blue Note. She is also an award-winning fashion designer. Along with her son, Greg Dunmore, they have created dramatic and stunning evening wear under the name Carlos Nina.

One of Jo Thompson's proudest moments was having jazz great Lionel Hampton present her one-woman show to benefit her late husband's scholarship fund, the Albert Dunmore Journalism Scholarship, at New York's internationally-acclaimed Carnegie Hall.

Jo Thompson
Pianist & Singer

Norman Thrasher
Detroit Music Legend

For more than five decades, Norman Thrasher has dazzled audiences nationwide. From humble beginnings, Thrasher's extraordinary musical abilities have led him to work with talent including Hank Ballard, Barry White, The Spinners, Chubby Checker and many other greats.

The earthy baritone began performing in the early 1950s with the Detroit Serenaders and the Royal Jokers. Thrasher climbed the R&B single charts as bass singer with Hank Ballard and the Midnighters. He worked as road manager for singer, Joe Tex and assisted with the promotion of Muhammad Ali's last professional fight.

Thrasher continued serving the entertainment industry as a record label executive, while operating his own public relations agency. He has proven flexibility in the industry on and off stage. Thrasher says he enjoyed helping other entertainers succeed, because he's been where they are trying to go. One of his fondest industry memories was being invited on-stage with Little Richard and the godfather of soul, James Brown.

Thrasher has expanded once more into the retail industry as owner of Thrasher and Ruth Fashions, Detroit's largest discount boutique store, according to Thrasher.

Ophelia Twine-Henry
Conference Coordinator
Leadership Summit on Race
New Detroit, Inc.

Ophelia Twine-Henry is an accomplished sales and marketing professional with more than 20 years of sales and management experience in downtown Detroit hotels.

In her new role as conference coordinator for New Detroit's Leadership Summit on Race, her sales and management experience is a key factor for the success of the Summit.Ophelia's success and longevity in sales and marketing can be attributed to building rapport with clients, having loyalty for clients, having clients feel appreciated and taking care of clients with integrity and respect. Known as the "Queen" of hospitality by her colleagues in Detroit and members of the National Coalition of Black Meeting Planners and the Religious Conference Management Association, she is a well respected and admired professional.

Ophelia received her education at Wayne County Community College District and Wayne State University. She has received the Marriott's Chairman Award, Marriott's Golden Circle Award and numerous sales training certifications from Westin Hotels & Resorts and Omni International Hotels.

A Georgia native, Ophelia is married to Edward Henry, is the mother of three and the revered grandmother of five.

Brian Walker
Account Executive
Conference and
Event Services
Detroit Metro Convention &
Visitors Bureau

Brian Walker is an account executive in conference and event services for the Detroit Metro Convention & Visitors Bureau (DMCVB). In this role, he advises meeting professionals and local host committees on available member and DMCVB services. Walker works with internal and external customers while serving as a liaison between the meeting professional, DMCVB industry partners, and Detroit's hospitality community. He secures the necessary contracted services to facilitate a successful and effective event.

Walker is a certified meeting professional with distinguished performance in operations, meeting planning, sales and marketing, and food and beverage. Prior to joining the DMCVB, he worked at the Detroit Marriott Renaissance Center, where he served in a variety of management positions including sales, events, convention services and banquet operations. In his various roles, he was responsible for negotiating contracts for the 1,300-room convention hotel and for daily banquet operations.

Walker received his bachelor of arts degree from Wayne State University in 1988.

K atrina Wesley is a mortgage loan officer for Charter One Bank and has worked in the banking and mortgage industry for the last 12 years. She has always had a desire to help others with their personal finances, especially in the area of homeownership. Her skills in the areas of finance and mortgage banking allow her to deliver exceptional service to all her clients, colleagues, realtors, family and friends.

Katrina received her bachelor's degree in business finance from Jackson State University and a master of business of administration degree from the University of Phoenix. She is a member of the Alpha Kappa Alpha Sorority, Inc., and assumes the duties of treasurer for the Jackson State Alumni Association of Detroit. Katrina is currently on a television commercial that advertises condominiums in downtown Detroit.

Katrina enjoys worshipping the Lord and fellowshipping with her church family at Family Victory Fellowship Church in Southfield, Michigan. Her hobbies include shopping, decorating, baking and walking for a cause.

Katrina G. Wesley
Mortgage Loan Officer
Community Lending
Department
Charter One Bank

A rthur Williams is the group sales manager for Hotel Pontchartrain. He is responsible for assisting tours, travel groups, family and class reunions, churches, fraternities and sororities with outstanding accommodations. At Hotel Pontchartrain, Arthur's resourcefulness is an asset to both company and clients. His attention to detail according to group specifications allows efficient servicing, and he excels at demonstrating how the hotel can assist guests with specialty needs. Arthur's groups, particularly the family reunions, consider his revered expertise in lodging and functional needs invaluable. He also supplies brochures showcasing a variety of directories featuring African-American entrepreneurship in Detroit.

A hotelier for more than 14 years, Arthur has received letters of thanks, certificates of appreciation, a R.O.S.E. (Recognition of Service Excellence) Award nomination, and one of Marriott's highest honors, the Tiefel Service Award Certificate.

Born and raised in Detroit, Arthur is the husband of Shanell Williams and is the loving father of their 19-month-old son, Christopher Carter Williams.

Arthur Williams
Sales Manager
Hotel Pontchartrain

You Are Always Welcome At

GREATER GRACE TEMPLE
(CITY of DAVID)
23500 WEST SEVEN MILE - DETROIT, MICHIGAN 48219
Bishop Charles H. Ellis III, Sr. Pastor

www.greatergrace.org
313.543.6000

Watch Us On
THE WORD NETWORK!

THE WORD
Network

Direct TV - Channel 373
and other digital cable outlets

Saturday
8:00 a.m. - 8:30 a.m.
Monday through Sunday
8:00 p.m. - 8:30 p.m. (EST.)

SCHEDULE OF SERVICES

SUNDAY
WORSHIP SERVICES
7:30 a.m. and 11:00 a.m.
CHRISTIAN EDUCATION
9:30 a.m.

WEDNESDAY
PRAYER SERVICES
11:00 a.m. and 6:00 p.m.
BIBLE CLASS "Growing In Grace"
12 Noon and 7:30 P.M.

RUNNING WITH THE *VISION!*

Bishop Charles H. Ellis III
& First Lady Crisette Ellis

Motown's
NEWEST HIT

African American **family**
FREE
MARCH 2006

Riding High
Local auto designer,
Ralph Gilles

Double Jeopardy
Black & Physically Challenged

Ballroom
Dance

To Advertise 248.398.3400

NOVATECH
COMPUTER SERVICES

Mission

Providing reliable
computer support services

Networking   Training   Web Design

Dependable
Solutions

Location
29829 Greenfield Rd.
Southfield , MI 48076

Contact
248.423.1170 T
248.423.1171 F
866.981.5750 Toll Free
www.4ncsi.com

Mark England
DE MODE
women's & men's clothing accessories

SHOPPING
Downtown Detroit

In-House Designers
Mark England
House of CEDi
Shionne Design Jewelry
Carolyn Ferrari Jewelry
By Sharrone
Franklin Rowe International

Custom Shirts and Suits
313.961.3991
@ Mark England De Mode
1253 Woodward Ave
Open 7 days a week - Next to Detroit Breakfast House Grille